LAW AND AUTHORITY IN BRITISH LEGAL HISTORY, 1200–1900

By presenting original research into British legal history, this volume emphasises the historical shaping of the law by ideas of authority. The essays offer perspectives upon the way that ideas of authority underpinned the conceptualisation and interpretation of legal sources over time and became embedded in legal institutions. The contributors explore the basis of the authority of particular sources of law, such as legislation or court judgments, and highlight how this was affected by shifting ideas relating to concepts of sovereignty, religion, political legitimacy, the nature of law, equity and judicial interpretation. The analysis also encompasses ideas of authority which influenced the development of courts, remedies and jurisdictions, international aspects of legal authority when questions of foreign law or jurisdiction arose in British courts, the wider authority of systems of legal ideas such as natural law, the authority of legal treatises, and the relationship between history, law and legal thought.

MARK GODFREY is Professor of Legal History at the University of Glasgow, where he teaches private law and legal history.

LAW AND AUTHORITY IN BRITISH LEGAL HISTORY, 1200–1900

Edited by

MARK GODFREY

CAMBRIDGE
UNIVERSITY PRESS

CAMBRIDGE
UNIVERSITY PRESS

University Printing House, Cambridge CB2 8BS, United Kingdom

Cambridge University Press is part of the University of Cambridge.

It furthers the University's mission by disseminating knowledge in the pursuit of education, learning and research at the highest international levels of excellence.

www.cambridge.org
Information on this title: www.cambridge.org/9781107122277

First published 2016

A catalogue record for this publication is available from the British Library

Library of Congress Cataloguing in Publication data
Law and authority in British legal history, 1200–1900 / edited by Mark Godfrey.
pages cm
Includes bibliographical references and index.
ISBN 978-1-107-12227-7 (hardback)
1. Law – Great Britain – History. 2. Authority. I. Godfrey, Mark, (Law teacher), editor.
KD606.L37 2016
349.41 – dc23 2015032899

ISBN 978-1-107-12227-7 Hardback

In Memory of
William M. Gordon
(1933–2012)
Emeritus Douglas Professor of Civil Law
University of Glasgow

CONTENTS

List of contributors *page* ix
Preface xi

1 The judicial interpretation of legislation in later thirteenth- and early fourteenth-century England 1

PAUL BRAND

2 The authority of parliament and the scope of the Statute of Uses 1536 13

N.G. JONES

3 Developing a prerogative theory for the authority of the Chancery: the French connection 33

IAN WILLIAMS

4 Authority and precedent 60

DAVID IBBETSON

5 Legislation and authority in early-modern Scotland 85

ANDREW R.C. SIMPSON

6 The sources of early Scots consistorial law: reflections on law, authority and jurisdiction during the Scottish Reformation 120

THOMAS GREEN

7 Conciliar authority and equitable jurisdiction in early-modern Scotland 140

J.D. FORD

8 Legal authorities as instruments of conflict management: the long endgame of Anglo-Hanseatic relations (1474–1603) 170

ALAIN WIJFFELS

9 History and the justification of governmental authority and individual rights in the age of John Locke and Samuel Pufendorf 192

ANDREAS THIER

10 The commissioners for claims on France and the case of the Baron de Bode, 1815–1861 212

MICHAEL LOBBAN

11 The authority of law in a bureaucratic framework: the nineteenth-century medicine stamp duty 250

CHANTAL STEBBINGS

12 The authority of treatises in English law (1800–1936) 274

STEPHEN WADDAMS

13 Maitland and Austin: legal history and legal thought in the late nineteenth century 293

JOHN HUDSON

Index 329

CONTRIBUTORS

PAUL BRAND is Emeritus Fellow of All Souls College and Professor of English Legal History at the University of Oxford.

J.D. FORD is Professor of Civil Law at the University of Aberdeen.

THOMAS GREEN is an Honorary Research Fellow in the School of Law, University of Glasgow. From 2011 to 2014 he was a British Academy Postdoctoral Fellow in the School of Law, University of Edinburgh.

JOHN HUDSON is Professor of Legal History at the University of St Andrews.

DAVID IBBETSON is Regius Professor of Civil Law at the University of Cambridge and President of Clare Hall.

NEIL JONES is Reader in English Legal History at the University of Cambridge, and a Fellow of Magdalene College, Cambridge.

MICHAEL LOBBAN is Professor of Legal History at the London School of Economics.

ANDREW SIMPSON is Lecturer in the School of Law, University of Aberdeen.

CHANTAL STEBBINGS is Professor of Law and Legal History at the University of Exeter.

ANDREAS THIER is Professor of Legal History, Ecclesiastical Law, Legal Theory and Private Law at the University of Zurich.

ALAIN WIJFFELS is a Senior Research Fellow of the French Centre National de la Recherche Scientifique at the University of Lille-2 and teaches legal history and comparative law at the universities of Leiden, Leuven and Louvain-la-Neuve.

IAN WILLIAMS is Lecturer in the Faculty of Laws, University College, London.

PREFACE

The papers in this book represent a selection of those given at the Twenty-First British Legal History Conference, held at the University of Glasgow between 10 and 13 July 2013 on the theme Law and Authority. The timing was significant for Glasgow, because 2013 marked the tercentenary of the foundation of the Regius Chair of Law at the University of Glasgow, celebrated with a programme of public lectures and other events, which included hosting the Twenty-First British Legal History Conference.

This was the second meeting of the conference in Glasgow. Indeed, a distinctive feature of the conference since its first meeting in Aberystwyth in 1972 has been an emphasis on legal history in all parts of the British Isles, and it has been held variously at venues in England, Ireland, Scotland and Wales. Its first Scottish meeting was in Edinburgh in 1977, organised by Professor Alan Harding (whom the conference was delighted to welcome back to Glasgow in 2013), but was held in Glasgow for the first time in 1989, organised by the late Professor William M. Gordon and Dr David Fergus. And as their successor in the role, I would like to record my gratitude to both Bill Gordon and David Fergus for their advice and support in the planning of the 2013 conference.

It is to the memory of Bill Gordon that this book is dedicated with both affection and esteem. He was an early supporter of the British Legal History Conference from its beginnings in the 1970s. He had planned to attend the 2013 conference, but after a short illness died on 1 September 2012, aged seventy-nine.[1] Bill was Douglas Professor of Civil Law at the University of Glasgow from 1969 to 1999, having begun his career at the University of Aberdeen, where perhaps uniquely he was a pupil of both

[1] See the memorial page at www.iuscivile.com/people/gordon/ which includes links to tributes from Dr Douglas Osler, Professor David Carey Miller and Professor Hector MacQueen, and a full bibliography.

David Daube and Peter Stein.[2] He occupied the chair with distinction and in retirement remained active as a scholar, the range of his interests being well represented by his last two books – *Roman Law, Scots Law and Legal History. Selected Essays* (Edinburgh, 2007), and the third edition of *Scottish Land Law* (Edinburgh, 2009).[3]

Aptly enough, the theme of Law and Authority around which the 2013 conference was based is one which Bill Gordon had himself addressed very suggestively at the Edinburgh conference in 1977 in a paper on 'Stair's Use of Roman Law'.[4] This paper analysed the approach to the authority of Roman law in Scots law taken by the most famous Scottish jurist of the early-modern period, James Dalrymple, Viscount Stair, in *Institutions of the Law of Scotland* (Edinburgh, 1681). Bill's argument was that 'insufficient stress has been laid on the role of natural law and equity in the Institutions, in mediating Roman law . . . '[5] This theme has been explored and developed considerably in scholarship of the last thirty years on the history of early-modern Scots law. In particular, John Ford's *Law and Opinion in Scotland during the Seventeenth Century* (Oxford, 2007) has opened up new perspectives in a remarkable way.[6] This corpus of recent work on Scottish legal history seemed fertile ground from which to generalise a theme for the 2013 conference in Glasgow, especially given that Bill Gordon was a Glasgow professor, John Ford is a Glasgow graduate, and Stair himself was both.[7]

Accordingly, with a suitably broad interpretation of the theme, a total of eighty-seven papers at the conference addressed the ways law has been shaped historically by different forms and ideas of authority, and explored how sources of law and frameworks for their application had developed

2 Omitted in Peter Birks' listing of Daube's pupils in 'Roman Law in Twentieth-Century Britain', in Jack Beatson & Reinhard Zimmermann, eds., *Jurists Uprooted. German-Speaking Émigré Lawyers in Twentieth-Century Britain* (Oxford, 2004), 250–251. For a first-hand account see William M Gordon, 'David's Teaching in Aberdeen', in Ernest Metzger, ed., *David Daube. A Centenary Celebration* (Glasgow, 2010), 88–100.

3 Volume 1 of *Scottish Land Law* appeared in 2009, co-authored with Scott Wortley; Volume 2 awaits publication. Bill's last publication to date appeared posthumously in 2013: William M Gordon, 'Communis error facit ius', in Andrew Burrows, David Johnston & Reinhard Zimmermann, eds., *Judge and Jurist. Essays in Memory of Lord Rodger of Earlsferry* (Oxford, 2013), 447–454.

4 William M. Gordon, 'Stair's Use of Roman Law', in Alan Harding, ed., *Law Making and Law Makers in British Legal History* (London, 1980), 120–126.

5 Gordon, 'Stair's Use of Roman Law', 121–122.

6 Reviewed by the writer in *Journal of Legal History* 29, 3 (2008), 369–372.

7 Stair did not hold a chair as such but was a regent at the university in the 1640s, having been a student there in the 1630s.

over time in relation to concepts of authority, or to the authority of other institutions, processes or actors within the legal order. Something like 180 delegates attended the conference, which was arranged in three parallel sessions over the four days of the meeting. The papers collected in this volume demonstrate the diversity of approaches in how the conference theme was explored, though in the interests of limiting the size of the volume as well as promoting thematic coherence the content was restricted to topics within the scope of British legal history. I am particularly sorry that the limit on the scope of the volume meant that papers by the many continental colleagues who attended the Glasgow conference are mostly not represented, though delighted that those of Andreas Thier and Alain Wijffels are included. The conference opened with John Ford's paper given as a keynote lecture in the first of three plenary sessions, the other two such lectures being given by Alain Wijffels and John Hudson. Sir John Baker also addressed the final plenary session on 'Dafydd Jenkins and the British Legal History Conference', though this is published elsewhere.[8] I am indebted to the four speakers in question for delivering these more extended contributions.

I am grateful to the School of Law at Glasgow for its significant sponsorship of the conference and practical support. I would also particularly like to acknowledge the help of my colleague Professor Ernest Metzger, and the generous advice and support of Dr Neil Jones of Magdalene College, Cambridge, in relation to how the previous conference had been organised in Cambridge in 2011. Cambridge University Press has been extremely patient and helpful too, and I am very grateful to Finola O'Sullivan for her help, advice and encouragement. Finally, the generosity of the other sponsors is also gratefully acknowledged – Glasgow University Court, Glasgow City Council, The Journal of Legal History, The Irish Legal History Society, The Selden Society, The Stair Society, The Welsh Legal History Society, Brill, Cambridge University Press, Duncker und Humblot, Edinburgh University Press, Hart Publishing, Oxford University Press, Routledge, University of Wales Press, The Faculty of Advocates and The Law Society of Scotland.

[8] Sir John Baker, 'Dafydd Jenkins and the British Legal History Conference', in Noel Cox & Thomas Glyn Watkin, eds., *Canmlwyddiant, Cyfraith a Chymreictod, A Celebration of the Life of Dafydd Jenkins 1911–2012* (The Welsh Legal History Society, Vol. XI, 2013).

1

The judicial interpretation of legislation in later thirteenth- and early fourteenth-century England

PAUL BRAND

The early history, or perhaps it is better called the pre-history, of the judicial interpretation of legislation goes back to at least the first quarter of the thirteenth century. We can certainly see the courts at work, for example, in the years after 1215 in giving a specific meaning to that clause of Magna Carta which had required that 'common pleas' should not 'follow our court' but be held 'in some certain place' (*in aliquo certo loco*).[1] A specific meaning needed to be attached by the courts to the term 'common plea',[2] and perhaps also to the requirement that such pleas be held 'in some certain place'.[3] It must also have been the courts and their justices who were responsible for, or at the very least responsible for accepting, the somewhat counter-intuitive interpretation of the 1237 legislation advancing limitation dates which is found within a few years of its enactment.[4] The legislation required (among other things) that counts of claimants in the writ of right should in future not go back as far as 1135 and the day of the death of Henry I (*tempore regis Henrici senis anni et diei*) but no further than the reign of Henry II (*a tempore regis Henrici avi domini regis*). This was to come into force as from Whitsun in the twenty-first regnal year (7 June 1237), but the legislation also said that writs which had been previously acquired might proceed (*et brevia prius*

Unless otherwise stated, manuscript sources are in the National Archives, London.

[1] c. 17 in the 1215 original charter; c. 12 in the 1216 and 1217 reissues; c. 11 in the 1225 reissue.

[2] For argument on this point see *Curia Regis Rolls*, xv, no. 1958 (1236) and for a ruling on this point see *CRR*, xvi, no. 8.

[3] For a 1260 enrolment of the king's claim to a manor against the prior of Wenlock in King's Bench where the prior sought the view and requested that he be given 'a certain day in a certain place' (*quod dies certus ei prefigatur et in loco certo*) and because the writ touched the right he was adjourned to a return day the following term before the justices at Westminster see KB 26/167, m. 4.

[4] *Close Rolls, 1234–7*, pp. 520–21. It soon became wrongly associated with the Provisions of Merton of 1236 and is c. 8 of the classic text of those Provisions.

inpetrata procedant). The obvious meaning would seem to be that the old limitation date would continue to be applicable in the case of writs then pending or which were acquired between the enactment of the legislation (probably in early February) and Whitsun 1237. The courts, however, allowed the continuation of any claim which had been brought prior to 1237 which had gone without a day for whatever reason (and however far in the past that had been)[5] provided there had been no permanent determination of that claim. As early as 1241 a claimant who had made a count based on the seisin of an ancestor in 1135 answered the tenant's objections that such a claim was statute-barred by showing that there had been litigation prior to the legislation which had gone without a day on the death of the claimant's father, and then further litigation brought by the claimant which had gone without a day on the death of the tenant's late husband. This was evidently accepted by the court as justifying the pre-1154 claim.[6] There was then a continuing trickle of such cases down to 1279, and this continued for a while even after the further change in limitation dates made in 1275 by the Statute of Westminster I, c. 39.[7]

It is, however, only in the reign of Edward I that it begins to be possible to see the engagement of individual named justices or groups of justices with the interpretation of statutes and their language in the context of the hearing of individual cases. This is mainly, but not exclusively, through surviving reports of those cases. The earliest known evidence, however, comes from the plea roll enrolment of a Common Bench case of Michaelmas term 1277.[8] In an action of attaint brought to reverse the verdict of a jury given in an action of cosinage in the 1274 Middlesex eyre, the defendants sought judgment of the writ on the grounds that the original verdict had been given before the enactment of c. 38 of the Statute of Westminster I in 1275, which had provided the statutory authority for the extension of

[5] A litigant in the 1268 Yorkshire eyre cited litigation brought by his ancestor Ivo against the tenant's grandfather supposedly before Rannulph de Glanville in 8 Richard I (1196–7) (though he had died in 1190). His opponent cited the 1237 legislation as though made at Runnymede before King John. For the case see *Henry of Carleton* v. *William de Arderne*: JUST 1/1050, m. 66d.

[6] *Matthew de Columbers* v. *Mabel de la Ryvere*: JUST 1/37, m. 7 (1241 Berks hire eyre).

[7] *Thomas of Rodborough* v. *Alan de Chartres and his wife Joan*: CP 40/30, m. 71d. For a discussion of these cases see Paul Brand, '"Time out of Mind": The Knowledge and Use of the Eleventh- and Twelfth-Century Past in Thirteenth-Century Litigation', in *Anglo-Norman Studies XVI* (Woodbridge, 1994), pp. 37–54, at p. 40; Paul Brand, 'Lawyers' Time in England in the Later Middle Ages', in Chris Humphrey and W M Ormrod, eds., *Time in the Medieval World* (York and Woodbridge, 2001), pp. 73–104, at pp. 99–100.

[8] CP 40/21, m. 63d. For the original case see JUST 1/538, m. 3d (Anglo-American Legal Tradition database image 3221).

the action of attaint beyond the limited range of actions (assizes only) in which it had hitherto been available.[9] The statute had not itself made clear whether or not it was to be retroactive, that is, whether it was to apply to jury verdicts which had been given prior to 1275. The point was settled in what may seem a curious way. A junior justice of the court (John de Lovetot) who had only been appointed to the court in Easter term 1275 (the very term during which the legislation was enacted) 'recorded' (*recordatur*) that it was 'not the king's intention' (*non est intencionis domini regis*) nor had it been at the time of the making of the statute (*nec existitit tempore confectionis statuti predicti*) that attaint juries be taken on inquisitions held before the statute was made. On that basis the action was dismissed. Whether this can properly be called 'judicial' interpretation of the statute is less clear, since what Lovetot seems to be doing here is acting as a channel for the king's authoritative ruling on the point at issue, based on his intention at the time of the making of the statute.

Clearer evidence of what may properly be called 'judicial' interpretation comes from law reports of the mid-1280s. In one of the earliest in the 1285 Northamptonshire eyre, Master Thomas of Siddington, the rector of the church of Passenham and, prior to this eyre, himself one of the justices of the same 'northern' eyre circuit, brought an action of annual rent to assert his title to certain annual rents owed to his church by the abbot of Grestein and two defendants and to claim fourteen years of arrears of those same rents. His only title to these rents was the seisin of his church and of his predecessors prior to his succession to the living. The defendants argued that he was not entitled to claim any arrears. In an intervention that did not itself quite amount to a judgment, Saham J. invoked c. 28 of the Statute of Marlborough of 1267 in favour of his erstwhile colleague's action and his right to claim arrears, saying that it was 'quite clear . . . that if a rector dies seised as of the right of his church, his successor (if someone withholds it from him) has his recovery and in this case damages will be adjudged to him . . . '[10] He seems to be referring to that part of c. 28 which referred to the possibility of an action and the recovery of damages but only in the case of intrusion into lands (not the withdrawal of annuities) during the time of a vacancy, and only for lands and tenements of which abbots and other ecclesiastical prelates, but not

[9] *Statutes of the Realm*, I, p. 38.

[10] *Earliest English Law Reports, vol. III, Eyre Reports to 1285*, 122 Selden Society, 2005, p. 233 (85 Northants. 9). For this chapter see Paul Brand, *Kings, Barons and Justices: The Making and Enforcement of Legislation in Thirteenth-Century England* (Cambridge, 2003), pp. 481–3.

parish priests, had died seised as of the right of their church.[11] It is difficult to know whether Saham's memory was at fault here or whether he was deliberately trying to extend a narrowly drawn clause to cover what he saw as an analogous situation. Saham also appears, but mainly through the possibly distorting effects of a complaint made against him for misconduct in 1290, as both significantly extending and significantly restricting c. 4 of the 1278 Statute of Gloucester, which had created the action of *cessavit per biennium*, through rulings made in a very briefly reported case in the 1286 Cambridgeshire eyre.[12] The statute clearly envisaged that the remedy be available only where the initial grant had created a tenurial relationship between grantor and grantee under which rent or the provision of estovers to a quarter of the value of the land was owed; where this rent or payment in kind had ceased; and where the land granted had lain fresh (so that no distress could be found on it) for two or three years.[13] Saham J. allowed the action to proceed even though the grant had been made merely in the hope (*sub spe*) that someone else (and not the grantee) would provide the grantor with food and clothing to a quarter of the annual value of the land in return for his service in a manor as a serjeant or hayward (and thus not as a rent or render payable by the defendant) and, according to the complainant, overruled an exception that the agreement had not created a rent and that the grantor had forfeited the food and clothing by his own wrongdoing when he had left the service of the lord concerned because he was in arrears on his account. Saham also refused to allow the exception that the land had not lain fresh but had been open to distraint. The legislation also specifically provided that if the defendant came before judgment, ready to pay arrears and damages and to find a suitable surety for the future observance of the terms contained in the writing, he was to keep his land. The report, however, indicates that, even though the defendant offered to fulfil the covenant and offered surety after a jury verdict passed against him it was Saham's view that this was too late, and this is also what the defendant later alleged had happened. The plea roll, however, tells a different, and possibly misleading, story: that the defendant had nothing in court when the verdict passed against him from which to satisfy the arrears (though it adds that he ought in any case to

[11] But note that the plea roll enrolment specifically refers to the other part of this chapter, supporting a right of action for withdrawals made in the time of a predecessor when the predecessor had not obtained justice.

[12] For the complaint see JUST 1/541B, m. 9d and the report and the enrolment of the original case *EELR*, vol. IV, pp. 381–2.

[13] *Statutes of the Realm*, I, p. 48.

have done this before the jury gave its verdict) and that he had no surety to offer for future performance.

Another case from the following year shows judicial interpretation of legislation at the hands of Thomas Weyland, then the chief justice of the Common Bench but soon after this himself a fugitive from justice. It is also concerned with the interpretation of the same legislation (c. 4 of the Statute of Gloucester).[14] In this 1287 case the grantor of land at fee farm sought to recover that land from the alienee of the person to whom he had granted it on the grounds that the original grantee had ceased performing the services owed for two years. The grantee had alienated the land to the tenant before the first term at which the rent was payable. The grantor thought that this meant that he was not able to distrain on the grantee because he had never been seised of this rent. Weyland, C.J. took a narrow view of the statute. The statute was intended to supply a remedy where the common law failed. Where the common law was adequate there was no need of the statutory remedy.[15] There was a common law remedy where a tenant failed to pay his rent. It was to distrain in his fee. The statute (as it itself made clear) only supplied a remedy if he was unable to find distresses in his fee, not where he thought he was unable to distrain for other reasons. Since that was not the case here the statutory remedy was not available. But there seems to have been no final judgment in the case.

Law reports become much more plentiful after 1290 and more particularly as from the summer of 1291, and this provides much more evidence about the nitty-gritty of the business of interpreting statutes. One thing they certainly show is that (from at least 1295 onwards) arguments about the meaning of statutory enactments and rulings on their meaning were being made with reference to the specific words of the statutory enactment. This is easier to see where the published text of the statute was in Latin and it is this Latin text which was being quoted in the French language report. In three reports of a 1295 formedon in the descender case (*William son of William de Ferrers* v. *Henry le Porter and his wife Ismania*) the tenant objected to a claim being made by the son and heir of the original donee in tail in which he was seeking to recover land alienated by

[14] *Early English Law Reports, vol. II, Common Bench Reports 1285–1289 and Undated Reports 1279*–1289, 112 Selden Society, 1996, pp. 265–8 (1287.1).

[15] In one report Weyland said this was the same principle as that which applied to writs of entry: no one could bring a writ of entry in the *post* (as created by the 1263 reissue of the Provisions of Westminster and by c. 29 of the Statute of Marlborough) where the writ of entry within the degrees was available. This is the principle affirmed by c. 40 of the Statute of Westminster I (1275): *Statutes of the Realm*, I, pp. 36–7.

the initial donee (his father). This was on the grounds that the claimant had counted that his father (the initial donee) had been seised under the grant in the reign of Henry III but that the statute of *de Donis* (chapter 1 of the Statute of Westminster II of 1285) applied only to entails created after 1285 since it specified that *ad dona prius facta non extenditur* ('it did not extend to gifts made before').[16] All three reports show that this was rejected by the court. One notes simply that 'it was supposed by the court that these words related solely to the (time of the) alienation and not to the time of the gift' (*E la fuist suppose de court qe cele parole ad solement regard al alienacion et nyent al tens del doun*). In the other two it was more specifically chief justice Mettingham who rejected it and who said (in the fuller of the two versions), 'If you understand that what the statute says of *ad dona prius facta etc.* relates to the initial gift you understand wrongly, but it relates to the alienation made by the one to whom the gift was made' (*Si vous entendez qe ceo qe le statut dyt . . . deyt aver relacion au primer doun vous entendez malement mes yl ad relacion a la alienacion fete par celi a qi le doun se tailla*). None of the reports shows the justices making what might seem to the modern reader the obvious point that the piece of the statute being quoted has been torn from its original context in which it is preceded by 'And it is to be known that this statute is to apply in respect of the alienation of the tenement contrary to the form of the gift made in future and . . . ' (*Et sciendum quod hoc statutum quoad alienacionem tenementi contra formam doni imposterum faciendum locum habet . . .*).

In 1298 there is the first reference in a report to a justice, or perhaps the justices, looking at a statute, doing more than just relying on their memory and examining the written text of the legislation being cited. It is a report of a replevin case (*Nicholas of Stillingfleet* v. *Parnel de Coygners*) in which the defendant had refused to gage the release of animals in the court because she had previously been adjudged the irreplevisable return of the animals taken in distraint by the Yorkshire county court after the plaintiff had twice been non-suited in replevin pleas brought there.[17] The defendant's serjeant (Sutton) said that the statute which had authorised irreplevisable returns only applied before the justices (*Le statut*

[16] BL MS. Additional 37657, f. 107r; LI MS. Miscellaneous 738, f. 106v; LI MS. Misc. 87, f. 18r. The plea roll enrolment is CP 40/110, m. 118d. For the legislation see *Statutes of the Realm*, I, pp. 71–2.

[17] There are two collatable reports of this case in BL MS. Additional 5925, f. 42r and LI MS. Hale 188, f. 38r. The enrolment is on CP 40/122, m. 114d.

ne sert fors qe devant justices). This is a reference to that part of the Statute of Westminster II, c. 2 which had first introduced the possibility of a judgment for return irreplevisable and whose words do indeed only talk in terms of litigation already removed into the king's court.[18] A little later it is Howard, J. who (in one version) is reported as looking at the statute (*How' regarda le statut*) and who in the other version spoke of himself and perhaps others as having done so (*Haward. Nous avoms regard le statut...*). He duly confirmed that it only applied before justices and not in the county court. He held that this meant that the county court could not adjudge an irreplevisable return and that the defendant must therefore gage the return of the distress.

The justices did not rely on the wording of legislation alone. In a suit brought by the judicial writ of *scire facias* (invented by the Statute of Westminster II, c. 45)[19] in King's Bench in Trinity term 1307 to enforce the terms of an earlier fine (of 1278) the question arose whether a life tenant who had sought the aid of a reversioner who was actually present in court was entitled to additional delay to have the reversioner summoned specifically for that purpose. The chief justice of the court, Roger Brabazon, was uncertain how to interpret the rather vague words of the chapter about the elimination of procedural delays. He decided that what was needed was consultation 'with our companions who were present at the making of the statute' (*voloms de ceste chose conseiller ove nos compaignons qe furent al statut fere*). The case was certainly adjourned to a later day, probably the same term, and it must be supposed that what he was intending to do was to consult with the justices not only of his own court but also of other courts who had been present at the making of the Statute of Westminster II.[20] What exactly that meant is less clear: was it those who were present when it was initially drafted? Or those who were present when it was discussed and approved in parliament?

Justices were certainly present in parliament when legislation was being discussed and probably took part in the discussion. The best evidence of this comes from a report of an assize of mort d'ancestor brought by Adam of Redlingfield against the chancellor and university of Cambridge for four messuages and twenty-six acres of arable in Cambridge heard

[18] *Statutes of the Realm*, I, p. 73. [19] *Statutes of the Realm*, I, pp. 93–4.

[20] *YB 33–35 Edward I*, pp. 577–87, at p. 585. The passage does not appear in other reports of the same case. For the record see KB 27/188, m. 45 [partially printed in *Select Cases of the Court of King's Bench vol. 3*, 58 Selden Society, 1939, pp. 165–8].

in the summer session of the 1299 Cambridgeshire eyre.[21] Counsel for the chancellor and university pleaded in bar a fine made in the previous Cambridgeshire eyre of 1286. Counsel for the claimant attempted to make the old and long accepted objection that the fine was not a bar since the claimant's brother and not the university had been seised before the making of the fine and when it was made. But c. 1 of the Statute of Fines published early in April 1299 had stated that this kind of objection was no longer to be accepted by the court and allowed to deprive fines of their effect.[22] The chief justice of the eyre, John of Berwick, had evidently been present at the Lent parliament of 1299 where this legislation had been enacted and he duly reported something of what had been said there less than six months earlier about the basic principle being enacted: 'when this statute was being made this argument was made: how can someone acknowledge tenements of which he was never seised to be the right of another who was never seised nor any of his ancestors? To this it was answered that since he acknowledged [it] one ought to understand that it was so, since who could better make estate than one who has the right in it.'[23]

The justices also interpreted legislation in the light of what they said, or what they deduced from the statute itself, to be its primary purpose. In a dower case brought in Trinity term 1291 Margery, widow of Philip of Bredicot, sued John of Bredicot in the Common Bench for one third of a messuage and a virgate in Bredicot near Worcester which she claimed as her dower. John said she was not entitled to dower as the land had been given to Philip and the heirs of his body and he had died without such an heir and had thus not been so seised that he was able to endow her.[24] The widow's counsel (Harle) cited Magna Carta as providing that the widow was to be entitled to have one-third of the land of which her husband had been seised. The heir's counsel (Warwick) argued that if she gained her dower that would be contrary to the will of the donor and

[21] BL MS. Additional 35116, ff. 56v–57v. The enrolment is JUST 1/96, m. 26d. It is not to be found in the other report of the same case in BL MS. Add. 5925, ff. 31r–v.

[22] *Statutes of the Realm*, I, pp. 128–9.

[23] *Berewyk. Quant ceo statut fust a fere home fist ceste reson: coment purra home conustre les tenemenz dount il ne fust unke seisi estre le droit autri qe unqes ne fust seisi ne nul de ses auncestres? A ceo fut respondu qe depus qil conust e home deit entendre qe auzi soit qar qi purra melz faire estate fors qe celui qe droit en ad.*

[24] CP 40/90, m. 87. There are reports of the case in multiple manuscripts: BL MSS. Harley 25, ff. 86v and 90v, Harley 572, ff. 142r–v, Harley 2183, f. 64r, Harley 2183, f. 65v, Stowe 386, f. 174v, Additional 31826, f. 148r, Additional 37657, f. 7r, Egerton 2811, ff. 107v–108r and Bodleian Library MS. Holkham Misc. 30, f. 60r.

'statute [meaning Westminster II, c. 1] provided that his wishes should be expressly kept in all matters' (*e lestatut veut qe sa volunte seyt en touz poynz expressment garde*). Harle argued that any issue of the husband would have inherited and since the wife was only a 'vessel to conceive' no failure could be ascribed to her. Warwick argued that since the husband had never had more than 'free tenement' (a life estate) she was not entitled to dower from this free tenement. Mettingham, C.J. then gave judgment. He said that the statute (he means Westminster II, c. 1) was made to prevent disinheritance since before the statute those who to whom land was given in tail could alienate the tenements so given once they had issue and exclude their issue and also exclude the donor's issue from the reversion. Its purpose was not to deprive widows of their dower contrary to Magna Carta (*pur eschuir celis durescis fut purveu statut e noun pas a toler damis lur douer encontir la Grant Chartre*). Since it was agreed by both sides that if there had been a child it would have inherited the tenement 'as of fee and right' even if the 'fee' concerned was only a 'fee tail' (*le fiz ust este enherite des tenement cum de fee e de dreit, coment qe le fee seit taille*) and any failure was not on her part, he gave the judgment of the court that she should recover her dower.

A related form of argument was that which identified those for whose benefit legislation had been made and said that they were the only group or groups who could benefit from it. Such an argument was, for example, made in the report of an assize of novel disseisin at an assize session of 1307 where the defendant had been distrained for arrears of a rent and had then replevied the distress. His counsel argued that the plaintiff's mother had given him the tenements concerned after the Statute of *Quia Emptores* of 1290 and thus the plaintiff (her heir) could not claim the rent as rent service. Higham, J. said that even if a tenant had been enfeoffed after the statute to hold of his feoffor and he had become seised of his services the tenant could not take advantage of the statute 'because if you wish to be aided by the statute it is necessary that you be the one for whose advantage the statute was made. But you know well that *Quia Emptores* was made wholly for the advantage of chief lords so that they do not lose wardships, reliefs and escheats. You are a tenant whom the statute does not aid'. And if one looks at the preamble to the statute that is exactly what this would lead you to conclude.[25] In modern terms, however, this was an *obiter dictum* since the matter then went to a jury verdict. This found that

[25] *Statutes of the Realm*, I, p. 106.

the enfeoffment had in fact preceded the statute of 1290 and the plaintiff's mother and the plaintiff had been seised until he was disseised.[26]

A second reported case (*Roger of Mersea and his wife Isabel* v. *Joan the wife of Robert Cope*) from Hilary 1305 unites both these approaches. A woman and her second husband brought a writ of entry *cui in vita* to recover fifteen acres of land granted to the woman and her first husband and allegedly alienated by that first husband.[27] In bar the tenant pleaded a final concord levied both by the wife and by the first husband with the alleged alienee in the 1287 Suffolk eyre, acknowledging the alienee's right to the land. In only one of the three reports is there an argument about the effects of that final concord. Counsel for the claimants said that the tenements had in fact originally been granted in fee tail to the wife and her first husband and the heirs of their bodies and that the alienation by fine had been made after the enactment of c. 1 of the Statute of Westminster II which had said that any final concord levied on land held in fee tail was in future to be held null and void (more pithily in the French *estatut veut qe la ou tenemenz sunt donez en fee tayle etc. e pus aliene en fee e sur ceo fyn se leve la fyn sait tenu pur nule*). That is indeed pretty much what the final sentence of c. 1 says but a little bit more fully.[28] It was counsel for the other side who rebutted this: 'the statute had been made to assist those to whom the reversion belongs and the heirs of the donee, and so he was not in the case of the statute' (*B dit qe statute est fet en ayde a ceus a qy la reversion apent e a les heyrs le done, dount il ne fut mye en cas de statut*). According to the same report it was Hengham, C.J. who in essence adopted this reasoning: 'You are not aided by statute and so the court adjudges that you take nothing by your writ' (*Vus nestes mye ayde par estatut par quai agard la cort qe vus ne prengnez ren par vostre bref*).

One other revealing, but anonymous, judgment of this period is known only from the plea roll enrolment. For once it is a criminal plea. It comes from the 1284 Leicestershire eyre and it takes us back to the interpretation of Magna Carta. Magna Carta (in clause 54 of the 1215 version and c. 34 of the 1225 version) had laid down as a rule that no one was to be arrested or imprisoned on the appeal (private criminal prosecution) of a woman for any death other than that of her husband. Annabel, the

26 The case is reported in BL MSS. Harley 572, f. 160v and Hargrave 375, f. 185r.

27 CP 40/154, m. 52d. The case is reported in BL MSS. Hargrave 375, f. 29v, Additional 31826, f. 375v and Stowe 386, f. 199r.

28 'Et si finis super hujusmodi tenementa imposterum levetur ipso jure sit nullus nec habeant heredes aut illi ad quos spectat reversio, licet plene sint etatis, in Anglia et extra prisonam, necesse apponere clamium suum'.

daughter of Robert of Nailston, had brought an appeal against William Bate of Nailston for the killing of her sister Isabel. Although the county court had entertained the appeal they had not outlawed him because she had appealed him for the death of someone other than her husband. Judgment was given against the county court by the justices in Eyre on the grounds that they 'had allowed the remedy (benefit) of the statute to those who had asked for no remedy, as they were absent' (*quia comitatus allocabat remedium statuti hiis qui nullum remedium pecierunt eo quod absentes fuerunt*). There are two points of interest here. One is the extended interpretation given by the county court to the clause of Magna Carta: In form it said only that no one was to be arrested or imprisoned on the appeal of a woman for the death of anyone other than her husband, not that no one was to be outlawed on the appeal of a woman for a killing. But it seems common for this clause to be extended beyond its terms, generally to disallow any appeal by a woman except for the death of her husband.[29] But the county court was not being penalised for this, for misinterpreting Magna Carta. What it was being penalised for was allowing the benefit of the statute to someone who had not asked for it. It is tempting to wonder whether this was because the king was the loser thereby, since the king potentially benefitted from any outlawry (from the year, day and waste of the outlaw's lands and the forfeiture of his chattels). It seems just possible, however, that there is a wider and more general rule being enunciated here and one which goes to the difference between the Common Law and Statute. Anyone was entitled to the benefit of the Common Law, but Statute (and perhaps especially Magna Carta, which took the form of a grant of liberties) needed to be invoked specially by those who wished to benefit from it.

The history of legislation in England goes back to the pre-Conquest period, indeed to well before there was a single kingdom of England. It is, however, only from the last decade of the twelfth century with the survival of the first plea rolls of the king's courts that we can see the courts beginning to engage in the business of the interpretation of legislation, of giving a more specific meaning to the words of legislative texts that might bear or be made to bear a variety of meanings, and only from c. 1270 onwards, with the beginning of unofficial law reporting, and on a larger scale from 1291 onwards with the beginnings of larger-scale law reporting that we can begin to see the contribution of individual royal justices in

[29] For evidence of this extension see TNA: PRO CP 40/10, m. 24; CP 40/17, m. 70; CP 40/125. m. 68.

and through their arguments and rulings and judgments to that process of interpretation. This paper has only been able to cite and use a small proportion of the surviving material, much of it as yet unpublished, but there is, I think, enough here to show that in these reports we can see the clear beginnings of a long, and as yet continuing, tradition of interaction between royal justices and authoritative legislative texts.

2

The authority of parliament and the scope of the Statute of Uses 1536

N.G. JONES

I. Introduction

Professor Baker has suggested that by Tudor times English legislation 'had undergone a significant change', that in this period 'in the temporal sphere parliament ventured to the limits of legal possibility', change being wrought by 'humanist legislators confident in their ability to improve things by the right use of power'.[1] One element in this exercise of authority by parliament was the Statute of Uses 1536,[2] the importance of which, as E.W. Ives has put it,

> is beyond doubt. The effect which its provisions had upon the development of English land law was revolutionary, and from it have grown the crucial doctrines of the trust. In the political field its importance was not less . . . when the rebels rose against Henry VIII in 1536, they demanded not only the abandonment of the king's religious changes, but the abandonment of the statute as well.[3]

Those who have sought to penetrate the thickets surrounding the 'brilliant and disreputable career'[4] of executed uses at common law after 1536 may perhaps doubt that in all respects the effect of the change wrought through

All manuscripts cited are in The National Archives: Public Record Office. Transcriptions from manuscript have been rendered into modern orthography.

[1] J.H. Baker, *An Introduction to English Legal History*, 4th edition (London, 2002), p. 207.

[2] 27 Hen. VIII, c. 10.

[3] E.W. Ives, 'The Genesis of the Statute of Uses', 82 *English Historical Review* (1967), p. 673, at p. 673. For the Statute of Uses and the northern rising known as the Pilgrimage of Grace see R.W. Hoyle, *The Pilgrimage of Grace and the Politics of the 1530s* (Oxford, 2001), pp. 155–156, 349, 352, 455, 462. The demand that the Statute of Uses be repealed may have been 'tangential to the main course of the Pilgrimage', *ibid.*, p. 352, but that means would be found to evade an unpopular statute clearly worried Thomas Cromwell; see Sir John Baker, *Oxford History of the Laws of England*, vol. 6, *1483–1558* (Oxford, 2003), pp. 680–681.

[4] S.F.C. Milsom, *Historical Foundations of the Common Law*, 2nd edition (London, 1981), p. 222.

the Statute of Uses was to 'improve things by the right use of power',[5] but a full understanding of the exercise of power represented by the statute requires assessment not only of its effects – which have been extensively considered[6] – but also of the context in which it arose. Quite what those responsible for the Statute of Uses supposed they were doing cannot be understood solely in hindsight. In the absence of a Chancery record before the mid-1530s,[7] this paper begins the process of examining the statute's context by considering a sample of some 130 bills in Chancery concerning uses from the chancellorships of Wolsey (1515–1529) and More (1529–1532), the last two complete chancellorships before the passing of the statute.[8] Chancery bills, of course, were subject to the imperatives of litigation, and even where pleadings survive beyond the bill the truth may remain elusive. But it is perhaps safe to assume that assertions made in pleading might bear some relation to the truth, and would at least not be obviously implausible.[9]

[5] For an outline discussion of legal executory interests, containing at their heart 'perhaps the deepest of all the mysteries of the common law' (that is, the doctrine of the *scintilla iuris*) see A.W.B. Simpson, *A History of the Land Law*, 2nd edition (Oxford, 1986), pp. 218 ff.

[6] For a general treatment of the statute's effect see Baker, *Introduction to English Legal History*, 4th edition, pp. 284–293. For the history of trusts in the immediate aftermath of the statute see N. Jones, 'Trusts in England after the Statute of Uses: A View from the Sixteenth Century', in R. Helmholz and R. Zimmermann, eds., *Itinera Fiduciae: Trust and Treuhand in Historical Perspective* (Berlin, 1998), pp. 173–205.

[7] The Chancery decree rolls (class C 78) contain cases from 1534 onwards; the Chancery entry books of decrees and orders (class C 33) begin in 1544.

[8] Bills have been identified from a word search under 'use' and 'uses' of the calendar of class C 1 (Early Chancery Proceedings, Richard II to Philip and Mary). In selecting bills for inclusion in the sample no account was taken of the information in the calendar concerning the contents of each bill beyond the fact that it included the term 'use' or 'uses'. In consequence of the respective lengths of the chancellorships of Wolsey and More, the substantial majority of the bills in the sample are from the chancellorship of Wolsey. The bills can be dated only from the name, style and titles of the chancellor to whom they were addressed. In consequence of this, in the period selected, bills fall into three date ranges: 1515–1518, 1518–1529, and 1529–1532. The events giving rise to a bill may, of course, have occurred long before the bill was exhibited, but an examination of bills in the period chosen gives access to questions and circumstances concerning uses which were being litigated in the years before the passing of the Statute of Uses.

[9] Litigated cases are in their nature exceptional, and thus not necessarily a complete guide to practice. Forming a fuller picture will therefore require examination of surviving conveyancing muniments from the period in addition to the evidence of litigation. In the absence of a Chancery record, judicial findings as to the truth of allegations in pleadings are generally not available. In consquence the focus in this paper is upon what might plausibly be alleged, rather than upon the truth or otherwise of the allegations. This being so, it has not been attempted to elucidate the true facts, though reference is made to pleadings

As is well known, the Statute of Uses operated to execute uses, passing legal title from the trustees (or feoffees to uses) to the beneficiary. It being generally impossible to make a will of freehold land at common law, in the late Middle Ages the practice became common of making *inter vivos* feoffments to the use of the feoffor and his heirs, or to the use of the performance of a last will,[10] the feoffor occupying and enjoying the land during his life, the feoffees holding the bare legal title and performing directions in the last will after the feoffor's death. Behind this practice lay the 'sub-plot'[11] of loss caused by such feoffments to the royal feudal revenue. In this context, following the decision of the judges in *Lord Dacre's Case* (1535)[12] that a will of a use of freehold land was void at common law, the Statute of Uses was passed.[13] As is also well known, it came to be understood that not all uses were executed by the statute, the exceptions (which might overlap) being uses of property other than freehold land; uses where the feoffees had active duties to perform; and uses upon uses.[14]

It seems from the provisions of the Statute of Enrolments 1536[15] that it was anticipated that uses would continue to arise after the Statute of Uses, the Statute of Enrolments operating to prevent the immediate execution of uses raised by implication in conveyances by bargain and sale.[16] The Statute of Enrolments concerned uses which, once raised by bargain and sale, would be executed by the Statute of Uses upon enrolment of the deed.[17] To what extent was it anticipated not merely that uses would

other than bills (in particular, answers) in cases in which such pleadings themselves shed light on what might plausibly be alleged.

[10] These provisions were interchangeable: Baker, *Oxford History of the Laws of England*, vol. 6, p. 653, n. 4.

[11] Milsom, *Historical Foundations of the Common Law*, 2nd edition, p. 208.

[12] Sir John Baker, *Baker and Milsom, Sources of English Legal History: Private Law to 1750*, 2nd edition (Oxford, 2010), pp. 127–132.

[13] For the practice of making feoffments to the uses of a last will, the effect of this on the royal feudal revenue, and the response leading up to the Statute of Uses see Baker, *Oxford History of the Laws of England*, vol. 6, pp. 654 ff.

[14] For these exceptions see *ibid.*, pp. 683–686.

[15] 27 Hen. VIII, c. 16.

[16] For discussion of the purpose of the Statute of Enrolments see J.M. Kaye, 'A Note on the Statute of Enrolments 1536', 104 *Law Quarterly Review* (1988), pp. 617–634.

[17] It may be that a view arose after 1536 that a conveyance by bargain and sale now took effect by force of the Statute of Enrolments, and not by the raising and execution of an implied use, a view which was rejected by the judges in the Court of Wards in *Tyrrel's Case* (1557), Dyer 155a; Benloe 28; 1 Anderson 37; Benloe with Dallison 61. See N.G. Jones, 'Tyrrel's Case (1557) and the Use upon a Use', 14 *Journal of Legal History* (1993), p. 75, at pp. 78–79.

continue to arise after the statute, but that some of them would not be executed?

Professor Simpson argued that upon the passing of the Statute of Uses it 'must have looked as though express conveyances to uses would die a natural death; now that it was no longer possible to separate the legal and the equitable estate, why bother to try?',[18] a view supported, Simpson suggested, by the failure of the legislature to make provision for the survival after 1536 of any type of use other than that implied in a bargain and sale. Given that this 'was the way the draftsman looked at the matter',[19] he might be blamed for having 'failed to word the first section [of the statute] so as to execute *all* uses',[20] with the result that 'his assumption that the separation of legal and equitable ownership would in future be impossible was wrong', and that after 1536 'there was still point in creating those uses which would not be executed by the statute'.[21]

In further weighing the blame which he attributed to the draftsman, Simpson made three points. First, that the later view that uses of leases were unexecuted because of a lack of seisin in the lessee would not have been clear in 1536, and that it was arguable at that date that some uses of leasehold were void in any event under the statute 3 Hen. VII, c. 4 (1487), which declared deeds of gifts of chattels 'of trust, to the use of' the makers of such deeds to be void.[22] Second, in relation to the 'discovery' after 1536

[18] Simpson, *A History of the Land Law*, 2nd edition, p. 193. [19] *Ibid.*

[20] *Ibid.* (emphasis in the original). In the immediate aftermath of the statute, John Boys, reading in Gray's Inn in 1536, took the view that 'every limitation of use made after the statute should have been void', for which view he was 'in trouble': W.H. Rowe, ed., *The Reading upon the Statute of Uses of Francis Bacon*, new edition (London, 1804), p. 41. In the same year Serjeant Mountague referred to the Statute of Uses as 'the Statute for extinguishing of uses' (Dyer, 23, pl. 148), though the Statute of Uses was still being referred to in Chancery pleadings in the 1560s as the statute 'made for the extinguishment of uses' (e.g. C 78/26/23, C 78/29/25, C 78/31/13, C 78/40/7). By that date it must have been clear that not all uses were executed, and unless a phrase originating in a misunderstanding had simply become hallowed by usage, it would seem that 'extinguishment' had a meaning closer to 'execution' than to 'abolition'. See also Baker, *Oxford History of the Laws of England*, vol. 6, pp. 674–675.

[21] *Ibid.* The identity of the 'draftsman' of the Statute of Uses is not certainly known. Lehmberg suggested that 'the prototype of the actual statute' was 'probably prepared by Thomas Wriothesley or another of Cromwell's drafting clerks'. It was followed by 'a draft written in a legal script and improved stylistically by Cromwell' which was 'virtually identical with the act as passed', Stanford E. Lehmberg, *The Reformation Parliament 1529–1536* (Cambridge, 1970), pp. 236–237, referring to SP 1/101, fos. 252–260 and 262–281.

[22] Simpson, *A History of the Land Law*, 2nd edition, p. 194. Further on the statute 3 Hen. VII, c. 4 see Baker, *Oxford History of the Laws of England*, vol. 6, pp. 541, 746–747. The statute seems to have been particularly aimed at deeds of gift of chattels to support debtors

of the non-execution of active uses, Simpson suggested that 'these uses did not generally form a large or important class, and represent only a minor fault in the statute', while accepting that uses for charitable purposes 'were important'.[23] Third, in relation to uses upon uses, Simpson supposed that the chancellor would not enforce such uses until the 1630s, and that uses upon uses in any event arose by accident, so that it would be 'unfair' to treat the draftsman's silence about them as 'a failing at all'.[24]

Some observations are required. As to leases, work on the Chancery record in the period after 1536 suggests that there was indeed some doubt about the execution of passive uses of leases until the 1590s, and that it may have been possible in the 1550s, and perhaps in the 1560s, to suppose that a passive use of a lease would be executed. In 1573 Christopher Wray JKB was noted as having said that he had heard 'that it has been the opinion of the Middle Temple that [a use of a lease] should be executed'.[25] But as early as 1547 a passive use of a lease appears to have been created in the belief that it was unexecuted, and to have been treated as such.[26] Probably the general view in the 1550s, and perhaps also in the late 1540s, was the later view that a passive use of a lease was not executed. There is insufficient evidence for the period between 1536 and the later 1540s to reach a firm conclusion in that period, but it seems at least possible that the non-execution of passive uses of leases, were they to be created, would have been foreseeable in 1536.[27] As to uses of freehold land in the form of a use upon a use, the view that they were not enforced in Chancery until the 1630s was merely the result of an accident of printing which gave apparent priority to *Sambach* v. *Daston* (or *Dalston*) (1635); and the supposition that they arose primarily, or even frequently, by accident is similarly open to question in the light of manuscript evidence, and was

fleeing to sanctuary, this mischief being set out in the preamble, though the statute itself provided generally that 'all deeds of gift of goods and chattels, made or to be made of trust to the use of that person or persons that made the same deed of gift, be void and of none effect'.

23 *Ibid.*, p. 195.

24 *Ibid.*, pp. 195–196. The reference to the 1630s in relation to uses upon uses is to *Sambach* v. *Daston* (or *Dalston*) (1635), Nelson 30, Tothill 188, pl. 168, on which see, J.E. Strathdene, 'Sambach v. Dalston: An Unnoticed Report', 74 *Law Quarterly Review* (1958), p. 550.

25 Baker, *Baker and Milsom, Sources of English Legal History*, p. 145. No indication is given as to when (or why) the Middle Temple had held this view.

26 *Jones* v. *Mustyn* (1566), C 78/3612, C 78/36/33, referring to a lease for twenty-one years made in 1547 by Hughe Whitforde to two trustees to his own use, following which the trustees 'did permit and suffer' Hughe to occupy the land and take the profits for 'a long time'.

27 For further detail see Jones, 'Trusts in England after the Statute of Uses', pp. 178–179.

encouraged by what seems to have been a misunderstanding of the reasons for the creation of a use upon a use in the conveyance by bargain and sale enrolled which led to *Jane Tyrrel's Case* (1557).[28] Simpson's reasons for regarding it as 'unfair' to blame the draftsman of the Statute of Uses for the non-execution of uses upon uses may thus be doubted. Whether uses upon uses existed before 1536, and were within the draftsman's contemplation, remains to be addressed.

Behind the detail of Simpson's approach, however, lies the deeper question of whether it is safe to suppose that it had ever been intended to 'execute *all* uses',[29] or that it had been assumed when the Statute of Uses was passed that 'the separation of legal and equitable ownership would in future be impossible'.[30] In relation to active uses of freehold land, Professor Milsom has suggested that they

> must have been within the contemplation of the draftsman. The commonest provisions by testators were those directing their feoffees to raise money out of their lands for the payment of debts, for marriage portions and the like, and for religious or other charitable works for the donor's soul. . . . The draftsman of the Statute of Uses . . . who supposed himself to be abolishing wills of land, may have thought that for the future such uses would just not arise,

and his failure to make provision for such uses already established in wills saved by the statute's transitional provisions may indicate that such uses were assumed to be outside the scope of the statute, and therefore that 'there may never have been any doubt about the propriety of truly active uses'.[31]

In relation to uses of personal property, including leases, Professor Milsom has suggested that while such property might have been devoted to charitable purposes or the like before 1536, this would normally have been by will – and the relevant jurisdiction therefore that over executors – and that since personalty could freely be devised at common law, there

[28] See Jones, 'The Use upon a Use in Equity Revisited' and Jones, 'Tyrrel's Case (1557) and the Use upon a Use'. For the report of *Jane Tyrrel's Case* see Baker, *Baker and Milsom, Sources of English Legal History*, pp. 141–142.

[29] Simpson, *A History of the Land Law*, 2nd edition, p. 193 (emphasis in original).

[30] *Ibid.*

[31] Milsom, *Historical Foundations of the Common Law*, 2nd edition, pp. 235–236. Section 9 of the statute provided that 'true and just' testaments and wills made by persons deceased, or who should die before 1 May 1536, 'shall be taken and accepted good and effectual in the law, after such fashion, manner and form as they were commonly taken and used' at any time within forty years before the making of the statute.

would have been no need to make transfers of it *inter vivos* to trustees to gain the effect of a will, these arguments presupposing both that there was a clear distinction between the jurisdiction in Chancery over trustees and the ecclesiastical jurisdiction over executors, and that there would have been no reason to create a use of personalty absent a necessity to do so to achieve the effect of a will.[32]

But in Milsom's view there was a deeper point. It was not 'just that uses of personal property were not intended to be executed by the statute', but that

> [t]he phrase itself would probably have seemed a contradiction in terms. Almost the only motive for an *inter vivos* arrangement which could be so described would be to defraud creditors; and an act of 1487, the latest of a series dealing with this, instead of speaking in terms of collusion as the others had, declared deeds of gift of chattels 'of trust, to the use of' the makers of those deeds to be simply void. Not until the middle of the sixteenth century does it seem to have been settled that this applied only to dispositions in fraud of creditors. And although it became clear that the Statute of Uses did not execute uses of leasehold, it appears that chancellors were reluctant to intervene on the ground that long terms could be employed to defraud the revenue. It is therefore possible that there was no continuity of equitable interests in personalty before and after the statute in the sense usually understood, and that the true trust of personalty began later . . . the draftsman of the Statute of Uses was not addressing himself to equitable interests as such: he was dealing with wills of land. To think of trusts of personalty as evidence that he did not intend to abolish uses, or as evidence that he did intend it but was incompetent, is to think in unreal terms.[33]

As to the reluctance of chancellors to enforce uses of leases, manuscript evidence suggests that there was no general policy of refusing enforcement to such uses in the period after 1536, and litigation concerning uses of leases was common in Chancery well before 1600. The earliest examples of uses of chattels personal in the Chancery record after the Statute of Uses date from the 1540s, and there is evidence of uses of leases being created

[32] Milsom, *Historical Foundations of the Common Law*, 2nd edition, p. 234. On the question of a distinction between the jurisdiction over executors and that over feoffees to uses see J. Biancalana, 'Testamentary Cases in Fifteenth-Century Chancery', 76 *Tijdschrift voor Rechtsgeschiedenis* (2008), pp. 283–306: 'In the fifteenth century Chancery asserted jurisdiction over testaments, oral last wills of chattels, trusts of chattels used as substitutes for testaments, and disputes involving executors and legatees', *ibid.*, p. 306.

[33] Milsom, *Historical Foundations of the Common Law*, 2nd edition, pp. 234–235, referring to the statute 3 Hen. VII, c. 4.

in the same decade.[34] If there was no continuity of 'equitable interests' in personalty before and after the Statute of Uses, the discontinuity after 1536 was not long. The position in Chancery in the decades before 1536 remains to be examined.

II. The evidence of the pleadings

1. *Freehold land*

To begin with freehold land, as expected, the sample of bills reveals a substantial number of allegations of conveyances to the uses of a last will. In *More* v. *Kyrkeham*,[35] for example, it was alleged that John Carowe, deceased, in his lifetime had enfeoffed several feoffees to the use of himself and his heirs, 'and to and for the performance' of his will, providing in the will that the feoffees should stand seised of the land after his death until they had raised from it £600, to be equally divided among his daughters for their marriages.[36] Such posthumous active duties upon feoffees of freehold to the uses of a last will were no doubt common. So in *Moile* v. *Kirton* it was alleged that the late John Moile had 'made and declared his last will' that his feoffees should take the issues of the land in question from which to make payments in specified sums to each of his three daughters.[37] And in *Parr* v. *Wanton* – indicating the difficulty of drawing a clear distinction between executors and feoffees to the uses of a last will – it was alleged that Sir George Hervy had suffered a common recovery of land to a group of trustees, to the use of Sir George and to the performance of his will. Two of the trustees were among those appointed executors of the will, which directed that for fifteen years following Sir George's death

[34] On trusts of leases in the decades after 1536 see Jones, 'Trusts in England after the Statute of Uses', pp. 179–181.

[35] C 1/545/30 (1518–1529).

[36] For further conveyances to the uses of a last will see, for example, C 1/451/7 (1515–1518); C 1/473/78 (1518–1529); C 1/484/28 (1518–1529); C 1/540/37 (1518–1529); C 1/545/2 (1518–1529); C 1/545/44 (1518–1529); C 1/556/1 (1518–1529); C 1/574/19 (1518–1529); C 1/596/27 (1518–1529); C 1/387/28 (1518–1529); C 1/383/62 (1518–1529); C 1/404/30 (1518–1529); C 1/408/10 (1518–1529); C 1/438/6 (1518–1529); C 1/438/16 (1518–1529); C 1/501/32 (1518–1529); C 1/505/51 (1518–1529); C 1/453/7 (1518–1529); C 1/478/20 (1518–1529); C 1/490/20 (1518–1529); C 1/382/20 (1518–1529); C 1/545/30 (1518–1529); C 1/565/323 (1518–1529); C 1/581/76 (1518–1529); C 1/599/55 (1518–1529); C 1/651/40 (1529–1532).

[37] C 1/545/44 (1518–1529).

the executors should take the revenues, issues and profits of the land to the intent that they should pay debts, and other legacies and bequests.[38]

But active duties in relation to freehold land were not confined to the performance of last wills.[39] Some active duties created *inter vivos* concerned payment of money. In *Vaughell* v. *Gibbs*, for example, it was alleged that Walter Toker, being seised of land, had enfeoffed four feoffees who were to 'receive and take the issues and profits' of the land 'and of the same to make payment to the churchwardens for the time being' of the church of Diptford, Devon, to 'the use of the... church'.[40] And in *Stukelegh* v. *Eston* it was alleged that the plaintiff's father, Nicholas Stukelegh, had enfeoffed Sir Thomas Greynfeld and John Eston, 'to the intent that... John Eston after the death of... Nicholas should take levy and perceive' £10 yearly from the issues and profits of the land to a total of £80 to the use of the plaintiff, then an infant, towards his exhibition and living.[41]

A number of bills concern an active duty upon feoffees, created *inter vivos*, to convey an estate. So in *Mennwenek* v. *Wylgarn* it was alleged that Thomas Mennwenek had 'of great trust only and for no other cause', enfeoffed the defendant and others 'to the intent to refeoff... Thomas or his heirs at such time as they should be thereto required'.[42] In other cases the re-conveyance was to be to persons other than the feoffor, so in *Cole* v. *Rawe* it was alleged that John Hyll had enfeoffed John Rowe, serjeant-at-law, and others 'upon this condition' that they should enfeoff the plaintiffs – Hyll's daughter and her husband – to them and the heirs of their bodies;[43] and in *Dormand* v. *Langham* it was alleged that William

[38] C 1/556/1 (1518–1529).

[39] Active duties in respect of realty were not limited to freehold land: the sample includes two active trusts of advowsons. In *Abbot of Tyltey* v. *Fanne*, C 1/582/29 (1518–1529) the trustees were to present the abbot for the time being of Tyltey, Essex, at each vacancy in the church of Great Easton, Essex, and in *Davys* v. *Kelik*, C 1/625/16 (1518–1529) the trustees were to present the plaintiff to the next vacancy of the church of Narberth, Pembrokeshire (the same matter appears also in C 1/495/20).

[40] C 1/587/26 (1518–1529).

[41] C 1/442/44 (1515–1518). The plaintiff was aged about eight at his father's death. The action was against John Eston's executor, the plaintiff alleging that Eston had retained the money to his own use, and that the plaintiff had no remedy at law for want of specialty to charge Eston's executor for the debt. It is possible that the alleged duty was specified in Nicholas Stukelegh's will, though neither the bill, nor the answer or replication (respectively C 1/442/45 and C 1/442/46), makes reference to a will, and it appears that the duty was imposed *inter vivos* upon the feoffment.

[42] C 1/430/12 (1515–1518).

[43] C 1/400/48 (1515–1519). The name of Serjeant Rowe (or Roo) is spelt 'Rawe' in the bill.

Norman had enfeoffed three feoffees 'to the intent' that they make estate 'at such time as they thereunto should be required', to William Massh and his heirs.[44] In light of such cases, and of those concerning duties to make payments of money, it is difficult to suppose that when the Statute of Uses was passed it could have been thought that if feoffments to the uses of a last will were abolished, active uses of freehold would thereafter 'just not arise'.[45]

No case in the sample concerns a passive trust of freehold expressed in the form of a use upon a use, though such trusts may have been known before 1536: in *Ebden* v. *Paris* it was found in Chancery in 1565 that in about 1527 John Huntingdon had purchased land in the name of Philip Paris, having, the plaintiffs supposed, 'for the more avoiding of suspicion . . . caused [the conveyance] to be made to the use of . . . [Paris] and his heirs', the land in consequence being held by Paris, to the use of Paris, to the use of Huntingdon.[46] It was also possible for a use upon a use to arise by the expressing of a use upon the use implied in a bargain and sale: in *Sherrard* v. *Mayor of London* it was alleged that Thomas and George Sherrard had bargained and sold land to Christopher Davison and John Hall, to the use of Davison and of his heirs.[47]

In contrast to the situation after 1536, it was possible before the Statute of Uses for a passive trust of freehold land, not in the form of a use upon a use, to persist unexecuted, and it was at the heart of the statute that such trusts to the uses of a last will should for the future be executed. But passive trusts of freehold beyond the scope of feoffments to the uses

[44] C 1/500/13 (1518–1520). Massh was brother to the two female plaintiffs. For a further example of duties to convey see *Whiteley* v. *Hall* (1518–1529) C 1/598/20 (in fulfilment of a marriage settlement, the groom was alleged to have enfeoffed feoffees to the intent to make estate to the bride for term of her life).

[45] Milsom, *Historical Foundations of the Common Law*, p. 235.

[46] C 78/31/21. To the extent that trusts in the form of a use upon a use were created in the period for purposes of secrecy such trusts would, in their nature, be unlikely to be evidenced in litigation.

[47] C 1/566/27 (1518–1529). An example of a use upon a use where the second use was active appears in *Thomas Elyot's Case* (1518–1529), C 1/501/34, where it was alleged that Sir William Fyndern had suffered a recovery of land by a group of recoverors, including Sir John Fyneux, Sir Robert Rede and Richard Elyot, serjeant-at-law, to the use of Sir William's last will, the will directing that the recoverors should for the period of sixteen years following Sir William's death suffer Sir John Cutt, Richard Elyot JCP, the Master of Clare Hall, Cambridge, and Master Robert Clayton, to receive all manner rents and farms going out of the land to the payment of his debts, legacies and other charges, and that the recoverors should thereafter make conveyances as directed. (C 1/501/32 and 33 concern related litigation.)

of a last will also appear in the sample. In some instances what appears at first sight to have been a passive trust may not have been intended as such. In *Lee* v. *Byrde*, for example, it was alleged that the two plaintiffs had stood jointly seised with Edward Byrde to the use of Edward Bardewell and Mary his wife for term of Mary's life, and after her death to the use of divers remainders made and tailed in the deed of feoffment.[48] It may be that in this and similar cases a conveyance of the legal title by the feoffees according to the terms of the settlement was expected,[49] such uses being intended to be transactions and not relationships, the trustees being subject to an active duty to convey.[50]

There are, nevertheless, clear allegations in the sample of subsisting passive trusts of freehold beyond the scope of feoffments to the uses of a last will. So in *Lord Daubeney* v. *Osgood* it was asserted in answer to the bill that the true terms of the feoffment had been to the use of Robert Walsh, Master of the Hospital of St John the Baptist, Bridgwater, the brethren of the hospital, and their successors for a term of sixty years, and thereafter to the use of Lord Daubeney and the heirs males of his body lawfully begotten, with remainder to Lord Zouch and his heirs forever, and that the feoffees had been and remained seised of the land, suffering the Master to take the profits.[51] In a number of cases provision for married women was made by subsisting passive trust of freehold. So in *Brudenell* v. *Worsop* it was alleged that Sir Robert Brudenell CJCP, Sir John More

48 C 1/537/26 (1518–1529).

49 Though if a conveyance had been expected in *Lee* v. *Byrde*, it had not yet been made, the prayer in the bill being for an order that one of the feoffees co-operate with the others in bringing actions at common law against trespassers. There are a substantial number of instances in the sample of bills exhibited to obtain a conveyance by feoffees to uses, there being no remedy at law to compel this. For example, in *Everard* v. *Tower* (1515–1518), C 1/405/51, it was alleged that a feoffee, being seised to the use of the plaintiff and his heirs, had refused a conveyance to the plaintiff; and in *Hercy* v. *Edyall* (1518–1529), C 1/ 518/15, it was alleged that John Stanley had suffered a recovery to the use of Sir Humphrey Stanley and the heirs of his body. The plaintiffs, heirs of the body of Sir Humphrey, had requested conveyance from the defendant, heir of the last surviving recoveror, who had refused to comply, contrary to right and good conscience 'and the trust before specified'. Whether a conveyance had been anticipated in such cases, or whether it had been expected that legal title would continue in the hands of the feoffees, is not clear.

50 Ambiguity between a passive arrangement within the scope of the Statute of Uses and an arrangement intended to give rise to an active reconveyance by the trustees became important after 1536. Warding off this ambiguity in the context of active trusts to reconvey seems likely to have been an early situation in which trusts were created in the form of a use upon a use after the statute. See Jones, 'The Use upon a Use in Equity Revisited', pp. 73–76.

51 C 1/625/1 (1529–1532).

JKB, Sir Edward Ferrers and Sir William Essex, 'of long time have been and yet be' seised to the use of Francis Cokayn and Dorothy his wife and the heirs of Dorothy.[52] And in *Wren* v. *Wetyngham*, it was alleged that Sir John Wilshire, having feoffees to the use of his last will, provided in his will that his widow should enjoy the premises for term of her life, remainder thereafter to his right heirs, and that following Sir John's death his widow, by sufferance of the feoffees, took and received the income of the land. The execution of such passive uses of freehold was presumably anticipated: the effect of the Statute of Uses on such uses was not to be confined to the context of feoffments to the uses of a last will.[53]

One further observation should be made in relation to uses of freehold. The second section of the Statute of Uses provided for cases in which cestui que use was included among the feoffees.[54] There are several instances

[52] C 1/385/45 (1515–1518). For Francis Cokayn see under Francis Cokayn I, Sir John Baker, *The Men of Court 1440 to 1550: A Prosopography of the Inns of Court and Chancery and the Courts of Law*, vol. 1 (Selden Soc. Suppl. Series 18(1)) (London 2012), p. 491. Dorothy his wife was daughter of Thomas Marow, serjeant-at-law. For other cases concerning married women see *Baldwyn* v. *Marmyon*, at n. 58 below; *Darcy* v. *Jenkynson* (1518–1529), C 1/498/47 (plaintiffs allege that they are seised to the use of Katherine, wife of Sir Thomas Burgh (the terms of the alleged use are not set out in the bill)); *Lee* v. *Byrde* (1518–1529), C 1/537/26 (alleged that feoffees were seised to the use of Edward Bardewell and Mary his wife, for term of the life of Mary, with remainders over, and that one of the feoffees had cut timber which he had no right to do during Mary's life).

[53] Execution might have the effect of diminishing protection for the interests of the offspring of a marriage. In *Blanderhasset* v. *Broke* (1515–1518), it was said in answer to the bill that in negotiation for marriage between George Blanderhasset and Anne Covert, and in return for payment of money, land had been conveyed to at least one feoffee to the use of George and Anne and the heirs of the body of George. George and Anne had a daughter, Mary. Anne now being dead, George had demanded conveyance of the land, to which the feoffee answering asserted that if a conveyance were made to George he would make estate to his second wife, which would be to the disinheritance of Mary during the life of the second wife, if George had no issue with the second wife and was survived by her. The feoffee was willing to convey, but wished this possible effect of doing so to be understood, C 1/386/24 (bill), C 1/386/25 (answer). Had the use in favour of George and Anne been executed, no such argument could have been made.

[54] 'And be it further enacted . . . that where divers and many persons be or hereafter shall happen to be jointly seised, of and in any lands tenements reversions remainders or other hereditaments, to the use confidence or trust of any of them that be so jointly seised, that in every such case that or those person or persons which have or hereafter shall have any such use confidence or trust, in any such lands tenements rents reversion remainders or hereditaments, shall from henceforth have and be deemed and adjudged to have, only to him or them that have or hereafter shall have such use confidence or trust, such estate possession and seisin of and in the same lands tenements rents reversions remainders or other hereditaments, in like nature manner and form condition and course as he or they had before in the use confidence or trust of the same lands tenements or hereditaments . . . '

of this in the sample, and it may not have been uncommon. An early example is provided by *Beaumont* v. *Cavell*,[55] where it was alleged that late in the time of Henry VII, John Caryll and Richard Brooke, serjeant-at-law, John Ernle, attorney-general, Andrew (or Sir Andrew) Windsor,[56] and Edmund Dudley, esquire, deceased, had recovered certain land to the only use of Edmund Dudley and his heirs, and to the performance of his last will. A more prosaic example of the same mechanism was alleged in answer to the bill in *Brende* v. *Odemse*:[57] Robert Babell and William Fountain, it was said, had together recovered certain land to the only use of Robert, his heirs and assigns. And in *Baldwyn* v. *Marmyon*, it was alleged that Anne Baldwyn, wife of John Baldwyn, was seised with Sir Thomas Fettiplace and divers others to the use of Anne for term of her life.[58]

2. *Terms of years and copyhold land*

Turning from freehold land to other forms of interest in land, there is one example in the sample of a use of a term of years, again a situation in which the alleged beneficiary of the use was among those holding legal title, in this case a use of a five-year lease of a parsonage.[59] Leaving aside common-form surrenders of copyhold land to the use of the grantee in the course

[55] C 1/473/78 (1518–1529).

[56] Andrew Windsor was presumably the brother of Dudley's first wife, Anne Windsor. He is referred to in the bill both as Andrew Windsor, esquire, and as Sir Andrew Windsor. See S. J. Gunn, 'Dudley, Edmund (*c.*1462–1510)', *Oxford Dictionary of National Biography*, Oxford University Press, 2004; online edition, May 2010, www.oxforddnb.com/view/article/8147, accessed on 29 April 2014.

[57] C 1/615/14 (1529–1532), answering the bill in C 1/615/13.

[58] *Baldwyn* v. *Marmyon* (1518–1529), C 1/477/22. Again here the beneficiary of the use was among the trustees. For further examples in relation to freehold see *Norwood* v. *Tylby* (1515–1518), C 1/453/7; *Culpeper* v. *Byston* (1518–1529), C 1/484/28; *Goddard* v. *Wattys* (1518–1529), C 1/513/39; *Holywell* v. *Davyson* (1518–1529), C 1/521/33; *Thomas* v. *Jenyns* (1518–1529), C 1/581/77 (answer to bill in C 1/581/76); *Quarell* v. *Grene* (1515–1518), C 1/438/6. In relation to a lease see *Bovell* v. *Sheriffs of London*, n. 59 below, and in relation to copyhold land see *Rowley* v. *Taylour* and *Feeld* v. *Breton*, nn. 61 and 62 below.

[59] *Bovell* v. *Sheriffs of London* (1515–1518), C 1/390/33 (Peter Carmelian, parson of St George's, Southwark, was alleged to have demised the parsonage in 1515 to John Farfurth, clerk, Thomas Pagett and John Smyth for term of five years to the only use of John Farfurth, yielding a specified sum yearly to Carmelian. Dispute arose from an allegation by Pagett and Smyth, Farfurth's co-lessees, that the lease had been made to the use of all the co-lessees, the use in favour of Farfurth only not being expressed in the indenture of lease).

of conveyancing in the manor court,[60] there are a number of examples of alleged uses of copyhold land. In *Rowley* v. *Taylour* it was alleged that John Rowley had surrendered copyhold land to the defendants to the use of his son – the plaintiff – if he were alive, and if not, to the use of the guild of Corpus Christi, York;[61] and in *Feeld* v. *Breton* it was alleged that Robert Feeld and William Breton were seised of copyhold to the only use of Feeld and his heirs.[62] Contemporary doubts of principle as to the possibility of uses of leases or of copyhold were not, it seems, borne out in practice.[63]

3. *Chattels personal*

Beyond interests in land, Professor Biancalana has shown that uses of money were handled in the fifteenth-century Chancery,[64] and the sample indicates that such uses continued to appear in Chancery in the decades before 1536, as they did in the contemporary ecclesiastical courts.[65] Some uses of money in the sample concern simple payment of money for transmission in the context of dealings at a distance. So in *Drew* v. *Chalke* it was alleged that William Chalke had by assent and commandment of the plaintiff received a sum in gold ducats at Rome to the use and behoof of the plaintiff in England.[66] But in other cases uses of money were alleged to have been created *inter vivos* in situations closer to relationship than transaction. In *More* v. *Eyre* it was alleged that the female plaintiff's father

[60] Doubt was possible to as whether surrender of copyhold land to the lord to the use of the grantee constituted a conveyance to the lord, and thus created a use of copyhold. The classic view was that there was no conveyance; as Coke put it, 'the lord is but an instrument to admit *cestuy que use*, for no more passes to the lord than to serve the limitation of the use; and *cestuy que use* when he is admitted shall be in by him that made the surrender, and not by the lord', Co. Litt. 59b.

[61] *Rowley* v. *Taylour* (1518–1529), C 1/561/100.

[62] *Feeld* v. *Breton* (1518–1529), C 1/508/45. Again we see cestui que use alleged to have been included among the trustees. For further examples of uses of copyhold see *Benett* v. *Hart* (1529–1532), C 1/612/37; *Brandon* v. *Bolles* (1515–1518), C 1/388/45; and *Smyth* v. *Tuke* (1515–1518), C 1/442/37.

[63] See Baker, *Oxford History of the Laws of England*, vol. 6, p. 684 and nn. 214 and 215, referring on copyhold to an undetermined demurrer in the Common Pleas in 1526, and a moot in Gray's Inn in the 1530s, where it was asserted that 'Of lands held by copy of court roll one may not be seised to the use of another', and on terms of years referring to moots in Gray's Inn *c.* 1520, though views diverged.

[64] Biancalana, 'Testamentary Cases in Fifteenth Century Chancery', pp. 295–296.

[65] R.H. Helmholz, 'Trusts in the English Ecclesiastical Courts 1399–1640', in R. Helmholz and R. Zimmermann, eds., *Itinera Fiduciae: Trust and Treuhand in Historical Perspective* (Berlin, 1998), pp. 161–162.

[66] C 1/498/30 (1518–1529). The money appears to have been the purchase price for a quantity of woad.

had delivered a sum of money to Stephen Eyre to the 'use and behoof' of the female plaintiff, and to deliver to her at the time of her marriage.[67] And in *Bassynwayt* v. *Mannoke* it was alleged that John Mannoke had offered marriage to the female plaintiff, who, having by reason thereof 'great trust and confidence' in Mannoke, had delivered to him the sum of £9 to keep to her use, and to the use of them both if it happened that they were married.[68]

Allegations of uses of personalty extended beyond uses of money. So in *Sherard* v. *Mayor of London*, again repeating the practice seen elsewhere of including the beneficiary among the trustees, it was alleged that Thomas and George Sherard stood bound jointly and severally in an obligation for payment of a specified sum to Christopher Davyson and John Hall, to the use of Christopher;[69] and in *Hales* v. *Sheriffs of London* it was alleged that Edith Darnall, widow, defendant in Chancery, supposed that William Wright had entered into an obligation in £60 to Edward Hales, 'to the use and profit' of Edith Darnall.[70] In *Benett* v. *Hert* it was alleged that the plaintiff's father, being possessed of certain chattels, including pots and pans of brass, feather beds, bolsters and blankets, had committed and appointed the plaintiff's uncle to have the possession, safe keeping, custody and use of the chattels and the increase and advantage of them to the use of the plaintiff;[71] and in *Brewster* v. *Grene*, it was alleged that a feather bed, three brass pots, and divers other goods, utensils and chattels, had been delivered to the defendant 'to keep and to deliver to the use' of the plaintiff.[72]

III. Conclusion

To return to the question of what those responsible for the Statute of Uses thought they were doing, in light of the evidence of the pleadings it

67 C 1/544/43 (1518–1529). 68 C 1/470/28 (1518–1529).

69 C 1/566/27 (1518–1529).

70 C 1/522/33 (1518–1529). For a further example see *Roberth* v. *Culpeper* (1518–1529), C 1/561/31.

71 C 1/612/37 (1529–1532). The action was against the uncle's executor, the plaintiff asserting (in standard form) that he had no remedy at common law for lack of knowledge of the details of the chattels.

72 C 1/476/47 (1518–1529). Here again the plaintiff alleged, in standard form, lack of remedy at common law for lack of knowledge of 'what goods and utensils and chattels were to him delivered nor no certainty of them'. That a common law action in detinue would have been available to the Chancery plaintiff had it been possible to assert the details of the items in question and how they were kept with sufficient specificity may not have been clear. See Biancalana, 'Testamentary Cases in Fifteenth-Century Chancery', pp. 294–295.

is difficult to accept Milsom's suggestion that before 1536 '[a]lmost the only motive for an *inter vivos* arrangement'[73] which could be described as a use of personal property would have been to defraud creditors, or to accept that anyone familiar with Chancery practice in the decades before 1536 would have considered a use of personal property 'a contradiction in terms'.[74] This being so, and given that the sample includes a use of a lease, and that it is difficult to support the view that after 1536 chancellors were generally reluctant for revenue reasons to intervene in uses (or trusts) of leases,[75] it is not easy to suppose that 'there was no continuity of equitable interests in personalty before and after the statute in the sense usually understood', or that 'the true trust of personalty began later'.[76] That said, it is difficult to imagine that it had ever been thought that uses of pure personalty would be executed: uses of money, of obligations, or of feather beds and brass pots, raised neither difficulty for the feudal revenue, nor serious questions of uncertainty of title. As has been seen, doubt was for some decades possible after 1536 about the execution of uses of leases, but the statute was plainly expressed in terms of seisin of hereditaments. As Milsom put it, 'the draftsman of the Statute of Uses was not addressing himself to equitable interests as such'.[77]

[73] Milsom, *Historical Foundations of the Common Law*, 2nd edition, p. 234.

[74] *Ibid.* It is worth noting in this respect that in his reading on the statute 4 Hen. VII, c. 17 in 1526 Thomas Audley defined a use as 'a property or ownership of land or something else, real *or personal*', Baker, *Baker and Milsom, Sources of English Legal History*, 2nd edition (Oxford, 2010), p. 118 (emphasis added). A question may arise here as to the meaning of 'use'. It could still be asked at common law in the 1590s 'whether a use of a [lease] was possible at all' (Simpson, *A History of the Land Law*, 2nd edition, p. 194), but the question concerned not a use or trust in the broad sense of a lease held to the benefit of someone else, which is the subject of this paper and of Milsom's discussion of the scope of the Statute of Uses, but a use in the narrow sense of a use separated from the possession (or legal title), as was clearly possible in the case of freehold land. For further discussion of this see Jones, 'Trusts in England after the Statute of Uses', pp. 180–181, and N.G. Jones, 'Uses, Trusts and a Path to Privity' [1997] *Cambridge Law Journal*, p. 175, at pp. 176–182.

[75] N.G. Jones, 'The Influence of Revenue Considerations upon the Remedial Practice of Chancery in Trust Cases, 1536–1660', in C. Brooks and M. Lobban, eds., *Communities and Courts in Britain 1150–1900* (London, 1997), p. 99, at pp. 106–111.

[76] Milsom, *Historical Foundations of the Common Law*, 2nd edition, p. 235.

[77] *Ibid.*, p. 235. The Statute of Uses referred to seisin to uses of 'honours, castles, manors, lands, tenements, rents, services, reversions, remainders or other hereditaments'. In 1536 it may not yet have been clear that there was no seisin of a lease (see N.G. Jones, 'Long Leases and the Feudal Revenue in the Court of Wards, 1540–1645', 19 *Journal of Legal History* (1998), p. 1, at pp. 3–6), though a lease for a term of years was clearly not an hereditament.

Turning to freehold land, we find, as expected, substantial numbers of feoffments to the uses of a last will. That these would be executed was, politically at least, the rationale of the statute. Outside the context of the posthumous duties of feoffees to the uses of a last will, active uses of freehold (and of other realty) appear in the sample, and the existence of such uses – in the context of charitable arrangements, even if not otherwise – must have been clear when the statute was drafted. That they would remain unexecuted must presumably have been clear also. It may not be insignificant in this respect that in a preliminary draft of the Statute of Uses, the mechanism of execution was expressed in terms that the beneficiary was to be deemed and adjudged to have such estate and interest in the land as he had in use, 'as if such estate or interest had been actually and sufficiently made granted and executed by the feoffees', a formulation not obviously applicable to feoffees seised to active duties.[78]

Beyond feoffments to the uses of a last will, and feoffments to active duties, we find cases in which feoffees are alleged to have been seised to passive uses of freehold land. The execution of these arrangements must presumably have been anticipated. To this extent, while the draftsman of the Statute of Uses was not addressing himself to equitable interests as such, neither was he simply 'dealing with wills of land'.[79] The statute's effect in relation to wills of freehold land was radical, the full difficulties of taking a legal problem 'out by the root, when the root is so reasonable and so universal a wish as to be able to provide for persons other than the heir' perhaps unforeseen.[80] But leaving aside the consequences for wills – and with the almost infinite complexities of legal executory interests still in the future[81] – the statute's effect on uses of freehold may have seemed less striking.

[78] SP 1/101 fo. 252, at fo. 258. Compare Simpson's argument that active uses were not executed because the feoffee could not in such a case convey the legal title to the beneficiary without a breach of trust, 'and the statute only did universally what the feoffee could himself have done privately without breaking trust' (*A History of the Land Law*, 2nd edition, p. 195). As enacted, the statute provided simply that the beneficiary should be deemed and adjudged 'in lawful seisin estate and possession . . . in such like estates as they had or shall have in use trust or confidence in or of the same'.

[79] Milsom, *Historical Foundations of the Common Law*, 2nd edition, p. 235.

[80] *Ibid.*, p. 221. For the immediate aftermath of the statute see Baker, *Oxford History of the Laws of England*, vol. 6, 679 ff.

[81] As Simpson put it, the new magic provided by statutory execution of uses was not lost on 'the conveyancers and the landowners who employed them, and the late sixteenth and early seventeenth centuries may justly be called the age of the fantastic conveyance' (*A History of the Land* Law, 2nd edition, p. 198).

It was clearly understood in the decades before 1536 that being seised of the legal title, and being cestui que use of freehold land, were not identical. In *Frodshame* v. *Lundysche*,[82] for example, it was alleged that the plaintiff had made a feoffment in the time of Edward IV to feoffees to use of himself and his heirs, but being now 'minded to be sole seised of the premises and thereof to die seised as of his own inheritance', had demanded a conveyance from the heir of the last surviving feoffee – thereby anticipating the effect of the Statute of Uses – which conveyance had been refused. But there was nevertheless a sense in which the position of cestui que use and the position of the freehold tenant at law might be assimilated, even before the execution of the use had the effect of uniting them in the hands of cestui que use. Well before 1536 it had become possible to speak of cestui que use as the 'owner' of the land: in his reading on uses in the Inner Temple in about 1490, Gregory Adgore repeatedly referred to cestui que use as the 'owner' of the land;[83] before 1536 it was possible to regard a use as an hereditament;[84] and a ground for doubting in the 1520s whether there could be a use of a lease (a doubt

[82] C 1/408/22 (1515–1518). In his answer the defendant alleged that he knew not whether his father had been seised to the plaintiff's use as alleged in the bill, and (as is not uncommon in the sample) asked that another who was claiming title be required to interplead, C 1/408/23. See also *Kynnarton* v. *Hykman* (1518–1529), C 1/531/24, where it was alleged that the plaintiff had enfeoffed two feoffees to the use of himself and his wife, their heirs and assigns for ever, and having required the feoffees to reconvey according to the use, had been refused. This appears to be a grant and regrant designed to alter the plaintiff's estate. He was clearly not content simply to have the land held to his use.

[83] Baker, *Baker and Milsom, Sources of English Legal History*, 2nd edition, p. 112. The word 'owner' appears in English (as opposed to law French) in notes of the reading. Likewise, reading in the Inner Temple in 1526 Thomas Audley defined a use as 'a property or ownership of land or something else, real or personal, depending solely upon confidence and trust between those who are in actual possession and are accounted owners by the common law of such lands and things whereon the use depends, and those who have a use in the same thing whereon the use depends', Baker and Milsom, *Sources of English Legal History*, 2nd edition, p. 118.

[84] It appeared from a note in YB Mich. 5 Edw. IV, fo. 7v, pl 17, perhaps of 1465, that there might be *possessio fratris* of a use. Referring to this in *Wimbish* v. *Tailbois* (1550), Mountague CJCP observed 'a use is an hereditament, and such an hereditament, whereof [the possession of the brother (*possessio fratris*) in fee simple shall make the sister an heir]'. See further N.G. Jones, 'The Trust Beneficiary's Interest Before R. v. Holland (1648)', in A. Lewis, P. Brand and P. Mitchell, eds., *Law in the City* (Dublin, 2007), p. 95, at pp. 96–99. For descent of the use to the heir of cestui que use see, for example, *Bright* v. *Joly* (1518–1529), C 1/472/38 (alleged that feoffees were seised to the use of Roger Symondes and his heirs, and that upon Roger's death without issue of his body, 'the use of the premises descended' to the plaintiffs as cousins and heirs of Roger).

which persisted after 1536), was that a use is real whereas a lease is but a chattel.[85]

This being so, it may not be surprising that there is some indication in the sample that a use of freehold land and the legal title to it might be seen as interchangeable. So in *Brown* v. *Howseden* it was alleged that William Howseden, being seised of land in fee, had bargained and sold it to Robert Wyse and his heirs, 'by force whereof the said William Howseden was seised of the . . . premises to the use of . . . Robert Wyse and of his heirs'. Robert Wyse then bargained and sold the land to the plaintiff, 'by reason whereof . . . William Howseden was and yet is seised . . . to the use of' the plaintiff: cestui que use had dealt simply with the use, allowing legal title to remain in the original bargainee.[86] In *Whiteley* v. *Hall* it was alleged that as part of marriage negotiations the groom's father had covenanted and agreed with the bride's widowed mother to grant certain land to the couple and the heirs of their bodies, promising, seemingly as equivalent alternatives, 'to make them estate' accordingly, or to do so to persons and their heirs 'to the use' of the couple and their heirs.[87] And in *Egerton* v. *Tychet* it was alleged that three persons were seised to the use of Dame Isabell Draycott for term of her life, the reversion thereof being said to belong and be expectant as of right to the plaintiff and his heirs males, either 'in use or possession'.[88]

In the case of personalty the statute made, and seems to have been understood to have made, no difference. The same seems to have been true of active uses of freehold. In the case of passive uses of freehold, Professor Baker has suggested that the Statute of Uses was the culmination of the process of treating cestui que use as though he were seised which

[85] For the doubt in the 1520s see Baker, *Oxford History of the Laws of England*, vol. 6, p. 684, n. 215. For later doubts see Jones, 'Trusts in England after the Statute of Uses', pp. 180–181. On the use as an interest in land see also Baker, *Introduction to English Legal History*, 4th edition, pp. 250–252: 'The beneficiary's interest was . . . assimilated to legal property concepts; it could be seen as a thing, a thing which descended to heirs on intestacy, a thing which could be bought and sold or settled on a succession of beneficiaries', *ibid.*, pp. 251–252; and Baker, *Oxford History of the Laws of England*, vol. 6, pp. 657–658.

[86] C 1/387/25 (1515–1518). It seems that the statute 1 Ric. III, c. 1 would not apply here, since the bargain and sale to the plaintiff was of the use only, albeit the bill refers to a bargain and sale of the land. For a similar case see *Fortescue* v. *Gilbert* (1518–1529), C 1/506/39 (alleged that recoverors had stood seised to the use of Roger Bolter, his heirs and assigns. Bolter bargained and sold the land to the plaintiff and his heirs. The recoverors thereafter stood seised to the use of the plaintiff, and one refused to join in conveyance to him).

[87] C 1/596/50 (1518–1529) (C 1/596/49 is closely related).

[88] C 1/629/16 (1529–1532).

had begun, in response to uncertainty of title, in the statute 1 Ric. III, c. 1 in 1484.[89] In some cases, and perhaps many, cestui que use was seised at law already: to the extent that it was common for cestui que use to be included among the feoffees, the effect of the statute was not, as is commonly said, to pass legal title from the feoffees and to vest it in the beneficiary. The beneficiary had legal title already, the statute doing no more than remove the additional feoffees. Where cestui que use was not included among the feoffees, he might nevertheless be regarded as the 'owner'. The statute 1 Ric. III, c. 1 gave him power to convey legal title good against that of his feoffees, and it may not have been uncommon to leave matters in use, cestui que use dealing with the use as though with legal title, use and possession being treated as interchangeable. Seen in this light, the effect of the Statute of Uses could be understood as being no more than to reconcile form with substance. This meant, of course, the re-imposition of primogeniture; but that is a slightly different story.

[89] Baker, *Oxford History of the Laws of England*, vol. 6, p. 662.

3

Developing a prerogative theory for the authority of the Chancery

The French connection

IAN WILLIAMS

The controversy involving the English Chancery in 1616 is well known.[1] A conflict over Chancery intervening after judgment at law led to debates about the propriety and legality of equitable intervention. Ultimately, the king supported the Chancery and Edward Coke was dismissed as Chief Justice of the King's Bench. There are two main strands which are identified in historical discussion of the dispute. The first concerns the relationship between law and equity and the supremacy of equity.[2] The

My thanks to Adolfo Giuliani, my LLM seminar group in the Historical Development of the Common Law and participants in the 2013 British Legal History Conference for their assistance and comments. I have used the following abbreviations: BL MS Add (British Library Additional Manuscript); BL MS Egerton (British Library Egerton Manuscript); BL MS Harg (British Library Hargrave Manuscript); BL MS Harl (British Library Harley Manuscript). References to William Lambarde's *Archeion* are to C. H. McIlwain and P. L. Ward (eds.), *Archeion or, a Discourse upon the High Courts of Justice in England by William Lambarde* (Cambridge MA: Harvard University Press, 1957). Quotations from Bodin's *République* are taken from K. D. McRae (ed.), *The Six Bookes of a Commonweal* (New York: Arno Press, 1979). This version of the text is the 1606 translation of the *République* by Richard Knolles, based on both the original French (1576) and the 1586 Latin text, which were substantially different (see McRae 'Introduction', in Bodin, *Six Bookes*, pp. A28–A38). I have compared the Knolles text to the third French printing of 1578 (J. Bodin, *Les Six Livres de la Republique* (Paris: Jacques du Puy, 1578)). Passages where the English translation arguably diverges from the French are noted in the footnotes, but do not affect the argument presented here.

1 J. P. Dawson, 'Coke and Ellesmere Disinterred: The Attack on the Chancery in 1616' (1941–1942) 36 *Illinois Law Review* 127; J. H. Baker, 'The Common Lawyers and the Chancery: 1616' (1969) 4 *Irish Jurist* 368; L. A. Knafla, *Law and Politics in Jacobean England* (Cambridge University Press, 1977), pp. 155–181.

2 For example, Baker, 'Common Lawyers'. In this paper I use 'equity' to describe the Chancery's jurisdiction which was based on the idea of *epieikeia*: justice which could not be provided in the regular courts by ordinary course of law. On *epieikeia* see J. L. Barton,

second regards the dispute as part of a conflict concerning the 'prerogative' courts, reflective of common law opposition to the arbitrary prerogative.[3] This paper considers why the authority of the Chancery was considered to be found in the royal prerogative.[4] In doing so, the paper reconsiders Elizabethan and Jacobean sources concerning the Chancery and equity and examines the changing conceptualisation of the prerogative from the late 1570s into the Jacobean period.

The argument in this paper is that the association between the Chancery and prerogative is a result of the changing conceptualisation of the prerogative from the late 1570s as well as James I's accession to the throne. Before the 1570s, common lawyers discussed the royal prerogative as a set of prerogatives: special royal rights in relation to property law. During the reigns of Elizabeth and James this view changed: royal powers generally were the prerogative and to challenge or restrict this prerogative was to undermine the king himself. This view meant that royal intervention to provide justice came to be seen as part of the royal prerogative, and as a consequence the Chancery became intellectually tied to ideas of prerogative. In addition to setting out the evidence of the change, the paper argues that a cause of this change can be identified in the influence of the writings of Jean Bodin. Direct evidence is too limited to demonstrate that Bodin's influence was the sole cause, but a number of writings about the Chancery demonstrably made use of Bodin, albeit without citation. Bodin's ideas about sovereignty and the authority of a ruler in relation to equity came to inform views about the authority of the Chancery itself.[5]

'Introduction', in T. F. T. Plucknett and J. L. Barton (eds.), *St German's Doctor and Student*, vol. 91 (London: Selden Society, 1974), pp. xliv–li. This meaning therefore excludes the 'equity of the statute' used by the common law courts in interpreting statutes and Halliday's recent use of 'equity' in relation to the prerogative writs in the common law courts c. 1600 (P. Halliday, *Habeas Corpus: from England to Empire* (Cambridge, MA: Harvard University Press, 2010), pp. 87–93).

[3] For example, J. S. Hart, *The Rule of Law 1603–1660: Crown, Courts and Judges* (Harlow: Pearson Education, 2003), p. 48.

[4] This is not to assume that the idea of a wider conflict between the common law and the prerogative is supported by the sources. For present purposes, it is sufficient to note that people interested in defending the Chancery's jurisdiction in 1616 clearly did see claims about the prerogative basis of that jurisdiction as important.

[5] The paper therefore also demonstrates the early influence of Bodin on English lawyers. For discussion of the influence of Bodin before the 1606 translation of the *République* see G. Mosse, 'The Influence of Jean Bodin's *République* in English Political Thought' (1948) 5 *Medievalia et Humanistica* 73. The evidence from Lambarde's *Archeion* (see nn. 52–72 below) antedates the earliest identified influence from Bodin in printed sources (Mosse, 'Influence', p. 75) by two years. Citations to Bodin's *Method* by English writers on history

I. Explaining the authority of the Chancery before the late 1570s

At first sight, links between the Chancery and the royal prerogative seem obvious. Historically, the Chancery did emerge from exercises of the royal power to do justice, a power which was accepted as a royal duty.[6] However, many discussions of Chancery and equity by lawyers make no reference to any specifically royal power at all. Probably the standard early-modern work on the Chancery, Christopher St German's *Doctor and Student*, is entirely silent on the source of the Chancery's authority, considering only the necessity of equity.[7] The same can be said about later works, such as William West's discussion of equity and the Chancery in *Symbolaeographia*.[8] If the prerogative has a role in these theories, it is not a role which is ever explained, nor is it a necessary role – the authority of the Chancery was dependent upon the need for equity, not the power of the monarch. Earlier debates about the jurisdiction of the Chancery to issue injunctions after common law judgment do not seem to have raised the issue of the link between the Chancery and the prerogative.[9]

can be seen from 1575 (see J. D. Alsop, 'William Fleetwood and Elizabethan Historical Scholarship' (1994) 25 *Sixteenth Century Journal* 155, p. 165).

[6] See, for example, W. H. Bryson, 'Introduction', in W. H. Bryson (ed.), *Cases Concerning Equity and the Courts of Equity 1550–1660*, vol. 117 (London: Selden Society, 2000), vol. 1, pp. xix–xxii.

[7] Plucknett and Barton, *St German's Doctor and Student*. This is not to say that the link between the king and equity was not made by others before the reign of Elizabeth, but that legal discussion of the Chancery did not mention the monarch's role. For a seemingly non-legal reference to the prince providing *epieikeia* in the fifteenth century see A. Cromartie, *The Constitutionalist Revolution* (Cambridge: Cambridge University Press, 2006), p. 7.

[8] W. West, *The second part of Symboleography, newly corrected and amended, and very much enlarged in all the foure seuerall treatises* (London: Thomas Wight, 1601), ff. 173v–177. West's discussion of equity used Hermann Vulteius' *Jurisprudentia Romana* (1590) (see M. R. T. Macnair, *The Law of Proof in Early-Modern Equity* (Berlin: Duncker & Humblot, 1999), p. 44.

[9] See J. H. Baker, *The Oxford History of the Laws of England, vol. VI, 1483–1558* (Oxford: Oxford University Press, 2003), pp. 174–175 for the Henrician period. The surviving material concerning *Finch* v. *Throgmorton* (1598), which raised the same legal issue as the 1616 controversy, does not refer to the prerogative, although all the surviving law reports were either written by Coke (E. Coke, *The Third Part of the Institutes of the Laws of England* (London: M. Flesher, 1644), p. 124; E. Coke, *The Fourth Part of the Institutes of the Laws of England* (London: M. Flesher, 1644), p. 86) or report Coke's references to *Finch* v. *Throgmorton* in later cases (3 Buls. 118; Cro. Jac. 344). Coke's own report of *Finch* v. *Throgmorton* (BL MS Harl. 6686, ff. 222v–227) does not mention the prerogative. Two tracts in relation to the 1598 debate do not link the Chancery and the prerogative (Henry E. Huntington Library Ellesmere Manuscripts 2920 (supporting the King's Bench) and 2986 (supporting the Chancery)).

Nevertheless, legal historians have linked the emergence of the jurisdiction of the Chancery with the prerogative.[10] The evidence of such a link is very limited, especially in terms of influencing the debates about the Chancery jurisdiction after 1600, which is when the association with the prerogative was explicit. Fortescue regarded the provision of equity as an exercise of the prince's *potestas absoluta* in his *De Natura Legis Naturae.*[11] This is the only explicit evidence of an association between the Chancery and royal power in the fifteenth century.[12] For purposes of considering the Chancery as a prerogative court in late-Elizabethan and Jacobean England, it should be remembered that Fortescue's *De Natura* was little known, if at all, to English lawyers in the sixteenth and seventeenth centuries, and none of the Elizabethan and Jacobean discussions about the Chancery even mentions or alludes to it.[13] Fortescue's views therefore had no impact on the early-modern debates.

The only other possible link is the reference to the Chancery proceeding according to 'absolute' power. This argument needs to be treated with

[10] See, for example, Macnair, *The Law of Proof*, p. 37.

[11] J. Fortescue, 'De Natura Legis Naturae', in T. Fortescue (ed.), *The Works of Sir John Fortescue, Knight, Chief Justice of England and Lord Chancellor to King Henry the Sixth*, 2 vols. (privately printed, 1869), vol. 1, c. 24 (Latin original at pp. 85–86, English translation at pp. 214–215).

[12] It is not clear when *De Natura Legis Naturae* was written; see R. McGerr, *A Lancastrian Mirror for Princes* (Bloomington: Indiana University Press, 2011), p. 118.

[13] In 1614, Edward Coke stated that he had a manuscript of 'a booke in defence of the title of king H.6' by Fortescue ('To the Reader', in E. Coke, *La Dixme Part des Reports de Sir Edw. Coke* (London: Societie of Stationers, 1614), sig. diiii). In 1616, John Selden observed that Fortescue had written three books, the *De Laudibus*, 'his *Difference* between *Dominium Regale* and *Dominium Politicum* and *regale*, and that *Declaration* touching the title of the Crowne'. The last two 'remaine Mss. in divers hands' ('To the Reader', in J. Fortescue, *De Laudibus Legum Angliae* (London: Companie of Stationers, 1616), sig. ¶iii^{v}). *De Natura* was one of a series of succession tracts so could be the work referred to by Coke and Selden, but this cannot be certain (see S. B. Chrimes, 'List of Fortescue's Works', in J. Fortescue, *De Laudibus Legum Anglie* (Cambridge: Cambridge University Press, 1949), p. lxxvi). Fortescue set out the idea of the *dominium politicum et regale* in *De Natura*, so *De Natura* could be the other work listed by Selden, but *The Governance of England* was also known as 'Of the difference between an absolute and limited monarchy' (Chrimes, 'List of Works', p. lxxvi). Selden did acquire a manuscript copy of the *De Natura* at some stage (see D. S. Berkowitz, *John Selden's Formative Years: Politics and Society in Early-Modern England* (Cranbury, NJ: Associated University Press, 1988), p. 313, n. 31). Selden was sent a manuscript of material by Fortescue by Thomas Allen in 1616, but according to Allen that was 'lyttle in hyt wiche is not in an olde prynte', suggesting that the manuscript consisted predominantly of *De Laudibus* (R. Beddard, 'Thomas Allen and John Selden and the 1616 edition of Fortescue's De Laudibus Legum Angliae' (2004) 53 *The Book Collector* 533, p. 541).

caution. A good example can be found in a yearbook report of a Chancery case in 1469.[14] Stillington C explains that there are two kinds of powers and processes, ordinary and absolute. Given that it was also recognised that the king had two types of prerogative, ordinary and absolute,[15] the link seems clear. However, the description of a power as 'ordinary', as Stillington explained, simply meant that a certain order was observed: the power was exercised according to a specified procedure or rules. The description of a power as 'absolute' meant that no such order was required. The distinction was well known in medieval Europe, featuring in both theology and canon law, even entering sermon literature.[16] Such an analytical model could be applied to the Chancellor; it could also be applied to different royal prerogatives, some of which were exercised according to law, while some were not. The fact that the same mode of analysis could be applied to the Chancellor, the king and God did not necessarily imply a causative link. The only early-modern writer who can be seen to have linked the Chancellor and the prerogative in this way is the controversial civilian John Cowell.[17]

The shared use of the language and idea of ordinary and absolute power does not mean that the equitable activities of the Chancery were seen as an application of the prerogative. Stillington did not draw that link, and nor did later common lawyers. William Lambarde's use of language

[14] (1469) YB T.9.Edw.4 f. 14 pl. 9. Macnair identifies the case as demonstrating that equity was an appeal to the 'absolute' power of the king (Macnair, *The Law of Proof*, p. 37), which seems to be a misreading.

[15] The earliest reference I have found to common lawyers discussing the 'absolute' prerogative is *The Case of Impositions on Cloth* (1559) Dyer 165, at f. 165v, where the 'absolute power' of Mary is mentioned. The general invisibility of the 'absolute' prerogative from legal sources is not surprising. Not only were exercises of the absolute prerogative not governed by law (and so unlikely to be of interest to lawyers), but sensitive matters such as the prerogative were often omitted from (printed) law reports (see J. H. Baker, 'Introduction', in J. H. Baker (ed.), *Reports from the Lost Notebooks of Sir James Dyer, Selden Society Publications*, vol. 109 (London: Selden Society, 1993), vol. 1, p. xlv). James Morice distinguishes between the king's 'absolute authoritie' and 'ordinary power in Administracion of Justice', in a context where the 'absolute authoritie' seems to be the king's prerogative (BL MS Egerton 3376, f. 27). For more discussion of Morice's reading see nn. 36–39 and 73–83 below.

[16] See F. Oakley, 'Jacobean Political Theology: The Absolute and Ordinary Powers of the King' (1968) 29 *Journal of the History of Ideas* 323. For the use of the distinction outside of the scholarly context see F. Oakley, 'The Absolute and Ordained Power of God in Sixteenth- and Seventeenth-Century Theology' (1998) 59 *Journal of the History of Ideas* 437, p. 443.

[17] J. Cowell, *The Interpreter: or Booke Containing the Signification of Words* (Cambridge: John Legate, 1607), sig. N2v.

is instructive. In the *Archeion*, when Lambarde refers to the 'absolute' power of the prince, there is never any contrast made with 'ordinary' power.[18] However, when Lambarde refers to the absolute power of the Chancellor to administer equity, this is in contrast to the 'ordinary' jurisdiction of the Chancery and there is no reference to the prince's absolute power.[19] Ellesmere similarly distinguished between the absolute power of the Chancellor and the ordinary power of the common law judges.[20] However, when discussing the prerogative, Ellesmere insisted that all aspects of the prerogative were a species of 'absolute' power.[21] Finally, William West's discussion of equity mentions the Chancellor's absolute power, but never even mentions the king and his power, let alone connects the king's power with equity.[22]

Before the texts discussed in this paper, there are two early-modern references which directly associate the Chancery with the royal prerogative. Both are found in a collection of material on Chancery associated with William Lambarde and they may have had some influence on Lambarde's view of equity as a prerogative function, although neither is alluded to in the *Archeion*.[23] The first is anonymous and undated. The text is entitled 'Curie Cancellariae prerogativa &c' and explains that 'The Courte of Chauncerye is the kings prerogative Royall and all other Courtes (except the Parliament) are inferior Courtes to the same for it is well knowne that the Courte of Chauncerie drawethe all manner of Accions from all other Courts as by the applicacions to his kingelie Maiestie'.[24] The author then explains this point: 'And so all other Courts have no iurisdicion to holde plea but they must receive their Originall from the Courte of Chauncerye', a point which the author substantiates by listing the types

[18] BL MS Lansd 621, ff. 78v, 81 and 83v (a letter about the Chancery from 1577) and Lambarde, *Archeion*, pp. 39 and 40.

[19] BL MS Lansd 621, f. 79v; Lambarde, *Archeion*, p. 32. In the *Eirenarcha*, Lambarde contrasts the Chancellor's 'absolute' power to 'limited' power (*Eirenarcha: or of the office of justices of peace* (London: Thomas Wight, 1581), p. 65).

[20] *Earl of Oxford's Case* (1615) 1 Chan. Rep. 14–15.

[21] 'A Coppie of a Wrytten Discourse by the Lord Chauncellor Elsemere Concerning the Royall Prerogative', in Knafla, *Law and Politics*, pp. 197–198.

[22] West, *Symboleography*, f. 177.

[23] BL MS Lansd 621. On the material Lambarde compiled about the Chancery see P. L. Ward, 'William Lambarde's Collections on Chancery' (1953) 7 *Harvard Library Bulletin*, p. 271.

[24] BL MS Lansd 621, f. 18. Ward explains that the text must date from before 1573 (see Ward, 'William Lambarde's Collections', p. 289, n. 75).

of actions and repeating for each one that a writ from the Chancery would be required before a court could hear the case. Similarly, justices of assize or *oyer et terminer* only had jurisdiction due to commission issued by the Chancery.[25] The text is not concerned with equity, and the reference to the royal prerogative at the outset is never mentioned again.

The second text is more significant. Henry, the second Lord Cromwell, 'one of the lesser and seedier Elizabethan peers', was a defendant in a Chancery suit and his behaviour led the Chancery to attach him for contempt.[26] Cromwell was eventually arrested, about which he complained in parliament in June 1572, raising the question whether a peer could be arrested for contempt of the Chancery. Nicholas Bacon defended the Chancery's jurisdiction and did so by associating the Chancery closely with the monarch. Bacon started from the accepted case of a peer who had shown contempt to the monarch, explaining that such a person would be subject to arrest. He then argued from analogy: disobedience to a Chancery decree is contempt of the prince and so a peer would be subject to arrest. The intellectual basis for this analogy is that 'the Prince by his prerogative hath powre to order causes otherwise then the lawe ys & to helpe the subiects in a cawse wherein he hath noe helpe by lawe whiche semes in reason as greate a prerogative as maie bee'.[27] Bacon expressly linked equity and the prerogative, a point which he reiterated in conclusion. Further arguments were made, but these did not concern equity or the prerogative.[28]

After consultation with the judges 'and others of the Queenes Majesties learned Councell', the (self-interested) House of Lords was unconvinced and Cromwell's protection from arrest remained intact. However, the conclusion of the Lords listed reasons by which their decision could be reviewed in a future parliament, including that 'there shalbee shewed sufficient matter that by the Queenes Prerogative . . . the persons of anie of the Lordes of Parliament in such case as this case of the Lord Cromwell is, ought to bee attached or attachable'.[29] The inference seems to be that the

[25] BL MS Lansd 621, f. 18v.

[26] On the proceedings see generally, M. A. R. Graves, 'Freedom of Peers from Arrest: The Case of Henry Second Lord Cromwell, 1571–1572' (1977) 21(1) *AJLH* 5–14.

[27] BL MS Lansd 621, f. 86.

[28] These arguments were based on custom, that otherwise Chancery would be ineffective, and that it would be absurd for Chancery to have power to hear and order cases, but not to execute judgment.

[29] BL MS Add 20700, ff. 158–158v.

House of Lords, following consultation with the common law judges, did not accept the claim that the jurisdiction of the Chancery was intimately connected with the royal prerogative, but that if the claim were substantiated, that would be a reason to allow attachment of peers. Elizabeth herself was also usually sensitive to encroachment on her prerogative, so the absence of royal concern about the case might also suggest that the claims about the prerogative were not altogether convincing.

However, by 1616, the links between Chancery, equity and the prerogative were clear. Francis Bacon advised James I to defend the Chancery (which Bacon described as 'the court of your absolute power') in the Star Chamber 'for the settling of your authority and strengthening of your prerogative according to the true rules of monarchy'.[30] The stress placed on the prerogative in 1616 may have been a tactic by supporters of the Chancery (or opponents of Edward Coke) to attract James I's personal attention to the jurisdictional dispute. This seems to have been the view of Timothy Tourneur (who clearly sided with the common law courts), who wrote that the Chancellor 'made grievous complaint.... to the King and the matter was much aggravated'. James was informed or persuaded that the Chancery 'was the very treasury of the ancient prerogative of the Crown and the mint of novel prerogative and that... the Lord Coke in this matter affronted principally the prerogative. And on this information, as was observed, the King was greatly incensed against the said Chief Justice'.[31] Tourneur thought that James had been persuaded that the Chancellor was 'only the instrument of his prerogative' and that 'his prerogative is transcendent to the common law'.[32] This would not be the first time that Ellesmere procured James's intervention on behalf of the Chancery in jurisdictional disputes, seemingly doing the same in the 1604 dispute between Chancery and the House of Commons over jurisdiction to judge the validity of election returns.[33] However, in 1604, James seems to have regretted his involvement and accepted the view of the House of Commons that the dispute was 'an usual controversy between courts about their pre-eminences and privileges'.[34] In 1616, James seems to have

[30] J. Spedding (ed.), *The Letters and the Life of Francis Bacon*, 7 vols. (Longmans, Green, Reader, and Dyer, 1869), vol. 5, p. 252.

[31] BL MS Add 35957, ff. 54v–55. [32] BL MS Add 35957, f. 55v.

[33] A. Thrush, 'Commons v. Chancery: the 1604 Buckinghamshire Election Dispute Revisited' (2007) 26(3) *Parliamentary History*, p. 301 and C. Russell, *King James VI & I and His English Parliaments* (Oxford: Oxford University Press, 2011), pp. 28–30.

[34] J. R. Tanner, *Constitutional Documents of the Reign of James I, 1603–25* (Cambridge: Cambridge University Press, 1930), pp. 224–225.

agreed with the arguments advanced that limiting the Chancery's jurisdiction was an attack on his own prerogative.[35]

Tourneur's belief as to the cause of James's intervention in the 1616 dispute reveals the significance of the association between the prerogative and the Chancery. Even if this link had been made before the late 1570s, it became explicit in the years around 1580. Furthermore, from 1578 onwards, common lawyers unconnected with the Chancery discussed the relationship between equity and the prerogative. These discussions seem to have been based on genuine intellectual conviction, rather than any jurisdictional self-interest. By binding together the prerogative, equity and the Chancery, 'an usual controversy between courts' instead touched upon matters of constitutional principle, as became apparent in 1616. This paper is concerned with the evidence showing when the association between the prerogative and equity emerged and suggests an explanation for this development in the influence of Jean Bodin.

II. Chancery, equity and prerogative from 1578

Three surviving texts suggest that the Chancellor's jurisdiction in equity was being explained by common lawyers as an aspect of the royal prerogative between 1578 and 1581. Unlike the remarks of Nicholas Bacon, none of these lawyers was directly associated with the Chancery. For these lawyers, the explanation of the Chancery as a prerogative court was not based simply on protection or expansion of the jurisdiction of the Chancery. Instead, the prerogative explanation for equity was derived from theory. Two of these lawyers, James Morice and William Lambarde, accepted the idea of the Chancery as exercising a prerogative power and for both of them we can identify influence from the work of Jean Bodin. The third lawyer, Robert Snagg, rejected the prerogative basis of the Chancery, but provides evidence that the idea was being discussed and may have been responding directly to Lambarde's work. This section ends by drawing attention to the emergence, in the 1580s, of the idea of the Chancellor applying the king's conscience, a development which relates closely to the prerogative theory of equity considered here.

This development required a change not just in the theory of equity, but also in the nature of legal discussions of the prerogative. James Morice's reading on the prerogative in 1578 is a new style of discussion of the subject. Morice's reading was based not on the text of *Praerogativa Regis*,

[35] See nn. 116–129 below.

but the Statute of Westminster I, c.50, which referred to the statute not prejudicing the king or his crown. From this text, Morice considered what rights the Crown held as prerogatives. By doing so, Morice's discussion of the prerogative moved away from the old focus upon property law, instead focusing on the king's powers more generally.[36] Morice's reading engaged with certain aspects of the 'absolute' prerogative, such as the monarch's role in law-making, producing 'what is probably the most complete analysis of the constitution by a common lawyer to have survived from the reign of Elizabeth'.[37] While there 'is no indication that the views he expressed in 1578 were particularly controversial', Morice's reading demonstrates a major change in common law discussion of (and perhaps even thinking about) the prerogative, a change which regarded all royal powers as aspects of the prerogative.[38] In undertaking his reading, Morice was breaking new ground. For present purposes, the significance of Morice's reading is that it provides evidence that in 1578 common lawyers were willing, and seemingly permitted, openly to discuss matters pertaining to the absolute prerogative. This new sphere of discussion meant that common lawyers could consider justifying, and elaborating upon, existing arrangements in terms of the royal prerogative.[39]

1. *William Lambarde*[40]

William Lambarde drew out the association between the Chancery and the monarch in his *Archeion*. Lambarde's views were the most fully developed and may have been influential. Not only did the *Archeion* circulate in manuscript before being printed in 1635,[41] but Lambarde became a Master in Chancery in 1592. Lambarde's influence on Egerton's work in

36 For this change see P. Halliday, *Habeas Corpus*, p. 66.

37 C. W. Brooks, *Law, Politics and Society in Early Modern England* (Cambridge: Cambridge University press, 2008), p. 79.

38 Brooks, *Law, Politics and Society*, p. 81.

39 For evidence that Morice also viewed equity as an aspect of the royal prerogative see nn. 73–74 below.

40 On Lambarde, in addition to other works cited here, see generally R. M. Warnicke, *William Lambarde, Elizabethan Antiquary 1536–1601* (London: Phillimore and Co., 1973).

41 G. R. Elton, 'Arthur Hall, Lord Burghley and the Antiquity of Parliament', pp. 88–103. in H. Lloyd-Jones, V. Pearl and B. Worden (eds.), *History and Imagination, Essays in Honour of H.R. Trevor-Roper* (London: Duckworth, 1981), p. 101.

the Chancery is often suggested, even if difficult to prove.[42] In relation to the Chancery and the prerogative, there is direct evidence of influence by Lambarde,[43] as well as more inferential evidence of both influence and rejection of Lambarde's views.[44]

The *Archeion* purported to be a historical description of various English courts. In the case of the courts of equity (for Lambarde, the Chancery and the Star Chamber), this historical description was associated with normative justification for the existence of such courts. Both the historical and normative contents associate equity with the monarch. While the historical content can be traced to a letter written by Lambarde in 1577, Lambarde's normative ideas are first evidenced in 1579 in a discussion of the Chancellor, Chancery and equity which is almost identical to that in the *Archeion*. The normative explanation in this later exposition could be derived from the earlier material associating the Chancery with the prerogative, to which Lambarde had access. However, the *Archeion* contains no reference to this material. Instead, the link is made or justified through ideas from the work of Jean Bodin.[45]

Lambarde's historical discussion claimed that both law and equity had been administered before the Conquest by the king's court, which Lambarde identified with the King's Bench.[46] In 1577, Lambarde explained that in the time when the king sat in the King's Bench personally, the 'kinge and his greate Consalior [referring to the Chief Justice] . . . did after an absolute power mittigate the rigor of the lawe accordinge to Conscience even as the kinge did before the Conquest and as the lorde keeper nowe dothe'.[47] While Lambarde identified a power to provide equity in the monarch, 'the lorde Chauncellors greatnes grewe by little and little although the tymes & moments of those increases be not knowne unto me'.[48] There is no explanation in the letter of 1577 as to the need for this absolute power, or its source. The language of 'absolute power' seems

42 See especially W. J. Jones, *The Elizabethan Court of Chancery* (Oxford: Clarendon Press, 1967), pp. 62 and 111–112.

43 See nn. 96–100 below.

44 For possible influence on Anthony Benn see nn. 110–114 below. For rejection of Lambarde's view see the discussion of Snagg, nn. 85–88 below.

45 Unless otherwise indicated, references to BL MS Lansd 621 following a reference to *Archeion* are to the 1579 draft. Alsop and Stevens were incorrect to claim that Lambarde was 'indifferent' to continental material and that it 'did little to serve his purpose' (J. D. Alsop and W. M. Stevens, 'William Lambarde and the Elizabethan Polity' (1986) 8 *Studies in Medieval and Renaissance History* 233, p. 251).

46 Lambarde, *Archeion*, pp. 17–18; BL MS Lansd 621, f. 78v (1577 letter).

47 BL MS Lansd 621, f. 79v.

48 BL MS Lansd 621, f. 81v. Similarly f. 83v.

to be the same as that used by Stillington in 1469, simply a power not governed by rules.

By contrast, in 1579 Lambarde's discussion of the Chancery explained the need for equity and why the provision of equity was a uniquely royal and sovereign power. Lambarde described the need for someone to 'supply the want, and correct the rigour of that Positive or written Law, which of it selfe neither is nor can be made such a perfect Rule, as that a Man may thereby truly square out Justice in all Cases that may happen', a traditional explanation of the need for equity. Fulfilling this need was a duty undertaken by the monarch through his coronation oath, and a consequence of the king's status as 'the immediate minister of Justice under God'.[49] Not only did Lambarde regard this as a duty placed on the monarch, but this was a 'soveraigne and preheminent Power'. Both the coronation oath and the king's place under God would ensure that this power was uniquely associated with the monarch.[50] In a passage which was written in 1589, Lambarde discussed a parliamentary petition from 1402, in which it was requested 'that none should be called before the Chancellor, or the Kings Councell, for any matter, but such onely as had no remedie at the Common Law'. Lambarde observed that when such petitions had been made in other parliaments, 'the Commons have seemed . . . to impugne this *Kingly Prerogative*' [emphasis added].[51]

From 1579, Lambarde referred to the Chancellor's authority as 'extraordinary, and absolute even as the Kings owne', associating the Chancery with the king's 'preheminent Power'.[52] In a section of the *Archeion* written after 1593, Lambarde explained that the king committed to the Chancellor 'his owne Regall, absolute, and extraordinarie preheminence of Iurisdiction in Civill Causes, as well for amendment as for supply of the Common Law'.[53] For Lambarde, the Chancellor was 'the Mouth, as it were, of the Prince'.[54] Consequently, 'his power is singular, and

[49] Lambarde, *Archeion*, p. 42; BL MS Lansd 621, ff. 98v–99.

[50] Lambarde, *Archeion*, p. 43; BL MS Lansd 621, f. 99.

[51] Lambarde, *Archeion*, p. 69. Although the petition, and Lambarde's commentary on it, considers the Chancery and equity, the passage occurs in Lambarde's discussion of 'criminal equity' in the Star Chamber. Folger MS V.a.207, dated 1589, is an autograph manuscript of Lambarde's material on the Star Chamber which came to form part of the *Archeion*.

[52] Lambarde, *Archeion*, p. 41, n. 26; BL MS Lansd 621, f. 98.

[53] Lambarde, *Archeion*, p. 39. See P. L. Ward, 'Appendix', in Lambarde, *Archeion*, p. 152 for discussion of the date of this section of the work.

[54] Lambarde, *Archeion*, p. 39. The idea of the Chancellor as the prince's voice is expressed in Thomas Smith's, *De Republica Anglorum* (London: Henry Middleton, 1584), pp. 36–37. *De Republica* was written between 1562 and 1565 (I. W. Archer, 'Smith, Thomas', in

of it selfe, which may rule the person which is commandable by the absolute and Regall Justice of the Prince'.[55] This association between the monarch, the prerogative and equity was influenced by the work of Jean Bodin, in particular Bodin's *République*, printed in 1576. The difference between Lambarde's 1577 letter and the 1579 text which became part of the *Archeion* can be directly linked with Lambarde's reading of a very recent publication.

This is demonstrated in Lambarde's discussion of the necessity of both law and equity.[56] Lambarde explains that 'if either this Arithmeticall Governement, (as they call it) by rigour of Law onely, or this Geometricall Judgment at the pleasure of the Chancellour or Praetor onely should bee admitted; and yet if they bee well compounded together, a most sweete and harmonicall Justice will follow of them'.[57] In the *République*, Bodin referred to the provision of arithmetic and geometric justice, resulting in justice as a form of musical harmony.[58] In doing so, Bodin mixed Aristotelian ideas of justice as proportion with mathematical theory and

H. C. G. Matthew and B. Harrison, *The Oxford Dictionary of National Biography*, 60 vols. (Oxford: Oxford University Press, 2004), vol. 51, p. 328). I can find no evidence that Lambarde had access to a manuscript copy of this work, although it did circulate. Ward has only found evidence of Lambarde using *De Republica* in his notes on the House of Commons, probably written in 1584, suggesting that Lambarde used the printed text and explaining why this remark does not appear in Lambarde's 1579 text (P. L. Ward (ed.), *William Lambarde's Notes on the Procedures and Privileges of the House of Commons (1584)* (London: HMSO, 1977), pp. 5 and 7; for the attribution of these notes to Lambarde see pp. 30–31). Lambarde seems to be the first person to use the idea of the Chancellor as the monarch's voice outside of the parliamentary context.

55 Lambarde, *Archeion*, p. 40.

56 Other evidence of the influence of Bodin upon Lambarde can be found in the *Eirenarcha*, where Lambarde observes that the justice of the peace 'may exercise sometimes *Legis actionem*, and sometimes *Iudicis officium*, or (which is all one) *Iudicium & Decretum*' (Lambarde, *Eirenarcha*, p. 63). The equivalence between the terms here is drawn from Bodin, *Six Bookes*, p. 333 (lib. III c. 5). The terms of *legis actio* and *iudicis officium* are also present in the printed marginalia to the French printing in the passage where Bodin discusses harmonic justice (Bodin, *Les Six Livres*, p. 749).

57 Lambarde, *Archeion*, p. 44; BL MS Lansd 621, f. 99v.

58 Bodin, *Six Bookes*, pp. 755–794 (lib. VI c. 6). The key passage is at p. 760. On Bodin's theory of harmonic justice, its wider intellectual background and significance see A. Giuliani, 'Metaphors of Justice. A Mathematical-Musical Image in Jean Bodin (1576)', unpublished paper presented at the 2009 British Legal History Conference. I am grateful to Dr Giuliani for providing me with a copy of his paper. Bodin also used the harmonic ratio in his earlier *Method for the Easy Comprehension of History* (New York: Columbia University Press, 1945), pp. 286–28. This was printed in 1566, and Lambarde acquired a copy in 1571 (see Ward, *William Lambarde's Notes*, p. 39, n. 14). However, the *Method* says nothing about equity or judging, so cannot be the source for Lambarde's discussion.

Pythagorean ideas of music as mathematical to produce the idea of justice itself as a form of musical harmony. References to arithmetic and geometric justice are not uncommon in the early-modern period,[59] but as Bodin himself made clear, with typical early-modern honesty, associating these ideas with musical harmony was a new step.[60] Unless Lambarde independently reached the same theoretical position as Bodin, in the three years after the *République* was printed, Lambarde's theoretical discussion of equity and the Chancery was informed by a reading of the French theorist.[61] The same idea of justice as musical harmony can also be seen in later writers on the Chancery, suggesting continued influence from Bodin (or perhaps Lambarde).[62]

A further suggestion that Lambarde's view of the Chancellor's powers may have been shaped by Bodin is visible in Lambarde's analogy between the Chancellor and the Roman praetor. This analogy seems to have been current in Elizabethan England, but was not disseminated in print until after Lambarde had formed his views.[63] Lambarde's comparison may have been formed by Bodin's use of the praetor as a prime example of equitable intervention in the application of the law.

A complication in applying Bodin's ideas to England lay in Bodin's background in the *ius commune*, where equity was associated with interpretation of textual law.[64] Much of Bodin's discussion of equity is based on this interpretative power.[65] In England, by contrast, much of the work of the Chancellor was concerned with the unwritten common law. This

59 In addition to the references to continental (especially French) material in Giuliani, 'Metaphors of Justice' see J. Hales, *An Oration in Commendation of the Lawes cheiflye of the lawes of this moste noble Realme of Englande* (BL MS Harl 4990, f. 1, at ff. 42–44), for an English example from the 1540s.

60 Bodin, *Method for the Easy Comprehension of History*, p. 286 and Bodin, *Six Bookes*, pp. 755–756 (lib. VI c. 6).

61 Lambarde seems to have been attracted to the metaphor of justice and music, even using it in a speech to a jury in his role as a Justice of the Peace in Kent (C. Read (ed.), *William Lambarde and Local Government, His "Ephemeris" and Twenty-nine Charges to Juries and Commissions* (Ithaca, NY: Cornell University Press, 1962), p. 124).

62 See nn. 110–114, 124–125 and 132 below. Alsop and Stevens suggest that the idea of law and equity leading to 'harmonicall Justice' may have been the 'coherent and orthodox moderate view' in Elizabethan England (Alsop and Stevens, 'William Lambarde', p. 247). If that is correct, this orthodox and moderate view came from Bodin.

63 The first reference I have found is in Smith, *De Republica Anglorum*, p. 54. For the evidence that Lambarde only had access to the printed version of this text (1584) see n. 54 above.

64 As Barton observes of *epieikeia*, '[p]rimarily, it was a canon of interpretation' (Barton, 'Introduction', p. xliv).

65 See, especially *Six Bookes*, pp. 763–764 (lib. VI c. 6).

difficulty in directly applying Bodin may have been noted by Lambarde, who solved the problem by incrementally changing the nature of the law in relation to equity, so that equity could operate in the context of the unwritten common law. Lambarde referred first to the need for equity in the context of 'written Lawes'.[66] Equity was then discussed in relation to 'Positive or Written law' and finally to 'the Positive and Common Law'.[67]

In the *République*, the mark of sovereignty was the power to make or unmake laws.[68] Consequently, certain aspects of equity were limited to a sovereign. Consequently, in relation to equity, 'the magistrat how great soever he be, cannot of himselfe derogat from the law, and much lesse abrogat the same: for these things we have shewed properly to belong unto soveraigntie'.[69] By contrast, 'equitie referred unto a soveraigne prince, is as much as for him to declare or expound, or correct the law', but equity referred to a magistrate could only permit the magistrate to 'asswage and mitigat the rigor of the law'.[70]

In Lambarde's work, the Chancellor mixed both the equitable powers in lesser magistrates and the equitable powers of the sovereign. According to Lambarde, the Chancellor could 'cancell and shut up the rigour of the generall Law', like magistrates in Bodin.[71] However, the king had also delegated to the Chancellor 'his owne Regall, absolute and extraordinarie preheminence of Jurisdiction in Civill Cause, *as well for amendment as for supply of the Common Law*' [emphasis added].[72] This power to amend the law was an element of sovereignty according to Bodin, albeit a form of sovereignty which as correction of the law was also described by Bodin as a form of equity. For Lambarde, such a correction of the law was a uniquely royal power, albeit delegated to the Chancellor.

Lambarde's association between the authority of the Chancellor and Chancery with the monarch was therefore a consequence of his reading

66 Lambarde, *Archeion*, p. 43; BL MS Lansd 621, f. 99.

67 Lambarde, *Archeion*, p. 44; BL MS Lansd 621, f. 99v.

68 Q. Skinner, *The Foundations of Modern Political Thought*, 2 vols. (Cambridge: Cambridge University Press, 1978), vol. 2, p. 289; M. P. Gilmore, *Argument from Roman Law in Political Thought 1200–1600* (Cambridge, MA: Harvard University Press, 1941), p. 104.

69 Bodin, *Six Bookes*, p. 335 (lib. III c. 5). The difference in the equity provided by the prince and by lesser magistrates in Bodin's thought has been noted by J. E. Shaw, 'Writing to the Prince: Supplications, Equity and Absolutism in Sixteenth Century Tuscany' (2012) 215 *Past and Present* 51, p. 54.

70 Bodin, *Six Bookes*, p. 763 (lib. VI c. 6).

71 Lambarde, *Archeion*, pp. 31–32; BL MS Lansd 621, f. 96.

72 Lambarde, *Archeion*, p. 39. This remark was added after 1593.

of Bodin's *République* between 1577 and his second discussion of the Chancery in 1579. Lambarde presented equity as a uniquely royal function and an inherent element of being sovereign, giving Chancery a privileged position in the legal system as a court which exercised the monarch's prerogative power of equity on his behalf.

2. *James Morice*

Although Morice never discusses equity in the surviving texts of his reading on the prerogative, he did state that he intended to discuss the Chancellor's role in the (undelivered) thirteenth division of the reading.[73] That division was given the heading 'What Prerogatives and Rights the king hath in and concerning the suites and accions of one Subiect against another'.[74] Morice therefore seems to have associated the Chancery, equity and the prerogative. On the basis of the surviving texts we cannot investigate the development of Morice's views any further, although there are tantalising hints that in other parts of his reading Morice was influenced by Bodin. Given that William Lambarde clearly used Bodin to associate equity with the prerogative, the same links may have been formed by Morice.

Evidence of influence from Bodin is found in Morice's discussion of the law-making prerogative. In his *République*, Bodin stressed that the mark of sovereignty was the power to make or unmake laws.[75] In Morice's reading, the first division is entitled 'What Righte of Prerogative and preheminencye the king hath in and concerning the making and establishing of lawes'.[76] This is the only heading which refers to the king's prerogative and pre-eminence, rather than just his prerogative.[77] The stress on

[73] BL MS Egerton 3376, f. 27v. [74] BL MS Egerton 3376, f. 9. [75] See n. 68 above.

[76] BL MS Egerton 3376, f. 8. The same heading appears in the version of the reading which Baker identifies as possibly Morice's autograph (J. H. Baker, *Readers and Readings in the Inns of Court and Chancery, Selden Society Supplementary Series* vol. 13 (London: Selden Society, 2000), p. 370, referring to BL MS Add 36081, f. 237), although Brooks is more sceptical (Brooks, *Law, Politics, and Society*, p. 79, n. 132).

[77] The language of pre-eminence is used by Morice as a definition of the prerogative (BL MS Egerton 3376, f. 8), but nowhere else in the text are the two words used for a single prerogative. Pre-eminence as an element of the definition of the prerogative was already to be found in the opening of Staunford's writing on the prerogative (*An Exposicion of the Kinges Prerogative* (London: Richard Tottel, 1567), f. 5), but not in the readings on *Praerogativa Regis* contained in McGlynn's study (M. McGlynn, *The Royal Prerogative and the Learning of the Inns of Court* (Cambridge: Cambridge University Press, 2003)). The prerogative was associated with the language of pre-eminence by at least 1534, when the

pre-eminence and the placing of this division as the first in the reading suggest that law-making was the most important of the monarch's powers, applying Bodin's idea of law-making as the key indication of sovereignty.

Furthermore, Morice's discussion of the law-making prerogative is reminiscent of Bodin in places.[78] In particular, he states that 'the begyning of the Parliament the continuance and the end thereof is by thonlie auc-thoritie of the Prince',[79] just as Bodin explains that the 'estates of England are never otherwise assembled . . . than by parliament writs, and expresse commandements proceeding from the king. Which showeth verie well that the estates have no power of themselves to determine, command, or decree anything; seeing that they cannot so much as assemble themselves; neither being assembled, depart, without expresse commaundement from the king'.[80] Such similarity is hardly determinative, but Morice's consideration of whether or not the king is bound by law echoes Bodin in significant ways. Morice reached the conclusion that 'rightly understood', the king is not bound by law, a conclusion which seems to be the same as that of Bodin.[81] However, this did not mean that the king could govern 'at his will and pleasure'. Morice referred to the coronation oath of the king, and asked 'What can be more meete or seeming to equite then the Prince to be bound by his owne law'?[82] Bodin also referred to the oath of kings to govern according to law and like Morice linked this to equity, explaining that 'the equitie of the law which he hath sworne to keepe, ceasing, he is no more bound to the keeping thereof, by his oath'.[83] There are clearly strong

two are listed together in the Act of Succession (Stat.25.Hen.8.cap.22) and in an oath sworn by new bishops (J. M. Gray, *Oaths and the English Reformation* (Cambridge: Cambridge University Press, 2013), p. 65).

78 It is in relation to law-making and sovereignty that Brooks also detects influence from Bodin on Morice (Brooks, *Law, Politics and Society*, p. 80).

79 BL MS Egerton 3376, f. 11.

80 Bodin, *Six Bookes*, p. 96 (lib. I c. 8). Bodin identifies his source as the English civilian and ambassador, Valentine Dale.

81 BL MS Egerton 3376, f. 13v. The question of how far Bodin's sovereign was constrained is a controversial one, but Bodin does seem to have recognised some limits on the monarch's powers. See Skinner, *Foundations of Modern Political Thought*, vol. 2, p. 293 for discussion and further references. Morice's detailed conclusion is not identical to that of Bodin, but the important point is the compatibility of the general view and approach to the discussion of the monarch.

82 BL MS Egerton 3376, f. 13v.

83 Bodin, *Six Bookes*, p. 93 (lib. I c. 8). The original French is 'la justice de la loy' (Bodin, *Les Six Livres*, p. 98), but the 1606 translation by Knolles' quoted here demonstrates that an early-modern Englishman might translate the French 'justice' as 'equity'. See n. 118 below for the Latin *iustitia* also being translated other than in the obvious literal sense.

parallels here between Morice's discussion of the law-making power and Bodin's discussion of sovereignty.

3. *Robert Snagg*

Snagg's *Antiquity & Original of the Court of Chancery*, printed in 1654, was probably originally delivered as a reading in the Middle Temple in 1581.[84] In it, Snagg raises the question of whether proceedings in Chancery complied with the *per legem terrae* requirements of Magna Carta.Were proceedings in the Chancery authorised by the law of England? Snagg's conclusion was that the authority of the Chancery and the Lord Chancellor derived from the law of England.

However, when referring to the Chancellor and the Chancery, Snagg observed that:

> looking into the course of the proceedings in the Chancery, by the Lord Chancellor of England, from time to time, it seemed as though that Office had been besides the Law, erected out of the absolute authority that the Conquerors claimed; and that it hath been continued from time to time against the Law, and the Provision of that Charter and Parliament, as it were *by a Prerogative above the Law*[85] [emphasis added].

While Snagg rejected his initial view, the link with the prerogative is clear.

There is some evidence that the remarks in Snagg's reading may have been a response to views on the Chancery. Snagg discussed the meaning of the word 'Chancellor', acknowledging 'wherein all agree, that he is called *Cancellarius, à Cancellando*. But what he may Cancell, whereby he had that honour, hath been doubted. Some have said, that he had authority *Cancellare iniquam Legem Communem, & judicare secundum Conscientiam*'.[86] In the *Archeion*, Lambarde explained that the Chancellor 'in his Court of Equitie, he doth (when the Case requireth) so cancell and shut up the rigour of the generall Law', a view which Snagg clearly rejected.[87] Lambarde's view was only expressed in 1579 and then the *Archeion*. In his 1577 letter on the Chancery, Lambarde referred to the Chancellor's name as referring to the cancellation of records (a point

[84] See Baker, *Readers and Readings*, pp. 610–611. For the controversy about the readership in the Middle Temple in February 1581 see *ibid.*, p. 354.

[85] R. Snagg, *The Antiquity and Original of the Court of Chancery, and Authority of the Lord Chancellor of England* (London: Henry Seile, 1654), p. 31.

[86] Snagg, *Antiquity*, pp. 43–44.

[87] Lambarde, *Archeion*, pp. 31–32; BL MS Lansd 621, f. 96.

he reiterated in the *Archeion*) and that he 'conteyneth the lawe within certen barres or boundes and mittigateth the suertie and Rigor thereof accordinge to aequum bonum to equitie & good conscience'.[88] There is no reference to cancelling the law here, although it might be implied.

4. *The idea of Chancery applying the king's conscience*

The idea of the Chancellor as the keeper of the 'king's conscience' is now largely treated as a commonplace.[89] But a focus on the monarch's conscience stands in marked conflict to the typical early-modern theory of conscience as in some way an objective standard.[90] Furthermore, so far as can be seen, the first identified reference to the Chancellor as the monarch's conscience was by Christopher Hatton, Lord Keeper between 1587 and 1591.[91] After Hatton, such language becomes more common.[92] As Chancellor, Lord Ellesmere referred to himself as applying the king's conscience in some cases.[93] By 1616, James I could say that the Chancery 'is called the dispenser of the King's Conscience', seemingly treating the description as a commonplace.[94] In 1621, Francis Moore wrote to Bishop Williams to remind him that as Chancellor he was to judge according to conscience, 'but that Conscience is the King's committed to the Chancellor', stressing that the Chancellor was to ignore his private conscience and to judge 'according to the King's Conscience'.[95] This change in the notion

[88] BL MS Lansd 621, f. 81.

[89] See, e.g., G. W. Thomas, 'James I, Equity and Lord Keeper John Williams' (1976) *EHR* 506, p. 514 ('[t]he chancellor, of course, was the keeper of the king's conscience').

[90] See generally DR. Klinck, *Conscience, Equity and the Court of Chancery in Early Modern England* (Farnham: Ashgate, 2010).

[91] G. Spence, *The Equitable Jurisdiction of the Court of Chancery*, 2 vols. (Philadelphia: Lea and Blanchard, 1846), vol. 1, p. 414 ('the holy conscience of the Queen, for matter of equity, that is in some sort committed to the Chancellor').

[92] Although never the only description of the nature of the conscience which was applied. Objective ideas remained, as did claims that the Chancellor was following his own conscience (see, e.g., Klinck, *Conscience, Equity*, p. 162).

[93] *Anon* (1612, Chancery) in W. H. Bryson (ed.), *Cases Concerning Equity and the Courts of Equity 1550–1660*, vol. 118 (London: Selden Society, 2001), vol. 2, p. 398; *Martin* v. *Marshall* (1615, Common Pleas) in *ibid.*, p. 444.

[94] I. James, 'A Speach in the Starre-Chamber, the XX of June. Anno 1616', in J. P. Sommerville (ed.), *King James VI and I: Political Writings* (Cambridge: Cambridge University Press, 1994), p. 214.

[95] D. Yale (ed.), *Lord Nottingham's 'Manual of Chancery Practice' and 'Prolegomena of Chancery and Equity'* (Cambridge: Cambridge University Press, 1965), p. 78.

of conscience which was to be applied in the Chancery stressed a link with the king.

III. Jurisdiction and prerogative in Chancery cases, 1595–1615

In two cases in 1595, references to the Chancery as a court deriving directly from the royal prerogative and the monarch can be found. This association with the prerogative was used to undermine other, inferior, courts which claimed an equitable jurisdiction. In *Cheyney* v. *Godfrey*, the Cinque Ports claimed an equitable jurisdiction to the exclusion of the Chancery, a jurisdiction not based upon any express grant. Two masters decided that 'this high court . . . has the dispensation of her Majesty's own pre-eminent and absolute judgment, from which no subject is or can be excused' and that only express words could found any exclusion of the Chancery jurisdiction.[96] The judgment of the Chancery was that of the monarch. The case was decided by two of the Masters in Chancery, one of whom is identified as William Lambarde. Lambarde's prerogative model of the Chancery, which he developed in the late 1570s under the influence of Jean Bodin, came to be directly applied by Lambarde himself when he became a significant figure in the Chancery.[97]

Bodin's influence may also explain the outcome of this particular case. For Bodin, in his discussion of equity, the power to give judgment other than by the law could only be given 'by vertue of his [a judge's] office' or from 'the princes rescript or commission'.[98] In England, it was clear that the judges did not have a power to judge by equity by virtue of their office (other than in matters of statutory interpretation). Such a power was therefore necessarily derived directly from the prince. This would explain Lambarde's decision in *Cheyney* v. *Godfrey* – without an express grant from the prince, no magistrate had authority to judge by equity.

However, it is not just in cases in which Lambarde's involvement can be proved that the association between the Chancery and the monarch can be seen. In the second case in 1595, *Dawborne* v. *Garbrand*, the Chancery

96 *Cheyney* v. *Godfrey* (1595), in C. Monro (ed.), *Acta Cancellariae* (London: William Benning & Co., 1847), pp. 25–26.

97 For other cases in the Chancery involving Lambarde as Master see Warnicke, *William Lambarde*, pp. 96–98.

98 Bodin, *Six Bookes*, p. 767 (lib. VI c. 6). Similarly, p. 763.

went further. The University of Oxford claimed an equitable jurisdiction. Here, even the effectiveness of an express grant of equitable jurisdiction was doubted on the basis that the Queen might not be able to delegate an inherent element of her prerogative: '[t]his court is not well satisfied that any such privilege as the said university claimeth for the cognizance and deciding of matters of equity can be by law granted by charter out of *the person and prerogative of the prince*, but that the cognizance and deciding thereof appertaineth to this honourable court' [emphasis added].[99] The Chancery here linked equity both with the person of the monarch, as in the claims to be the monarch's conscience, and with the prerogative itself. By basing the court's authority on an inherent aspect of the monarch's own power and authority, the Chancery was able to assert its jurisdictional exclusivity.[100]

In the second decade of the seventeenth century, similar arguments can be seen. In 1612, it was held that the Chancery always retained jurisdiction to hear equity cases, even if they should have been heard in other equity courts, such as the court of the Duchy of Lancaster. This was explained as the king retaining a 'supreme power' to provide equity.[101] In Michaelmas term 1615, when arguing that the city of York could not establish a court of equity by prescription, it was explained that counties palatine 'have *jura regalia* and, by consequence, a court of chancery'.[102] In both of these cases, any Chancery jurisdiction was fundamentally tied to the king's special royal power to provide equity, indeed was a consequence of this uniquely royal power.

99 *Dawborne* v. *Garbrand* (1595) in Monro, *Acta Cancellariae*, pp. 680–681. Coke was similarly adverse to the creation of new equity jurisdictions, but not because of the prerogative basis of equity courts. For Coke, the king could not create an equity court by letters patent because an equity judge would be 'without controulment' (*The Case of the Lords President of Wales and York* 12 Co. Rep. 51, f. 52).

100 This is similar to Edward Coke's use of the prerogative to justify the King's Bench's jurisdiction in *habeas corpus*. See Halliday, *Habeas Corpus*, pp. 12–13. Francis Bacon also described equity as an element of the royal prerogative, but used this to justify the king's power to establish equity courts other than the Chancery (in this case, the provincial councils). Bacon referred to this prerogative as the king's 'sovereign power', a power which included the 'power to stay suits at the common law; yea *pro bono publico* to temper, change, and control the same' (Bacon, 'A View of the Differences in Question betwixt the King's Bench and the Council in the Marches' (1607), in Spedding, *The Letters and the Life*, vol. 3, pp. 371 and 373).

101 *Anon* (1612, Chancery), in Bryson, *Cases Concerning Equity*, vol. 2, p. 398.

102 *Martin* v. *Marshall* (1615, Common Pleas), in Bryson, *Cases Concerning Equity* vol. 2, p. 444, at 445.

IV. Bodin, prerogative and the Chancery in 1615/1616

When defending the Chancery during the controversy of 1615/1616, participants in the debates typically took one of two positions. The first was a narrow defence focused on the particular arguments made, and statutes relied upon, by the supporters of the common law courts.[103] The second approach was to stress the status of the Chancery as a prerogative court, challenges to which were challenges to the prerogative itself. If the notion of the prerogative lying behind the provision of equity was associated with ideas of sovereignty from Bodin, this would explain why the Chancery necessarily needed to prevail over the common law courts: if the common law courts were able to prevent the application of equity, the king would have lost an element of sovereignty.

Three texts from the 1616 controversy about the Chancery reveal continuing influence from Bodin.[104] Two of these texts stress the association between the Chancery, equity and the prerogative. The third sought to undermine the Chancery, and to do so engaged with material from Bodin.[105] None of the texts draws out the association between ideas of sovereignty, English equity and the Chancellor as clearly as Lambarde. Arising in a different context and for different purposes, the arguments are less clear, but there is evidence that Bodin remained an influence on thinking about the unique authority of the Chancery. The texts continue

[103] Ellesmere's 'A Breviate or Direccion for the Kinges Learned Councell collected by the Lord Chauncellor Ellesmere' (in Knafla, *Law and Politics*, pp. 319–336) is an excellent example. See also William Hakewill's discussion, BL MS Lansd 174, ff. 226–235v.

[104] Given that by 1580, Gabriel Harvey thought it very likely that on entering a scholar's study one would find him reading either Bodin's *République* or Le Roy's *De l'excellence du gouvernement royal* (1575), the appearance of Bodin in the early seventeenth century is not especially surprising (E. J. L. Scott (ed.), *Letter-Book of Gabriel Harvey. AD 1573–1580*, Camden Society New Series vol. 33 (London: Camden Society, 1884), p. 79).

[105] Not all participants in the debate, even on the side of the Chancery, used the same ideas from Bodin as Lambarde. Most notably, Lord Chancellor Ellesmere did not focus on the prerogative (contrary to the assertions of Timothy Tourneur), nor the idea of justice as musical harmony. Ellesmere's contributions seem to have been resolutely technical, focusing on the meaning of the statutes in question (see BL MS Stowe 415, ff. 37v-40v). Ellesmere did know Bodin's work (see Knafla, *Law and Politics*, pp. 75 and 319), but chose not to use the discussion of equity found there and seems generally to have rejected the practical application of theory about the prerogative (Russell, *King James VI and I*, p. 152). This may explain why the prerogative was not a concern in *Finch* v. *Throgmorton* (see n. 9 above) – the parties to the debate were not those interested in seeing equity in the Chancery as an issue of political theory.

to make reference to the role of equity in providing justice as musical harmony, suggesting a continuing influence from Bodin.[106]

1. *Anthony Benn*

Benn was a lawyer whose surviving writings are generally supportive of royal authority against the common law courts. Benn wrote a tract in support of the Chancery in which he stressed the association between the Chancery and the prerogative.[107] Benn refers to the Chancery, the Exchequer and letters under the Privy Seal from the King's Council as 'Courts of Prerogative'.[108]

Benn's discussion includes the musical metaphor from Bodin of the relationship between law and equity, albeit in different terms from those seen in Bodin and Lambarde. While for Bodin and Lambarde the Aristotelian underpinnings of the theory are apparent, Benn changes the metaphor. For Benn, 'Justice is her [equity's] plaine song, as it is the plaine song of the lawe, the descant is manyfold, yet no other then such as the law also makes her musick of; It is with equity as with law'.[109]

Brooks has observed that Benn's writings reveal links with Bodin's thought, and so the appearance of the musical metaphor, and the association of equity with the prerogative, may not be surprising.[110] However, it may be that in this particular instance Benn was being influenced not by Bodin directly, but by Lambarde. In addition to using the idea of music in association with justice, Benn refers to a parliamentary petition from the reign of Henry IV which complained about the use of subpoenas from the Chancery and the king's response.[111] The same petition and response are found in Lambarde's *Archeion*, near the end of a section showing the complaints made against the Chancery and other royal interventions in the legal system, with some of the royal responses

[106] Not all such prerogative arguments made use of Bodin's ideas (or at least do not do so in a manner which can be identified). Most obviously, Francis Bacon's letter to James clearly associated the Chancery with the prerogative, but does not explain this link (see above, n. 30).

[107] BL MS Lansd 174, ff. 205–215. [108] BL MS Lansd 174, f. 211v.

[109] BL MS Lansd 174, ff. 211v–212. At this point is his discussion, Benn rejects the argument of uncertainty in equity, arguing that equity is no more uncertain than law, hence the description of equity as 'like' the law. Baker dismisses this passage as 'florid' language, but in fact it reveals the influences on Benn (Baker, 'The Common Lawyers and the Chancery', p. 382).

[110] Brooks, *Law, Politics and Society*, p. 141. [111] BL MS Lansd 174, ff. 211–211v.

to them.[112] It is in this section that Lambarde refers to the role of the Chancery as 'prerogative',[113] and it is in this context that Benn also refers to the Chancery as a prerogative court.[114]

2. *James I*

Timothy Tourneur seems to have regarded the king as someone manipulated into his intervention in the dispute over the Chancery's jurisdiction.[115] Even if James was originally provoked into action, the result was his *Speach* in the Star Chamber in 1616, a speech in which James revealed some of his own views on the relationship between law, equity and prerogative in the English context. It seems likely that James agreed with Francis Bacon's recommendation to use the Star Chamber to resolve the Chancery dispute; the *Speach* was another opportunity for James to demonstrate to the wider world his understanding of the 'true rules of monarchy'.[116] The *Speach* enabled James to show that he could not only write *The Trew Law of Free Monarchies*, but that he could apply this true law as a king.

In the *Speach*, James revealed a strong association between the Chancery and the royal prerogative. James described the Chancery as 'mixing Mercy with Justice', and then stated that 'the Kings Throne [is] established by Mercy and Justice'.[117] This idea seems to be a combination of Proverbs 20.28 (where the throne is established by mercy) and the Latin vulgate of Proverbs 25.5 (in which the throne is established by *justitia*, although early-modern English translations use 'righteousness').[118] For James, the Chancery therefore performed an essential biblical function on his behalf, securing the throne in a way which the common law courts, which 'proceed onely according to the strict rules of Law', did not and could not.[119] This special role for the Chancery led James to explain that 'as I am bound in my Conscience to maintaine every Courts Jurisdiction, *so especially this*' [emphasis added], further privileging the Chancery.

While James did not explicitly refer to the Chancery as prerogative court, the discussion of the Chancery was part of a disquisition as to

[112] *Archeion*, pp. 68–73, at 71–72. [113] See n. 51 above. [114] See n. 109 above.

[115] See nn. 31–32 above. [116] See n. 30 above. [117] James I, *Speach*, p. 214.

[118] Benn explicitly referred to Proverbs 20.28 in his discussion of the Chancery ('mercy and trueth preserve the King and his throne shalbe established by equity'), BL MS Lansd 174, f. 206. The marginal note is to Proverbs 20. Bacon also referred to Proverbs 20.28 to demonstrate that 'by the ordinance of God' the power to establish courts of equity belonged inherently to the king (Bacon, 'A View of the Differences', pp. 372–373).

[119] James I, *Speach*, p. 214.

the limits to which judges of the common law courts were subject. 'First, Incroach not upon the Prerogative of the Crowne'.[120] The second limit was 'not to invade other Jurisdictions'.[121] Although these two topics appear unrelated, after stating the jurisdictions of the King's Bench, Common Pleas and Exchequer, James then instructed the judges that while they were 'to give me no more right in my private Prerogative, then you give to any Subject . . . as for the absolute Prerogative of the Crowne, that is no Subiect for the tongue of a Lawyer, nor is lawfull to be disputed'.[122] James then discussed the jurisdiction of the Chancery. The structure of the *Speach* therefore suggests that James did associate the Chancery with the absolute prerogative, an impression strengthened by James's claim that the Chancellor should not 'exceed his limite' but that if he were to do so 'the King onely is to correct it', suggesting that the Chancery was part of the 'absolute Prerogative of the Crown' which was not to be disputed, especially as James described any such jurisdictional litigation as 'in contempt of our Authoritie'.[123]

The *Speach* shows considerable influence from Bodin. Most obviously, James used a musical metaphor in relation to the Chancery and other courts, but without any evidence of the underlying Aristotelian theory. James proclaimed that '[i]t is a speciall point of my Office to procure and command, that amongst Courts there bee a concordance, *and musical accord*' [emphasis added],[124] later encouraging the judges to 'labour to keepe that *sweete harmonie*, which is amongst those sisters the Muses' [emphasis added].[125]

Furthermore, Bodin recommended that sovereigns should not themselves act as judges, largely for pragmatic reasons.[126] In his *Speach*, James explained that to intervene in a case which directly concerned him or was a 'great cause' might cause people to suspect partiality either towards James himself or one of the parties, and that to intervene in a 'meane cause was not worthy of me'.[127] Impliedly, James could intervene in this dispute as a 'great cause' not concerning any particular parties. Rather, the dispute between the common law courts and Chancery concerned 'a speciall point of my Office'.[128] In the *République*, Bodin stated that because equitable intervention 'greatly concerned the rights of soveraigntie, princes . . . reserved unto themselves the expounding and correcting

[120] *Ibid.*, p. 212. [121] *Ibid.*, p. 213. [122] *Ibid.*, p. 214.
[123] *Ibid.*, p. 215. [124] *Ibid.*, p. 215. [125] *Ibid.*, p. 217.
[126] Bodin, *Six Bookes*, pp. 506–517 (lib. IV c. 6). [127] James I, *Speach*, p. 207.
[128] *Ibid.*, p. 215.

of the laws, especially in cases doubtful, betwixt the Law and Equitie',[129] just as James was doing in the *Speach*. James therefore seems to have used an idea from Bodin both to justify his intervention to his domestic audience and to explain his departure from Bodin's own advice.

3. *Francis Ashley*

In his 1616 reading on Magna Carta and the meaning of *lex terrae*, Ashley, like Snagg, concluded that equity was part of the *lex terrae*, not an alternative or competitor to it.[130] The reading was delivered in Michaelmas 1616, after Coke had been dismissed from his post. The prefatory speech to the reading strongly hints at Ashley's support for Coke. Not only did Ashley cite the preface to Coke's *Eighth Reports* on the importance of Magna Carta, he explicitly relied on Magna Carta to declare that the king cannot delay justice by orders under the great or privy seal, impliedly supporting Coke's conclusion on this point concerning the writ *non procedendo rege inconsulto* and perhaps in the *Case of Commendams*.[131]

Interestingly, Ashley also makes use of the musical metaphor about law and justice. However, unlike writers in support of the Chancery, Ashley uses the metaphor in relation to Magna Carta and other laws in England. According to Ashley, 'The old statutes which were the auntient Common Lawes are the body and the Text, and all Records and Reports are but Commentaryes and exposicions upon them, and so is this law in effect the ground, and the rest subsequent but florishes upon it, *this the base and others the descant*' [emphasis added].[132] Ashley subverts the musical

[129] Bodin, *Six Bookes*, p. 764 (lib. VI c. 6). Bodin's view was probably informed by C.1.14.1.

[130] On Ashley's reading see Halliday, *Habeas Corpus*, pp. 145–147.

[131] BL MS Harl 4841, f. 3. Halliday notes that '[t]he timing [of Ashley's reading] may have mattered', but does not directly consider the content of the reading in this regard (Halliday, *Habeas Corpus*, p. 394, n. 27). On the controversy concerning the writ *non procedendo rege inconsulto* see Hart, *The Rule of Law*, pp. 104–105. The *Case of Commendams* did not involve a sealed order from the king, merely a letter, and so was not directly covered by Ashley's point. However, for an early-modern common lawyer to accept that justice could not be delayed by a formal writ but could be delayed by letter seems unlikely, suggesting Ashley was alluding to the *Case of Commendams*. For the letters and debates see *Acts of the Privy Council of England 1615–1616* (London: HMSO, 1925), pp. 595–609.

[132] BL MS Harl 4841, f. 3. The reference to the old statutes as the text of the common law and reports as commentaries is taken from the preface to Coke's eighth reports (E. Coke, *La Huictme Part des Reports de Sir Edw. Coke* (London: Societie of Stationers, 1611), sig. Aii). Lambarde referred to the three estates in parliament as being 'harmonicall', 'because from such, and so well-tuned a Base, Meane, and Treble, there proceedeth a most exquisite consent, and delicious melodie' (Lambarde, *Archeion*, p. 126), which

idea of justice found in Bodin to suit his own ends. For Ashley, equity was a part of *lex terrae*, but at best one part of the 'descant' of the harmony of justice. That harmony depended upon Magna Carta. Equity, which was clearly associated with the prerogative in the 1616 debates, could not work against Magna Carta if justice were to flourish. The controversial implication about the relationship between the prerogative and Magna Carta is clear, but not made explicit.

V. Conclusion

By the 1650s, the Chancery's association with the prerogative, and the use of Bodinian terms, seems to have been widely accepted. Henry Robinson's proposal to abolish the Chancery condemned the court as 'such an absolute Prerogative Royall, as that every knave, oppressor, or revengefull person is able . . . to commence and continue a suite'.[133] An anonymous pamphlet in support of the Chancery could, by contrast, praise the court as the 'conscience of the Supreme Authority', language which echoes Bodin's concept of the sovereign, while avoiding awkward questions about who or what was the supreme authority in Interregnum England.[134] While it was possible to discuss equity and the Chancery without reference to questions of sovereignty, the influence of Bodin, perhaps via Lambarde (whose *Archeion* was printed in 1635), intertwined questions of equity with matters of prerogative and fundamental political authority. As the harmony of the commonweal gave way to discord in the mid-seventeenth century, the prerogative itself came to be challenged and criticised. The Chancery's existence came to be threatened by an association with the prerogative, an association which had protected the Chancery a few decades earlier.

may suggest Ashley's use of the musical terms originated in Lambarde. Lambarde's discussion here is reminiscent of Bodin's reference to musical harmony in relation to a royal monarchy (Bodin, *Six Bookes*, p. 755 (lib. VI c. 6)). Alternatively, the reference to the 'descant' may be a response to Benn's argument (see n. 109 above).

133 Henry Robinson, *Certaine proposals in order to a new modelling of the lawes and law-proceedings for a more speedy, cheap, and equall distribution of justice throughout the common-wealth* (London: M. Simmons, 1653), p. 4.

134 Anon., *Considerations touching the dissolving or taking away the court of chancery and the courts of iustice depending upon it* (London: Thomas Heath, 1653), p. 4.

4

Authority and precedent

DAVID IBBETSON

It is a commonplace, almost a caricature, among comparative lawyers that English law, like all common law systems, is based on case law, built up of binding precedents or authorities, whereas continental European legal systems pay relatively little heed to this. Legal historians can too easily suppose that this is a deeply rooted distinction, with common lawyers focusing on the law applied in courts while their continental counterparts focus on doctrine and the development of the rules of Roman and canon law. More recently, however, legal historians working within the continental traditions have begun to examine the role of case law before the codifications of the nineteenth century. In Italy in particular, building on the pioneering work of Gino Gorla, there have been several studies devoted to the case law of particular courts;[1] and some comparative work has revealed the complexity of the position between the sixteenth and eighteenth centuries.[2] The present paper aims to elucidate this aspect of legal reasoning in the early-modern period. It was at this time that the printing press made it a practical possibility routinely to have access to at least a selection of reasoned decisions, so it is unsurprising that it was at this time that there appeared the first traces of the idea that special weight might attach to the judgments of superior courts. The dissemination of printed volumes of *decisiones* across continental Europe

Thanks are due in particular, subject to the usual disclaimer, to John Baker, Paul Brand, Dolores Freda, Adolfo Giuliani, Lorna Hutson, Neil Jones, Jonathan Rose, Guido Rossi, Alain Wijffels and Ian Williams.

1 G Gorla, 'I Tribunali Supremi degli Stati Italiani, fra i Seec. XVI e XIX, quali Fattori della Unificazione del Diritto nello Stato e della Sua Informazione fra Stati', in *La Formazione Storica del Diritto Moderno in Europa* (Florence: Olschki, 1977), 447; M Ascheri, *Tribunali, Giuristi e Istituzioni dal Medioevo all'Età Moderna* (Bologna: Il Mulino, 1989), 85–183; D Freda, *La Dottrina dei Lawyers: Le Raccolte di Giurisprudenza nell'Inghilterra dei Tudor* (Naples: Satura, 2009), 9–20, with the further works there cited.

2 See in particular the introduction to A Wijffels, ed., *Case Law in the Making* (Berlin: Duncker & Humblot, 1997), vol. 1. The point is well made by Professor Baker: 'English Law and the Renaissance' (1985) *Cambridge Law Journal* 46, 53–56.

made it possible for ideas developed in one place to spread to others; and in England the wholesale shift from pre-trial discussions of pleading to post-trial arguments in arrest of judgment and *non obstante veredicto* heightened the focus on the centrality of the judicial decision.

An indication of the sheer volume of reports in continental Europe is provided by the list of reporters given by Agostino Fontana in his *Amphiteatrum Legale* published in 1690, about 800 in total, of whom approximately 400 were Italians.[3] Before 1600, some thirty-two collections had been published in Italy, most of them large folio volumes reprinted several times;[4] by contrast, leaving aside the Year Books, England knew only the collections of Plowden and Dyer. Even including the printed Year Books, and not ignoring the circulation of manuscripts within the tight-knit community of English lawyers centred on Westminster Hall and the Inns of Court, the amount of decision-based literature available in England before 1600 was still only a fraction of that found in Italy. At the very least, we can be sure that the interest in decisions was not a phenomenon limited to England. As well, outside England, works of legal dialectic flourished in the sixteenth century,[5] providing an opportunity for self-conscious reflection on the nature of legal argument. Such works appeared rather later in England and show influence from their continental counterparts. So far as the long-term picture is concerned, it may be more pertinent to ask why authority- or precedent-based legal reasoning lost its hold in continental systems rather than why it took hold in England.

Two preliminary observations are necessary. First, although there was a movement towards the assimilation of the language of precedent/precedents and that of authority/authorities, it is necessary to keep the terminology separate. The process of assimilation of the two sets of ideas is one of the central features which need to be explored, not something that can be taken for granted. Second, the paper is concerned not so much with the way in which courts in practice reached decisions in particular cases as with what it was said that they were doing, whether this was said by judges, advocates, writers on legal dialectic or anyone

[3] A Fontana, *Amphiteatrum Legale* (1690), part 3, 358–380; Ascheri, *Tribunali, Giuristi e Istituzioni*, 89.

[4] M Ascheri, in H Coing, *Handbuch der Quellen und Literatur der Neueren Europäischen Privatrechtsgeschiche* (Munich: Beck, 1976), vol. II/2, 1179–1182.

[5] V Piano Mortari, 'Dialettica e Giurisprudenza. Studio sui Trattati di Dialettica Legale del Sec XVI' (1957) *Annali di Storia del Diritto* 1, 293; H J Berman, *Law and Revolution, II* (Harvard University Press, 2003), 100–130; J Schröder, *Recht als Wissenschaft* (2nd edition; Munich: Beck, 2012), 47–50.

else. As has been pointed out in studies of the Italian *decisiones* literature, those lawyers publishing collections of decisions might be predisposed to exaggerate their worth;[6] and, more generally, any attempt to articulate the implicit assumptions behind any social practice will necessarily introduce distortions, so that the study of the practice itself and the study of its description are two very different enterprises.

I. The *argumentum ab auctoritate*

The argument from authority was very common in the Middle Ages. It had its source in Aristotle's *Topics*, where the basic distinction was made between demonstrations and dialectical deductions.[7] In the former, the premises of the argument were true in and of themselves and hence the conclusions were also undoubtedly true provided only that the argument was formally sound. Dialectical deductions were different, in so far as there the premises of the argument were only opinions, and the truth of the conclusions depended on the quality of the premises. Their plausibility depended on the reputability of the opinions which lay at their base. For these to have any value they had to be opinions 'accepted by everyone or by the majority or by the wise, i.e. by all or by the majority, or by the most notable and reputable of them'. It was this reputability that turned opinions into authorities, *auctoritates*. Cicero handled the matter very slightly differently. For him, the crucial feature was whether the premises were simply true in and of themselves and where they depended on facts external to the argument.[8] Such extrinsic facts might be undoubtedly true, most notably (when applied in a Christian context) the texts of scripture, but they were nonetheless *auctoritates*.

In the hands of the medieval philosophers, building on these, an argument from authority might be *necessary*, in the sense that its premises could not be questioned, or it might be *probable*, in the sense that it was based on premises which might or might not be true. The difference between something that is true and something that might be true looks significant at first sight, but in the medieval context it might not have been too substantial. The whole justification for the argument from authority was that those who were recognised as very skilled in their art or science

6 M N Miletti, *Stylus Judicandi* (Naples: Jovene, 1998), 101–192, especially at 142.

7 *Topics*, 1.1, in J Barnes, ed., *The Complete Works of Aristotle* (Princeton University Press, 1984), 1.167.

8 *Topica*, 4.24.

were deserving of being believed, so that even probable arguments were likely to be true, and hence their conclusions had a provisional validity.[9] The normal way to oppose an argument from authority was not simply to produce contrary authorities and claim that these were stronger than one's opponent's, or to claim that the opponent's texts did not have authoritative status, though undoubtedly some authorities might carry more weight than others. Rather, the authorities would typically be accepted as such but then reinterpreted to show that they were not, in truth, incompatible with one's own position.[10]

The jurists of the medieval *ius commune* recognised the value of arguments from authority.[11] The late-fifteenth-century civilian Giovanni Battista Caccialupi collected together references from Justinian's *Corpus Iuris* to illustrate the proposition that those very learned in their art should be believed: saints, medical doctors, philosophers and poets as well as jurists.[12] The authority of poets was particularly problematic since the only art in which they could be said to have any specific expertise was that of writing poetry, something which would rarely come into account in any legal argument.[13] Moreover, even in the ancient world, it was recognised that poets were an unreliable guide to the truth. Nonetheless, Homer and Virgil had been cited in the Digest and the Institutes, so that it could hardly be argued by lawyers that their works were of no authority.

Perhaps the most substantial treatment of the argument from authority for medieval lawyers was found in Bartolus's commentary on Digest 12.1.1. He drew the distinction between, on the one hand, descriptive authorities, such as the writings of historians and chroniclers, which should be believed in so far as they were reputable, and, on the other hand, prescriptive authorities, such as the writings of Aristotle on philosophy or

[9] J Buridan, *Summulae de Dialectica*, 6.5.10, G Klima, ed. (Yale University Press, 2001), 482.

[10] J Marenbon, *Later Medieval Philosophy (1150–1350): An Introduction* (London: Routledge, 1991), 29–30.

[11] V Piano Mortari, 'L'Argumentum ab Auctoritate nel Pensiero dei Giuristi Medievali', in *Dogmatica e Interpretazione: I Giuristi Medievali* (Naples: Jovene, 1976), 77–91; N Horn, 'Argumentum ab Auctoritate in der Legistischen Argumentationstheorie', in O Behrends, et al., eds., *Festschrift für Franz Wieacker zum 70. Geburtstag* (Göttingen: Vendenhoeck & Ruprecht, 1978), 261.

[12] S Caprioli, 'De Modis Arguendi Scripta Rariora' (1963), *Studi Senesi* 75, 30; (1965) *Studi Senesi* 77, 355, at 372.

[13] G Van den Bergh, 'Auctoritas Poetarum: The Fortunes of a Legal Argument', in A Watson, ed., *Daube Noster* (Edinburgh: Scottish Academic Press, 1974), 27. For the classic medieval responses to the authority of poets see gl *poeta Homero* to Inst 1.23.2 and gl *Virgilius* to D.1.8.6.5.

Hippocrates on medicine. The opinions of lawyers fitted into this second category and could themselves be divided into two types. First, there were statements made by the Roman jurists who, according to Justinian's *Corpus Iuris*, had been given the power to create law;[14] since these had the authority of the Emperor they constituted necessary authorities, and the conclusions derived from them by formally valid arguments were straightforwardly true. Second, there were the writings of the medieval glossators and doctors, which had only probable authority and hence could be ranged one against another.

This distinction between the necessary authority of the Roman jurists and the probable authority of the medieval and modern lawyers was something of a commonplace for the sixteenth-century writers on legal dialectic.[15] Writers such as Peter Gammarus and Jean Bellon, for example, did little more than briefly restate what had been orthodoxy for several centuries.[16] Later in the century, Nicolas Vigelius was similarly conservative if less brief. For him, statute (*lex*) and custom (*consuetudo*) were necessary authorities, but the only human opinions which had such necessary authority in point of law were the writings of the Roman jurists included in Justinian's *Corpus Iuris*, since it had been expressly laid down that they had the force of imperial constitutions. As for the rest – the writings of other lawyers, the *communis opinio doctorum*, *regulae iuris*, as well as the non-legal writings of philosophers, orators, medical men, poets and the like and common proverbs – these had only probable authority.[17]

The argument from authority was treated at length by the Dutchman Nicolas Everaerts (Everardi) in his *Topica*, first published in 1516, with a considerably expanded second edition appearing in 1552.[18] At its core was the orthodox maxim that the expert should be believed in his own science, *expertus in sua scientia credendum est.*[19] From this it followed that reputable historians were to be followed in matters of history, reputable philosophers in matters of philosophy, reputable medical men in matters of medicine, and so on. Reputability in this context was to be determined

[14] C.1.17.1.6. [15] Above, n. 9.

[16] Gammarus, *Dialectica Legalis* (ed. 1545), 214–215; Bellon, *De Argumentis Legum* (Lyons, 1551), 180–182.

[17] Vigelius, *Dialectices Iuris Civilis* (ed. Basel, 1573), 112–121.

[18] For the textual history of the work see O M D F Vervaart, *Studies over Nicolaas Everaerts (1462–1532) en zijn Topica* (Arnhem: Gouda, 1994), 69–82, 235 (English summary). In what follows page references to the first version are to the Basel edition of 1544, the second version to that of Lyons of 1564.

[19] *Topicorum seu Locorum Legalium Opus de Inventione* (ed. Basel, 1544), 243–254.

according to the opinion of scholars or those in the universities. Statutes and binding customs (i.e. practices satisfying the formal criteria laid down in the *Corpus Iuris*) constituted necessary authorities, as more generally did the instructions of those who had the power to create law; but other sources, including the gloss, the writings of the medieval *doctores* and their *communis opinio*, were only probable authorities. These, it was said, could be countered by binding texts or by reason, *ratio necessaria*. It was not, however, sufficient to treat all probable authorities as equivalent: some had greater weight than others. In theological matters, for example, Saint Augustine was the strongest authority in matters of doctrine, Saint Gregory in matters of morals and Saint Jerome in matters of translation. In law, all other things being equal, the judge should follow the gloss or the *communis opinio* of the learned lawyers; moreover, if he did so he was free from the risk of personal liability for giving a false judgment even if more expert analysis showed that the authority should in truth have been displaced.

A slightly different approach is visible in the *Topica Legalia* of the Basel humanist Claudius Cantiuncula. For him, the argument from authority was just one facet of the argument from precedents, *praeiudicia*, and his discussion was based not on the traditional legal sources but on Cicero and Quintilian.[20] The argumentative force of these precedents, whether they were found in previous judgments or in the writings of reputable authors, depended on two factors: the authority of the person who was to be followed and the similarity between the previous instance and the present question. That decisions might be authorities was already clear in the first version of Everaerts' *Topica*, where it was said that the authority of decisions of the Roman Rota and similar courts was only probable, not necessary,[21] but in the second version the equivalence of the two ideas was brought very much into the foreground. Here the argument *ab auctoritate* and the argument from precedent, *a praeiudiciis vel pronuntiatis*, were essentially interchangeable terms, visible in the opening words of the section:

> Ab autoritate seu exemplo maiorum, vel ut alii volunt, a praeiudiciis seu pronunciatis . . .[22]

[20] C Cantiuncula, *Topica Legalia* (ed. Basel, 1545), 5–8.

[21] *Topicorum seu Locorum Legalium Opus de Inventione* (ed. Basel, 1544), 248.

[22] *Loci Argumentorum Legales* (ed. Lyons, 1564), 581 (text reads *provinciatis* for *pronunciatis*, a clear misprint); and 582: 'Haec argumentatio ab autoritate seu exemplo maiorum, vel *si malis* a praeiudiciis seu pronuntiatis'. [emphasis added].

These precedents could count as either necessary or probable authorities: necessary where those deciding the case had the power to create law, probable where they did not.

However, alongside this and independent of it, it was being said in the sixteenth century that decisions of supreme courts had the force of *lex*, reinterpreting (or conflicting with) the explicit Roman rule that one should judge according to *lex* rather than *exempla*, applying the law rather than reasoning from concrete cases.[23] Although this view was commonly attributed to Baldus, he did not go quite so far, saying only that decisions by the ruler (*princeps*) had the force of *lex* and that legislation by the Senate would have the force of *lex* if confirmed by the ruler.[24] More important were the express statements in the Neapolitan *Decisiones* of Matthaeus de Afflictis, first published in 1499, that judgments by the *Sacrum Consilium* of Naples had the force of general statutes.[25] The reason for this was clear, that they were given in the name of the king and hence had the same force as decisions by the king himself.[26] Elsewhere, where there was no similar provision giving legislative force to decisions, the Neapolitan example could not be followed so easily. Hence, in the preface to his collection of decisions from Piedmont, Antonio Tesauro argued that the Senate there had no law-making power since none had been granted to it by the prince, the only person with the ability to create law. It followed that its decisions were not in themselves law.[27] When in 1561 it was prescribed that the judges of the Roman Rota should not adjudicate contrary to the practice and decisions of the Rota which were in print, '*contra stylum et decisiones factas in Rota quae impressae habentur*', without strong reason and after discussion, and only then if two-thirds of the judges agreed, it was clear that previous decisions had weight but there was no question that

[23] C.7.45.13.

[24] Baldus, ad C.1.14.12, *Si Imperialis*, ad C.1.14.8 *Humanum* in *Opera Omnia* (ed. Venice, 1615), vol. 5, 69–70.

[25] Afflictis, *Decisiones*, 96 no. 11, 169 no. 9, 383 no. 8. Similarly, Vivius, *Decisiones Regni Neapolitani*, Decisio 91; Maranta, *Consilia*, 25; *id.*, *Speculum Aureum*, Part 6, *Et quandoque appellatur*, no. 252; Muscatellus, *Sacri Regii Consilii Magnaeque Curiae Vicariae Praxis Civilis*, f.8 no. 109. See G Vallone, *Le 'Decisiones' di Matteo d'Afflitto* (Lecce: Milella, 1989), 47–53.

[26] It had been laid down by Ferdinand I in 1493 or 1494 that the *sententiae* of the *Consilium* should be given in the name of the King: *Pragmaticae ac Reformationes Tribunalium in hac Civitate Neapolitanae Existentium* (Naples, 1559), f.6, § Sacrum praeterea concilium.

[27] Thesaurus, *Novae Decisiones Sacri Senatus Pedemontani*, praefatio, num. 32. Osascus, *Decisiones Senatus Pedemontani*, Decisio 1 no. 44.

they had any binding force equivalent to statutes.[28] Hence, in the 1620s, Sigismundo Scaccia could assert that the decisions of the Neapolitan *Consilium* had greater authority than those of the Roman Rota since the former were given in the name of the king but the latter were not given in the name of the pope.[29]

But if Naples was precocious, by the seventeenth century other Italian territories were following its lead:[30] in Milan, for example, it was said simply that decisions of the Senate constituted *lex*;[31] in Savoy, the Senate was described as representing the person and majesty of the prince;[32] and even Tesauro in Piedmont and Asinio in Florence, while denying any general legislative force to decisions of the Senate, were willing to accept that in some circumstances they should be treated as *lex*.[33] This was not purely an Italian phenomenon. We find it stated explicitly in Portugal, for example,[34] and in the Netherlands.[35] Even in Germany, whose 'commitment to legal science' has been described by John Dawson,[36] the Neapolitan example was cited by Hermann Vultejus in 1602, saying that 'today there is hardly anybody in the Roman Empire who doubts that the decisions and precedents of the Imperial Chamber [i.e. the *Reichskammergericht*] have the force of law'.[37] France was more

[28] E Cerchiari, *Capellani Papae et apostolicae sedis, auditores causarum sacri palatii apostolici, seu sacra romana Rota ab origine ad diem usque 20 septembris 1870: Relatio historica-iuridica* (Rome, 1919), vol. 3, 297, at 299. For the *authoritas* of the Rota contrasted with that of the *communis opinio doctorum* see the comments of Jerónimo Cucalón on Decius, *De Regulis Iuris*, lex *Iura Sanguinis* (ed. Lyons, 1557), 84.

[29] Scaccia, *De Sententiis et Re Iudicata* (ed. Lyons, 1628), Gloss 14 q. 24, especially at nos. 18, 57–58.

[30] Ascheri, *Tribunali, Giuristi e Instituzioni*, 97–99.

[31] Clarus, *Practica Criminalis* (ed. Venice, 1568), q. 38, § Vidi aliquando.

[32] *Codex Fabrianus*, lib. 9 tit. 29 def. 5 n. 4 (p. 1203).

[33] Thesaurus, *Novae Decisiones Sacri Senatus Pedemontani*, praefatio, num. 32; Asinius, *Judiciorum Praxis*, s. 22 c. 16.

[34] Gamma, *Decisiones Lusitaniae*, Decisio 33 no. 2, Decisio 228; Cabedo, *Practicarum Observationum*, Part 1, Decisio 212.

[35] Christinaeus, *Commentaria in Leges Municipales Mechlinienses* (ed. Antwerp, 1657), 409; Christinaeus, *Practicarum Quaestionum Rerumque in Supremis Belgarum Curiis Actarum* (ed. Antwerp, 1661), Decisio 1.

[36] J P Dawson, *Oracles of the Law* (Ann Arbor: University of Michigan, 1968), 148.

[37] Vultejus, *Consilia sive Responsa Doctorum et Professorum Facultatis Juridicae in Academia Marpurgensi*, vol. 4 (ed. Frankfurt, 1631), cons. 54, no. 158 (p. 1338); essentially repeating vol. 3 (1607), cons. 19 nos. 93–94 (p. 142), cons. 29 no. 108 (p. 341). For a more conservative view expressed by the Law Faculty of Nürnburg see Rittershausen, *Consilia sive Responsa Altorfina de Iure* (ed. Hanau, 1603), resp. 55, p. 266–267, expressly denying that

ambiguous and may not have gone quite so far as Germany. In the first half of the century, Budé had said that the French Parlement had all the powers of the Roman Senate, together with the judicial powers of the Emperor, and this view had been followed by Nicolas Bohier and approved in the early seventeenth century by Georges Louet.[38] On the other hand, in the second decade of the seventeenth century, the Justinianic rule that one should judge according to *lex* rather than by *exempla* was said to remain in force despite the practice of following previous cases.[39] But whatever the theory of the matter, the reality was that decisions might have legislative weight: the opinion of Rebuffus that a decision contrary to the *stylus curiae* was a nullity[40] would have produced a result similar to the Italian experience, and the practice of the judges of the Parlement resolving particularly important question 'in red robes' elided the distinction between adjudication and legislation.[41]

The core of the dominant line found in continental Europe by the early seventeenth century was the Neapolitan rule that decisions of the *Sacrum Consilium* had the force of statute since they were given in the name of the King, but alongside this we find a variety of other partial explanations: if the king or prince had been present and the decision reached with his consent, this could be treated as a ruling by him; the senate or other superior court might represent the prince, even though he was not there; if the same decision had been reached three or four times (or perhaps even only twice), then it could be treated as a binding custom or as the *stylus curiae*, which should not be departed from; where legislation was ambiguous, or its detail required filling out, the supreme court's decision as to its meaning could be conclusive; the fact that the judges of the court were learned men, *doctores*, might give their rulings the status of *communis opinio* which ought to be followed; or simply that respect should be paid to the decisions of the supreme court, whose judges were wise and learned.

these *praeiudicia* had the *auctoritas* of *lex*, but recognising the practice of citing previous decisions and approving the following of them in cases where the law was otherwise doubtful.

38 Budaeus, *Annotationes in Pandectas*, Ex l. ultima, de Senatoribus (ed. 1542, p. 128); Boerius, *[Additiones in Montanus,] Tractatus de Authoritate Magni Concilii et Parlamentorum Galliae*, in *Decisiones Burdegalenses* (ed. Lyons, 1566), nos. 178–179; Louet, *Arrêts*, note to Decision N.4.

39 Autonne, *La Conference du Droict Francois avec le Droict Romain* (Paris, 1615), 855.

40 Rebuffus, *Commentaria in Constitutiones seu Ordinationes Regiae* (ed. Lyons, 1613), Art. II gloss 13 no. 44; Dawson, *Oracles of the Law*, ch. 3.

41 Dawson, *Oracles of the Law*, 313–314.

We may summarise the continental European tradition, as it had developed by the late sixteenth and early seventeenth centuries, in three propositions. First, the texts of the law, whether the writings of scholars or decisions in cases, were authorities in the Aristotelian sense that they constituted an acceptable base for legal argument; but they were differentiated from statutes and formally recognised customs in that they might only be probable authorities, not necessary ones. Moreover, there was a linguistic overlap between precedents and authority/authorities: according to the Saxon Benedict Carpzov, in common usage *praeiudicia* were the same thing as *auctoritates* of judgments,[42] and it was commonly said that decisions had authority.[43] Second, decisions made by supreme courts and other tribunals which had legislative as well as adjudicative power could be regarded as binding, having a statutory force which would be applied in similar cases in the future. And third, explicitly stated in the ordinance regulating the Roman Rota, the argumentative weight of decisions might depend on the fact of their having been printed.

II. The argument from authority in England

With all this background in mind, we turn to sixteenth-century England. The first thing to be said is that the argument from authority, in its medieval form, was absolutely ubiquitous. Religious polemicists almost beyond count harangued each other with the authorities of the church fathers and of pagan philosophers as well as with scriptural citations. Medieval chroniclers and historians, and medieval lawyers such as Bracton, could be used as authorities for what had occurred in the past, the latter all the stronger when it was confirmed by the laws of Edward the Confessor and William I.[44] Some wrote explicitly of the force of authorities in an unmistakeably medieval way. So, Thomas Bell, in his *Motives concerning Romish Faith and Religion*, described arguments based on the

[42] *Iurisprudentia Forensis Romano-Saxonica*, preface: 'rerum judicatarum autoritat[es] (quae praeiudicia vulgo nominantur)'.

[43] Ascheri, *Tribunali, Giuristi e Instituzioni*, 90, 117, citing Ludovicus, *Decisiones seu Diffinitiones Causarum Perusinarum et Provinciae Umbriae*, Trivisanus, *Decisiones Causarum Civilium, Criminalium et Haereticarum Venetiis in Palatio Apostolico Tractatae* (1595), Mastrillus, *Decisiones S. Regiae Conscientiae Regni Siciliae* (1606), Barzius, *Decisiones Almae Rotae Bononiensis* (1603). See too Christinaeus, *Practicarum Quaestionum Rerumque in Supremis Belgarum Curiis Actarum*, Studioso ac Candido Lectori; Borelli, *Decisionum Universarum et Totius Christiani Orbis Rerum Omnium Iudicatarum*, Praefatio, no. 207.

[44] R Broughton, *An Ecclesiastical Protestant Historie* (St Omer, 1624), 61, 118.

writings of the ancient philosophers or the doctors of the church as merely probable, whilst arguments derived from canonical scripture produced necessary conclusions.[45]

Writers of treatises on medicine relied on the authorities of Aristotle, Galen and Hippocrates,[46] as did those writing about the benefits or evils of tobacco.[47] When Thomas Morley wrote his treatise on practical music in 1597, he relied on the authorities of Franchinus, Jordanus and Peter Aron, and among the more modern writers of Glareanus, Losius, Listenius and Berhusius. He was admittedly a little diffident about this, but if writers on law could cite the authorities of Paul and Ulpian, Bartolus and Baldus, he asked, then why should he not confirm his opinions with authorities of those who were no less famous as musicians?[48] Thomas Wilson, in *The Rule of Reason*, his little treatise on logic published in 1551 and several times republished, devoted a section to the argument from authority, otherwise known as the sentences of the sage, that is to say testimonies brought to confirm any proposition, taken out of old authors or in common usage. These included, he said, 'sentences of noble men, the laws in any realm, proverbs . . . histories of wise philosophers, the judgments of learned men, the common opinion of the multitude, old custom, ancient fashions, or such like'. Still though, the basic division was between those authorities which came from God, which had of necessity to be treated as true, and those which came from man, which might be rejected; though they should not be set aside rashly, since 'every cunning man must be believed in his own art'.[49]

In such an environment, it would have been truly shocking if English lawyers had not used arguments from authority. And of course they did. The Elizabethan and Jacobean reports give us many examples of what are called authorities being cited as the basis of arguments; but we do not seem to find this before the Tudor period, and it is important briefly to examine the pre-Tudor background to put the later texts into perspective.

[45] *Thomas Bel's Motives Concerning Romish Faith and Religion* (London, 1593), 126–127.

[46] For example, H Crooke, *Mikrokosmographia* (London, 1616), 86, 150 and *passim*; N Gyer, *The English Phlebotomy* (London, 1592), 29; J Hart, *The Anatomie of Urines* (London, 1625), 91.

[47] J Deacon, *Tobacco Tortured* (London, 1616), 35, 37; R Marbecke, *A Defence of Tabacco* (London, 1602), 31, 45; Philaretes, *Work for Chimny-Sweepers* (London, 1602), To the Reader (nb the allusion to the dialectical tradition here: 'Authorities of expert and learned men in their art . . . ').

[48] T Morley, *A Plaine and Easie Introduction to Practicall Musicke* (London, 1597), 28, 183.

[49] T Wilson, *The Rule of Reason* (London, 1551) (unpaginated), sig Mv i^{v}.

When the language of authority is used in the Year Books, it had a very sharp focus on the power to command or permit, or the consequence of the exercise of that power: the King or parliament might have authority, an individual might act on the authority of King or parliament.[50] In addition, at least by the start of the fifteenth century, it could be said that one might act by 'authority of law', when something was authorised by the ordinary course of the common law;[51] but it is the authority of the law that was called upon here, not the authority of previous cases or texts. This is not to say that earlier cases could not be relied on to show what the law was, and as early as the reign of Edward I, it could be said that a decision in a case would be used in future cases of the same type;[52] but the terminology of authority is not used to refer to these.

So far as I know, the first clear usage of the word 'authority' in something approaching its dialectical sense occurs in the printed Year Book for 1494.[53] The plaintiff had brought an action of debt against an executor in an inferior court, and had continuance until the Monday next before the Feast of St Boniface. In a writ of error after judgment for the plaintiff, it was argued that the continuance was not good since the Feast of St Boniface had already passed before the continuance had been granted. Against this, it was said that there were two feasts of St Boniface in the printed calendar, though only one in the 'Mertlage', or Martyrology, which was used by the church in England. Brian CJ inclined towards seeing this as an error: 'car le kalender en print n'est d'ascun authoritie', 'for the calendar in print is of no authority'.[54] The reference here is clearly to a text rather than to an authorising body, but the idea of authority which it reveals is of something which determines an outcome, rather than something which could be used as a foundation of an argument. The same is true of an entry in Fitzherbert's Abridgment referring to Bracton.[55] Bracton, it was

50 For the Year Books, I have relied heavily on David Seipp's analytical database, www.bu.edu/law/seipp/.

51 The first usage of this which I have found is YB H. 11 Hen IV f. 45 pl.18.

52 YB 32 & 33 Edw I (RS) 30 (the word 'authority'appearing in the English translation is not in the original French).

53 YB H. 9 Hen VII f.14b pl.1. There may be an earlier example in YB P. 1 Hen VII 14 pl. 2, at 16, where Fineux CJ says that there are many authorities and ways (*auctorites et voies*) of drafting a deed; but the meaning here is rather opaque.

54 Reading from the 1555 and 1597 printings of the Year Book; the Vulgate reads 'autheur'. See J H Beale, 'Judicial Notice and the Law of Evidence' (1890), *Harvard Law Review* 3, 285, 297–298.

55 Fitz, *Garde*, 71, abridging YB H. 35 Hen VI f. 52 pl 17 (where the reference to Bracton does not appear). See D E C Yale, '"Of No Mean Authority": Some Later Uses of Bracton',

said, had suggested that the age of majority for males and females was the same, but the judges in the Exchequer Chamber disagreed: 'Bracton ne fuit unques tenus pur auctor en nostre ley'. '*Auctor*' here can only mean 'authority', a usage which is found from the fourteenth century.[56] As with the case of 1494, we seem to be at a stage where the idea of authority is referring to a text but at the same time having the sense of something which could determine an outcome.

This ambiguity in the treatment of Bracton remains visible in Plowden's report of *Stowel* v. *Lord Zouch*.[57] On the one hand, Catlin and Dyer CJJ are reported as citing 'divers authorities' from Bracton, Hengham and others on the nature of fines,[58] while, on the other hand, Saunders CB and Catlin CJ stressed that Bracton was not 'an author in our law', but was only cited where he agreed with the law or as an ornament in support of better authority.[59] Yet this ambivalence about medieval writers on English law is not reflected, or at least not reflected explicitly, in the use by Weston J of St Augustine, or in the citation by Catlin CJ of Cato or his giving a Latin definition of *pax* (from an unidentified source), or in drawing a somewhat strained parallel between Janus or Noah and the Statute of Fines.[60] Each of these usages would have constituted an argument *ab auctoritate* within the medieval dialectical tradition, though it is notable that Plowden does not himself employ the language of authority in describing them. The word 'authority' is being restricted to legal texts.

By the last quarter of the sixteenth century, we may see with some confidence both what counted as 'authorities' in the law and also what was meant by 'authority' in this context. Very clearly, the only things that counted as authorities were legal materials. Only one counter-example has been found in the printed reports, where 'various authorities' were cited out of Latin authors to show that the word *puer* might include females as well as males.[61] Apart from this, when 'authorities' were referred to, it was legal texts that were meant: reported cases predominantly, but also

in M S Arnold, et al., eds., *On the Laws and Customs of England* (Chapel Hill: University of North Carolina, 1981), 383 and 384.

56 *Oxford English Dictionary*, sub verb author, noun, 4.

57 (1569) Plo 353v. 58 At 357v, 368v–369.

59 At 357, 358v–359. 60 At 368v, 369v.

61 *Humphreston's Case* (1574) 2 Leon 216, 219. See also *Morris* v. *Webber* (1587) 2 Leon 169, 172, where Dr Goldingham is reported to have cited 'divers authorities out of the canon law'; but the argument here concerned the canon law of marriage, in which context these were straightforwardly legal citations. *The Case of Mines* (1567) Plo 321v, 339, may appear to say that the *De Re Metalli* of Agricola was (or had) authority, but this is only in the English translation; the original French has simply '*accordant al luy*', 'according to him'.

Bracton and other common law writers.[62] So, in his long argument in *Tresham's Case*,[63] Plowden based his reasoning on a series of cases reported in Year Books, Fitzherbert's *Abridgment* and his own *Commentaries*, together with Littleton's *Tenures* and Frowyk's reading on *Prerogativa Regis*. The defendant's argument in *Shelley's Case*,[64] reported *in extenso* by Coke, who was counsel, was based on dozens of cases, Bracton, Littleton's *Tenures* and Perkin's *Profitable Book*. In *Englefield's Case*,[65] reported at length by Francis Moore, one of the counsel in the case, a range of medieval and sixteenth-century cases were cited, not all of them from printed reports, and also the *Old Natura Brevium*, *Doctor and Student*, and Staunford's *Exposition of the Kinges Prerogative*. In the third and final argument, as reported, Popham A-G adopted the 'authorities' of Egerton S-G the previous term, while Serjeant Drewe adopted the 'authorities' of Francis Moore and Edward Coke.[66]

Perhaps more importantly, we may see what was meant by 'authority' in this context. It was not a simple black-and-white matter, but was rather a matter of weight. In his argument in *Tresham's Case*, Plowden put great emphasis on a Year Book case of 1426, since as a decision of the Exchequer Chamber, it was 'of the greatest authority there could be in our law';[67] and in *Sir William Pelham's Case*, Manwood B said that not all reported cases were equally law, but that the authority of the particular case had to be examined.[68] In Plowden's *Commentaries*, truly binding authority attached only to legal maxims, axioms whose validity could not be brought into question: for him, these were 'principles and authorities in themselves'.[69] In none of this was there any visible attempt at theorisation.[70]

The turning point seems to have come in 1600, with the publication of William Fulbeck's *Direction or Preparative to the Study of the Law*. Here we do find something approaching a theory of authorities. While in principle

62 For a very full study of the authority of cases at this time see I Williams, *English Legal Reasoning and Legal Culture, c1528–c1642* (Cambridge University PhD thesis, 2008), 39–106.

63 (1583) CUL MS Ff 5.4 f.344.

64 (1581) 1 Co Rep 93b, 96.

65 (1591) Moo 303.

66 Moo 303, 326, 331.

67 CUL MS Ff 5.4, at f.357v, referring to YB H. 4 Hen VI f. 12 pl. 9.

68 *Sir William Pelham's Case* (1589) 2 Leon 60, 65.

69 *Colthirst* v. *Bejushin* (1550) Plo 21, 27. For this approach to maxims in English law see P Stein, *Regulae Iuris* (Edinburgh University Press, 1966), 160–162; cf. 170–174 for the rather different approach of Francis Bacon.

70 Nor was there in Abraham Fraunce's *Lawyers' Logic* (London, 1588), though since this was an attempt to apply the theories of Peter Ramus to law rather than an attempt to elucidate the nature of legal reasoning we should not put any weight on this.

the lawyer should proceed by seeking out the reason of the law, the *ratio legis*, and applying that, it was not always easy to discern what the reason was. One solution was for the opinions of jurists to be formally treated as having the authority of imperial enactments, as had been laid down in Roman law, though that was not the case in England. Nonetheless, he seems to be saying, English law did have its authorities. 'I would wish', he says, 'that the authorities and cases of the learned writers of the law should rather be weighed than numbered'.[71] Though Fulbeck was a common lawyer, he had an unusually substantial knowledge of the civil law, and his book, aimed at young common lawyers, was shot through with civilian learning. What he says about authorities was quite explicitly drawn from the writings of modern civilians, the Italian humanist Alciatus and more directly Oxford's Regius Professor Alberico Gentili.[72] Like most writers in the orthodox civilian tradition, Gentili had been concerned about the authority of the medieval doctors, carefully distinguishing between the strength of their reasoned opinion and that of their *obiter dicta*, but Fulbeck followed writers like Cantiuncula, Everaerts and Vigelius and extended Gentili's thinking so that it applied also to the authority of cases. But the cases did not have authority which could be discovered and applied in a crude way; rather, the lawyer seeking to use them had to seek out the *ratio* of each of them and weigh them against each other.

III. Authority and precedent

As happened in the works of the continental writers on legal dialectic,[73] in England too there was a degree of assimilation of reasoning from authority and reasoning from precedent.[74] This had three aspects. First,

[71] W Fulbeck, *Direction or Preparative to the Study of the Law* (London, 1600), 84.

[72] A Gentili, *Lectionum et Epistolarum ad Ius Civile Pertinentes Libri* (London, 1584), Book 3 cap 17 (= p. 217). Fulbeck's reference to Alciatus is probably a blind citation from Gentili.

[73] Above, n. 5.

[74] For reasoning from precedent in English law see in particular Sir John Baker, *Oxford History of the Laws of England*, vol. 6 (Oxford University Press, 2003), 486–489, I Williams, 'Early-Modern Judges and the Practice of Precedent', in P Brand and J Getzler, eds., *Judges and Judging in the History of the Common Law and Civil Law: From Antiquity to Modern Times* (Cambridge University Press, 2011), 51. The complex question of the relation between Elizabethan and Jacobean English law and the humanist traditions of dialectic and rhetoric is explored in Williams, *English Legal Reasoning and Legal Culture*, 9–38, and L Hutson, 'Rhetoric and Early Modern Law', in M MacDonald, ed., *Oxford Handbook of Rhetorical Studies* (Oxford University Press, forthcoming). I am grateful to Professor Hutson for the opportunity to read her essay before publication.

there was a shift in the idea of precedent from any formal source of law specifically towards the judicial decision. Second, when the authority of case law was in issue there was a similar movement in the direction of giving primacy to judicial decisions rather than to mere arguments. And third, the corollary of the last point, it was the reasoning that led to the judicial decision that was important, not off-the-cuff remarks of judges. The confluence of these three strands generated a distinctive approach to authoritative precedent. Moreover, as Ian Williams has noted, at this time argument from authority began to be more important in practice than argument from reason.[75]

The dominant sense of 'precedent' in legal contexts in the mid-sixteenth century was an exemplar of a formal text, for example, a medieval charter,[76] a recognisance,[77] a writ[78] or a form of pleading.[79] The showing of a precedent did not entail that it should be followed; it depended on the weight to be ascribed to it. Hence, in *Waterhouse* v. *Woodstreet* in 1597, counsel produced precedents of 1589, 1594 and 1596, but the Exchequer Chamber adjourned the case pending the production of more ancient precedents.[80] By contrast, according to Brook CJ in *Buckley* v. *Thomas*, the fact that a form of pleading was in the printed book of entries meant that it was 'a good precedent settled by learned counsel', and hence was worthy to be followed.[81] Judgments recorded in the plea rolls were formal texts, and hence counted as precedents in themselves,[82] and, no less importantly, they gave weight to other precedents: if a form of pleading approved by grave and learned counsel was weighty, how much more was a form of pleading approved by grave and learned judges? So, in a case of 1588 in the Court of Common Pleas, Serjeant Puckering showed to the court a precedent of a King's Bench decision of the previous year, and the reporter duly noted that the court relied on that precedent in

[75] Williams, *English Legal Reasoning and Legal Culture*, 13.

[76] *Grendon* v. *Bishop of Lincoln* (1577) Plo 493, 503; *The Case of Mines* (1568) Plo 310, 317, 318; *Anon* (1582) 2 Leon 162, 165; *Stowel* v. *Lord Zouch* (1569) Plo 353, 360.

[77] *Anon* (1579) Dyer 364.

[78] *Wimbish* v. *Willoughby* (1552) Plo 73, 75; *Willion* v. *Berkley* (1561) Plo 223, 229; *R* v. *Archbishop of York* (1591) Cro El 240, 241.

[79] *Buckley* v. *Thomas* (1555) Plo 118, 128; *Eccleston's Case* (1573) Dyer 320, 321; *Grendon* v. *Bishop of Lincoln* (1577) Plo 493, 497; *Clavell* v. *Mallory* (1590) Cro El 208; *Smith* v. *Stapleton* (1573) Plo 426, 432; *Playter's Case* (1583) 5 Co Rep 34, 35; *Corbyson* v. *Pearson* (1596) Cro El 457.

[80] (1597) Cro El 592.

[81] (1555) Plo 118, 128.

[82] For early usages in this sense see N Doe, *Fundamental Authority in Late Medieval English Law* (Cambridge University Press, 1990), 22–25.

giving judgment.[83] The courts were conscious that a decision in one case might be a precedent in others, and were sometimes reported as taking especial care because of this.[84] A court might follow a series of precedents, saying that were it not for the precedents the law would have been taken to be different.[85] But for all the weight that might be put on precedents, they did not generate binding rules or mandate particular conclusions: as Solicitor-General Egerton put it in *Charnock* v. *Worsley*, 'Presidents are not so holy, *quod violari non debeant*'.[86]

By the early seventeenth century there is a clear tendency, so far as judicial reasoning is concerned, for precedents to be equated with judgments. This is most easily visible in Coke's report of *Slade's Case*, which contains a substantial disquisition on reasoning from precedent.[87] According to Coke, the principal reason for the decision in the case was conformity with the 'infinite precedents'. This reflects Coke's own arguments in 1597 and 1601, and possibly also in 1602;[88] and it is noteworthy that Coke's manuscript dates the case to Trinity term 1602 (as does the printed report), the final term in which the case was argued – by Coke himself – rather than Michaelmas term, when the judgment was given. Nonetheless, it may not misrepresent the thrust of judicial opinion: Popham CJ is known to have relied on the 'infinite precedents' in a judgment of 1597;[89] one report of the 1597 argument in *Slade's Case* suggests, if we understand it correctly, that the judges were minded to change their opinion on

[83] *Anon.* (1588) BL MS Lansd 1076 f.129.

[84] *Ratcliff's Case* (1565) Plo 267, 268; *Babington* v. *Babington* (1589) Cro El 157.

[85] *Emmot* v. *Fulwood* (1575) 1 and 49. Similarly in Chancery: *Rogland* v. *Wilgosse* (1592) PRO C33/85 f.79v (a reference I owe to Dr Neil Jones): '. . . the matter ys of great waight and importance and may hereafter be vouched for a precedent in other like cases And therefore would requier good deliberacion before any resolute order or Judgment should be geven'.

[86] *Charnock* v. *Worsley* (1589) 1 Leon 114, 116; Williams, 'Early Modern Judges and the Practice of Precedent', might see the precedent as having been more determinative, though see his qualifications at 58–59.

[87] *Slade's Case* (1602) 4 Co Rep 92b, 93a–94a; BL MS Harl 6686 f.526, 527–528v.

[88] 1597: CUL MS Ll 3.9 f.504v, 505v; Harvard Law School MS 1004a f.2v, 3; BL MS Harg 5 f.67, 68. 1601: LI MS Misc 492 f.313v, 318, Yale Law School MS GR 29.16 f.70v, BL MS Add 25203 f.391v. The only report I know of his argument of 1602 is that in Thomas Coventry's reports, BL MS Add 25203 f.496, 498v, LI MS Misc 492 f.313v, 319, which is brief and does not refer specifically to this; but the contrary argument of Francis Bacon seems to be answering the point: J H Baker, 'New Light on Slade's Case' [1971] CLJ 51, 66.

[89] *Barkley* v. *Foster* (1597) BL MS Harl 4552 f.110, quoted by J H Baker, 'New Light on Slade's Case' [1971] CLJ 213, 222.

sight of the precedents;[90] and one report of the judgment of Popham CJ in Michaelmas term 1602 refers to his saying that there were many precedents.[91]

Our concern at the moment is not with the force to be given to precedents in legal argument,[92] but with the question what counted as precedent for these purposes. In this respect, there is an important difference between Coke's position as we can reconstruct it from the reports of his arguments in 1597 and 1601 and his position as it appears in his own Reports, both in print and in his own manuscript.[93] In 1601, in particular, Coke put considerable weight on the 'notable precedents' in the Register of Writs and Fitzherbert's *Natura Brevium*, alongside cases in the Year Books and Dyer's Reports.[94] In the polished report, by contrast, he is concerned solely with *judicial* precedents.[95] The infinite precedents that are referred to are 'precedents of judgments',[96] it is only when precedents are judicial that it is said that they can be relied upon; and it is the multitude of *judicial* precedents that prove the case at bar.[97] We may see this as an important watershed in the re-focusing of the idea of precedent onto decisions of judges, reflected in other usages in the first and second decades of the seventeenth century: in *Calvin's Case* it was said that to assert that those born in Scotland after the union of the crowns were aliens would have been 'against so many judgments, resolutions, authorities, and *judicial precedents*',[98] and in *The Case of the Marshalsea* 'judicial records and precedents' took their place in Coke's list of authorities in law.[99] While the linguistic focus may be more marked in Coke's usage

[90] CUL MS Ll 3.9 f.504v, 506; it is possible that the report is simply reproducing Coke's argument that judges in the past had changed their minds when presented with contrary precedents.

[91] BL MS Lansd 1061 f.42v.

[92] Below, text at n. 115.

[93] Except at one point (below, n. 95) the printed text accurately reflects the manuscript version in BL MS Harl 6686 f.526, at all relevant points.

[94] Yale Law School MS GR 29.16 f.70v, 71v.

[95] Note too Co Litt 11a, where the argument 'from originall writs in the Register' is recognised as something distinct from the argument from authority.

[96] The printed text, 4 Co Rep 92b, 93b, reads 'precedents *and* judgments' ('presidents *et* iudgements' in the Law French original), but the manuscript, BL MS Harl 6686 f,526, 527, seems to read '*presidents de iudgements*', which makes more sense.

[97] 4 Co Rep 92b, 94a. Coke's concern with the nature of precedent is revealed by his heading 'Presidents' to a note of a reference by Popham CJ in 1592 to a decision reported with *Reade* v. *Rochforth* (1555) Dyer 120, a case later cited by him in his report of *Slade's Case*: BL MS Harl 6686 f.39v.

[98] *Calvin's Case* (1608) 7 Co Rep 1, 23b.

[99] *The Case of the Marshalsea* (1614) 10 Co Rep 68b, 75a (below, n. 104).

than elsewhere, there is no doubting the gravitational pull towards treating judicial decisions as precedents *par excellence*. So, in *Slade* v. *Drake*, Hobart CJ speaks of the lack of 'authenticall President, much less Judgement or grave opinion' to support an argument;[100] and in his speech in *Calvin's Case*, Lord Chancellor Ellesmere, although giving a somewhat wider meaning to the word 'precedent', stated explicitly that where there were no unchallengeable principles or maxims, the common law was to be known by 'former judgements given in like cases', seen by him as the equivalent of the Romans' *responsa prudentium* (which, as has been seen,[101] were treated as having the force of imperial constitutions).[102] If it was the judgment that mattered rather than the fact that there was a formal exemplar, then there was little reason to give priority to its being in the plea rolls ahead of the existence of a report of it. Hence, as Ian Williams has demonstrated,[103] by the early seventeenth century there was a clear tendency towards the citation of reports of decisions rather than the formal records of the courts.

This concern with judicial decisions was reflected in the development of the idea of authority in legal argument. Again, it is Coke who provides the best evidence of this, though there is no necessary reason to suppose that he was the originator of this shift of emphasis. Already this is clear in the Preface to his *Third Reports*, published in 1602, where he placed decisions in cases ahead of legal treatises, giving preference to reported decisions ahead of decisions recorded in the plea rolls because of their greater perspicuity,[104] but the clearest starting point to understand his position is the statement in his report of *The Case of the Marshalsea*:

> And as to authorities in law, they are copious and of several natures. 1. The year-books. 2. Books written of the laws of England. 3. Judgments

[100] *Slade* v. *Drake* (1617) Hob 295, 300. [101] Above, n. 14.

[102] *The Speech of the Lord Chancellor in the Exchequer Chamber Touching the Post-Nati* (1609), 36, in L A Knafla, *Law and Politics in Jacobean England* (Cambridge University Press, 1977), 218. For the wider meaning given to 'precedents', equivalent to 'past practice' or 'formal exemplars' see *Speech of the Lord Chancellor*, 39 (Knafla, 219), 41 (Knafla, 220), 83 (Knafla, 238), 108 (Knafla, 249). This wider meaning is still in use today: law libraries are replete with volumes of 'forms and precedents'.

[103] Williams, 'Early-Modern Judges and the Practice of Precedent'.

[104] Coke, *Third Reports*, Preface, ii–iv^{v} (following the pagination of the 1776 edition, where the Latin and English texts of the preface are in parallel columns, rather than that of the French edition, where the English appears after the Latin).

> in Parliament: and all these are *thesauri aperti*. 4. Judicial records and precedents: and these are *thesauri absconditi*.[105]

The first noteworthy feature of this catalogue is its inclusion of the Year Books and its exclusion of the more modern reports of Plowden, Dyer and Coke himself. Unless Coke is being unwontedly modest, the most plausible explanation of this is that the cases in these reports were not authoritative in themselves, but because they fell into his final category of judicial records or precedents. Their weight rested in the decision rather than in the fact of the report.[106] It is noteworthy that both Plowden and Coke published the records of the cases alongside their reports, and that Thomas Egerton marked *quaere* in the margins of his copy of Dyer's *Reports* opposite the reports of cases where no judgment was recorded.[107] The curiosity perhaps lies more in the explicit inclusion of the Year Books rather than the exclusion of the modern reports, but this is explicable since these did not typically consist of decisions at all, but of arguments by judges and counsel, yet their centrality in legal reasoning meant that they could not be ignored. Consistently with this focus on the judicial decision rather than the report, in 1596, in the Court of Common Pleas, Anderson CJ, Beaumont and Owen JJ rejected an argument of Walmsley J on the basis that in none of the authorities which he had vouched was there 'any judgment or settled opinion';[108] in *Slade* v. *Drake*, Hobart CJ rejected the authority of *Wimbish* v. *Talboys*, reported by Plowden, because the judges there were split two against two and hence nothing had been decided;[109] and in *Doctor Leyfield's Case*, the King's Bench rejected the authority of *Austin's Case* since the point in issue had not actually been determined there one way or the other.[110]

The inevitable corollary of this concern with judicial decisions was that opinions which were not directly relevant to a decision had relatively little

105 *The Case of the Marshalsea* (1614) 10 Co Rep 68b, 75a. The language of *thesauri absconditi* is found in notes to R Agricola, *De Inventione Dialectica, cum Notis Alardi Aemstelredami* (Cologne, 1539), 130, but the language is sufficiently vague that we cannot say with any degree of confidence that this was Coke's source.

106 Contrast the argument in *Wright* v. *Swanton* (1604) BL MS Harg 29 f.94 (translated in Sir John Baker, *Baker and Milsom, Sources of English Legal History* (Oxford University Press, 2010), 479, where it was Coke's report of *Slade's Case* that was relied upon rather than the judgment itself. Other manuscripts also refer specifically to Coke's report.

107 I am grateful to Ian Williams for this information.

108 *Banyster* v. *Trussel* (1596) Cro El 516.

109 *Slade* v. *Drake* (1617) Hob 295, 300; *Wimbish* v. *Talboys* (1550) Plo 38.

110 *Doctor Leyfield's Case* (1611) 10 Co Rep 88a, 94a; *Austin's Case* (1555) Dyer 115.

weight. We find references in the reign of Elizabeth to there being 'direct' authority for some proposition,[111] perhaps pointing in this direction, though at least so far as we can see from the printed reports it was not until the early seventeenth century that it was made explicit. This paralleled the civilian downgrading of *obiter dicta* visible in Alberico Gentili's writing and reflected in Fulbeck's *Direction or Preparative to the Study of the Law.*[112] Hence, in *The Earl of Northumberland's Case*, Houghton J said that the only authority against the conclusion for which he was arguing was *Boulston's Case*, but this was 'only on the bye' and hence was no disproof;[113] in *Foster* v. *Jackson* a statement in an earlier case 'not upon solemn argument of the Judges' was said not to be comparable to other authorities which had been cited;[114] and in *Dalton* v. *Bishop of Ely* it was observed that there was no authority for an argument, but only an opinion *obiter.*[115]

Stefan Vogenauer has observed that it was at the time of Coke that English law was most receptive to arguments from methods drawn from continental Europe.[116] Coke's treatment of the argument from authority is a good example of this, and the continental theory in its turn casts light on his understanding of authority.[117] The first hint of this occurs in the Preface to his *Third Reports*, first published in 1602. Here, expatiating on legal method, he said that in reaching a reasoned opinion or judgment, one should set down 'all authorities, precedents, reasons, arguments and inference that may be probably applied to the case in question'.[118] There are two hints here, if subtle ones, that Coke is thinking in terms of the old argument from authority of the medieval dialecticians. First, the Latin reads *auctoritates* and *exempla* for 'authorities' and 'precedents'. *Exemplum* is a reasonable equivalent of precedent, though we might have expected to see *praeiudicium*, but the collocation of *auctoritates* and *exempla* is very common in Everaerts' treatment of the argument from authority in his *Topica*: the section heading in the first version,

[111] See, for example, *Colgate* v. *Blyth* (1586) Goulds 12, 14.

[112] Above, text at n. 71.

[113] *The Earl of Northumberland's Case* (1618) Poph 141; *Boulston's Case* (1597) 5 Co Rep 104b.

[114] *Foster* v. *Jackson* (1610) 2 Br & Gould 311, 314, *per* Dodderidge Sjt.

[115] *Dalton* v. *Bishop of Ely* (1624) W Jones 46, 50.

[116] S Vogenauer, *Die Auslegung von Gesetzen in England und auf dem Kontinent* (Tübingen: Mohr Siebeck, 2001), 766.

[117] For the use of authority contrasted with reason see Williams, *English Legal Reasoning and Legal Culture*, 22–26.

[118] Coke, *Third Reports*, Preface, iii^{v}.

Ab authoritate, seu exemplo maiorum, locus, transparently treats them as equivalent.[119] Second, the word-order of the English version, reading 'be probably' rather than the more natural 'probably be' points to the use of the technical terminology. In his report of *Bunting* v. *Lepingwell*, published in 1604 in his *Fourth Reports*, he refers to the maxim 'Cuilibet in sua arte perito est credendum', clearly a reference to the dialecticians' rule that an expert ought to be believed.[120] The hint is yet clearer in his *Commentary on Littleton*. Here he refers to reasoning '*Ab authoritate, et pronunciatis*', again reflecting the language of Everaerts.[121] Echoing this, at another point in the text he justifies treating book cases as the best proofs of what the law is by saying that '*Argumentum ab authoritate est fortissimum in Lege*',[122] unmistakeably adopting the terminology of dialectic. The same language was used by him in parliament in 1628, adding that '*Argumentum ab authoritate, valet affirmative*'.[123] This also is a clear reflection of, or perhaps a near-direct borrowing from, Everaerts.[124] While we cannot say for certain that Everaerts was Coke's source, the similarities to the *Topica* strongly suggest that he was influenced at least indirectly by it or a related work.

The evidence for Coke's having been influenced by works of dialectic (and also rhetoric) is very strong.[125] As is all too commonly the case with his writings though, it is hard to know whether we are seeing his own thoughts or more generally accepted ideas of lawyers for which he is the

[119] *Topicorum seu Locorum Legalium Opus de Inventione* (1544), 243 (*cf.* above, n. 18).

[120] *Bunting* v. *Lepingwel* (1585) 4 Co Rep 29 (already in his manuscript report, BL MS Harl 6687D f.701, a reference which I owe to Professor Baker); above, n. 9. The same maxim is quoted, alongside a quotation from Aristotle's *Topics*, in his report of *Calvin's Case* (1608) 7 Co Rep 1a, 19a.

[121] Co Litt 11a. For Everaerts' use of this terminology see above, n. 19. The link between *pronunciata* and *testimonia ab authoritate profecta* is found in J Seton, *Dialectica* (1584) (unpaginated), a work which Coke had in his library: W O Hassall, *The Library of Sir Edward Coke* (Yale University Press, 1950), 62. For Seton's dependence on the treatise of the Dutch Rudolph Agricola see J R McNally, '"Prima Pars Dialecticae": The Influence of Agricolan Dialectic upon English Accounts of Invention' (1968) 21 *Renaissance Quarterly*, 166.

[122] Co Litt 254a. *Cf.* G Brunner, *Synopsis Locorum Legalium Nicolai Everardi a Middelburgo* (1554), 134, where the argument from authority is said to be '*utilissimus*', a close parallel with Coke's *fortissimum*.

[123] S Sheppard, ed., *The Selected Writings of Sir Edward Coke* (Indianapolis: Liberty Fund, 2003), vol. 3, 1244.

[124] *Topicorum seu Locorum Legalium Opus de Inventione* (1544), 250; *Loci Argumentorum Legales* (1564), 591.

[125] See further, Hutson, 'Rhetoric and Early Modern Law'.

mouthpiece. Whichever of these was the case, it was reflected in the leading English treatment of legal logic of the early seventeenth century, in John Dodderidge's *The English Lawyer.*[126] Dodderidge's purpose was to show the importance of logic over mere authorities, since the authorities out of which legal arguments were commonly drawn were rarely sufficient to lead to a firm conclusion in any controversial case;[127] but in doing this he could not avoid making reference to the use of authorities as the basis of argument, referring along the way to the sixteenth-century writers on legal dialectic who had described the argument *ab auctoritate.*[128] His citations may be seen as complementing Coke's express statements of the role of authorities in the common law. Taken together, Coke and Dodderidge provided a clear theoretical underpinning for what was already the practice of the common lawyers of the later sixteenth century.

In early-modern England, then, case law fitted into the framework of the argument from authority, which was familiar to educated Englishmen in all fields. This was a framework within which authority was either necessary or probable;[129] and in these terms, as Edward Coke clearly hinted in the Preface to his *Third Reports*, legal authorities were probable.[130] It followed from this that there was a high degree of flexibility in the use of these texts, a flexibility which would not have existed if they had been necessary. It meant that there was no need to differentiate among the categories of authorities listed by Coke in *The Case of the Marshalsea*:[131] Year Books and writings on law had probable authority, as did judicial decisions, whether known from reports or from plea rolls. It meant too that there was no formal problem caused by conflicting decisions, something which must commonly have occurred in a system where a large number of cases were being decided and a relatively small number reported, even if only in manuscript, and where the plea roll would rarely reveal whether a case had actually had judicial discussion at all. It allowed for the shift of emphasis from the record of a case to the report,[132] since it was the

[126] J Dodderidge, *The English Lawyer* (London, 1631), pp. 55–148.

[127] *The English Lawyer*, 65; cf. *The Lawyers Light* (London, 1629), p. 93.

[128] *The English Lawyer*, 61. As well as Everaerts and Cantiuncula, he cited Hegendorphinus, Fregius, Gambraeus, Apellus, Bellonus, Oldendorpius, Nevisanus, and Grammara.

[129] Above

[130] It may be no coincidence that John Seton's *Dialectica*, which Coke owned and would almost certainly have studied at Trinity College, Cambridge, focuses from the start on dialectic's concern with arguments *probabiliter*, though this might better be translated as 'provability' than 'probability'.

[131] Above, n. 104.

[132] Williams, 'Early-Modern Judges and the Practice of Precedent'; above, n. 102.

reasoning behind the judgment that gave a case its weight and not simply the fact that it had been decided. And this concentration on argument, rather than mere result, goes some way to explain the clear preference of the courts for printed texts, perhaps licensed by the judges or at any rate approved by them, over manuscript reports which would not be so reliable.[133]

IV. Conclusions

By the 1630s, in England, the twin strands of reasoning from authority and reasoning from precedents had run together. Authorities were precedents, with a marginal role being given to treatise literature. The theoretical justification for this form of reasoning can be traced back to medieval dialectical theory, and in the terms of this theory, precedents, like treatises, had probable rather than necessary authority. In other words, decided cases did not in themselves determine the outcome of future law suits but pointed towards the correct result. As a result, English law had a flexible approach to authority- or precedent-based reasoning. Decided cases, and the reasoning which led to the decisions, could exercise a constraint on future judges without emasculating them. Nothing in the theory created any clash with judicial practice: there was room within it to allow other forms of argument, based, for example, on 'reason' or on consistency with moral values, without generating any stress with authority or precedent.

In continental Europe, the theory emanating ultimately from late-fifteenth-century Naples where decisions of superior courts had statutory force, whether this was justified on the Neapolitan basis that the superior court had legislative power or on some other basis, pointed in the direction of cases generating rules which did determine the outcome of future law suits. The sources of this theory were wholly distinct from the medieval argument from authority, which was treated alongside it in works concerned with legal dialectic. In contrast to English law, such an approach did not provide a flexible framework within which judges could recognise a degree of constraint without having their hands tied

[133] I Williams, 'He Creditted More the Printed Booke: Common Lawyers' Receptivity to Print, c1550–1640' (2010) 28 *Law and History Review*, 39. A Star Chamber decree of 1586 requiring licensing by the two chief justices may not have been a total dead letter (p. 64), though it was not until 1637 that there was introduced a licensing system which was apparently observed in substance: J H Baker, 'English Law Books and Legal Publishing', in J Barnard and D McKenzie, eds., *The Cambridge History of the Book in Britain Volume IV: 1557–1695* (Cambridge University Press, 2002), 474, 492–493.

unacceptably tightly. Arguments based on reason and the like could not be integrated within a theory which effectively gave legislative force to decisions, and this lack of flexibility prevented precedent-based reasoning from undermining the Roman rule that one should judge according to *lex* rather than *exempla*.

5

Legislation and authority in early-modern Scotland

ANDREW R.C. SIMPSON

I. Introduction

In 1566, Mary, Queen of Scots, appointed a commission of noblemen, clergymen and leading lawyers to print all of the ordinances that had been promulgated by the monarchs of Scotland on 'the auise of the thre Estatis in Parliament'.[1] It was initially hoped that the resulting printed volume would include all of the surviving statutes of the realm, and also certain medieval legal treatises. In the event, only the statutes that had been promulgated since 1424 were actually published in 1566.[2]

Why was the decision taken to print these laws in 1566? One possible explanation may be found in the political turbulence of the time. During the mid-sixteenth century, a series of rebellions seriously threatened the

I am grateful to Professor John Ford, Professor Robin Evans-Jones, Professor Hector MacQueen, Dr Mátyás Bodig, Dr Adelyn Wilson, Mr Eddie Simpson and Mr Malcolm Combe for their comments on this article, and to Mr Greg Gordon, Dr Angus Campbell and Dr Douglas Bain for their thoughts concerning an earlier draft. Any errors are my own. I am also grateful to the W M Tapp Studentship of Gonville and Caius College, Cambridge, and the Clark Foundation for Legal Education, for funding the original doctoral research that underpinned this study.

[1] *The Actis and Constitutiounis of the Realme of Scotland... Anno. Do. 1566* [Imprintit at Edinburgh be Robert Lekpreuik, the xij day of October the zeir of God ane thousand fyue hundreth thre scoir sax zeiris], Sig. A2r–A2v. I have used the version of the Actis printed in October 'Imprintit at Edinburgh be Robert Lekpreuik, the xij day of October the zeir of God ane thousand fyue hundreth thre scoir sax zeiris'; see *Actis and Constitutiounis... 1566* [October], f.181v. A further version of the Actis was published in November 1566, which omitted legislation concerning the suppression of heretics; see *The Actis and Constitutiounis of the Realme of Scotland... 1566*; the date of the work is to be found at f.182r. On this see George Nicol's short appendix at the end of the volume of the *Actis and Constitutiounis... 1566* [October] held in the NLS (shelfmark H.33.c.20(1)), www.eebo.chadwyck.com (EEBO), site accessed 30 July 2013. See also Klaus Luig, ed., *The Acts and Constitutions of the Realm of Scotland, Edinburgh 1566: "Black Acts"*, Mittelalterliche Gesetzbücher Europäischer Länder in Faksimiledrucken Band 3/im Auftrag des Max-Planck-Instituts für Europäische Rechtsgeschichte, Glashütten, 1971.

[2] *Actis and Constitutiounis... 1566* [October], Sig A3r–A3v.

survival of several Scottish governments.[3] Each of these insurrections had subtly different causes and goals, but frequently the rebels sought to justify their actions on the grounds that the government of the day was ignoring the traditional laws and liberties of the Scottish polity. The Protestant Reformers employed this argument during their rebellion of 1559–1560[4] against the regime led by Mary of Guise, the mother of Mary, Queen of Scots; in this way, they hoped to attract the support of Scots who were not altogether sympathetic to their religious ideology.[5] Similarly, when two further rebellions took place against the regime of Mary, Queen of Scots herself in late 1565 and in early 1566, the queen's enemies justified this by claiming that she was following the advice of counsellors who had no knowledge of the laws of the Scots.[6]

Of course, the causes of these rebellions were much more complex than these comments might suggest. So, the Protestant-led rebellion of 1559–1560 sought to challenge the power of the Catholic Church, which had long been a partner in government with the Stewart monarchy. The Reformers were prepared to justify this rebellion in various ways, and some of the Protestant preachers had begun to ask searching questions about the foundations and limits of royal authority, which contributed further to the instability of the time. Additionally, leading members of the nobility were frequently prepared to exploit the turbulent situation to

[3] See, for example, Gordon Donaldson, *Scotland. James V–James VII*, The Edinburgh History of Scotland, vol. 3 (corrected edition, Edinburgh, 1971), 83–131; Jenny Wormald, *Mary, Queen of Scots: A Study in Failure* (London, 1991); Julian Goodare, 'Mary (1542–1587)', in *Oxford Dictionary of National Biography* (Oxford, 2004); online edition, May 2007, www.oxforddnb.com/view/article/18248; site accessed 30 July 2013; Jane E Dawson, *Scotland Re-Formed 1488–1567*, The New Edinburgh History of Scotland vol. 6 (Edinburgh, 2007), 155–263.

[4] As regards this rebellion see, for example, Gordon Donaldson, *The Scottish Reformation* (Cambridge, 1960), 1–182; J H Burns, *The True Law of Kingship: Concepts of Monarchy in Early Modern Scotland* (Oxford, 1996), 122–184; Roger A Mason, *Kingship and the Commonweal: Political Thought in Renaissance and Reformation Scotland* (East Lothian, 1998), 139–164; Keith M Brown, 'The Reformation Parliament', in Keith M Brown and Roland J Tanner, eds., *The History of the Scottish Parliament Vol. 1: Parliament and Politics in Scotland 1235–1560* (Edinburgh, 2004), 203.

[5] Donaldson, *Scotland James V – James VII*, 100–101 (see also 96–97); R Mason, 'Covenant and the Commonweal: The Language of Politics in Reformation Scotland', in N Macdougall (ed.), *Church, Politics and Society: Scotland 1408–1929* (Edinburgh, 1983), 97, particularly at 109–110; Burns, *True Law* (Oxford, 1996), 153–168; see also Pamela E Ritchie, *Mary of Guise in Scotland, 1548–1560: A Political Career* (East Lothian, 2002), 205–244; Dawson, *Scotland Re-Formed*, 189–190.

[6] Donaldson, *Scotland James V–James VII*, 118–122; Gordon Donaldson, *Mary, Queen of Scots* (London, 1974), 85.

their own ends.[7] Nonetheless, following the rebellion of early 1566, Queen Mary seems to have felt that there was a need to respond to the allegations that the ancient laws and liberties of the realm were being ignored under her government. It was at this point that she granted the commission mentioned above to print the laws of her ancestors, clearly a very public way for Mary to respond to the allegation that those ordinances were being ignored.

But arguably there was more to the decision to publish the laws than a purely political exercise in public relations.[8] The commission was inspired by a suggestion made to the Queen by a leading Scottish lawyer, John Leslie, Bishop of Ross, and the commissioners who actually carried out Mary's orders were also significant jurists.[9] As will be explained below, their interest in the study of the medieval Scottish laws seems to have gone beyond fulfilling the Queen's commands. Furthermore, in 1566, one lawyer, David Chalmers of Ormond, sought to create an heuristic device for practitioners that summarised those laws, together with judicial decisions, in alphabetical topics. This came to be labelled as his *Dictionary of Scotch Law* in the nineteenth century, but the editors of the sole surviving manuscript currently plan to publish it under the less anachronistic title of Chalmers's *Compendium of the Laws of Scotland.*[10] This is how it will be referred to here. Other anonymous texts that may date from the 1560s

[7] See nn. 1 and 2 above, and also Burns, *True Law*, 122–152.

[8] See also Julian Goodare, *The Government of Scotland* (Oxford, 2004), 70–86. I hope to develop elsewhere the conclusions advanced in this article to engage further with Goodare's highly insightful account of this period.

[9] *Actis and Constitutiounis . . . 1566* [October], Sig A3r–A3v; on the jurists referred to here see, for example, Rosalind K Marshall, 'Lesley, John (1527–1596)', ODNB, www.oxforddnb.com/view/article/16492 site accessed 2 August 2013; Julian Goodare, 'Chalmers, David, of Ormond (*c*.1533–1592)', ODNB, www.oxforddnb.com/view/article/5069, site accessed 2 August 2013; Marie-Claude Tucker, 'Henryson, Edward [Henry Édouard] (1522–*c*.1590)', ODNB, www.oxforddnb.com/view/article/12982, site accessed 17 August 2013; J Durkan, 'Henry Scrimgeour, Renaissance Bookman', 5 *Edinburgh Bibliographical Society Transactions* (1971–87), 1, at 2–4 (I am grateful to Professor Hector MacQueen of Edinburgh University for referring me to this last article); Thomas M Green, ed., *The Consistorial Decisions of the Commissaries of Edinburgh, 1564 to 1576/7* (Stair Society 60) (Edinburgh, 2014), xxxiii–xxxiv.

[10] David Chalmers, *A Dictionary of Scotch Law*, British Library (BL) MS Additional 27472. On this manuscript see Gero Dolezalek, *Scotland Under JusCommune. Census of Manuscripts of Legal Literature in Scotland, mainly between 1500 and 1660* (Stair Society 57) (Edinburgh, 2010), vol. 3, 342–345. The manuscript has been transcribed by Dr Julian Goodare and Dr. Winifred Coutts, and I am currently working on the transcript with them and will be contributing to the introduction to the work.

also sought to render the medieval laws more accessible.[11] Thus there was apparently a concerted effort to promote the study of those laws at this time, which seems to have been absent in the immediately preceding decades. So what brought about this development?

Focusing on the decades immediately following the 1560s, several historians have attempted to explain lawyers' interest in the study of the statutory law of medieval Scotland, and also lawyers' efforts to promote legal codification at that time.[12] Cairns, Fergus and MacQueen have argued that these efforts were at least partly facilitated by 'essentially Renaissance notions of sovereignty' which allowed jurists 'to explain, justify, and rationalise the materials used by Scots lawyers'.[13] Specifically, these legal historians have suggested that those early-modern lawyers conceptualised the authority of their statutes in a manner that partly anticipated, and then embraced, Bodin's theoretical position, according to which all law-making depended upon an exercise of sovereign will.[14] More recently, Ford has shown that one can question this account of how late sixteenth-century lawyers conceptualised legal authority, and consequently his argument challenges the attempt made by Cairns, Fergus and MacQueen to explain the more intensive study of the Scottish legal texts during this period. Ford has argued that at least some sixteenth-century Scottish lawyers believed that when Scottish legal experts relied upon their collective legal learning to reach consensus that a proposition of law was just or reasonable, then the proposition in question acquired binding legal force.[15] So did lawyers draw inspiration from Renaissance notions of sovereignty when promoting the study and the codification of the laws of Scotland at this time? Alternatively, did they somehow utilise the idea

[11] Consider National Library of Scotland (NLS) MS Advocates 25.4.11 f.10r–92v; British Library (BL) MS Additional 48032, f.15r–130v; and British Library (BL) MS Additional 48050, f.1r–106v, as discussed in Gero Dolezalek, *Scotland Under* Jus Commune. *Census of Manuscripts of Legal Literature in Scotland, mainly between 1500 and 1660* (Stair Society 56) (Edinburgh, 2010), vol. 2, 303–315 and in Dolezalek, *Census*, vol. 3, 347–350, 351–355; Dolezalek shows the first and the last of these three manuscripts were written after 1555.

[12] Consider Arthur H Williamson, *Scottish National Consciousness in the Age of James VI* (Edinburgh, 1979), 64–85; John W Cairns, T David Fergus and Hector L MacQueen, 'Legal Humanism and the History of Scots Law: John Skene and Thomas Craig', in John MacQueen, ed., *Humanism in Renaissance Scotland* (Edinburgh, 1990), 48; Goodare, *Government of Scotland*, 70–86.

[13] Cairns, Fergus and MacQueen, 'Legal Humanism', 66.

[14] Cairns, Fergus and MacQueen, 'Legal Humanism', particularly at 62, 66–67.

[15] J D Ford, *Law and Opinion in Scotland during the Seventeenth Century* (Oxford, 2007), in particular at 2–5, 32–33, 215–246.

that legal learning was in some sense intrinsically authoritative to justify their efforts? Or did they adopt an altogether different approach?

One aim of this chapter is to engage with this debate by exploring lawyers' attitudes to the laws that were published in print in 1566. The chapter will first examine juristic attitudes to those laws in the decades immediately preceding their publication. It will be argued that, during the 1540s, it was frequently accepted in practice that a lawyer could rely on learning in Roman law and canon law in order to interpret narrowly the medieval laws of Scotland, so as to limit their effect in practice. The next section of this chapter will consider the reasons given by lawyers in 1566 for publishing the Scottish laws. It will be argued that those reasons reveal that a subtle, but significant, shift had taken place in lawyers' attitudes towards the laws of the realm over the previous twenty years. While many judges during the 1540s had been prepared to rely upon their legal learning to construe the local laws narrowly, in 1566 some of their successors sought to utilise the same authoritative learning to promote the wider use and study of the Scottish legal tradition in practice. To this end, at least one of the jurists involved re-conceptualised the local tradition as a body of learning, like that found in the *ius commune*.

Having explored these matters, the chapter will then seek to offer some explanation for the apparent change in attitude to the local laws that took place between the 1540s and the 1560s. It will be shown that the centrality of legal learning in the attempts made in 1566 to explain the authority of Scots law may indicate that Ford is correct to argue that consensus amongst local legal experts possessed the binding force of law in the Scottish courts. Nonetheless, the importance attributed to statutory law and codification during this period could simultaneously have prepared the way for a reception of Bodin's ideas on legislative sovereignty later in the sixteenth century.

II. The legal context prior to the 1560s

Prior to 1532, the judges known as the Lords of Session acquired *de facto* supreme jurisdiction over all Scottish civil cases. In 1532, the Session was reconstituted as a College of Justice.[16] The surviving evidence of decisions of the College of Justice makes it possible to explore contemporary attitudes amongst lawyers to some of the laws that were subsequently

[16] See generally A M Godfrey, *Civil Justice in Renaissance Scotland. The Origins of a Central Court* (Leiden, 2009); the foundation of the College of Justice is discussed at 94–160.

selected for publication in print in 1566. In particular, Sinclair's *Practicks* is useful in this regard.[17] This work contains a series of decisions of the Lords of Session noted by one of their number, John Sinclair, between 1540 and 1549.[18]

Sinclair's work reveals that Scots lawyers drew upon a variety of sources in their disputes. Citations of the texts of Roman law and canon law were very common.[19] Yet it is also clear that lawyers utilised the texts of the older medieval Scottish legal tradition in argument. References were made to the collections of local royal ordinances and statutes[20] and to medieval Scottish treatises such as the fourteenth-century *Regiam Majestatem*,[21] which were selected for publication in print in 1566. Additionally, lawyers drew upon the local laws of the realm in that they cited past decisions of the Lords of Session in order to support their arguments.[22]

17 For the provisional text of *Sinclair's Practicks*, edited by Athol L Murray and by Gero R Dolezalek see www.uni-leipzig.de/~jurarom/scotland/dat/sinclair.htm, accessed 14 August 2013. I have relied on this transcript except where indicated.

18 For Sinclair's *Practicks* see, for example, A L Murray, 'Sinclair's Practicks', in Alan Harding, ed., *Law-Making and Law-Makers in British History: Papers Presented to the Edinburgh Legal History Conference, 1977* (London, 1980), 90; Gero Dolezalek, 'The Court of Session as a Ius Commune Court – Witnessed by "Sinclair's Practicks", 1540–1549', in Hector L MacQueen, ed., *The Stair Society Miscellany Four* (Stair Society 49) (Edinburgh, 2002), 51. It should be mentioned here that the text of Sinclair's *Practicks* that survives today may have been revised and augmented by the author during the 1550s. As Murray explained in an unpublished paper presented to the Scottish Legal History Group on 4 October 2008, at times Sinclair wrote in such a way as to indicate that he was recalling the dates of cases long after they were decided. Furthermore, the text of his work includes a reference to a statute of 1555. Consequently, it could be argued that the final version of the *Practicks* might conceivably have been composed after 1555. For these points, I am grateful to Dr Murray, who generously shared with me a copy of his paper 'Sinclair Revisited: Further Thoughts on Sinclair's Practicks', the abstract of which is reported in 'Scottish Legal History Group Report 2008', 30 *The Journal of Legal History* (2009), 81, at 81–82. To Dr Murray's comments it may be added that Sinclair died on 9 April 1566, and consequently any amendments made to his collected decisions after that date must have been added by another hand. Nonetheless, regardless of when Sinclair composed the final version of his work, the level of detail that it contains concerning the debates before the Lords during the 1540s indicates that it must have been based on very substantial notes made during that decade. Broadly speaking, therefore, it may be relied upon as representative of legal practice at that time – at least as the author understood it. For the date of Sinclair's death see Athol Murray, 'Sinclair, John (c.1510–1566)', ODNB, www.oxforddnb.com/view/article/25624, accessed 10 October 2014.

19 See Dolezalek, 'Court of Session as a Ius Commune Court'.

20 Consider Dolezalek and Murray, *Sinclair's Practicks*, cns. 58, 346, 465, 484, 503.

21 Consider Dolezalek and Murray, *Sinclair's Practicks*, cns. 84, 187–188, 419.

22 Consider Dolezalek and Murray, *Sinclair's Practicks*, cns. 282, 295, 460–461; see also Dolezalek, 'Court of Session as a Ius Commune Court', 59–62.

Various factors hindered the practical application of the medieval laws of the realm. First, as MacQueen has noted, much of the older medieval literature had been transmitted to sixteenth-century practitioners in confused and voluminous manuscript traditions, making it difficult to search through the texts in order to find solutions to the legal questions that arose in the College of Justice.[23] Second, many of the older texts were concerned with the enforcement of certain types of feudal rights through procedure on brieve. As Godfrey has shown, those rules were largely out of use by the 1540s.[24]

Additionally, there were more complex problems associated with using the medieval laws. These were bound up with the way in which many of the judges conceptualised the authority of the Scottish legal literature, and the law more generally. In order to explain this claim, it is necessary to consider several decisions in which they could have applied the laws of the Scottish realm to resolve the disputes in question, yet chose not to do so.

1. *The 'commoun law' and the laws of the Scottish realm*

Dolezalek has already analysed a series of cases that considered the scope and legal force of a Scottish rule found in *Regiam Majestatem*, which provided *minor non tenetur placitare super hereditatem.*[25] In other words, a minor was not bound to plead in court in matters concerning heritage before he or she attained majority.[26] Sinclair's *Practicks* reveal that Lords of Session sometimes disregarded the rule on the ground that its application in certain circumstances would have been inconsistent with equity and right reason. An example of this can be found in *Queen's Advocate* v.

[23] Hector L MacQueen, 'Regiam Majestatem, Scots Law, and National Identity', 74 *The Scottish Historical Review* (1995), 1, at 14–15. Whether or not anyone knew of the relationship between *Regiam Majestatem* and *Glanvill* in 1566 has not been established; on this see Hector L MacQueen, 'Glanvill Resarcinate: Sir John Skene and Regiam Majestatem', in A A MacDonald, M Lynch and I B Cowan, eds., *The Renaissance in Scotland: Studies in Literature, Religion, History and Culture Offered to John Durkan* (Leiden, 1994), 385. I am grateful to Professor MacQueen for discussing this point with me.

[24] Godfrey, *Civil Justice*, 268–354, 449–453.

[25] Dolezalek, 'Court of Session as a Ius Commune Court', 61–62, 78–79; see also Dolezalek's commentaries on the relevant decisions in Dolezalek and Murray, *Sinclair's Practicks*, cns. 101, 315, 403, 459, 460–461, 513.

[26] For a brief commentary on the rule see Lord Cooper, ed., *Regiam Majestatem and Quoniam Attachiamenta. Based on the Text of Sir John Skene* (Stair Society 11) (Edinburgh, 1947), 230–233.

Morton (1543).[27] In this case, the third Earl of Morton complained that James V had compelled him to resign his earldom into the king's hands by unlawful *metus* or duress. James V had died in 1542, and had been succeeded by his infant daughter Mary, Queen of Scots. Morton now sued the Queen's Advocate for the reduction of the resignation in favour of the king. He based his claim upon Roman texts attributed to Ulpian and Gaius in the *Digest*,[28] which provide that deeds done under duress should be given no legal effect, if the duress was such that it would have overcome the will of a constant and resolute man. The exact order of the arguments in this case is not entirely clear, but the Queen's Advocate seems to have responded that the Queen was not bound to answer the allegation at this juncture because, as an infant, she benefited from the *minor non tenetur* rule. The Queen's Advocate also cited two decisions of the Lords of Session to show that this rule had been applied in practice, perhaps to demonstrate that it had not fallen out of use. Regardless, the Lords of Session held that it would be 'ovirrigorous just or unjust, gif the erle of Mortoun and his airis suld vant his heritage wranguslie, as wes allegit, tane fra him *utpote per metum cadentem in constantem virum*'.[29] As Dolezalek shows, the Latin passage quoted includes a direct allusion to the *Digest*. The point seems to have been that the 'ovirrigorous' application of the *minor non tenetur* rule could have led to the perpetuation of what the Lords, on the basis of ideas drawn from Roman law, recognised to constitute an inequity. Thus, they refused to apply the *minor non tenetur* rule. The application of a Scottish rule could be limited on the basis that it would give rise to an inequity, and the relevant standard of equity and reason was revealed in part by Roman law.

Similarly, in *Seaton* v. *Cockburns*, probably decided in 1549, Alexander Cockburn had transferred lands to his son which he had allegedly acquired by defrauding Lady Seaton.[30] When his son was challenged to answer for the lands, he pleaded *minor non tenetur*. The Lords refused to allow this exception, citing the principle drawn from canon law and Roman law that no minor should be enriched at the expense and harm of another

[27] Dolezalek and Murray, *Sinclair's Practicks*, cns. 315–316, 541.

[28] Alan Watson, ed., *The Digest of Justinian* (Pennsylvania, 1985), 4.2.1 (Ulpian); 4.2.6 (Gaius). All further references to the *Digest* hereafter are to this version, unless otherwise indicated.

[29] See Dolezalek and Murray, *Sinclair's Practicks*, cn. 315; the reference was to *Digest* 4.2.6 (Gaius).

[30] Dolezalek and Murray, *Sinclair's Practicks*, cns. 459–461. The date of the case is not given, but it is included between two cases dated to 1549.

(*quod minor non debet locupletari cum iactura aliena*), especially where this had arisen out of the fraud of his father. It would have been a great inequity if men could have successfully defrauded others – at least for a time – simply by transferring to their infant sons the property they had gained dishonestly. Consequently, it was stated, 'the judge may lawfully depart from the strict severity of that municipal law of Scotland'.[31] Again, the rule in *Regiam* was set aside at least partly on the basis that it was inconsistent with ideas of justice and equity drawn from canon law and Roman law.

Additionally, a comparable reliance on canon law can arguably be found in *Commendator of St Andrews Priory* v. *Bishop of Dunkeld* (1542).[32] Here the pursuer sought reduction of a tack or lease made in favour of the defender. The defender claimed that, as a clergyman, he was not bound to answer before the civil court of the Lords of Session. The pursuer replied that according to the practice of Scotland, the Lords of Session were judges of all such leases, regardless of the identities of the parties involved. He produced an act or decision of the Lords to 'verafie' the claim that this represented the consuetude of the realm. The Lords were not certain that the decision actually indicated the existence of a practick that supported the pursuer's case. But they commented that even if it did, they would not have upheld it. This was because, as they put it, the alleged consuetude was not 'trew in the selff'. Thus, they decided to proceed 'conforme to the commoun law' – that is, the canon law principle found in the *ius commune* that enabled clergymen to benefit from the *privilegium fori*, and so to answer such claims before ecclesiastical tribunals.[33] It seems

[31] For this translation see Murray, 'Sinclair's Practicks', 100.

[32] Dolezalek and Murray, *Sinclair's Practicks*, cn. 284–285.

[33] See Walter Ullmann, *Law and Politics in the Middle Ages* (Cambridge, 1975), 183; for a helpful treatment of the point see Dolezalek, 'Court of Session as a Ius Commune Court', 71–72. Not all manuscripts state that the Lords decided to proceed 'conforme to the commoun law'. These words are found in Edinburgh University Library (EUL) Laing MS III.388a f.70v, which Murray and Dolezalek used in their edition of Sinclair's *Practicks*. Other early manuscripts give different readings; EUL Laing MS III.429 f.28v states that the Lords proceeded according to the 'commoun cannon lawis', and National Libray of Scotland (NLS) MS Advocates 24.1.11 f.23r states that they made their decision according to the 'common Canon Lawis'. However, the point made here is unaffected; all three manuscripts state that the Lords chose to rely on the canon law because the alleged consuetude was not 'trew in ye selff'. Dolezalek states that the version of Sinclair found in EUL Laing MS III.429 can be dated to about 1618 (Dolezalek, *Census*, vol. 3, 262–263) and that the version of Sinclair found in MS Advocates 24.1.11 was probably copied during the first half of the seventeenth century (Dolezalek, *Census*, vol. 2, 178–180).

that the canon law was a better guide to what was 'trew in the selff' than a past decision of the College of Justice, at least for some Lords of Session. Of course, such a decision could alternatively have been seen as representative of the emergence of a Scottish customary law.[34]

2. *Explaining the approach found in Sinclair's Practicks*

Evidently, the judges in the College of Justice were, on occasion, prepared to construe the local laws of the Scottish realm narrowly, or even to ignore them altogether. This could happen where the Lords did not believe those laws to constitute authoritative statements of equity, justice or legal truth. They reached such conclusions by making reference to standards of 'equity' and 'justice' that were drawn from sources other than the local laws themselves – namely, the scholarly traditions of ideas that had grown up around the texts of Roman law and canon law, with which the *libri Feudorum* were closely associated.[35] These traditions will collectively be referred to here as the learned laws, or the *ius commune.*

Such attitudes can be explained with reference to certain fundamental assumptions that were held by an influential group of medieval jurists, whose attitudes were shaped by the *mos Italicus.* The *mos Italicus* was a method designed to assist lawyers to study the law, and it was developed above all through the work of two great fourteenth-century jurists, Bartolus of Sassoferrato and Baldus de Ubaldis.[36] Specifically, the method was intended to enable lawyers to do various things. First, the *mos Italicus* guided them in the interpretation of the voluminous texts of the *Corpus Iuris Civilis,* the great compilation of Roman law produced by the Emperor

[34] See Ford, *Law and Opinion,* 305–312.

[35] On the *libri Feudorum* see Peter Stein, *Roman Law in European History* (Cambridge, 1999), 61–62.

[36] On the *mos Italicus* see S E Thorne, 'Statuti in the Post-Glossators', 11 *Speculum* (1936), 452, 452–458; W Ullmann, 'Bartolus on Customary Law', 52 *Juridical Review* (1940), 265; Peter Stein, 'Bartolus, the Conflict of Laws and the Roman Law', in Peter Feuerstein and Clive Parry, eds., *Multum Non Multa. Festschrift für Kurt Lipstein Aus Anlass Seines 70. Geburtstages* (Heidelberg, 1980), 251; Peter Stein, 'Civil Law Reports and the Case of San Marino', in Okko Behrends, Malte Diesselhorst and Wulf Eckart Voss, eds., *Römisches Recht in der europäischen Tradition. Symposion aus Anlaß des 75. Geburtstages von Franz Wieacker* (Ebelsbach, 1985), 323, at 331–332; Stein, *Roman Law in European History,* 38–72; O F Robinson, T D Fergus and W M Gordon, *European Legal History. Sources and Institutions,* 3rd edition (London, 2000), 63–70. For an example of Bartous's approach see J A Clarence Smith, 'Bartolo on the Conflict of Laws', 14 *American Journal of Legal History* (1970), 157, 247, particularly at 163–174.

Justinian in the sixth century, which was studied in the universities.[37] Second, some leading proponents of the method also sought to show how the complex and sometimes conflicting traditions of Roman law and the canon law of the Catholic Church could be reconciled.[38] Apparent contradictions were to be resolved by employing the techniques of scholastic logic.[39] But why were these lawyers so keen to reconcile the provisions outlined in the texts? Followers of the *mos Italicus* treated the texts of these traditions – that is to say, the learned laws – as highly authoritative repositories of learning concerning the normative standards of justice, equity and legal truth.[40] They taught that the validity and binding force of all law depended upon its conformity with such standards.[41] Thus, one aim of the proponents of the *mos Italicus* was to enable lawyers to discover the principles of justice, which, it was believed, were to be found through the rigorous study of authoritative texts, such as the *Corpus Iuris Civilis* and the works of the canon law. But, of course, contradictory interpretations of two authoritative texts from these traditions could not both be true; hence the need for a harmonious interpretation in the attempt to reveal the legal truth within the laws.[42]

The third purpose that the *mos Italicus* sought to realise was connected with the increasing interest in the use of academic knowledge of Roman law and canon law in order to resolve practical disputes in the many jurisdictions of Europe. The courts increasingly turned to university-trained lawyers for advice concerning legal problems, and the lawyers utilised their training in the learned laws to provide solutions.[43] But if the force of all law depended upon its conformity with legal truth, and if legal truth was primarily discerned through the harmonious interpretation of

37 See Robinson, Fergus and Gordon, *European Legal History*, 63–64. On the *Corpus Iuris* see Stein, *Roman Law in European History*, 32–36.

38 See Randall Lesaffer, *European Legal History* (Cambridge, 2009), 265–266.

39 Lesaffer, *European Legal History*, 239–241, 265–266, 283–284.

40 See W Ullmann, *The Medieval Idea of Law* (London, 1946), 74–76; Joseph Canning, *The Political Thought of Baldus de Ubaldis* (Cambridge Studies in Medieval Life and Thought, Fourth Series, 6, 1987), 154–158; Franz Wieacker, *A History of Private Law in Europe with Particular Reference to Germany* (trans. Tony Weir, Oxford, 1995), 55–57; Manlio Bellomo, *The Common Legal Past of Europe*, 2nd edition (trans. Lydia G. Cochrane, Washington, 1995), 190–195; Stein, *Roman Law in European History*, 38–74; Ford, *Law and Opinion*, 18, 125 and (importantly) at 310–312.

41 On the general proposition that the validity of local laws in this period depended upon their conformity with justice, equity and legal truth see Ullmann, *Medieval Idea of Law*, 1–6, 65–66, 112–122; Canning, *Political Thought of Baldus*, 154–158.

42 Lesaffer, *European Legal History*, 239–241, 265–266, 283–284.

43 Lesaffer, *European Legal History*, 259–260.

certain authoritative texts, then what force could be accorded to a local law that diverged from the standards of the authoritative learning? Bartolus argued that such local laws could possess binding force, and indeed greater force than the learned laws, meaning that a lawyer looking at any legal problem should first consider what the local law had to say about it. But he was very careful to outline several important caveats to this general rule.[44]

Bartolus began by pointing out that the textual learning of the *ius commune* itself permitted the development of laws which departed from its precepts in certain circumstances.[45] This reinforced his argument that a lawyer who was seeking to resolve a legal dispute in a particular jurisdiction should begin by considering local laws that applied there. But Bartolus also explained that any local law that was inconsistent with the learning of the *ius commune* should be presumed to be 'bad'.[46] It followed that it was not to be applied in practice.[47] However, he accepted that the presumption against the validity of the local law could be rebutted, and explained that this would happen if it could be shown that the local law somehow modified the Roman law in order to uphold its basic principles in light of local circumstances.[48] In such cases, the local law could be held to be just and therefore applicable in practice.

Nonetheless, Bartolus and his followers, the proponents of the *mos Italicus*, were generally wary of extending by analogy local laws that departed from the *ius commune*. It was frequently argued that such laws had to be interpreted narrowly and applied to as few cases as possible.[49] It was evidently feared that the broad interpretation of such laws might be unjust.[50] This last point is readily intelligible, given the assumptions outlined above. If a jurist accepted that a local law could only legitimately depart from

[44] Stein, *Roman Law in European History*, 71–72; Robinson, Fergus and Gordon, *European Legal History*, 68–69.

[45] See the sources cited in n. 36 above, and also Clarence Smith, 'Bartolo on the Conflict of Laws', 168–169; for Baldus's development of these ideas see Canning, *Political Thought of Baldus*, 93–131.

[46] Clarence Smith, 'Bartolo on the Conflict of Laws', 167–168.

[47] Clarence Smith, 'Bartolo on the Conflict of Laws', 167–168.

[48] See Stein, 'Bartolus, the Conflict of Laws and the Roman Law', 251; Stein, 'Civil Law Reports and the Case of San Marino', 331–332; Stein, *Roman Law in European History*, 71–72; Clarence Smith, 'Bartolo on the Conflict of Laws', 163–174.

[49] Stein, *Roman Law in European History*, 72; Robinson, Fergus and Gordon, *European Legal History*, 69; Ford, *Law and Opinion*, 125.

[50] See Andreas Alciato, *De Verborum Significatione Libri IIII. Eiusdem in titulum XVI. Lib. L. Digestorum commentarii, Postrema hac editione quanta fieri potuit diligentia, collatione autographi, castigati* (Lyons, 1572), 27.

the justice of the *ius commune* in certain specific circumstances, then he might also have concluded that its broad interpretation to cover other circumstances by analogy could result in inequity.

In summary, jurists who followed the *mos Italicus* assumed that the force of law depended upon its consistency with legal truth, which could primarily be discerned through the learning of the *ius commune*. Thus, laws which were inconsistent with that learning could be presumed to be bad, and, in theory at least, ignored in practice; this would follow unless the presumption against their inequity were to be rebutted. Furthermore, it was thought that even valid laws that departed from the *ius commune* should be construed narrowly. These attitudes seem to be closely reflected in the decisions of the Lords of Session cited here.[51] The overall aim of the Lords seems to have been to give effect to equity and legal truth in their decisions. To this end they placed great reliance on the learning of the *ius commune*, and they were prepared to ignore or construe narrowly local laws that departed from that standard of justice.[52]

Why was it that Bartolus and his followers treated the *ius commune* as a reliable repository of learning concerning justice, equity and legal truth? The sources of the traditional learning provided part of the answer. The *Corpus Iuris Civilis* was revered partly because its origins lay in the supposedly sacred and universal authority of the Roman Empire.[53] But lawyers' reverence for the texts also flowed from their assumption that an individual with a reputation for expertise in a particular field was to be trusted to uncover truth in questions relating to that field where there was uncertainty or doubt. It was believed that those who were learned in the existing law and who had a reputation for recognising justice could rationally be trusted to give just judgments. Additionally, it was thought that where consensus had emerged amongst a community of such reputed experts concerning the nature of justice and reason, then that expert consensus was particularly authoritative as a guide to truth. The learned traditions of the *ius commune* were believed to have been produced by such communities of jurists over many centuries, in ancient Rome, in the Catholic Church and in the medieval universities. It was partly for this reason that they were viewed as trustworthy sources of learning concerning equity. Those who were steeped in the learning of

[51] For a similar argument see Ford, *Law and Opinion*, 200–203, 210–211.

[52] See Dolezalek and Murray, *Sinclair's Practicks*, cns. 284–285, 315–316, 460–461, as discussed above.

[53] Wieacker, *History of Private Law*, 31.

those traditions and who remained in some sense faithful to them would themselves become experts. Once they reached consensus concerning the just solution to a new legal problem, this would possess great authority.[54]

It is argued here that this approach can be traced in the decisions cited from Sinclair's *Practicks*. The Lords of Session in those disputes were prepared to accord binding force to that which they collectively recognised to be just and equitable on the basis of their learning in the *ius commune*. In other words, their decisions possessed legal force *because* they represented the Lords' consensus concerning the nature of legal truth, which arose from their communal expertise in a highly reputable tradition of legal learning. They thought that such expert consensus could even have greater legal force than the local laws of the realm, including passages drawn from *Regiam* and the customary laws that might have been evinced by their past decisions. This also explains why they were willing to ignore any of their past decisions that they did not now collectively recognise as 'trew'. It seems that the force of an individual decision as an expression of the law rested on the extent to which they believed it expressed legal truth.

3. *The Lords' attitudes to the local laws prior to 1566*

It seems that the Lords of Session treated the traditions of the *ius commune* as reputable bodies of learning, which could enable them to develop their expertise so as to recognise legal truth and thus that which possessed binding force of law. But on the basis of the evidence cited above from Sinclair's *Practicks*, they did not accord the same authority to the local laws; these could be presumed to be unjust where they were inconsistent with the learned laws.

However, this may not quite be the whole picture. While the *mos Italicus* was evidently highly influential in the work of the court, there was a late

[54] On the concept of expertise outlined here see, for example, E Foster (trans.), *Aristotle's Topica* (Loeb Classical Library 391) (Cambridge, MA, 1960), 100a18–100b23, 104b1–104b5; P Slomkowski, *Aristotle's Topics*, Leiden, 1997; Ann Moss, *Printed Commonplace-Books and the Structuring of Renaissance Thought* (Oxford, 1996), 1–23 (particularly at 13–23); John I Jenkins, *Knowledge and Faith in Thomas Aquinas* (Cambridge, 1997), 49–50, 78–98 (particularly at 88–89); Mary Carruthers, *The Book of Memory. A Study of Memory in Medieval Culture*, 2nd edition (Cambridge, 2008), 261–263. On the role of such expertise in contemporary legal thought see, for example, Ullmann, *Medieval Idea of Law*, 1–6, 74–76, 112–122; John P Dawson, *The Oracles of Law* (Michigan, 1968), 124–147; Stein, *Roman Law in European History*, 38–74; Ford, *Law and Opinion*, 4–5, 18, 25, 32–33 and (importantly) 310–312; Lesaffer, *European Legal History*, 235–266.

medieval tradition that the laws of the Scottish realm also constituted a body of learning.[55] One decision recorded in Sinclair's *Practicks* gives a tantalising hint that at least some judges were prepared to accord some respect to this view. In *McClachelan* v. *Laird of Lewmond* (1547), the Lords of Session considered whether or not tailzies were lawful.[56] Tailzies arose where a feudal title was completed with a clause known as a 'destination', in which a superior and his vassal agreed that the feu would pass to a particular heir 'of tailzie' on the death of the vassal, rather than to the vassal's heirs by the ordinary course of the law.[57] One of the authorities cited in favour of the view that the tailzie represented a lawful departure from the normal order of succession was a treatise that can probably be dated to the mid-fifteenth century. This explained that tailzies were lawful because no one in Scotland had found them harmful 'past mynd or memour of man'.[58] The wording of the treatise was paraphrased in Sinclair's account of the Lords' reasoning, and it may indicate that some were prepared to recognise that the local tradition possessed its own learning concerning what was, and was not, harmful and unjust. Part of the difficulty here is that the author of the treatise on tailzies also justified the authority of customary law, and so this particular custom, with clear allusions to canon law and Roman law.[59] Yet the approval given to his argument leaves open the possibility that some Lords of Session were prepared to recognise learning in the medieval tradition of Scots law. It may also reveal that they were aware that past generations of Scots lawyers had relied upon their knowledge of canon law and Roman law to establish that their own legal system was a repository of learning.

[55] See National Library of Scotland (NLS) MS Advocates 25.4.15 f.5r; National Library of Scotland (NLS) MS Advocates 7.1.9 f.50v–51r; see also Hector L MacQueen, *Common Law and Feudal Society* (Edinburgh, 1993), 87–88.

[56] Dolezalek and Murray, *Sinclair's Practicks*, cns. 418–420.

[57] George L Gretton, 'Feudal System', in Kenneth G C Reid, ed., *The Law of Property in Scotland* (Edinburgh, 1996), para. 41, at para. 111.

[58] See National Library of Scotland (NLS) MS Advocates 7.1.9 f.48r; British Library (BL) MS Harley 4700 f.256v–257r. It seems reasonable to conclude that this was the treatise that Sinclair had in mind. Before citing it, he stated that in the law of Scotland 'tailyeis ar usit and previt past memour of man and sua lesum', and exactly the same claim was made in the treatise on tailzies cited here. Furthermore, Sinclair's version of the treatise was bound together with a copy of *Regiam Majestatem*, as are all surviving copies of the treatise on tailzies mentioned here. No other text has been identified thus far that could have been Sinclair's treatise.

[59] I discuss this at more length in Andrew R C Simpson, *Early Modern Studies of the Scottish Legal Past: Tradition and Authority in Sixteenth Century Scots Law*, unpublished PhD dissertation, University of Cambridge, 2011, 17, n. 87.

Nonetheless, while some Lords may have adopted the attitude outlined here to the authority of the local laws, there is little evidence to suggest that they made any sustained attempts to remedy the significant problems associated with the use of those laws in practice. During the 1540s and the 1550s, no serious, concerted efforts were made by the Lords to address either the confusion of the laws or the fact that many of the texts in which they were presented assumed a procedural framework that was now out of date. Furthermore, no evidence has been found to suggest that lawyers mounted any significant challenge at this time to the *mos Italicus* assumptions that could undermine the authority of the local laws.

III. Promoting the study of the medieval laws in 1566

This all changed quite radically during the mid-1560s. In 1566, several Lords of Session sought to remedy the problems associated with utilising the local tradition in legal argument, and secured royal support for this aim.[60] One was Bishop John Leslie of Ross, a canonist, Privy Councillor and Lord of Session. Leslie was aided by Edward Henryson, a former teacher of Roman law at Bourges, who was a Lord of Session and the holder of a commission to lecture law, Greek and Latin to the people of Edinburgh.[61] As noted above, also in 1566, another commissioner and Lord of Session, David Chalmers of Ormond, wrote an heuristic device for practitioners that summarised in alphabetically-arranged topics the laws of the realm.[62] Other lawyers were also involved in the project to promote the study of the laws, including the judges Sir Richard Maitland of Lethington[63] and Sir James Balfour of Pittendreich.[64] Yet the most detailed accounts of the purposes of the 1566 project can be found in Henryson's *Preface* to the statutes printed in 1566,[65] and in two *Epistles*

[60] *Actis and Constitutiounis . . . 1566* [October], Sig. A2r–A3v. On the biographical details of the commissioners given here see the sources cited in n. 9 above.

[61] On this commission see John Durkan, 'The Royal Lectureships under Mary of Lorraine', 62 *Scottish Historical Review* (1983), 73; on Henryson's biography see also Durkan, 'Henry Scrimgeour, Renaissance Bookman', 2–4.

[62] Chalmers, *Compendium*, BL MS Add. 27472. Chalmers stated that he had organised the laws of the realm in common-places at f.1v–2r.

[63] On Sir Richard Maitland see Michael R G Spiller, 'Maitland, Sir Richard, of Lethington (1496–1586)', ODNB, www.oxforddnb.com/view/article/12982, accessed 14 August 2013.

[64] On Sir James Balfour see Peter G B McNeill, 'Balfour, Sir James, of Pittendreich (*c.*1525–1583)', ODNB, www.oxforddnb.com/view/article/12982, accessed 14 August 2013.

[65] *Actis and Constitutiounis . . . 1566* [October], Sig. A3r–A3v.

Chalmers included in his *Dictionary*. Chalmers's *Epistles* were addressed to the Queen and his readers.[66] Here the focus will be on a few important elements of what those sources reveal.

1. *Addressing the confusion of the texts*

Henryson and Chalmers expressly drew attention to the confusion of the texts in which the medieval laws were contained. Henryson stated that the laws were 'throuch Ignorance of the copistis confusit and full of errouris';[67] printing an authoritative edition of the legal texts was an obvious solution. He explained that only the laws promulgated on the advice of parliament after 1424 were printed in 1566, because the older texts were by far the most confused, and required more detailed study before they could be printed.[68] Similarly, in his book Chalmers, presumably referring to the pre-1424 texts in particular, commented that they were 'confusit and oft repeittit without ony or small augmenta[tio]un or d[i]min[u]tioun'.[69] He then stated that this was one of the reasons that he had written his heuristic work.[70] Through the re-organisation of the materials of the tradition in alphabetical topics, Chalmers hoped to make it easier to search through the local literature.

2. *The problem of out-of-date law*

Yet, Henryson and Chalmers did not apparently seek to remedy the problem that many of the older laws were no longer in use. Henryson included out-of-date legislation in the printed acts of 1566.[71] Similarly, Chalmers drew attention to the possibility that many of the laws he included in

66 Chalmers, *Compendium*, BL MS Add. 27472, f.1r–2r (*Epistle to the Queen*); f.3r (*Epistle to the Redar*).

67 *Actis and Constitutiounis . . . 1566* [October], Sig. A3r.

68 *Actis and Constitutiounis . . . 1566* [October], Sig. A3r–3v.

69 'diminutioun' is probably what is meant here, but the script is a little unclear.

70 Chalmers, *Compendium*, BL MS Add. 27472, f.1v. In quoting Chalmers's works, I have expanded contractions and added punctuation in order to make the meaning of his arguments clearer.

71 Consider *Actis and Constitutiounis . . . 1566* [October], f.76v-77r, c.124, in light of Godfrey, *Civil Justice*, 65–66. Other statutes presumed the existence of a framework of remedies that had been superseded by developments in the practick of the Lords of Session – on this development see Godfrey, *Civil Justice*, 268–354, 449–453). Relevant statutes include that found at f.108v–109r, concerning the brieve of right, and that found at f.55v, and entitled 'Anent breuis pleidabill'.

his *Dictionary* were 'presentlie ... not in use'. Nonetheless, he maintained that the 'knawlage thereof is necessar and worthie to be wnderstand and will serff at the leist In place of ane histoir'.[72] Elsewhere, he stated that his aim had been to include in his work all surviving laws that had been promulgated since the first kings reigned in Scotland, supposedly in the fourth century BC.[73] His desire to produce a detailed historical account of the Scottish legal tradition will be examined in more detail shortly.

Why were Henryson and Chalmers more concerned with an attempt to address the confusion in the medieval legal texts than with the production of an up-to-date account of the law in force? Part of the answer may lie in what were, arguably, their conscious attempts to engage critically with the *mos Italicus* assumptions adopted by some of their colleagues in the College of Justice, and to reconceptualise the authority of the local laws in the process.

3. *Challenging the* mos Italicus *in Henryson's preface*

Henryson's *Preface* opened with the following claim:

> IT is maist certane, that na thing is swa eirnistlie to be socht and straitlie keipit, as the knawlege of the Lawis and thair authoritie. Because the Lawis rychtlie disponis, and ordouris to the best baith godlie, and manlie effairis, and banisis thairout all iniquitie.[74]

This passage resembles the opening words of Justinian's *Constitutio Deo Auctore* from near the beginning of the *Digest*:

> Whereas, therefore, nothing amongst all matters is learnt [*inuenitur*] so eagerly as the authority of laws, which sets in good order affairs both divine and human, and casts out all injustice ...[75]

[72] Chalmers, *Compendium*, BL MS Add. 27472, f.3r.

[73] Chalmers, *Compendium*, BL MS Add. 27472, f1v. Chalmers implicitly endorsed the claim that the monarchy had originated in the fourth century BC at f.169r by referring to a law that had supposedly been promulgated by one of Scotland's kings at that time. On this mythical king see Chalmers's source, Hector Boece's *Scotorum Historiae a Prima Gentis Origine* ... (Paris, 1527), f.12v–15v.

[74] *Actis and Constitutiounis* ... 1566 [October], Sig. A.3r.

[75] *Digest, Constitutio Deo Auctore* 1 (translation slightly altered); the Latin text reads '*Cum itaque nihil tam studiosum in omnibus rebus inuenitur quam legum auctoritas, quae et diuinas et humanas res bene disponit et omnem iniquitatem expellit* ...'. See also Hughes de la Porte, ed., *Corpus Iuris Civilis* (Lyons, 1558–1560), *Codex* (1560), http://amshistorica.unibo.it/diglib.php?inv=176&int_ptnum=4, accessed 19 August 2013, 1.20.

Henryson continued by making the following remarks:

> Thay [the laws] ar the gift of God, the statute and decreit of wyse men, the amending and rychting of forthoct, and suddane faultis, the commoun promeis, band, and obligatioun of the Realme, and of ilk member thairof to uther, efter the quhilk it apportenis all the saidis members to leid thair lyfe, gif thay will not onlie leif, bot als manerlie, weill, and godlie leif.[76]

This translated a passage from the *Digest*, which was originally drawn from Demosthenes's oration *Against Aristogeiton*:

> For Demosthenes the orator also defines it thus: "Law is that which all men ought to obey for many reasons, and chiefly because all law is a discovery and gift of God, and yet at the same time is a resolution of wise men, a correction of misdeeds both voluntary and involuntary, and the common agreement of the *polis* according to whose terms all who live in the *polis* ought to live."[77]

Taken together, these two passages formed part of Henryson's general exhortation to his readers to acquire knowledge of 'the Lawis and thair authoritie'. They were encouraged to do this for various reasons. The laws constituted the 'commoun promeis' of each member of the realm to the other; the laws had been decreed by 'wyse men' and were 'the gift of God'; and they revealed to the people how to live in a 'godlie' manner. Thus, to know the authority of the law was to appreciate that it was God-given, infused with wisdom and upheld through the 'commoun promeis, band, and obligatioun' of the realm. A further element of the authority of the law was hidden from all but Henryson's more learned readers, who would have known that he was quoting from the *Digest*. They would have discerned a claim that to know the authority of the laws of the Scottish realm was to appreciate that it was in some way similar to that possessed by the laws of ancient Rome and Athens. Later, Henryson expressly compared Queen Mary's actions in publishing the laws to the proclamations of laws in ancient Israel, Athens and Rome.[78]

Henryson developed these ideas further later in his *Preface*. Here he exhorted the literate populace at large to study and then manifest in their lives their duty as expressed in the printed 'Law buke' – indicating that his comments applied to the statutory laws of the realm in particular. He told them to search 'heirout doctrine of treuth and obedience to the Princeis, thair Magistratis, and Officiaris of Justice: Off honest lyfe, of

[76] *Actis and Constitutiounis . . . 1566* [October], Sig. A.3r. [77] *Digest*, 1.3.2.

[78] *Actis and Constitutiounis . . . 1566* [October], Sig. A.3r.

abstinence fra iniuring and hurting ane a uther: Off geuing to ilk persoun his awin'.[79] The claim was that Scots law revealed 'doctrine of treuth' according to which the people could discern their duty and live godly and just lives in their dealings with one another. In other words, Henryson argued that Scots law constituted a body of legal learning. But his learned readers would have recognised the equally explicit claim that the laws of the Scots expressed Ulpian's fundamental principles of justice, which were apparently upheld in Roman law.[80] Again, a link was made between the authority of the laws of the realm and that of the learned laws.

Yet, what is easy to overlook here is precisely *how* Henryson was using the learned authority of Ulpian's principles. He was undoubtedly encouraging the lay populace to read the laws promulgated with the advice of parliament, and so to discover legal truth on their own. His exhortation looks, *prima facie*, like that of a more radical Protestant preacher encouraging his flock to read scripture for themselves, guided by conscience alone, to discover how to lead a godly life.[81] It might even be argued that it constituted a subtle attack on the notion that the populace required the help of expert lawyers to enable them to discern legal truth. But Henryson also provided his readers with fundamental legal principles drawn from his learning in Roman law, to guide them in their interpretation of the Scottish texts.[82] This indicates that he believed that legal expertise still had a significant role in enabling the people to learn 'doctrine of treuth'. In discovering the doctrine of truth and their duty to one another, they were to seek out the rules that explained the meaning of Ulpian's principles.[83]

Simultaneously, Henryson's statement that the people should utilise the Roman precepts of justice to guide their interpretation of the Scottish texts reinforced the claim that Scots law constituted a body of legal learning. Ulpian's vague principles could only be given meaning in the context of a legal framework that defined their constituent terms, like harm, and what

[79] *Actis and Constitutiounis . . . 1566* [October], Sig. A.3v.

[80] *Digest*, 1.1.10.1 ('*Iuris praecepta sunt haec: honeste uiuere, alterum non laedere, suum cuique tribuere*'). The claim that David I of Scotland had ruled according to such precepts was advanced by the medieval Scottish chronicler Wynton; see MacQueen, '*Regiam Majestatem*, Scots Law, and National Identity', 8, n. 27. I am grateful to Professor MacQueen for this point.

[81] On this approach to the discovery of truth in the scriptures see, for example, P Harrison, 'Philosophy and the Crisis of Religion', in J Hankins, ed., *The Cambridge Companion to Renaissance Philosophy* (Cambridge, 2007), 234, at 239–243.

[82] Leading Protestants came to accept that the laity would need help to interpret the scriptures; see Harrison, 'Philosophy and the Crisis of Religion', 240.

[83] *Digest*, 1.1.10.1.

was a man's due. Which body of learning could one trust to explain the meaning of those terms in a manner consistent with legal truth? Some of Sinclair's colleagues would evidently only have accorded this status to the *ius commune*, and conceptualised the learning and so authority of the local laws according to their *mos Italicus* assumptions. Henryson rejected this view. For him, the laws of the Scottish realm, and in particular the statutory laws of the realm, constituted trustworthy repositories of legal 'treuth' and learning. To know the authority of the laws of the Scots was, apparently, to know that they expressed wisdom and the same sort of learning as that found in the laws of ancient Rome. While some of his predecessors in the College of Justice had used their legal learning to limit the force of the medieval laws of the realm, Henryson was now utilising his learning in Roman law to *promote* the authority of the local legal tradition.

4. *The foundations of Chalmers's argument in his* Epistles

Chalmers's *Epistle to the Queen* conveys the strong impression that he, like Henryson, wished to engage critically with the sort of *mos Italicus* approach found in the College of Justice in the 1540s. Early in his *Epistle* he addressed Mary, Queen of Scots, and argued that it was

> without all contrauersie that zour majestie and zour most noble progenitors, as alsua all wther princis[84] not recognoscand ony superiors, hes alss grete powar & auchtoritie within zour awin realmess to statut mak lawes and ordinances for the politie and gouernament of zour commoun welthis & contrayis – As ewer had ony empreor within thair empyre.[85]

Chalmers's point was that Mary had the same authority as the emperor to promulgate laws *because* she and her predecessors had never recognised any superiors. In making this claim, Chalmers not only referred to the maxim *rex in regno suo est imperator*, but also its theoretical foundations in the *ius commune*. By his time many expert jurists agreed that the right of the monarch to exercise the powers of the emperor (whether *de facto* or

[84] This word could read 'princis', 'princs', 'printis' or 'prints', but only 'princis' or 'princs' makes sense in the context.

[85] Chalmers, *Compendium*, BL MS Add. 27472, f.1r–1v. I have added punctuation to Chalmers's original text for the sake of clarity. Chalmers's thought, as reconstructed below, is also discussed in Andrew R C Simpson, 'Power, Reason and Equity. Two Juristic Accounts of Royal Authority in Sixteenth-Century Scotland', in Jørn Øyrehagen Sunde, ed., *Constitutionalism before 1789. Constitutional Arrangements from the High Middle Ages to the French Revolution* (Oslo, 2014), 128–146, at 128–136.

de iure) ultimately arose from the *ius gentium*. This directed each people to provide for their governance, which could be achieved through the institution of an hereditary monarchy. Where a dynasty had exercised such governance over a people for a long period of time, without recognising superiors, its right to govern could be fortified by prescription. Many of the authoritative texts that were used to establish these points were drawn from the *Corpus Iuris Civilis* compiled by the Roman Emperor Justinian.[86]

Thus, Chalmers relied upon learned authority to explain that the power of the Queen to promulgate laws was uncontroversial. Having asserted the importance of the principle *rex in regno suo est imperator*, he continued:

> Quhair fore findis not neidfull, bot express againis all equitie and reasoun, that salang as ony questioun uccurrand can be decidit be ony wreittin Lawes or statuttis sufficientlie maid be zour hienes or predicessors as zit not abrogate, nor zit be ony Lovable consuetude or commoun practik, that ony Recurss suld be had to quhatsumeuer wther Lawes maid be ony emperors or wther forregn princes.[87]

Chalmers's point was that those who ignored laws that proceeded from Scottish royal power, and so simultaneously ignored the principle *rex in regno suo est imperator*, acted in a manner that was contrary to all 'equitie and reasoun' – that is to say, the equity and reason revealed by the *ius commune*, which the judges of Sinclair's time had claimed to uphold. It should also be noted that in the passage just cited, Chalmers outlined a hierarchy of the sources of Scots law that was reminiscent of a passage in the *Digest* attributed to the jurist Julian, which was briefly mentioned above:

> What ought to be held to in those cases where we have no applicable written law is the practice established by customs and usage. And if this is in some way deficient, we should hold to what is most nearly analogical to and entailed by such a practice. If even this is obscure, then we ought to apply law as it is in use in the City of Rome. Age-encrusted custom is not undeservedly cherished as having almost statutory force, and this is the kind of law which is said to be established by use and wont... it is absolutely right to accept the point that statutes may be repealed not only by vote of the legislature but also by the silent agreement of everyone expressed through desuetude.[88]

[86] See, for example, Canning, *Political Thought of Baldus*, 64–70, 93–131, 209–221. On the maxim in Scotland see, for example, Leslie J Macfarlane, *William Elphinstone and the Kingdom of Scotland, 1431–1514: The Struggle for Order* (Aberdeen, 1985), 40–44, 188–189, 302.

[87] Chalmers, *Compendium*, BL MS Add. 27472, f.1v.

[88] *Digest* 1.3.32.pr.-1.

Julian argued that, failing written law, judges should apply the 'practice established by customs and usage'. Commenting on this passage, Bartolus had identified the *ius commune* with the written law, which applied in so far as it had not been superseded by developments in customary law, meaning the laws that had grown up in each European polity following the fall of the Roman Empire.[89] There is evidence to suggest that some judges in Sinclair's time endorsed this way of conceptualising the local law.[90] In contrast, assuming he did have Julian's argument in mind, Chalmers identified written law with the statutes promulgated by the Scottish monarchs, and the customary law with the consuetude of the realm and the 'commoun practik' – this was probably a reference to the law emerging from the decisions of the College of Justice.[91] Like Henryson, Chalmers was apparently using a text of Roman law, and his legal learning more generally, to rationalise and promote the authority of Scots law. He too did this in a manner that departed from the *mos Italicus* approach of some of his predecessors among the Lords of Session.

Chalmers relied upon the learning of the *ius commune* to establish the force of the tradition of laws promulgated by the Scottish monarchs. He also reinterpreted an authoritative text of Roman law to outline a hierarchy of the sources of Scots law. Yet those who favoured the *mos Italicus* might still have replied that the local laws, while perhaps meriting more attention than they had received, were still not as authoritative as the *ius commune* as a body of learning concerning equity and reason. A learned lawyer like Henryson had drawn upon his own knowledge of Roman law to argue that this was incorrect, but did Chalmers also anticipate such an objection?

5. *Chalmers on the learning and history of Scots law*

Chalmers was much less explicit than Henryson when it came to the question of whether or not the Scottish tradition constituted a body of legal learning. Yet arguably he too thought this was the case. He did this by implying that there was some link between the authority of the local

89 Clarence Smith, 'Bartolo on the Conflict of Laws', 167–169; Stein, 'Bartolus, the Conflict of Laws and the Roman law'; Stein, 'Civil Law Reports', 331–332; Ford, *Law and Opinion*, 18.

90 See Dolezalek and Murray, *Sinclair's Practicks* cn. 503, which refers to the Leases Act 1449 as 'customary' law. For the act, see K M Brown, et al., eds., *The Records of the Parliaments of Scotland to 1707*, www.rps.ac.uk, accessed 5 August 2013, 1450/1/15.

91 On this meaning of the word 'practick' see Ford, *Law and Opinion*, 85–86, 305–312. See also Godfrey, *Civil Justice*, 179–180, 204–206.

tradition and that of Roman law. It has been suggested here that he thought one could appreciate the force of Scottish statutes and customary laws by viewing them through the prism of texts concerning the force of Roman *ius scriptum* and consuetude. Additionally, as has been seen, Chalmers compared the authority of the Queen to promulgate laws with that of the emperors of Rome. But he also made various claims about the project to promote the study of the medieval laws of Scotland that would almost certainly have given his more learned readers the impression that he was drawing parallels between that project, on the one hand, and Justinian's attempt to create an authoritative statement of Roman law, on the other. A few examples of this approach will suffice here. First, the sixth-century compilers of the *Digest* accepted that it was difficult to apply the laws of ancient Rome in practice because of the confused and voluminous nature of the texts in which they were found.[92] Chalmers made the same point about Scots law. Second, Justinian had consequently commanded the reduction to order of all of the surviving laws of the Romans that had been promulgated from the time of Romulus, the legendary founder of Rome in the eighth century BC, down to his own time.[93] Similarly, Chalmers emphasised that he had sought to reduce to order all surviving written laws promulgated 'seyn the first begonneng of any kingis within this realme',[94] who had supposedly reigned during the fourth century BC. Third, Justinian also claimed that by virtue of his great authority, which rested on the *imperium* transferred to him by the consent of the Roman populace in the *lex Regia*, he could rectify defects in the ancient laws.[95] Likewise, Chalmers indicated that it was necessary to reform the 'auld & commoun custum' in light of 'wertew', and implied that this could only be done with the Queen's 'authorisment' because 'ane grett number' within the realm would prefer to retain 'wice'.[96]

The implication is that Chalmers wished to draw various parallels between Scots law and Roman law as it had stood in the time of Justinian, in terms of the authority possessed by both legal systems and in terms of aspects of their historical development. This reinforces the argument advanced above that Chalmers relied upon his learning in Roman law, and his knowledge that Scottish lawyers respected the authority of that body of law, to promote the authority of the local legal tradition. But

[92] *Digest, Constitutio Deo Auctore*, 1. [93] *Digest, Constitutio Deo Auctore*, 1–2, 4–5.
[94] Chalmers, *Compendium*, BL MS Add. 27472, f.1v.
[95] *Digest, Constitutio Deo Auctore*, 7.
[96] Chalmers, *Compendium*, BL MS Add. 27472, f.2r.

can anything else be concluded from the points noted here concerning whether or not Chalmers conceptualised Scots law as a body of learning? One way of tackling this question is to reiterate some of the arguments advanced above in order to establish what can be said about how he conceptualised the authority of Roman law. It should be recalled here that Chalmers treated the maxim *rex in regno suo est imperator* as a statement of 'equitie' and 'reasoun'. It was noted that this maxim arose from an expert consensus concerning the correct interpretation of certain authoritative texts, many of which were drawn from the *Corpus Iuris Civilis*. It is clear that Chalmers was aware of this, because he alluded to the theoretical foundations of *rex in regno suo*. His statement that it was 'without all contrawersie' may even have been a nod in the direction of the fact that it expressed a widespread consensus amongst learned lawyers. From these points seems to follow the conclusion that, on this occasion, Chalmers treated expert consensus concerning the correct interpretation of the texts of Roman law as an authoritative guide to 'equitie' and 'reasoun'. But one must be careful here. Chalmers made clear the complexity of his position when he immediately went on to use the 'equitie' that the experts had discerned in establishing the maxim *rex in regno suo est imperator* in order to suggest that the Bartolists had misinterpreted Julian's account of the hierarchy of laws, at least in the Scottish context in which he wrote. Yet, while Chalmers was unwilling to follow blindly Bartolist interpretations of the texts of Roman law, he clearly regarded expert interpretation of those texts as a means of discerning equity and reason. This in turn could reveal who, in law, had the power to promulgate ordinances and statutes.

The authority of Roman law for Chalmers thus lay in its status as a repository of learning concerning equity. It also seems correct to say that Chalmers believed that Scots law was effectively to be regarded as a system that had developed so as to parallel Roman law as it stood before Justinian's reforms, both in terms of its authority and its history. It appears to follow from this that Chalmers, like Henryson, believed that Scots law constituted a body of learning. While he drew attention to the equity revealed in the learned laws to explain why the local laws should be applied, he seems to have thought the application of the local laws themselves would also be consistent with right reason. This impression may be reinforced by the way in which Chalmers presented his account of Scots law. Like Henryson, Chalmers included much material which he admitted was probably out of date. One plausible explanation for Chalmers's decision to do this was that he was simply unsure which laws were in force and which were not. Yet if this is so, he clearly thought that he could make a virtue out of this necessity, because he hoped that the resulting work would 'serff at the leist In place of ane histoir'.[97] What Chalmers meant by 'ane histoir' can be illustrated by examining his individual titles. For example, in his title 'Counsall',[98] it was possible to see how the law connected with the administration of justice had gradually been developed, with some policies being upheld over time and some being rejected. The impression given was that Scots law represented the product of a long process of trial and testing of individual statutes and ordinances; but such a claim could only be conveyed through the inclusion of out-of-date law.[99] If Chalmers meant to convey this impression, then it seems likely that he, unlike some of his predecessors in the College of Justice during the 1540s, thought Scots law constituted a body of learning. Henryson's reasons for including out-of-date statutes remains unclear, but it is possible that he was motivated by considerations similar to those outlined here.

IV. Rethinking authority in Reformation Scotland

So why did Henryson and Chalmers depart from the *mos Italicus* assumptions of their predecessors? Why did they utilise their legal learning in order to argue that the laws of the realm in some senses possessed the same sort of authority as the learned laws? Clearly, the promotion of the authority of the Scottish statutes formed part of a public relations effort on behalf of Queen Mary. Furthermore, it is possible that the increasing numbers of practitioners in the College of Justice, from about ten in the late 1540s, to about twenty in the late 1550s, may have created greater demand for literature on the local law.[100] Additionally, Chalmers and Henryson may have been influenced by much older, medieval accounts of Scots law, which did locate learning in the local tradition. Yet their challenges to the *mos Italicus* framework employed by some judges in

97 Chalmers, *Compendium*, BL MS Add. 27472, f.3r.

98 Chalmers, *Compendium*, BL MS Add. 27472, f.102r–105v.

99 The pragmatic use of history was commonplace in early modern Europe; see Quentin Skinner, *The Foundations of Modern Political Thought*, 2 vols. (Cambridge, 1978), vol. 1, 168–170, vol. 2, 284–301; Donald R Kelley, 'The Theory of History', in Charles B Schmitt, Quentin Skinner, Eckhard Kessler and Jill Kraye, eds., *The Cambridge History of Renaissance Philosophy* (Cambridge, 1988), 746, at 753–761; John M Najemy, 'Society, Class, and State in Machiavelli's Discourses on Livy', in John M Najemy, ed., *The Cambridge Companion to Machiavelli* (Cambridge, 2010), 96.

100 See John Finlay, 'Advocates Unlimited: The Numerus Clausus and the College of Justice in Scotland', 82 *Historical Research* (2009), 206, at 218. I am grateful to Professor John Finlay of Glasgow University for this suggestion.

the 1540s, and their reconceptualisations of the authority of the law of Scotland, perhaps require further explanation.

First, it may be asked what it was that focused these lawyers' efforts *at this particular point in time* to promote the study of the laws of the realm promulgated with the advice of parliament? Arguably, the answer lies in the crisis of authority which manifested itself in the revolutions of the 1550s and the 1560s, and which forced Mary to present herself as the defender of the laws and liberties of the Scots.[101] Both Henryson and Chalmers went to some length to justify their claims that the authority of royal laws promulgated on the advice of parliament was uncontroversial.[102] In this regard, they were starting from a claim that virtually all members of the Scottish polity would have found difficult to refute. Even the radical Protestants relied upon the statutory recognition of their interpretation of scriptural truth as the legal basis of the Reformation.[103] In fact, the only Scots who might realistically and effectively have challenged the authority and scope of an individual statute would have been lawyers who endorsed the *mos Italicus* precepts that can be traced in the College of Justice in the 1540s. Some judges at this time had relied upon their legal learning in the *ius commune* to limit the force of the medieval laws of Scotland in certain situations. Cleverly, Henryson and Chalmers relied upon texts and propositions drawn from the same legal learning in order to argue that the local laws of Scotland possessed the same sort of authority as the learned laws.

Second, it may be asked how Henryson and Chalmers would have justified their claims. It is worth reiterating briefly the manner in which they were advanced. It was observed above that during the medieval period, various authoritative texts of Roman law had been used to describe the authority of the *ius commune* and to explain the limited force of the local laws of the European jurisdictions as they stood in relation to that pan-European learning. For example, Bartolus used the *Digest* text attributed to Julian to explain the relationship between the authority of the learned *ius commune* and the local laws of the European jurisdictions. But now Henryson and Chalmers simply used such authoritative texts of Roman law to describe the authority possessed by the laws of Scotland.

101 On the effects of the religious revolutions of the 1550s and 1560s on jurisdictions and legal institutions within Scotland see now Green, *Consistorial Decisions*, xxvi–xxxi, xxxvii–xlv.

102 *Actis and Constitutiounis . . . 1566* [October], Sig. A.3r; Chalmers, *Compendium*, BL MS Add. 27472, f.1r–1v.

103 See Goodare, *Government of Scotland*, 75; see also *The Records of the Parliaments of Scotland to 1707*, www.rps.ac.uk, accessed 17 August 2013, A1560/8/3, A1560/8/5.

The texts of Roman law were no longer employed to reveal that Scots law was simply a local customary variant of a pan-European *ius commune*. Rather, they were used to explore the nature of Scots law as a legal system that resembled and even paralleled Roman law. For example, Henryson stated that Scots law expressed the same sort of legal truth as Roman law. Put another way, that which could be said about the authority of Roman law could now be said about Scots law. What motivated this element of these jurists' approach?

1. *Eguinaire Baron on French law and Roman law*

One possible way to explain the attitudes of these Scottish lawyers can be found in the work of Eguinaire Baron, who was one of Henryson's teachers.[104] Baron himself was a follower of Andreas Alciato (1492–1550),[105] who is frequently referred to as the founder of the 'humanistic jurisprudence', later known as the *mos Gallicus*.[106] In their academic work, jurists like Alciato argued that Bartolus and the commentators had distorted the meanings of the texts of Roman law through erroneous interpretations. Armed with a rich knowledge of the classics, the proponents of the *mos Gallicus* sought to purge the texts of these errors and to discover what they meant in their original historical context. As Stein observes, there were certain parallels here between their work and that of the Protestant preachers, who sought to recover the meaning of the text of scripture without making reference to the traditions of interpretation which they now thought of as erroneous. Like the Protestants, these jurists also wanted to enable their readers to approach the meaning of the texts directly for themselves, without the apparent distractions of glosses and commentaries.[107] There were also clear parallels between these aspects of the aims of Alciato and his followers and the goals of Henryson and Chalmers outlined above. They too sought to establish an authoritative account of medieval Scots law, purged of confusion and errors, which would be directly accessible to a broad audience. Of course, it has long

[104] See also Durkan, 'Henry Scrimgeour, Renaissance Bookman', 3–4.

[105] Donald R Kelley, 'Gaius Noster: Substructures of Western Social Thought', 84 *The American Historical Review* (1979), 619, at 631.

[106] See, for example, Peter Stein, 'Legal Humanism and Legal Science', 54 *Tijdschrift voor Rechtsgeschiedenis* 297; Stein, *Roman Law in European History*, 76–79; Lesaffer, *European Legal History*, 350–351.

[107] Stein, 'Legal Humanism', 300–301.

been known that elements of the attitudes of Alciato and his followers were endorsed by many Scottish jurists during the sixteenth century.[108]

Like his colleagues at the University of Bourges, Baron sought to recover the original historical meanings of the texts of Roman law. But his interest in history extended to the study of the development of French law and French institutions. He sought to study the histories of both traditions together, according to what Kelley terms 'a unique and self-consciously comparative method', which Baron referred to as '*commentaria bipertita*'. He claimed to have 'accommodated civil law to French customs and legislation', and explored 'parallels and contrasts' between the two legal systems.[109] He made it very clear that he thought Roman law and French law could be analysed as legal systems that had developed along similar lines. For example, he commented that in establishing laws, the French king followed 'almost the same method [*ratio*]' as the Roman emperor. This could be said because the French king formed his *constitutiones* 'having applied closely the advice of the nobles [*proceres*]', and because those laws were not thought to acquire binding force until they had been read aloud in the 'praetorian prefecture', which term Baron subsequently translated into French as 'La court de parlement'.[110]

Here Baron attempted to compare certain institutions through which the law was developed and refined during the late Roman Empire with apparently similar institutions in sixteenth-century France. Early-modern writers had cause to believe that past Roman emperors had granted both

[108] See Cairns, Fergus and MacQueen, 'Legal Humanism'; the commission of 1566 is discussed, along with other such commissions, at 50–52.

[109] Quoted in Kelley, 'Gaius Noster', 632.

[110] See Eguinaire Baron, *Institutionum ciuilium ab Iustiniano Caesare editarum lib. IIII. Bipartito commentario quam breuissime illustrati, cuius pars altera Romanum, altera Gallicum ius ad singulos titulos complectitur*..., Poitiers, 1546, VI. The Latin text referred to here reads: '*Regem Francum Romano Principi opponimus: qui in legibus constituendis, & promulgandis, eandem fere rationem sequitur, quam Imperator. Etenim constitutiones, adhibito fere procerum consilio, totius Regni communes, edit: quae non prius vim legum obtinere creduntur, quam in praefecturis praetorianis recitentur, homologentur, & in acta referantur. Quo illa verba pertinent quae subscribi solent, Lecta, publicata, & regesta, & c. Mores regionum, & municipiorum leges, epistola) quas patentes literas dicimus) Tribunianis quibusdam, & Theophilis mandare solet specialiter: alia epistola ad praefecturam praetorianam,* La court de parlement, *data, (ad quam illa regio pertinet) mandare recognitionem, & homologationem, idem Rex solitus est*'. I have not reproduced side-notes or accents on the Latin text. I am grateful to Alison Simpson for discussing the translation of this passage with me. On this text see also Donald R Kelley, 'Law', in J H Burns with Mark Goldie, eds., *The Cambridge History of Political Thought 1450–1700* (Cambridge, 1991), 66, at 80.

the noblemen (*proceres*) in their retinue and also the Senate the right to be consulted concerning the content of all laws that were to be promulgated in the future. The text in the *Code* that stated this was the case also indicated that the emperors had declared such laws would not receive binding force until they had first been approved by the Senate – and possibly also the nobility – and then subsequently read out in the imperial consistory.[111] Frequently, these ordinances were addressed to individual praetorian prefects, who represented the emperor in the four prefectures into which the empire was divided; the prefect then generally had the duty to publish the law.[112] Baron compared these rules with the ways in which laws were brought into force in sixteenth-century France. There it was thought that the effectiveness of royal ordinances depended upon their being registered by the *Parlement* of Paris.[113] Importantly, the *Parlement* was prepared to refuse to register royal edicts when its magistrates somehow found such edicts inequitable or contrary to law, on the basis of their expertise.[114] Ultimately, the French monarch had the ability to force the *Parlement* to register his edicts by means of *lettres de jussion* or by means of the ceremony known as the *lit de justice*.[115]

Baron's point was that the monarchs of France followed the same sort of method as the Roman emperors when promulgating their ordinances. The French constitutions were informed by the counsel of the nobility, and the laws were also open to refinement by the expertise of the magistrates of the *Parlement*. His arguments implied that if his readers thought Roman law constituted a body of learning because of the methods followed by the Roman emperors when promulgating their laws, the same claim could

[111] See *Codex* (1560), 1.17; see also the equivalent version of the Latin text (*Codex* 1.14.8), http://webu2.upmf-grenoble.fr/DroitRomain/Corpus/CJ1.htm#14 and the rather loose translation by C P Scott of this passage at http://webu2.upmf-grenoble.fr/DroitRomain/ (site accessed 19 August 2013). I have also referred to the translation of this passage found at www.uwyo.edu/lawlib/blume-justinian/, accessed 14 October 2014. It is not absolutely clear from this text that the consent of the *nobility* (as opposed to the Senate) was required in order for new laws to receive force, but the passage can be read in that way. On the procedures adopted during the Dominate in the promulgation of laws see H F Jolowicz and Barry Nicholas, *Historical Introduction to the Study of Roman Law*, 3rd edition (Cambridge, 1972), 460–461.

[112] Jolowicz and Nicholas, *Historical Introduction*, 423–424, 460. Note that here Baron cited X.1.2.2; for this see the *Corpus Iuris Canonici* (1582), http://digital.library.ucla.edu/canonlaw/.

[113] See J H Shennan, *The Parlement of Paris*, 2nd edition (Stroud, 1998), 159–161, 210–211; Ford, *Law and Opinion*, 313–315.

[114] Shennan, *Parlement*, 159–160.

[115] Shennan, *Parlement*, 161.

be advanced for French law. The legal systems paralleled one another in their respective authority.

2. *The wisdom and learning of the Scottish clergy and nobility*

Is it possible that this sort of approach influenced Baron's student Henryson when he came to explore the authority of Scots law? Both men relied upon their learning in Roman law to promote the authority of their own local legal traditions. Furthermore, they both did this in such a way as to distance themselves from Bartolus's approach. To reiterate, Bartolus had argued that the learned laws revealed why lawyers faced with practical problems in the European courts should examine any local sources of law first before turning the *ius commune* itself for guidance. But his approach retained the assumption that the true standard of legal truth, according to which the justice and equity of all laws could be judged, was revealed in the *ius commune* and not in the individual legal traditions of the European jurisdictions. In contrast, Baron and Henryson advanced claims that implied that their own local legal traditions, in France and Scotland, were traditions of legal learning in their own right. They were prepared to utilise their learning in Roman law in order to *confirm* this to be so, but they did not indicate that it was necessary to test each proposition of local law against the learning of Roman law in order to establish its equity and reason. They challenged the idea that legal truth could only be found in one authoritative tradition of legal learning. Additionally, like Baron and Henryson, Chalmers utilised his legal learning in order to promote the authority of Scots law and to argue that it had developed in parallel with Roman law. It was argued above that he too identified the local tradition as a repository of equity and reason.

Furthermore, is it also possible that the Scottish jurists who promoted the authority of the Scottish tradition in 1566 were influenced by the notion that French law constituted a body of learning *because* it had been open to refinement according to expert and wise counsel? Admittedly, there is little direct evidence to suggest that Henryson was influenced by this view. For example, Henryson's claim that Scots law expressed 'the statute and decreit of wyse men'[116] does not demonstrate that he had Baron's argument in mind. And yet there is evidence to suggest that Henryson's colleagues who were appointed to the commission of 1566 may have come to adopt such a view. In 1579, Chalmers emphasised

[116] *Actis and Constitutiounis . . . 1566* [October], Sig. A.3r.

that the monarchs of the Scots ruled with the advice of grave and wise individuals drawn from the ranks of the nobility and the clergy, who enjoyed the right to vote in the Scottish parliaments;[117] the implication was that their wisdom and expertise infused the laws of the realm. In 1578, Bishop Leslie argued that the power of passing or annulling laws in Scotland was expressed in the votes of the three estates, confirmed by the assent of the king.[118] He had already stressed that traditionally the government of the realm had been informed by the divine power and learning that inhered in the authority of the clergy, on the one hand, and by the venerable and wise counsel of the nobility, on the other.[119] He noted that this learning and wisdom had recently been harnessed in the College of Justice, which included representatives of both the nobility and the clergy, whose combined spiritual and temporal prudence enabled the Scottish polity to flourish.[120]

What this shows is that, by the late 1570s, Chalmers and Leslie were prepared to argue that the laws of Scotland had been framed so as to embrace some of the learning and wisdom of the clergy and the nobility, which was expressed in parliaments and in the Session. It may be that this

[117] David Chalmers, *La Recerche des Singularitez plus Remarquables, Concernant l'Estat d'Escosse*... (Paris, 1579), f.8v, 11v, 14r. I have used the copy of the *Recerche* printed by Jean Feurier; two other printers printed the work in Paris in 1579 (Michel Gadoulleau and Robert Coulombel), but the minor variants in these texts do not affect the point made here. It was widely believed in sixteenth-century Scotland that the Scottish nobility constituted the 'monarch's natural born counsellors', seized of 'a political birthright that entailed both a duty to counsel the king and a responsibility to ensure the welfare – the commonweal – of the realm as a whole'. This belief in 'aristocratic conciliarism' is reflected in some of the works of George Buchanan. For this see Roger A Mason, 'Beyond the Declaration of Arbroath: Kingship, Counsel and Consent in Late Medieval and Early Modern Scotland', in Steve Boardman and Julian Goodare, eds., *Kings, Lords and Men in Scotland and Britain, 1300–1625* (Edinburgh, 2014), 265–282, at 277–281; the passages quoted can be found at 278.

[118] John Leslie, *De origine, moribus, et rebus gestis Scotoum libri decem* (Rome, 1578), 71; see also E G Cody, ed., *Leslie's Historie of Scotland* (Scottish Text Society, Series 1, 5, 1888), 120. Cody checked and corrected a translation of Leslie's text made by one Father James Dalrymple in 1596, which I used in conjunction with the Latin text.

[119] See Leslie, *De origine*, 62–70, particularly at 62, 64, 66; Leslie, *Historie*, 105–118, particularly at 105–106, 108–109, 111. I intend to explore elsewhere the significance – if any – of John Knox's claim that Leslie once said in a disputation concerning Catholic doctrine, 'I knaw nothing but the Cannoun Law: and the greatest reassone that ever I could ever fynd thair, is *Nolumus* and *Volumus*'. For this see David Laing, ed., *The Works of John Knox*, 6 vols. (Edinburgh, 1846–1864), vol. 2, 138–141. Elsewhere Leslie undoubtedly promoted the notion that the authority of the law was bound up with its status as a body of learning and truth. For this see Simpson, 'Power, Reason and Equity', 137–146.

[120] Leslie, *De origine*, 74–75; Leslie, *Historie*, 126–127.

sort of attitude informed Chalmers's apparent decision in 1566 to treat Scots law as a body of learning that was comparable to Roman law.[121] If so, the ultimate inspiration for such an approach, which would at least have been consistent with the comments Henryson made concerning the authority of the law, could have come from the work of an author like Henryson's old teacher Baron. It may be that the laws of the Scots were collectively treated as a guide to legal truth because they were thought to have been open, at the stage of their formation, to the influence of the same sort of wise and expert counsel as the laws of the Romans. At present this thesis is highly tentative, but it does seem to make sense of much of the available evidence.[122] Nonetheless, as I have argued in more detail before now, it is possible to explain the decisions of Leslie, Henryson and Chalmers to treat the Scottish legal tradition as a body of learning in other ways.[123] I intend to explore this matter more fully elsewhere.

V. Conclusion

As was explained above, Cairns Fergus and MacQueen argue that renaissance notions of sovereignty, themselves often associated with French humanist thought, may have helped Scottish lawyers writing towards the end of the sixteenth century to conceptualise the authority of the local laws.[124] More specifically, they suggest that these jurists may have anticipated, and then embraced, Bodin's theoretical position that all law-making depends upon an act of sovereign will. But the evidence cited above reveals that at least some sixteenth-century Scottish lawyers sought to promote the authority of their laws on a different basis. These jurists drew upon their legal learning in the *ius commune* in order to argue that the statutes and texts of the Scottish legal tradition possessed the same sort of authority as Roman law, and the learned laws more generally. Henryson made clear his conviction that Scots law was a body of learning, just

[121] Chalmers stressed that it was critical for Scottish monarchs to listen to noble counsel in his *Compendium*; see Chalmers, *Compendium*, BL MS Add. 27472, f.102r.

[122] Further information about Henryson's general thinking concerning the authority of law might be gleaned in the future from a study of his earlier works, which were not specifically concerned with Scots law. These are his treatises entitled *Commentatio in Tit. X. Libri Secundi Institutionem De Testamentis Ordinandis*..., 1555, and *Pro Eg. Barone Adversus A. Goveanum De Jurisdictione Libri II*..., 1554, both of which are printed in Gerardi Meerman, *Novus Thesaurus Juris Civilis et Canonici*..., 7 vols. (Hague, 1751–1753), vol. 3 (1752), 424–482.

[123] See Simpson, *Early Modern Studies of the Scottish Legal Past*, 55–101, 136–154, 224–229.

[124] Cairns, Fergus and MacQueen, 'Legal Humanism'.

like Roman law, and it has been argued that Chalmers believed the same. Those who relied upon Scottish legal texts in disputations before the College of Justice could rest assured that their arguments were based on truth, equity and reason. This would clearly have been significant for any practitioners and judges who continued to endorse an assumption found in the College of Justice during the 1540s, which was that the authority of the law rested upon its conformity with justice and legal truth. No evidence has yet been found to suggest that anyone seriously challenged that assumption during the period considered here. In fact, the appeals made by Henryson and Chalmers to legal learning as a means of promoting reliance on the local laws in practice may reinforce the suggestion that they believed this concept of legal authority was widely held in the Session at this time.

Various arguments could be advanced against this attempt to distinguish the approaches of Henryson and Chalmers from that of Bodin. Bodin did, after all, state that the legislator owed a duty to God to enact laws that were consistent with natural law.[125] Perhaps, Henryson and Chalmers were simply drawing the Queen's attention to a rich source of equitable legal ideas in the local legal tradition, which she, as the legislator, could then adopt or amend. Indeed, as was noted above, Chalmers himself spoke of the need for legal reform under the guidance of the Queen. But what marked out Bodin's concept of legislative sovereignty was his insistence that the binding force of the law did not, and could not, rest upon collective expert recognition of legal truth, but only upon an exercise of sovereign will.[126] This sort of thinking is simply absent from the works of Henryson and Chalmers.

Another argument might be advanced against the attempt made here to distinguish the approach of Chalmers from that of Bodin. Chalmers did state that Queen Mary possessed the same legislative powers as the Roman emperor, and that she was like another Justinian. Furthermore, Chalmers was not as explicit as Henryson was when the latter advanced the claim that Scots law constituted a body of learning. To such objections it can be replied that Chalmers was content to discern and defend the Queen's legislative power through reliance on the learned laws. The truth of the maxim *rex in regno suo est imperator* rested upon the collective recognition of expert lawyers. Furthermore, his primary objection against those who sought to ignore the Scottish legal tradition was that this in itself would

[125] See, for example, Skinner, *Foundations*, vol. 2, 294–295.
[126] See Skinner, *Foundations*, vol. 2, 289–291.

undermine the 'equitie' and 'reasoun' laid down in the learned laws. Seen in this light, Chalmers's arguments look less like those of Bodin and rather like those of a man working within a more traditional framework of legal thought.

Of course, these arguments do not prove that Cairns, Fergus and MacQueen are wrong to suggest that Bodin's theory of legislative sovereignty may have influenced some lawyers practising in Scotland during the second half of the sixteenth century. It remains possible that it did. It is even possible that the emphasis on the authority of the statutory laws of the realm that can be traced in the works of Henryson and Chalmers facilitated the reception of Bodin's ideas later in the century. Yet the argument advanced here tends to support Ford's view as stated above, which is that many lawyers at this time were prepared to accept that the binding force of law in Scotland could be attributed to that which experts in the College of Justice recognised to be just, that is to say legally true.

Even if Henryson and Chalmers did not anticipate the theoretical views of Bodin, their position had shifted subtly from that held by lawyers like Sinclair earlier in the century. Like Sinclair, Henryson and Chalmers accepted the view that learning concerning justice and equity could enjoy the binding force of law. But simultaneously they maintained that the Scottish legal tradition was a repository of legal learning, just like the textual traditions of the *ius commune*. The learned laws no longer represented the sole authoritative standard through which one could discern the meaning of legal truth. Contemporary debates concerning the dissolution of a unitary European *ius commune* in the early-modern period may perhaps be usefully informed by this aspect of the Scottish experience.[127]

[127] So, to some extent, these arguments may serve to complement Osler's claim that during the sixteenth century 'the legal unity of Europe was shattered by the twin forces of the Reformation and the growing power of the emerging national state'. See Douglas J Osler, 'The Jurisprudence of the Baroque', in *Jurisprudence of the Baroque: A Census of Seventeenth Century Italian Legal Imprints, Studien zur europäischen Rechtsgeschichte*, vols. 235–237/Bibliographica Iuridica 4 (Frankfurt am Main, 2009), vol. 1, IX–XXII; the argument pursued at IX–XVI is particularly relevant here. I intend to explain my own view on the subject more fully elsewhere.

6

The sources of early Scots consistorial law

Reflections on law, authority and jurisdiction during the Scottish Reformation

THOMAS GREEN

Within the context of Scots law, consistorial law is that branch of the law which traditionally has concerned marriage, divorce and legitimacy. Prior to the Reformation, the consistorial jurisdiction was the preserve of the courts of the Catholic Church in Scotland, and as such the consistorial law of Scotland was the medieval Canon law of the Catholic Church.[1] During the Reformation crisis of 1559–1560, these courts were suppressed by the Protestant Lords of the Congregation.[2] There followed a brief period during which the earliest tribunals of the Protestant Kirk assumed the consistorial jurisdiction[3] and began to administer what may be conceived of as the early consistorial law of the Church of Scotland.[4] This development of the Protestant Kirk's consistorial jurisdiction was arrested

1 For the workings of these courts see Simon Ollivant, *The Court of the Official in Pre-Reformation Scotland* (Edinburgh: The Stair Society, 1982). Those consistorial decisions of these courts which are still extant have been published in Cosmo Innes, ed., *Liber Officialis Sancti Andree* (Edinburgh: Abbotsford Club, 1845).

2 The traditional thesis that these courts were suppressed by the Papal Jurisdiction Act of 1560 has recently been disproved. See Thomas Green, *The Court of the Commissaries of Edinburgh: Consistorial Law and Litigation, 1559–1576* (PhD Thesis, University of Edinburgh, 2010), 7–13. This thesis may be downloaded free of charge and subject to copyright from the Edinburgh Research Archive at www.era.lib.ed.ac.uk/handle/1842/5456.

3 This was first noted and discussed by the peerage lawyer and genealogist John Riddell, *Inquiry into the Law and Practice in Scottish Peerages: Together with an Exposition of our Genuine, Original Consistorial Law* (Edinburgh: Thomas Clark, 1842), i, 430–433. It was again noted by Gordon Donaldson, 'The Church Courts', in *An Introduction to Scottish Legal History* (Edinburgh: The Stair Society, 1958), 363–373, at 367; and explored further in the seminal article by Sheriff David, B. Smith, 'The Spiritual Jurisdiction 1560–64', *Records of the Scottish Church History Society*, 25 (1995), 1–18, at 4 *et seq*. For some recent remarks on this head see Green, *Court of the Commissaries of Edinburgh* (2010), 82–88.

4 Although the earliest tribunals of the Kirk often purported to enforce 'the law of God' rather than their own unique law. Moreover, the consistorial jurisdiction of these early

by the appointment of the Commissaries of Edinburgh in February 1563/1564.[5]

The Commissaries of Edinburgh were appointed directly by Mary Stewart about half- way through her personal reign,[6] and were entrusted with various national and local jurisdictions previously exercised by the pre-Reformation Courts of the Officials and Officials' Commissaries. Among the new Commissaries' national jurisdictions was an exclusive jurisdiction in all actions concerning marriage, divorce and legitimacy.[7] Since this new central court, and the general system of inferior local Commissary Courts over which it enjoyed an appellate jurisdiction, survived until the second quarter of the nineteenth century,[8] it was the consistorial law of the Commissaries of Edinburgh, and the Commissary system as a whole, which became the unchallenged consistorial law of Scotland. This consistorial law was a mixture of pre-Tridentine Canon law,[9] Roman

courts has often been conflated with the disciplinary jurisdiction which kirk sessions and Superintendents' courts exercised over Protestant congregations.

5 Although the Commissaries consistorial jurisdiction appears to have been resisted by the Protestant Superintendent of Fife, Fotherick and Strathearn sitting at St Andrews (Green, *Court of the Commissaries of Edinburgh* (2010), 222–223; D. H. Fleming, ed., *Register of the Minister, Elders and Deacons of the Christian Congregation of St Andrews* (Edinburgh: Scottish History Society, 1889–1890), i, 267–270).

6 Which ran from her return to Scotland in August 1561 to her forced abdication in July 1567. As is well known, Mary had been sent to France in her childhood to prevent her from being married to Henry VIII's son, Edward, at a time when Scotland was repeatedly invaded by English armies in a series of military engagements know as the Rough Wooing. Mary was subsequently married to Francis Valois, the eldest son of Henry II of France. As is also well known, Mary was Queen of Scots from her earliest infancy, following the death of her father James V, shortly after the Battle of Solway Moss. Mary's first husband was granted the crown matrimonial by the Scottish three estates in 1558, and upon the death of Henry II in 1559, the young couple became king and queen of France as well as Scotland. However, Mary was forced to return to Scotland following her husband's untimely death in December 1560.

7 For which see the founding charter of the Court of the Commissaries of Edinburgh in P. G. B. McNeill, ed., *The Practicks of Sir James Balfour of Pittendreich* (Edinburgh: The Stair Society, 1962–1963), ii, 670–673. An English translation of this charter has been offered in Green, *Court of the Commissaries of Edinburgh* (2010), 254–264. Cf. Fredrick Walton, 'The Courts of the Official and the Commissary Courts 1512–1830', in *An Introductory Survey of the Sources and Literature of Scots Law* (Edinburgh: The Stair Society, 1936), 133–153, at 145–148.

8 For brief details concerning the demise of the Commissary Courts see *Guide to the National Archives of Scotland* (Edinburgh: The Stationery Office & The Stair Society, 1996), 153–155.

9 The reforms of the Council of Trent were never countenanced in Scotland. Most notably, the canon *Tametsi* of 1563, which made clandestinity an impediment to marriage and thereby provided a ground for the annulment of all irregularly contracted marriages, was not enforced in Scotland.

law, the 'law of God', Scottish statute and Scottish 'practick', and various explanations as to the precise blend of these sources as countenanced and enforced by the Commissaries of Edinburgh may be offered.

The religious, political and legal contexts within which the first Commissaries of Edinburgh were appointed, and within which they created early Scots consistorial law through their earliest decreets, or definitive sentences, were highly complex. The deceptive simplicity of the Commissaries' charter of constitution, according to which they were appointed by virtue of nothing more than the 'inaction or absence of the ecclesiastical jurisdiction of the Officials and [pre-Reformation] Commissaries within the Scottish realm', made no explicit mention of the Wars of the Congregation,[10] of the Reformation Parliament of July to August 1560,[11] nor of the consistorial jurisdiction of the tribunals of the Protestant Kirk, yet the contexts created by these events were nevertheless reflected in the consistorial law of the first Commissaries of Edinburgh.

The most important features of the legal context dictated by the tumultuous progress of the Scottish Reformation, prior to appointment of the Commissaries of Edinburgh, may be briefly summarised. The Law of Oblivion, enacted by the first Parliament of Mary Stewart's personal reign in June 1563, consigned to oblivion forever all memory of all actions committed contrary to law from 8 March 1558/1559 until 1 September 1561.[12] This period encompassed the Wars of the Congregation of May 1559 to July 1560, during which the Lords of the Congregation had deposed Mary of Guise from the office of Regent of Scotland, claimed her authority for themselves and presumed to issue ordinances in the names of Mary and Francis, queen and king of Scots, as though they were the Privy Council. At least two such ordinances were the instruments by which the courts of the Catholic Church in Scotland were suppressed during the autumn

[10] The Scottish Reformation began with the Wars of the Congregation, which were a series of military actions carried through by a number of what were initially leading Protestant nobles and their followers. Since the Scottish reformers could not avail themselves of the traditional Protest model of reform by godly prince or magistrate (since the king and queen of Scots and their Regent in Scotland were all Catholics), Protestant reform in Scotland had to be initially carried out by nobles in armed rebellion against the authority of the Regent, Mary of Guise. For the best narrative account of the Wars of the Congregation and the early Scottish Reformation see John Spottiswoode, *The History of the Church of Scotland* (Edinburgh: The Spottiswoode Society, 1847–1851; reprinted New York, AMS Press, 1973), i, 263 *et seq.*

[11] For the best legal discussion of which see Peter McNeill, '"Our Religion, Established Neither by Law or Parliament": Was the Reformation Legislation of 1560 valid?', in *Records of the Scottish Church History Society*, 35 (2005), 68–89.

[12] For the Act see Keith Brown, et al., eds., *Records of the Parliament of Scotland [forthwith RPS]* (St Andrews, 2007), www.rps.ac.uk, A1563/6/1.

of 1559.[13] This period also encompassed the holding of the Reformation Parliament, during which the three estates had attempted to abrogate papal authority in Scotland,[14] and also the period prior to Mary Stewart's return to Scotland, when Scotland had been governed by a provisional government of questionable legitimacy. During these 'years of oblivion', the earliest tribunals of the Protestant Kirk had begun to assume the consistorial jurisdiction, a process which was augmented and enhanced by the appointment of Protestant Superintendents by the General Assembly of the Church of Scotland and the 'Privy Council' active during the year of the provisional government which ruled Scotland between the Reformation Parliament and Mary Stewart's return in August 1561.

While there can be no doubt that, from the perspective of the Protestant party, both clerical and lay, the events of the years 1558/1559 to 1561 had been legitimate, the opinion of many lawyers and of many members of the government of Mary's personal reign was that they had been rebellious, constitutionally invalid and unlawful. The progress of the Reformation prior to Mary's return was nevertheless a religious and political reality, which the sovereign prudently acknowledged upon landing at Leith in August 1561, upon her return from France, through the issuing of something akin to an edict of toleration in favour of the Protestant faction. This 'Proclamation of Leith' of 25 August 1561 accepted the *de facto* consequences of the Reformation crisis by stating that no subjects of the realm should undertake any innovation by which the state of religion, as found universally standing at Mary's return, should be altered.[15] This in effect meant that while the Reformation was not to proceed further, neither were its gains to date to be repealed, nor was the old Catholic order, so imperilled by the 'uproar for religion', to be restored.

The alterations in the religion of Scotland, including the suppression of the courts of the Catholic Church and the development of the early kirk sessions and Superintendents' courts by which the consistorial jurisdiction had been at least partly assumed, were therefore given some form of legal validity by the twin buttresses of the Proclamation of Leith and the Law of Oblivion. Nevertheless, it is clear that, following Mary's return, the nascent Church of Scotland, as yet bereft of proper endowment and

[13] For which see Robert Keith, *History of the Affairs of the Church and State in Scotland* (Edinburgh: Spottiswoode Society, 1844–1850), i, 232–238, 247–248; Cf. Green, *Court of the Commissaries of Edinburgh* (2010), 11–13.

[14] For the Papal Jurisdiction Act of 1560 see *RPS*, A1560/8/4.

[15] J. H. Burton, et al., eds., *The Register of the Privy Council of Scotland* (Edinburgh, 1877), i, 266–267.

establishment, struggled to administer its consistorial jurisdiction, and as such petitioned Mary's Privy Council through the General Assembly, to the effect that some proper order might be taken in that respect.[16]

The response of Mary's government was indirectly to relieve the Church of Scotland of its consistorial jurisdiction through the appointment of the Commissaries of Edinburgh, who were declared by their charter of constitution to be the heirs of the spiritual jurisdiction of the courts of the Catholic Church in Scotland; the charter passed over the role of the Church of Scotland in silence. This was clearly the approach recommended by the commission appointed by the Privy Council in 1563 to advise on the order that should be taken in respect of the 'inaction' of the old courts spiritual, headed by Henry Sinclair, at that time Bishop of Ross and Lord President of the College of Justice.[17] Since the Commissaries' charter of constitution made no explicit mention of the Reformation, the Church of Scotland[18] or the extensive consistorial jurisdiction of the early tribunals of the Church of Scotland, the Commissaries were in effect given no official guidance as to what their policy ought to be in respect of the Canon law of the old consistorial courts, and the early law of the tribunals of the Protestant Kirk.

This situation was further complicated by the fact that in the years immediately following the appointment of the Commissaries of Edinburgh it was still possible for litigants to bring consistorial actions before two other authorities besides the Commissaries themselves, who, as has already been mentioned, were supposed to be exercising an exclusive national jurisdiction in all consistorial actions within the realm. For example, during the period 1565–1567, actions for divorce could be and indeed were heard by John Winram, the Protestant superintendent of Fife, Fotherick and Strathearn at St Andrews,[19] by John Hamilton, the

16 See Donaldson, 'Church Courts' (1958), 368; Smith, 'Spiritual Jurisdiction' (1995), 16–17.

17 *Register of the Privy Council*, i, 252; Green, *Court of the Commissaries of Edinburgh* (2010), 23–25.

18 A relative silence in respect of the Church of Scotland in official state documentation during Mary's personal reign has also been noted by Gordon Donaldson, in James Beveridge and Gordon Donaldson, eds., *Registrum Secreti Sigilli Regum Scotorum* (Edinburgh: Her Majesty's Stationery Office, 1957), volume V, Introduction from page i.

19 For example, Fleming, ed., *Register of the... Congregation of St Andrews* (1889–1890), i, 254–255, 12 December 1565, *Smyth* v. *Duplyn*. This sentence of divorce may be presumed to have been pronounced by the Superintendent's court at St Andrews, rather than just the kirk session there, because the General Assembly had ordained on 31 December 1562 that only Superintendents hear such actions thereafter (Duncan Shaw, ed., *The Acts and Proceedings of the General Assemblies of the Church of Scotland, 1560–1618* (Edinburgh: The Scottish Record Society, 2004), i, 38).

Roman Catholic Archbishop of St Andrews[20] and by the Commissaries of Edinburgh themselves; Superintendent Winram purported to enforce the law of God, Archbishop Hamilton the pre-Tridentine Canon law and the Commissaries a combination of both. In the event, it was the Commissaries who emerged victorious from this period of jurisdictional conflict and whose law therefore endured as the consistorial law of Scotland.

Within this context, the nomination of the four men of law who became the first Commissaries of Edinburgh was highly prudent. In general, while some and perhaps all were Protestants, they were more importantly moderates, who could be expected to steer the consistorial law and jurisdiction away from the potentially radical excesses of the early Church of Scotland, and towards a more conservative retention of the older customs and traditions of the long-accepted norms of the Canon law. The most senior of these men of law, James Balfour, was ideally suited to this role. On the one hand, Balfour had been a radical Calvinist in his youth and had likely studied in Lutheran Wittenberg in the early 1540s. Nevertheless, he had been punished for his membership of the Protestant 'Castilians' who had held St Andrews castle following the murder of David Beaton, Cardinal and legate of Scotland, Archbishop of St Andrews, in 1546,[21] and had been pressed into service in the French fleet;[22] it may be speculated that his time at the oars with John Knox for company may have cured him of his more radical ideas. In any event, by 1553, he was a spiritual judge in the Catholic Church, sitting in St Giles' collegiate church in Edinburgh as – what proved to be – the last holder of the office of Official of Lothian.[23]

[20] Hamilton famously authorised the successful action of annulment on the ground of undispensed consanguinity in the fourth degree, brought by James Hepburn, fourth earl of Bothwell, against his countess, Jane Gordon, in 1567, as a prelude to the former's marriage to Mary, Queen of Scots (for a readable account of which see John Stuart, *A Lost Chapter in the History of Mary Queen of Scots Recovered* (Edinburgh: Edmonston and Douglas, 1874), from p. 9). Although the annulment was granted, it is notoriously known that the impediment of consanguinity standing between Hepburn and Gordon had in fact been dispensed by the Archbishop in February 1565/6. Considerable searches were made for the dispensation during the nineteenth century, and it was successfully located by Stuart at Dunrobin Castle, whence it had likely been conveyed by Jane Gordon, who, subsequent to her divorce from James Hepburn, had married Alexander Gordon, twelfth earl of Sutherland (*ibid.*, 93–94, 5).

[21] For a brilliant account of the cardinal's murder see Margaret H. B. Sanderson, *Cardinal of Scotland: David Beaton, c.1494–1546* (Edinburgh: John Donald, 1986), 225–228.

[22] For a brief account of this stage of Balfour's life see *Balfour's Practicks*, ed. McNeill (1962–1963), i, pp. xii–xiii; cf. Peter G. B. McNeill, 'Balfour, Sir James, of Pittendreich (c.1525–1583)', *Oxford Dictionary of National Biography* (www.oxforddnb.com/view/article/1188, accessed 5 August 2013).

[23] Donald E. R. Watt and Athol L. Murray, eds., *Fasti Ecclesiae Scoticanae Medii Aevi ad annum 1638* (Edinburgh: Scottish Record Society, 2003), 423.

The seeming enigma of Balfour, the Protestant radical, and Balfour, the Catholic judge, may perhaps be explained by his time at Wittenberg, where he may have observed certain features of Lutheranism which fitted him for his role as senior Commissary of Edinburgh. As is well known, Luther and Lutheranism had rejected the Canon law out of hand during the heady years of the first great revolt from the authority of the medieval Church, but by the 1530s had enthusiastically re-embraced 'the accursed papal law' on pragmatic grounds. Indeed, by the time Balfour is thought to have been a student at Wittenberg, the text-book on Canon law used there contained a commendatory preface by none other than Luther himself.[24] There could well have been parallels with the early Scottish Reformation in Balfour's mind, in that the early Protestant Kirk had rejected the Canon law, preferring instead to enforce the 'law of God' in its own tribunals, with all the radical potential this involved.[25]

As to the other Commissaries, it may be said that Balfour was not alone as to quality. On the bench beside him was Edward Henryson, doctor of laws, who had taught civil law at Bourges, and had held a Royal Lectureship in law and Greek at Edinburgh under Mary of Guise. Despite Henryson's considerable credentials as a 'legal humanist', as may readily be anticipated, there is little trace of such learning affecting the workings of the actual sixteenth-century Scottish court over which he presided.[26] Next on the bench was Clement Little, a graduate of Leuven, and a known Protestant convert prior to the crisis of 1559–1560. Little was clearly a pillar of the early Protestant establishment in Edinburgh, who as well as acting as a procurator to the General Assembly of the Church of Scotland, bequeathed his considerable library of theological works to Edinburgh to aid in the work of the training of ministers.[27] The last Commissary, Robert Maitland, is little known beyond his office of Dean of Aberdeen (although he was not a pre-Reformation cleric) and

[24] See John Witte, 'Canon Law in Lutheran Germany', in M Hoeflich, ed., *Lex et Romanitas: Essays for Alan Watson* (Berkeley, CA: Robbins Collection Pub., 2000), 181–224 generally, and 183 for Luther's commendatory preface to the canon law textbook.

[25] For a brief discussion of Scottish Protestant radicalism, the Lutheran example and Balfour see Green, *Court of the Commissaries of Edinburgh* (2010), 89–91.

[26] For Henryson see Marie-Claude Tucker, 'Henryson, Edward [Henry Édouard] (1522–c.1590)', *Oxford Dictionary of National Biography* (www.oxforddnb.com/view/article/12982, accessed 5 August 2013). It should be noted that Henryson was a Protestant and not a moderate Catholic as Tucker has speculated (James Kirk, *Patterns of Reform: Continuity and Change in the Reformation Kirk* (Edinburgh: T & T Clark, 1989), 42).

[27] See Shaw, *Acts and Proceedings* (2004), i, 145; Kirk, *Patterns of Reform* (1989), 40–45, 60 *et seq.*

his later elevation, along with Balfour and Henryson, to the College of Justice.[28]

Having sketched the context within which the first Commissaries of Edinburgh were appointed, and intimated something of the judges' quality and experience, it may now be inquired as to what their early consistorial law was, and as to what authorities were cited before them in litigation during the 1560s and 1570s. As those with experience of sixteenth-century Scottish court records will know, legal authorities are not cited explicitly before the courts as often as might be expected, or indeed hoped for. With respect to the consistorial law of the early Commissaries of Edinburgh, a search through the early manuscript registers of acts and decreets of their court reveals relatively few explicit citations of legal sources. Nevertheless, there is a wealth of general appeals to authority and, perhaps most interesting of all, and despite the Reformation, an almost tranquil acceptance of many Canon law principles as self-evidently the law of Scotland.

There is perhaps a propensity among legal historians approaching the sixteenth century to think of law in terms of sources of law, and the authority of those sources. So in respect of the Canon law contained in Scots consistorial law, it is natural to call to mind Thomas Craig of Riccarton, who as a young man was a procurator before the first Commissaries of Edinburgh,[29] and who was later to reflect in his *Ius Feudale* that 'in Scotland, notwithstanding that we have thrown off the papal yoke, the authority of the Canon Law endures: so much so, that, where it differs from the Civil Law... we follow the Canon Law'.[30] This tantalising suggestion of something approaching a hierarchy of sources in the minds of sixteenth-century Scots lawyers, by which the composition of early Scots

[28] For a full account of these judges and the other personnel of the court over which they presided, including a discussion of religious and political persuasions see Green, *Court of the Commissaries of Edinburgh* (2010), 42–59. It should also be noted that Balfour was replaced on the bench in October 1565 by Alexander Sym, who had also been a royal lecturer in the laws during the regency of Mary of Guise, and who, along with Clement Litill, was appointed as one of the procurators of the Church of Scotland in 1567 (Shaw, *Acts and Proceedings* (2004), i, 145).

[29] Craig was a procurator before the Commissaries from the earliest times (i.e. National Records of Scotland, CC8/2/1, 55v–56r, 12 June 1564, *Cathcart* v. *Cunningham*). His most famous series of cases before the Commissaries concerned the tortuous attempts of Archibald Campbell, fifth earl of Argyll, to rid himself of his first countess, the remarkable Jane Stewart, natural daughter of James V (as is discussed below in respect of the Divorce Act 1573).

[30] Cited in David Sellar, 'A Historical Perspective', in Meston, Sellar and Cooper, eds., *The Scottish Legal Tradition* (Edinburgh: The Saltire Society and The Stair Society, 1991), 29–64, at 41.

consistorial law might be rendered harmonious and rational, does not seem to be borne out by the sources. In fact, given the context faced by the first Commissaries, it may reasonably be anticipated that it would be anachronistic to conceive of them as sitting in the Tolbooth of Edinburgh next to St Giles', having academic discussions about the authority of the sources they were incorporating into early Scots consistorial law. Rather, they were charged with containing the fallout from a fairly chaotic revolution, during a period when the formally established religion of the kingdom was in doubt.

On the one hand, it might be argued that although the Catholic Church had been severely impaired by the Reformation crisis, is was by no means clear that it had been formally disestablished. For lawyers like Balfour and Henryson, the legislation of the Reformation Parliament of 1560, which had purportedly abrogated papal authority, outlawed the Mass, and accepted the Protestant Scots Confession of Faith as defining the religion of the realm, was not to be countenanced[31] – i.e. recognised, sanctioned, acknowledged or enforced – with wide-ranging implications for the position of the Church of Scotland.[32] Indeed, as long as Mary remained Queen of Scots, the Catholic cause could not be considered to be entirely lost and beyond restoration, and nor could the future of the Church of Scotland be regarded as secure.[33]

Within this context, it may be more correct to say that the Commissaries' principal concern was with lawful jurisdiction rather than abstract

[31] Most famously, Balfour and Henryson were among those appointed to a commission during Mary's personal reign to 'visit, sight, and correct the laws of Scotland', which resulted in the publication of the Acts of Parliament from 1424–1564, in 1566, from which volume the legislation of the Reformation Parliament of 1560 was omitted (John Cairns, 'Historical Introduction', in Kenneth Reid and Reinhard Zimmermann (eds.), *A History of Private Law in Scotland* (Oxford: Oxford University Press, 2000), i, 14–182, at 95; *The Actis and Constitutiounis of the Realme of Scotland* (Edinburgh: Robert Lekprevik, 1566), of which a facsimile edition has been printed as *The Acts and Constitutions of the Realm of Scotland* (Glashütten/Taunus: Verlag Detlev Auvermann, 1971)).

[32] For example, the failure of the Church of Scotland to achieve formal establishment until after Mary's personal reign caused the Kirk considerable financial difficulties prior to 1567, including the securing of manses and benefices for ministers in, and pertaining to, the parishes where they served (for a general discussion and detailed specific example of which see Thomas Green, 'Scottish Benefices and the Commissary Court of Edinburgh: The Example of *McGibbon* v. *Struthers*', in Hector L. MacQueen, ed., *Miscellany VI* (Edinburgh: The Stair Society, 2009), 45–61).

[33] It has recently been argued that the order represented by the Commissaries of Edinburgh was temporary, and had been in fact constituted in such as way as to be capable of future reform or indeed abolition, depending on which of the potential religious futures facing Scotland during Mary's personal reign came to pass (Green, *Court of the Commissaries of Edinburgh* (2010), 26–30).

conceptions of the authority of law. Following this line of thought leads to the reflection that the Commissaries enjoyed a full appellate jurisdiction in respect of the decisions of the old courts spiritual.[34] This meant that if the Commissaries had to enforce the terms of a pre-Reformation consistorial sentence, or, for example, hear an action of reduction against a pre-Reformation sentence of divorce, they enforced the law which had been enforced by that jurisdiction at that time. That is to say, law reforms introduced during the Reformation were not retrospectively applied to pre-Reformation cases by the Commissaries, so that when dealing with pre-Reformation cases they administered pre-Tridentine Canon law in its entirety.[35]

From this perspective, the question becomes at what point had pre-Reformation consistorial law changed as far as the Commissaries were concerned by virtue of the Reformation, if indeed it had been changed at all. Given that the Commissaries had been appointed on the assumption that the old courts spiritual were simply inactive, that is to say *de facto* suppressed but not lawfully abolished, while at the same time restricted from discussing the causes of such inaction on account of the Law of Oblivion, it could readily follow that they saw themselves as administering the old consistorial jurisdiction until such time as the courts spiritual became active once again. Since it is known that the two most senior Commissaries of Edinburgh would not countenance the Papal Jurisdiction Act of 1560, it could also follow that, until that Act was ratified in December 1567, the Commissaries did not even consider the inherent authority of the Canon law to have been rejected in Scotland.

Within this specific context it is noteworthy that, of the various consistorial 'law reforms' introduced by the early tribunals of the Church of Scotland, the Commissaries initially accepted only Scottish Protestant divorce on the ground of adultery, which allowed the innocent divorced party to remarry at once.[36] This reform appears to have been accepted

[34] See the charter of constitution of the Commissaries of Edinburgh, at n. 7 above.

[35] Interestingly, a litigant before the Commissaries of Edinburgh did attempt to argue that the new type of Protestant divorce ought to be retrospectively applied to pre-Reformation divorces *a mensa et thoro*, but this attempt appears to have failed (see Thomas Green, *The Consistorial Decisions of the Commissaries of Edinburgh, 1564–1576/7* (Edinburgh: The Stair Society, 2014), Item no. Appendix 2, *Forrester* v. *Abernethy*). Other cases brought before the Commissaries demonstrate the principle that Reformation law reforms could not be retrospectively applied to pre-Reformation cases (i.e. *ibid.*, Item no. 64, *Morton* v. *Morton*), which principle was also confirmed by the post-Marian statutes discussed below.

[36] It would appear that the new kind of Protestant divorce allowed the innocent party to remarry at once, in the same way as the old divorce *a vinculo matrimonii*, while the guilty party remained bound to the marriage until such time as they were freed to remarry by

by the Commissaries principally because the Privy Council had explicitly commissioned various kirk sessions and Superintendents' courts to hear actions of the new type of divorce during the period between the suppression of the old courts spiritual and the appointment of the Commissaries of Edinburgh.[37] As such, when Protestant sentences of divorce pronounced by virtue of Privy Council commissions were produced in litigation before the Commissaries, they appear to have been accepted as having been competently pronounced by a valid jurisdiction, which brought with it an implicit acknowledgement of the legal basis of the new divorce law.

A particularly striking example of this procedural acceptance of law reform occurred in *Hardy* v. *Rutherford*. Here an action for Scottish Protestant divorce had been pursued 'befoir the minister, eldaris and deaconis of Jedburcht [i.e. Jedburgh], be verteu of ane commissioun grantit be the Lordis of Secreit Counsale [i.e. the Privy Council] to thame thairupoun . . . Quhilk actioun of diuorce being concludit befoir the saidis minister, eldaris and deaconis, reddy to the avysing thairwith and geving furth of thair decreit thairin, thai, in respect of the erecting of the jurisdiction of the said Commissarie [i.e. the Commissaries of Edinburgh], on na wyis will pronunce the samyn'. The case was in effect remitted to the new Commissaries, who accepted the process led before the kirk of Jedburgh, and accordingly pronounced a sentence of divorce which conformed to the same on 11 April 1565 in the pursuer's favour on account of the defender's proven adultery.

The legal basis for *Hardy* v. *Rutherford*, as stated in the pursuer's libel contained in the Commissaries' decreet, nevertheless, made no explicit reference to an acknowledged source of law, but rather made only a vague reference to the law or word of God, the main argument being that the new action of divorce was relevant 'sen the ward of God is now sinceirlie

the death of their innocent spouse, rather as though the guilty party had been divorced *a mensa et thoro* only. The reasons for this are complex, but have been discussed in Riddell, *Inquiry into the Law and Practice in Scottish Peerages* (1842), i, 408–409 and in Green, *Court of the Commissaries of Edinburgh* (2010), 103–142.

37 The tribunals of the Kirk also seem to have acted upon their own purported authority from time to time. The jurisdictional aspect of the legacy of the brief ascendancy of the Protestant Kirk in the consistorial jurisdiction is complex, since not all sentences of the Kirk accepted by the Commissaries had proceeded by virtue of Privy Council commissions. Other themes such as the validity of the jurisdiction of Catholic bishops who conformed to the Reformation may also have been at play: for a full discussion of these complexities see Green, *Court of the Commissaries of Edinburgh* (2010), 83–88.

and treulie prechit and His trew kirk erectit in thir partis'.[38] Various other decreets of Protestant divorce on the ground of adultery pronounced by the Commissaries did, however, make direct reference to the word or law of God, although again no specific citations from scripture were ever recorded in the Commissaries' decisions. Various precise forms were offered in support of the new divorce law, usually making general reference to the 'law of God',[39] but also to 'the law of God and justice',[40] 'the law of God and man',[41] and perhaps most notably to 'the law of God and daily practick now observed and kept'.[42] As with other branches of early Scots consistorial law, appeal could also be made simply to the 'the laws of this realm' and 'the laws and practick of this realm'.[43]

Yet although it is clear that the Commissaries accepted what was essentially the early tribunals of the Church of Scotland's understanding of the 'law of God' in respect of the new kind of divorce, there was a good deal more of this 'law of God' as enforced by the Kirk which did not become part of the law of the Commissaries. The obvious example concerns solemnisation on the ground of deflowered virginity. This was based upon Exodus 22:16, which held that he who deflowered a virgin must marry her, unless the girl's father absolutely refused to let the man marry his daughter, in which case the deflowerer was to pay compensation. This was incorporated into the *First Book of Discipline*, and was variously enforced by the kirk session and Superintendent's court at St Andrews, and by the General Assembly of the Church of Scotland.[44] However, this principle, manifestly enjoined by the 'law of God', was never countenanced by the Commissaries of Edinburgh,[45] and faded from the law and practice of

[38] For a full transcription and summary of this decreet see Green, *Consistorial Decisions* (2014), Item no. 15; cf. Item no. 9.

[39] *Ibid.*, Item nos. 11, 16 and 113. [40] *Ibid.*, Item nos. 103 and 117.

[41] *Ibid.*, Item no. 28. [42] *Ibid.*, Item no. A2. [43] *Ibid.*, Item nos. 119, 148 and 94.

[44] J. K. Cameron, ed., *The First Book of Discipline* (Edinburgh: Saint Andrew Press, 1972), 193; Shaw, *Acts and Proceedings* (2004), i, 59 (Thomas Duncanson case); Fleming, ed., *Register of the... Congregation of St Andrews* (1889–1890), i, 185–186, *Reid* v. *Cuthbert.* These cases seemed to have given the deflowered virgin the option of whether to marry or to receive some pecuniary compensation; but if the deflowered virgin wished her deflowerer in marriage, he was to be compelled thereto. I gratefully acknowledge permission to consult Dorothy Anderson's fascinating study *'The Blessed Ordinance of God': A Study in the Decisions of the General Assembly in Relation to Marriage, December 1560–March 1573* (BD dissertation, School of Divinity, University of Edinburgh, 2004), a copy of which was procured for me some years ago by Professor Jane Dawson.

[45] Fortunately for Scots law. To have introduced such a law would have undermined the central importance of the giving of valid consent in the contracting of marriage, and

the Church of Scotland during the 1570s.[46] Clearly, then, the 'law of God' as countenanced by the Church of Scotland did not possess an irresistible authority in and of itself by virtue of the Reformation in relation to the consistorial law of the Commissaries of Edinburgh. Rather, the only innovation based upon this source actually accepted by the Commissaries during Mary's personal reign was Scottish Protestant divorce for adultery,[47] which appears to have been accepted by the Commissaries principally on the basis of the Privy Council's acknowledgement of the temporary consistorial jurisdiction of the Church of Scotland by which such divorces were first introduced into Scotland.

Other areas of the 'law of God' as understood by the Church of Scotland did, however, become part of the law of Scotland by virtue of Acts of Parliament, but in respect of consistorial law this occurred only after Mary's personal reign and the ratification of the legislation of the Reformation Parliament. This process by which the three estates in Parliament sought to recognise the 'law of God' as part of Scots law was distinct from the Commissaries of Edinburgh's jurisdictional approach and provided a secondary layer of legal interpretation of the consequences of the Reformation for Scots consistorial law. The use of statute to regulate which aspects of the 'law of God' would and would not form part of the law of Scotland began in 1563, with the criminalisation of adultery, which was made a capital offence, although the Act made only general reference to 'commandments of God'.[48] In criminal law, this process was continued with the Incest Act of 1567, which did provide an explicit reference to 'the 18th chapter of Leviticus'.[49]

Of more direct relevance for the Commissaries was the Marriage Act of 1567, which was passed by the 'second Reformation Parliament' of December 1567, which ratified the legislation of the Reformation Parliament of August 1560, thereby in effect retrospectively abolishing papal jurisdiction, outlawing the Mass and accepting the Scots Confession of Faith as of August 1560. As part of this process by which the Protestant

would have led to a multitude of difficulties as to proving not only *copula*, but also prior virginity.

46 Cameron (ed.), *First Book of Discipline* (1972), 193, n. 51.

47 See Green, *Consistorial Decisions* (2014), Item nos. 1–22 for the consistorial decreets pronounced prior to the 'second Reformation Parliament' of December 1567.

48 *RPS*, A1563/6/10.

49 *RPS*, A1567/12/14; for an excellent discussion of which see W. D. H. Sellar, 'Marriage, Divorce and the Forbidden Degrees: Canon Law and Scots Law', in W. N. Osborough, ed., *Explorations in Law and History: Irish Legal History Society Discourses, 1988–1994* (Dublin: Irish Academic Press, 1995), 59–82, at 76 *et seq.*

party ascendant sought to define and legitimate the revolution of 1559–1561, the Marriage Act of 1567 addressed the forbidden degrees of consanguinity and affinity, declaring 'that seconds in degrees of consanguinity and affinity, and all degrees outwith the same contained in the word of the eternal God and that are not repugnant to the said word, might and may lawfully marry at all times since 8 March 1558/1559'.[50] Again, no explicit citation of scriptural authority was given, but rather a general reference to the law and word of God. This Act demonstrates an interesting aspect of the role of Parliament in consistorial law, at least prior to the Divorce Act of 1573, in that the three estates sought only to acknowledge the law of God and to declare the date from which it had been applicable in Scotland, rather than to alter the law by virtue of any assertion of the inherent authority of the three estates to alter consistorial law.[51]

The importance of stating an 'appointed day' for the reception of innovations into Scots consistorial law by virtue of the Reformation may be seen in an action of bastardy, *Morton* v. *Morton*, heard by the Commissaries in 1569. The alleged bastard argued, relevantly, that although his parents had married within the prohibited degrees of consanguinity according to the Canon law prior to the Reformation, nevertheless, they had continued to live together as husband and wife after the 'Reformation of Religion' and as such could be considered to have contracted marriage anew, in conformity with the Marriage Act of 1567, thereby legitimating their issue *per subsequens matrimonium*. The alleged bastard proved this to have been the case, and as such was decerned legitimate by the Commissaries.[52]

While the Marriage Act of 1567 had sought to acknowledge the law of God and to determine a date from which it had applied in Scotland, the Divorce for Malicious Desertion Act of 1573 also purported to do the same, when it, in fact, simply prescribed new law. The Divorce Act resulted from the marital difficulties of the fifth earl of Argyll, whose first countess, Jane Stewart, natural daughter of James V, refused to adhere to him,

[50] *RPS*, A1567/12/15. The 'appointed day' of this Act appears to have recalled the start date of the period encompassed by the Act of Oblivion of 1563. The General Assembly of the Church of Scotland had stated what the 'law of God' was in respect of the forbidden degrees of consanguinity and affinity on 21 December 1560 (Shaw, *Acts and Proceedings* (2004), i, 5).

[51] This is an interesting distinction, which suggests that the three estates, having rejected the legislative authority of the bishops of Rome in respect of Canon law, did not move directly to assume the papal legislative competence in respect of consistorial law, but rather sought to acknowledge laws conceived of as having been directly legislated by God as being part of Scots law.

[52] See Green, *Consistorial Decisions* (2014), Item no. 64.

despite the earl having obtained a decreet of adherence against her from the Commissaries of Edinburgh in January 1571/1572.[53] Various further diligence was done against the countess to compel her adherence, but she proved singularly resistant to them all. Since the earl had neither legitimate issue, nor could procure his lawful wife's adherence, he determined to obtain a sentence of divorce which would grant him licence to remarry at once, by virtue of which subsequent lawful marriage he hoped to produce legitimate issue. The difficulty lay in the fact that obstinate or malicious desertion was not clearly a ground for Protestant divorce in Scotland. Rather, it may be demonstrated that, prior to the Divorce Act of 1573, neither the Commissaries of Edinburgh nor the General Assembly of the Church of Scotland could positively assert that malicious desertion was a ground of Scottish Protestant divorce, in addition to adultery.[54] Nevertheless, in 1573, the three estates in Parliament declared Scottish Protestant divorce on the ground of malicious desertion to have been the law of Scotland 'in all times past, since the true and Christian religion was publicly preached, avowed and established within this realm, namely, since the month of August 1560'.[55] Curiously, there was not even a general mention of the law or word of God, as had been the case in earlier Acts, and the 'appointed day' of this Act was almost a year and a half later than that contained in the Marriage Act of 1567. Nevertheless, the Commissaries of Edinburgh pronounced a decreet of divorce, in conformity with the Divorce Act of 1573, in the earl of Argyll's favour on 22 June 1573.[56]

Apart from Scottish Protestant divorce on the grounds of adultery and malicious desertion, together with a reduction of the forbidden degrees of consanguinity and affinity, no other obvious law reforms were introduced into Scots consistorial law, which for the remainder was therefore still held by the Commissaries to be Canon law.[57] This meant, for example, that

[53] For a transcription of which see *ibid.*, Item no. 95.

[54] See Riddell, *Inquiry into the Law and Practice in Scottish Peerages* (1842), i, 546 *et seq*; Jane Dawson, 'The Noble and the Bastard: the Earl of Argyll and the Law of Divorce in Reformation Scotland', in J Goodare and A. A. MacDonald, eds., *Sixteenth-Century Scotland: Essays in Honour of Michael Lynch* (Leiden: Brill, 2008), 147–168, at 162–164; Shaw, *Acts and Proceedings* (2004), i, 314; Green, *Court of the Commissaries of Edinburgh* (2010), 144–146.

[55] *RPS*, A1573/4/2.

[56] For a transcription of which see Green, *Consistorial Decisions* (2014), Item no. 111. This was the first known divorce of its kind for malicious desertion pronounced in Scotland.

[57] Some aspects of the old Canon law, such as *cognatio spiritualis* and the relation between religious vows and promises of marriage, simply ceased to be raised before the Commissaries. Whether or not such abeyance actually removed such principles from the law of Scotland seems to have been decided in *Gordon* v. *Gordon* (1697), when the Court of

pre-Tridentine laws concerning irregular marriages were retained entirely by the Commissaries of Edinburgh, and indeed remained the law of Scotland until 1940.[58] However, the Canon law was never explicitly cited to support the law of irregular marriage, except on one occasion, during the first twelve years worth of cases brought before the first Commissaries of Edinburgh. In *Dunlop* v. *Brown* (1564/1565), the defender had excepted to an action of Scottish Protestant divorce on the ground of adultery that she was irregularly married to her alleged paramour. It was alleged that this irregular marriage had been predicated upon an exchange of promises of marriage in words of the future tense, which promises had been fortified by an oath, and which had subsequently been ratified by copulation. In this respect, it was relevantly argued that this was a lawful marriage 'quod sponsalia defuturo si sequuta est copula carnalis efficiunt matrimonium indissolubile, ut capitulum veniens etc, et in capiteis qui fidem dedit de sponsalibus et matrimoniis, speacillie si sponsalia confirmata sint iuramento, as is contenit at mair lenth in capite ex literis syluanj de sponsalibus et matrimoniis'. These three citations are taken from Book IV, title I of the *Decretals of Pope Gregory IX*, namely X. 4.1.15, 30, and 10, respectively.[59] This argument and its attendant citations were accepted by the Commissaries as stating the law of Scotland, and accordingly admitted to the defender's probation, although in the event she failed to prove the same.[60]

There is only one other case where the Decretals of Gregory IX (or any of the other constituent parts of what went on to be known as the *Corpus Iuris Canonici*) were explicitly cited in litigation before the Commissaries,

Session held, contrary to the Commissaries of Edinburgh, that divorce *a mensa et thoro* remained a competent remedy for adultery in Scots law, despite the fact that such a remedy had not been sought since the Reformation (James Fergusson, *A Treatise on the Present State of the Consistorial Law in Scotland* (Edinburgh: Bell & Bradfute, 1829), 190 (treatise pagination) *et seq*; Patrick Fraser, *Treatise on Husband and Wife, According to the Law of Scotland* (Edinburgh: T & T Clark, 1876–1878), ii, 904–905).

58 W. D. H. Sellar, 'Marriage by Cohabitation with Habit and Repute: Review and Requiem?', in D. L. Carey Miller and D. W. Myers, eds., *Comparative and Historical Essays in Scots Law. A Tribute to Professor Sir Thomas Smith QC* (Edinburgh, 1992), pp. 117–136. The two forms of irregular marriage countenanced in pre-Tridentine Canon law were abolished in Scotland by the Marriage (Scotland) Act (1939). As is well known, a third type of irregular marriage, possibly unique to Scots consistorial law, namely marriage by cohabitation with habit and repute, continued in Scotland until abolished by the Family Law (Scotland) Act (2006).

59 For which see A. Friedberg, ed., *Corpus Iuris Canonici* (Graz: Akademische Druck-u. Verlagsanstalt, 1959), ii, 664, 666–667, 672.

60 For a transcription and summary of this case see Green, *Consistorial Decisions* (2014), Item no. 11.

and that arose in an action for adherence, *Thornton* v. *Sanderson*, where the defender relevantly excepted that he had been justified in deserting the pursuer, since 'repellitur vxor petens restitutione si notorie fornicata est'.[61] This was a direct quote from the *Decretals* 4.19.4, the principle being that a wife who petitions for the return of her husband is to be repelled if she is a notorious fornicator, so long as her husband has remained continent.[62]

In the main, these and other parts of Scots consistorial law founded directly on Canon law appear to have been simply accepted as being part of the law and daily 'practick' of the realm. Thus, in *Crawfurd* v. *Crawfurd* (1564) it was argued relevantly by an alleged bastard that his parents had married after his birth 'and sua be the commone law and dailie practik of this realme, howbeit the said [alleged bastard] had bene gottin and borne in fornicatioun, zit be the mariage foirsaid, following thaireftir betuix his said father and mother, he wes maid lauchfull and thairfoir aucht to be decernit lauchfull and to succeid to his landis, gudis, and heretage'.[63] So while the alleged bastard might have reasonably cited Book IV, title 17 of the *Decretals of Gregory IX*, he chose instead to assert that the principle of legitimation *per subsequens matrimonium* should be observed by virtue of the common law and daily 'practick' of Scotland.

Other Canon law principles seem to have been accepted into early Scots consistorial law with no reference to any source of law whatsoever, as was the case with reconciliation. Reconciliation of an innocent party with his or her adulterous spouse was a relevant exception to an action of divorce on the ground of adultery before the Commissaries; however, no authority was even cited in support of this principle, although both Roman and Canon law could have been cited explicitly.[64]

The early tribunals of the Church of Scotland are also known to have held reconciliation to be relevant in respect of disregarding any adultery committed prior to reconciliation. In a fairly complex and unique case, heard by John Willock, Superintendent of Glasgow, and decided in August 1563, it was argued by the pursuer that he ought to be divorced from his

61 *Ibid.*, Item no. 23. It is noteworthy that this decreet was pronounced on 7 January 1567/8, twenty-three days after the three estates had ratified the Papal Jurisdiction Act of 1560 (i.e. *RPS*, A1567/12/1).

62 Friedberg, ed., *Corpus Iuris Canonici* (1959), ii, 721.

63 Green, *Consistorial Decisions* (2014), Item no. Appendix A1a.

64 For example, Codex 9.9.11 states that a husband may not accuse his wife of adultery if he has continued in marriage with her after the offence, while in Gratian's *Decretum*, Case 32, question 1, chapters five to seven permit reconciliation following adultery, but only after due penance (Friedberg, ed., *Corpus Iuris Canonici* (1959), i, 1116–1117).

wife on the grounds of her adultery. Against this it was excepted that the pursuer had also committed adultery. To this it was replied that he had indeed committed adultery, but had been reconciled to his wife, after which reconciliation she had committed adultery, and as such only her adultery was pertinent in litigation. This was in the event found relevant and proven, and the couple were divorced and the husband granted licence to remarry, which licence he exercised almost immediately. Within six months of the pursuer's second marriage, his second wife gave birth to a child, acknowledged by both to be theirs. The first wife therefore pursued for reduction of the Superintendent's sentence of divorce before the Commissaries of Edinburgh (who had been appointed in the interim), on the ground that her husband must also have committed adultery after the date of the reconciliation, as evidenced by the date of birth of the child to the second wife, and that as such he had been likewise guilty of adultery at the time of the pronouncing of the Superintendent's sentence of divorce, which ought therefore to be reduced.[65]

This argument was found relevant and in the event proven, since the other classic defence to an action grounded on adultery both before and after the Reformation, was recrimination, or mutual guilt of adultery. While this principle was not supported by a citation in *Hamilton* v. *Maxwell & Lindsay*,[66] it was, however, explicitly supported before the Commissaries by a direct citation from Roman law in *Fleming* v. *Fleming* (1569). In that case, the defender to the action, having admitted committing adultery, nevertheless argued relevantly that the pursuer 'havand comittit the like offence with [a named paramour], can not be hard to persew hir for the allegit adultery libellit be him, bot ane offence aucht tobe recompensit with the vther, *cum de jure paria delicta mutua compensatione tolluntur*'.[67] This is a direct citation from Justinian's Digest 23.3.39, which holds like moral faults to cancel each other out.[68]

65 For a transcription and summary of this litigation see Green, *Consistorial Decisions*, Item no. 12, *Hamilton* v. *Maxwell & Lindsay* (1564/5).

66 Or indeed in various other cases heard by the Commissaries, i.e. *ibid.*, Items nos. 23, 97, 115, 128, 157, 178.

67 *Ibid.*, Item no. 56.

68 'Where a husband and wife accuse each other of immorality in court and it is declared that both of them have given cause for repudiation, the decision should be taken to mean that since they have both treated the law with contempt, neither can make use of it in their claims, as their faults disappear when set against each other' (*The Digest of Justinian*, trans. and ed. Alan Watson, et al. (Philadelphia: University of Pennsylvania Press, 1998), ii, 725). Reference could also have been made to Gratian's *Decretum*, Case 32, question 6, chapter one (*Corpus Iuris Canonici*, ed. Friedberg (1959), i, 1139).

From the foregoing reflections, it may be said that the Commissaries of Edinburgh, as inheritors, or possibly even temporary administrators, of the consistorial jurisdiction of the Catholic Church in Scotland, continued to enforce the entire Canon law in respect of any matters which came before them pertaining to the period prior to the Reformation. After the date of the Reformation, howsoever determined, it was held that various parts of the 'law of God' were now the law of Scotland. Only in respect of Scottish Protestant divorce on the ground of adultery did the Commissaries directly accept the purported law of God to be the law enforced in their own court, and that likely because that specific aspect of the 'law of God' and the attendant jurisdiction by which it had been first introduced into Scotland had been explicitly acknowledged by the Scottish Privy Council prior to the Commissaries' appointment. This would suggest that for the Commissaries themselves, the central principle governing the composition of early Scots consistorial law was not their understanding of the authority of the sources of which that law was composed, but rather their understanding of their own consistorial jurisdiction in relation to the consistorial jurisdictions of the pre-Reformation Church and of the Protestant Kirk. Any further reforms to early Scots consistorial law were explicitly declared by post-Marian Parliaments to have occurred by virtue of the Reformation, fairly convincingly in respect of the forbidden degrees in 1567, and less so concerning malicious desertion in 1573, both of which Acts were nevertheless enforced by the Commissaries of Edinburgh. In this respect, statute formed a secondary layer of legal interpretation of the Reformation, which augmented and overlaid the Commissaries' earlier interpretation based upon lawful jurisdiction. As to the rest of the early consistorial law of Scotland, it was consistent for the Commissaries to continue to enforce the law they were obliged to acknowledge as the law of Scotland up to the Reformation, namely pre-Tridentine Canon law, with the traditional ancillary support from Roman law. As has been noted, this allowed litigants to cite legal principles relevantly from the *Decretals of Pope Gregory IX* and from the *Digest of Justinian* before the Commissaries of Edinburgh.[69] Nevertheless, in the vast majority of cases where the norms of the old Canon law continued to be applied, appeal was made either to the authority of 'the laws and daily practick of this realm', or no appeal to authority was made at all.

[69] It may be presumed that other sources of Canon and Roman law could also have been cited relevantly before the Commissaries, but there is no explicit evidence to this effect during the era of the Reformation.

In these respects, it would seem that what made sense for the Commissaries of the mixture of Canon law, Roman law, the 'law of God', statute and 'daily practick' which underpinned early Scots consistorial law was not any abstract idea about the authority of these sources, but rather in the first instance the authority of the jurisdictions by which these laws had been variously enforced in Scotland prior to the Commissaries' appointment, and in the second instance the authority of the three estates to declare what the legal consequences of the Reformation had been. Within this context, the early consistorial law of the Commissaries of Edinburgh can be seen as the product of the learning and conservatism of the bench, overlaid with the more mechanical, and sometimes less historically accurate, impositions of the three estates. Beyond these more theoretical considerations, there is a profound sense that the old Canon law, having been for so long part of the law and practick of Scotland in the minds of judges, men of law and the laity, was held to be self-evidently the received law of Scotland. This sense of custom, of old familiar usage and even of Scottish-ness may well have transcended abstract notions of authority, even papal authority, and provided the vehicle by which the old ideas, alongside the new, endured in Protestant Scotland.

7

Conciliar authority and equitable jurisdiction in early-modern Scotland

J.D. FORD

In his *Basilikon doron*, James VI instructed his elder son and heir 'to haunt your Session, and spie carefully their proceedings', believing that his own presence in the supreme civil court of Scotland had served to prevent partiality and to encourage expedition in the handling of cases.[1] The court comprised fifteen judges generally known as 'lords of council and session', though since 1532 they had become formally designated 'Senators of the College of Justice'.[2] Originally appointed under the auspices of parliament or council to determine disputes that could not be brought within the ordinary legal process, the lords of council and session had become by the later sixteenth century judges of law as well as equity, with the primary role of administering justice according to law.[3] James recognised as much in proceeding to instruct his son that he must 'discerne betwixt Justice and equitie', not redistributing wealth between the rich and the poor (as Cyrus, in Xenophon's account, had been chided for doing), but protecting the rights of his subjects.[4] The future king of Scots was always to be mindful that 'Justice, by the Law, giveth every man his owne', whereas 'equitie, in things arbitrall, giveth every one that which is meetest for him'.[5] James did not explain what he meant by 'things arbitrall', or how far the lords of session might legitimately deal with such matters, but he did identify a question that still needs to be answered by anyone intent on providing a satisfactory explanation of the role of the lords of

[1] C. H. McIlwain, ed., *Political Works of James I* (Cambridge, MA, 1918), p. 39.

[2] A. M. Godfrey, 'Scotland: The Court of Session from its Foundation to 1800', in A. A. Wijffels, ed., *European Supreme Courts: A Portrait through History* (London, 2013), p. 190.

[3] A. M. Godfrey, *Civil Justice in Renaissance Scotland: The Origins of a Central Court* (Leiden, 2009).

[4] Xenophon, *Cyropaedia*, 2 vols., trans. W. Miller (Cambridge, MA, 1914), 1.3.17.

[5] *Political Works of James I*, p. 39 (punctutation and spelling slightly adjusted here and elsewhere).

session in the legal system of early-modern Scotland. To what extent did they continue to enjoy the equitable jurisdiction that had been exercised by their predecessors on the strength of the conciliar authority devolved to them by one branch or another of the *curia regis*? The aim of this paper is not to offer the kind of answer to the question that is ultimately required, based on painstaking analysis of the voluminous records of the early-modern court, but is rather to examine a number of different ways in which contemporary observers began to address the question. Each approach adopted involved a particular view of the relationship between law and authority, and while the focus here is on how these different views informed discussion of the role of the lords of session in Scotland, it will be apparent that the different views outlined have broader significance in the legal history of Britain and beyond. In other words, the Scottish experience should serve to exemplify some of the modes of thought examined more widely in this volume.

I. A historical perspective

In offering instruction on kingship to his son, James was inevitably mindful of the instruction he had himself been offered by his former tutor, the humanist scholar George Buchanan.[6] In his *Rerum Scoticarum historia*, dedicated to James in 1582, Buchanan had remarked that the foundation of the College of Justice had proved to be a disappointment.[7] He explained that in Scotland there were virtually no laws (*leges*) except acts of parliament (*conventuum decreta*), that these acts were not normally introduced on a permanent basis (*non in perpetuum, sed in tempus facta*) and that the judges did all they could to obstruct further legislative intervention (*lationem legum impediant*). The consequence was that property rights (*omnium civium bona*) were entrusted to the will (*arbitrium*) of fifteen men, whose power seemed wholly tyrannical (*imperium plane tyrannicum*) since their rulings alone served as laws (*arbitria sola sunt pro legibus*). The lords of session therefore failed to administer justice according to law and were in effect *quindecim tyranni*, a complaint that was revived and widely recirculated a century later.[8] 'Buchanans observation

6 Although James encouraged his son to become 'well versed in authentick histories', he immediately added that he did not mean 'such infamous invectives, as Buchanans' (*ibid.*, p. 40).

7 *Rerum Scoticarum historia* (Edinburgh, 1582), f. 147v; *The History of Scotland*, 2 vols., trans. J. Aikman (Glasgow, 1827), vol. 2, p. 306.

8 *A Representation to the High Court of Parliament, of Some of the Most Palpable Grievances in the Colledge of Justice* (n.p., n.d.), pp. 1–2; [George Mackenzie, earl of Cromarty], *A*

upon thair institution is still the same', one writer lamented in 1674, 'that as they desyre no lawes to be thair rule but thair owne opinions, which they may alter and use as they pleas, so they would willingly wish they had no superior to mack them lawes to be thair rules in thair sentences and interloquitors'.[9]

An eighteenth-century editor of Buchanan's *Historia* found his account of the Scottish *collegium iudicum* reminiscent of Livy's account of the Carthaginian *iudicum ordo*, in which the domination of those *perpetui iudices* over the people (*res fama vitaque omnium in illorum potestate erat*) was brought to an end by Hannibal's enactment of legislation (*legem extemplo promulgavit*).[10] Like Hector Boece, whose *Scotorum historia* he was to some extent intent on updating, Buchanan certainly aimed in writing about Scotland to rework classical models like Livy's history of Rome, and recollection of this passage would help to explain his remark that the property rights of the people were placed under the *perpetua potestas* of the judges.[11] Another, and more obvious, source was Justin's epitome of the lost *Historiae Philippicae* of Pompeius Trogus, which was not unusual among ancient histories in maintaining that nations subjected themselves to princes before they were subjected to laws, but was unique in stating that until laws were introduced, *arbitria principum pro legibus erant.*[12] Elsewhere in his book, Buchanan tended to use the word *arbitrium* to signify unlimited discretion or mere caprice.[13] As an example of tyrannical

Friendly Return to a Letter Concerning Sir George Mackenzie and Sir John Nisbet's Observation and Responce on the Matter of the Union (n.p., 1706), pp. 22–3; [Thomas Spence], *The Testamentary Duty of the Parliament of Scotland, with a View to the Treaty of Union Now on Foot and Considerably Advanced betwixt the Two Kingdoms* (n.p., 1707), pp. 8–9.

9 National Library of Scotland, MS 9375, f. 22v.

10 Buchanan, *Rerum Scoticarum historia*, J. Mann, ed. (Aberdeen, 1762), p. 409; Livy, *Ab urbe condita*, 14 vols., trans. B. O. Foster, et al. (Cambridge, MA, 1919–59), 33.46.

11 I. D. McFarlane, *Buchanan* (London, 1981), pp. 416–17 and 424–6; J. MacQueen, 'Aspects of Humanism in Sixteenth- and Seventeenth-Century Literature', in J. MacQueen, ed., *Humanism in Renaissance Scotland* (Edinburgh, 1990), p. 10, at pp. 20–28; N. R. Royan, 'The *Scotorum historia* of Hector Boece: A Study', D.Phil. dissertation (Oxford, 1996), pp. 116–45.

12 Marcus Iunianus Iustinus, *Epitoma historiarum Philippicarum Pompei Trogi*, ed. O. Seel (Leipzig, 1935), 1.1.2; Justin, *Epitome of the Philippic History of Pompeius Trogus*, trans. J. C. Yardley (Atlanta, 1994), p. 14; *The Roman Antiquities of Dionysius of Halicarnassus*, 7 vols., trans. E. Cary (Cambridge, MA, 1937–50), 10.1; Tacitus, *Annals*, 3 vols., trans. J. Jackson (Cambridge, MA, 1931), 3.26. Cf. Livy, *Ab urbe condita*, 37.54.

13 *Rerum Scoticarum historia*, ff. 2r, 11v, 18v, 34r, 41v, 43r, 57v, 69v, 82r, 86v, 92v–3r, 109r, 128r, 139r, 140r, 143, 165v–6r, 167v, 170v–1r, 174r, 184r, 196r and 203v–4r; *History of Scotland*, vol. 1, pp. 8, 61, 104, 186, 226, 233, 311, 375 and 441, and vol. 2, pp. 16, 50, 126, 215, 267, 270, 285, 289, 390, 392, 399, 416–17, 430, 474, 527, 560 and 563. Less often Buchanan used the word to mean the rulings of arbiters (e.g., *Rerum Scoticarum historia*,

behaviour, he mentioned a mythical king who *ad suum arbitrium causas capitales revocat*, and after later recalling that the acts of the Reformation parliament had been refused ratification by James VI's mother, whose deposition he meant to justify, he remarked that this was her first *manifesta tyrannidis professio.*[14] Conscious that they had no laws except acts of parliament (*nullas habeant leges, praeter conventuum decreta*), the Scots had been alarmed at the prospect of life under a queen *cuius arbitrium pro legibus habendum esset.* In another attempt to justify Mary's deposition, still on the basis of *veterum sententiae*, Buchanan argued again in his *De iure regni apud Scotos dialogus* that it was their experience of a time *cum libido regum pro legibus esset* (another phrase from Justin) that induced people to enact laws, and that afterwards it was the touchstone of tyranny for kings to dispense with the laws enacted.[15] Throughout his *Historia* he contrasted examples of kings who enacted and enforced sound *leges* with those who nullified and neglected them.[16]

In distinguishing in this way between the *legitimum imperium* of rulers who adhered *ad legum praescriptum* and the *tyrannis* of others who directed their rule *ad unius libidinem* Buchanan pursued the same line of argument as Hector Boece and his slightly earlier successors, the lords of session John Leslie and David Chalmers.[17] However, these earlier historians had not only contrived to give the impression that the legislation of the Scottish kings had been rather more extensive and diverse than Buchanan's references to *conventuum decreta* suggested, but had also indicated that the Scots had many *consuetudines veteres, mores maiorum* and *prisca instituta*, which were understood to derive at least some binding force from *tacitus consensus populi.*[18] Buchanan also made reference to the

ff. 30v, 80v, 96r and 208v; *History of Scotland*, vol. 1, pp. 168 and 435, and vol. 2, pp. 65 and 584).

14 *Rerum Scoticarum historia*, ff. 36v and 190r; *History of Scotland*, vol. 1, p. 200, and vol. 2, p. 502.

15 Buchanan, *A Dialogue on the Law of Kingship among the Scots*, ed. R. A. Mason, trans. M. S. Smith (Aldershot, 2004), pp. 14–15 and 34–5; Iustinus, *Epitoma historiarum Philippicarum*, 2.7.3; Justin, *Epitome of the Philippic History*, p. 34.

16 *Rerum Scoticarum historia*, ff. 29r, 30r, 32v–3r, 34r, 50r, 51r, 52r, 56v–7r, 58v, 59v, 60, 64r, 100v, 102v, 106, 124r, 126v, 178v, 182r, 185v and 197r; *History of Scotland*, vol. 1, pp. 161, 164, 166, 180–1, 186, 272–3, 278, 284, 307, 309, 316, 321, 324–5, 327 and 344, and vol. 2, pp. 87, 95, 113, 197, 209, 449, 465, 482 and 529.

17 *Rerum Scoticarum historia*, f. 185v; *History of Scotland*, vol. 2, p. 482. On Chalmers especially, and also Leslie see the contribution to this volume by Andrew Simpson.

18 Boece, *Scotorum historia* (Paris, 1575), ff. 16, 20, 22–3r, 24v–5r, 58r, 76v–7r, 79r, 82v, 93v, 102v, 200v–1v, 215r, 220, 231–2, 234r, 238v–9r, 250v–1r, 256, 260r, 275, 279v–80r, 298r, 348v and 349v; Boece, *Scotorum Historia*, trans. D. F. Sutton (www.philological/bham.ac.uk), 2.12–14, 2.23, 2.29, 2.31, 2.38–9, 4.25, 5.15, 5.22, 5.34, 6.23, 6.51, 10.55–8, 10.98,

ancient customs, habits and institutions of the Scots, to which he clearly attached some importance, but he never described any of them as a kind of law.[19] The closest he came to doing so was in a passage concerned with the law (*lex*) regulating the succession to the throne, which he described as giving new force to an existing custom (*vetustam Scotorum consuetudinem nova sanctione confirmasse*), yet his purpose here was to prove that the law was just by arguing that the Scots had conducted their affairs in the way later stipulated even when they were not obliged (*obstricti*) to do so.[20] In a passage from his *Dialogus*, he imputed to his interlocutor Thomas Maitland, an advocate before the lords of session, the opinion that custom could acquire the force of law (*diuturnae consuetudinis tanta vis est, ut apud me legis vigorem obtineat*).[21] Although Maitland's words were borrowed from the jurist Callistratus, who had claimed to be relaying the words of the emperor Septimius Severus, Buchanan dismissed the opinion with the remark that custom was a form of tyranny.[22] In his own opinion, where *leges* were lacking, there could be nothing except *arbitria* and thus tyranny, for what he referred to as *legum auctoritas* was the only authority he was prepared to recognise behind laws.[23]

Buchanan's apparent reluctance to regard *tacitus consensus populi* as a source of legal authority needs to be considered further in connection

11.14, 11.45–50, 11.54, 11.68, 12.12–15, 12.31, 12.41, 13.24, 13.41, 14.21, 17.10 and 17.14; Leslie, *De origine, moribus et rebus gestis Scotorum* (Rome, 1578), pp. 74–7, 83, 84, 86, 96, 103, 108, 142–3, 145, 150, 182, 197, 200, 202–4, 213, 246, 274, 300, 306, 333, 343, 376, 522, 524 and 573; Leslie, *The Historie of Scotland*, 2 vols., trans. J. Dalrymple (Edinburgh, 1888–95), vol. 1, pp. 118–24, 131, 133, 136–7, 152–3, 162, 171, 218–19, 222–3, 230, 275, 184, 294, 297, 300–303 and 314–15, and vol. 2, pp. 69, 110–11, 121, 223, 355, 358–9 and 448; Chalmers, *Histoire abbregée de tous les roys de France, Angleterre et Escosse* (Paris, 1579), ff. 4r, 5, 8v, 18v, 21v, 24r, 60v, 100v, 103r, 104v, 116v, 121v, 126r and 186v, and *La recerche des singularitez plus remarquables, concernant l'estat d'Escosse* (Paris, 1579), ff. 2 and 21v–7r.

19 These concepts feature in many of the passages cited in n. 16 above, and see too *Rerum Scoticarum historia*, f. 62v; *History of Scotland*, vol. 1, pp. 337–8, where, in the space of a single page, *lex* is used to mean law while *consuetudo* appears to mean no more than behaviour.

20 *Rerum Scoticarum historia*, f. 120; *History of Scotland*, vol. 2, pp. 49–52.

21 *Dialogue on the Law of Kingship among the Scots*, pp. 108–9. On this passage see J. W. Cairns, T. D. Fergus and H. L. MacQueen, 'Legal Humanism and the History of Scots Law: John Skene and Thomas Craig', in J. MacQueen, *Humanism in Renaissance Scotland*, p. 48, at pp. 62 and 64.

22 *Digest*, 1.3.38, in *Corpus iuris civilis*, 3 vols., eds. T. Mommsen et al. (Berlin, 1875), and *The Digest of Justinian*, 4 vols., ed. A. Watson (Philadelphia, 1985).

23 *Rerum Scoticarum historia*, f. 201r; *History of Scotland*, vol. 2, p. 549. On this point see further below.

with a passage in his *Dialogus* that has attracted a great deal of attention. Having argued that kings must rule in accordance with laws and must not be trusted to make laws for themselves, Buchanan added that he did not mean to entrust law-making instead to the people at large (*universi populi iudicio*).[24] His idea, broadly in keeping with Scottish practice (*prope ad consuetudinem nostram*), was that representatives of every class of people should meet with the king in council (*ex omnibus ordinibus selecti ad regem in consilium coirent*), and that any bill (*προβουλευμα*) they approved should be placed before the people for final approval (*ad populi iudicium deferretur*). To several readers, it has seemed that Buchanan was recommending here the use of some form of referendum process, though it is difficult to see how this reading can be reconciled with his claim to be reflecting present practice.[25] To other readers, it has seemed that he was thinking of the normal practice in Scottish parliaments of electing a committee known as 'the lords of the articles' to prepare bills for approval by the whole assembly.[26] One difficulty with this reading is that it involves a distinction between the *universus populus*, whose *iudicium* was not exercised in the passing of legislation, and the *populus*, whose *iudicium* was exercised when bills were passed, though the epithet *universus* would appear to apply more naturally to the people when assembled in a parliament.[27] A more serious difficulty is that while the phrase *ad regem in consilium coirent* may be taken to describe quite accurately the assembling of the people in a parliament, it can only be taken to describe the meeting of the lords of the articles if they are reckoned to have been members of the king's council who directed the business of parliament on his behalf.[28] The difficulty is that recent research has shown this

24 *Dialogue on the Law of Kingship among the Scots*, pp. 54–5.

25 W. S. McKechnie, 'De iure regni apud Scotos', in G. Neilson, ed., *George Buchanan: Glasgow Quatercentenary Studies* (Glasgow, 1907), p. 211, at pp. 243–4; J. H. Burns, 'The Political Ideas of George Buchanan' (1951) 30 *Scottish Historical Review* 60, at pp. 63–4; J. Goodare, 'The Estates in the Scottish Parliament' (1996) 15 *Parliamentary History* 11, at pp. 18–19.

26 R. A. Mason, '*Rex stoicus*: George Buchanan, James VI and the Scottish Polity', in J. Dwyer, R. A. Mason and A. Murdoch, eds., *New Perspectives on the Politics and Culture of Early Modern Scotland* (Edinburgh, 1982), p. 9, at pp. 19–20; J. H. Burns, *The True Law of Kingship: Concepts of Monarchy in Early-Modern Scotland* (Oxford, 1996), pp. 200–202; Cairns, Fergus and MacQueen, 'Legal Humanism and the History of Scots Law', p. 62.

27 Burns, *True Law of Kingship*, p. 202.

28 C. S. Terry, *The Scottish Parliament: Its Constitution and Procedure, 1603–1707* (Glasgow, 1905), pp. 103–20; R. S. Rait, *The Parliaments of Scotland* (Glasgow, 1924), pp. 356–74; J. J. Scally, 'Constitutional Revolution, Party and Faction in the Scottish Parliaments of Charles I' (1996) 15 *Parliamentary History* 54, at pp. 57–8.

conventional view to be untenable.[29] In an attempt to preserve the second reading of the passage, it has been suggested that Buchanan was drawing no more than a rough parallel between Scottish practice and the constitution of ancient Athens, which provided for the approval by a popular assembly (*ekklesia*) of motions (*probouleuma*) prepared by a council (*boule*) it had appointed.[30] An acknowledged difficulty with this suggestion is that the Athenian *ekklesia* comprised the entire people, while the *boule* was a more representative body comprising several hundred, so that the more obvious parallel would have been between the *boule* and the Scottish parliament.

Another possible reading is that Buchanan was mindful in addition of the constitution of ancient Rome, where at one time *leges* were approved by assemblies of the entire people (*comitia*) after first being refined by the senate.[31] The title of Justinian's *Digest* containing the opinion of Callistratus imputed to Maitland also contained the opinion of Julian that customs had the force of laws (*leges*) because laws were themselves binding through popular approval (*quod iudicio populi receptae sunt*).[32] Julian thought it should make no difference whether this *iudicium populi* (the phrase used by Buchanan) was exercised by voting in a legislative assembly or by behaving in a consistent manner, adding that this was why statutes were able to lose force not only by being formally repealed but also by being allowed to fall into desuetude (*tacito consensu omnium per desuetudinem*). If Buchanan knew that advocates like Maitland were inclined to accept the view expressed by Callistratus, he must also have known that they were even more inclined to accept the view expressed by Julian, and that Acts of Parliament drawn to the attention of the lords of session were sometimes found to be in desuetude and thus invalid.[33]

[29] I. E. O'Brien, 'The Scottish Parliament in the Fifteenth and Sixteenth Centuries', Ph.D. dissertation (Glasgow, 1981), pp. 88–141; R. Tanner, 'The Lords of the Articles before 1540: A Reassessment' (2000) 79 *Scottish Historical Review* 189; A. R. MacDonald, 'Deliberative Processes in Parliament, c.1567–1639: Multicameralism and the Lords of the Articles' (2002) 81 *Scottish Historical Review* 23, at pp. 40–50 especially.

[30] R. A. Mason, 'Introduction', in *Dialogue on the Law of Kingship among the Scots*, p. xv, at pp. lix–lx.

[31] A. Lintott, *The Constitution of the Roman Republic* (Oxford, 1999), pp. 40–64.

[32] *Digest*, 1.3.32.1. Although an imperial jurist active in the reign of Hadrian, Julian was widely believed during the early-modern period to have been thinking of the republican constitution in this text.

[33] Julian's text was fundamental to the thinking of early-modern Scots lawyers on the sources of their law. Even an author who disliked the notion of desuetude like Sir George Mackenzie of Rosehaugh felt obliged to admit in his *Observations on the Acts of Parliament* (Edinburgh,

Buchanan seems to have had this in mind when he observed in his *Historia* that one old law had been either *lege abrogatum vel sponte abolitum*, and he may have had the same notion in mind again when he observed in his discussion of the College of Justice that the acts passed by the Scottish parliaments tended to be *non in perpetuum, sed in tempus facta*.[34] The third possible reading of the difficult passage in his *Dialogus* is thus that he believed the statutes enacted in the Scottish parliaments needed not only to be approved by the king, when he touched them with the royal sceptre, but also to be approved by the people, when they followed them in practice. This reading would fit quite neatly with the view that Buchanan was an author of republican tendencies who was keen to identify a balance in the Scottish constitution between the rule of the one, the few and the many.[35]

Although there are also difficulties with the third reading, they are not perhaps insuperable. One is that allowing the people at large to decide whether or not to abide by acts of parliament is not obviously reconcilable with Buchanan's insistence that he did not mean to entrust law-making to the people instead of the king. However, the explanation may be that there is a difference between allowing *tacitus consensus populi* to play a part in the legislative process and allowing it to give rise independently to customary laws.[36] Buchanan's assertion that he was not leaving the making of laws to *universi populi iudicium* would be consistent with his observation that acts passed in parliament should be referred *ad populi iudicium* if he accepted that laws could be deprived of force through desuetude without accepting that they could come into force through consuetude.[37] A second difficulty is that Buchanan was clearly objecting to the current state of affairs when he wrote that the acts of the Scottish parliaments tended to be *non in perpetuum, sed in tempus facta*. He was complaining that the adjudication of the lords of session was tyrannous partly because such

1686) that many of the statutes promulgated during the fifteenth and sixteenth centuries were in desuetude, some having lost force, others never having been in force.

34 *Rerum Scoticarum historia*, ff. 30v and 147v; *History of Scotland*, vol. 1, p. 168, and vol. 2, p. 306.

35 A. H. Williamson, *Scottish National Consciousness in the Age of James VI: The Apocalypse, the Union and the Shaping of Scotland's Public Culture* (Edinburgh, 1979), pp. 115–16.

36 For reflections on how the Scottish practice of allowing statutes to fall into desuetude could be accommodated within a theory of legislative authority see J. Goldsworthy, *Parliamentary Sovereignty: Contemporary Debates* (Cambridge, 2010), pp. 270–72.

37 A reluctance to accept the central thrust of Julian's argument would help to explain the lack of any more open reference to his text than the repeated employment of the expression *iudicium populi*.

statutes as were enacted could later be deprived of force, which is not easily reconciled with a belief that the force of statutes ought to depend on their acceptance into practice by those to whom they were applicable. It may be, however, that he was comfortable with the idea that statutes would only come into force if accepted by the people, but uncomfortable with the idea that once statutes had come into force they might later lose force again through popular disregard.[38] It may also be that his complaint about the acts of the Scottish parliaments lacking permanent validity was connected with the complaint he proceeded to make about the lords of session obstructing further statutory intervention. At this point, he may have been thinking of particular instances of obstructive behaviour by lords of session, or connecting Mary's refusal to ratify the legislation of the Reformation parliament with the support she received from judges like Leslie and Chalmers. Alternatively, he may have been thinking of the repeated failure in the fifteenth and sixteenth centuries of commissions appointed by parliament to codify the law of Scotland.[39] In 1575, the purpose of these commissions had been declared to be the provision of a 'certain writtin law to all oure soverane lordis jugeis and ministeris of law to juge and decyde be'. As lords of session like Leslie and Chalmers were not merely involved in these commissions but instrumental in steering them towards the production of new editions or digests of the current law, it may be that Buchanan blamed them for diverting their colleagues away from the task of producing a legislative code covering both 'that quhilk is alreddy statute' and 'thay thingis that wer meit and convenient to be statute'.[40]

The repeated attempts to codify the law of Scotland have been connected with the more successful redaction of the customary laws of northern France, and the eighteenth-century editor of the *Historia* already

[38] Of course, the possibility remains that the statements made in Buchanan's *Historia* and *Dialogus* simply were inconsistent. But to some extent these two works shared the same polemical purpose, and in any case the crucial point for present purposes is that in both passages Buchanan was commenting on current practice in Scotland, so that the inconsistency would need to be in his perceptions of reality rather than his argumentative positions.

[39] Records of the Parliament of Scotland (www.rps.ac.uk), 1426/13, 1469/34, 1473/7/17, A1575/3/7 and 1578/7/18; T. Thomson and C. Innes, eds., *The Acts of the Parliaments of Scotland*, 12 vols. (Edinburgh, 1814–75), vol. 1, pp. 28–30, vol. 2, pp. 10, 97 and 105, and vol. 3, pp. 40, 89 and 105; *The Actis and Constitutiounis of the Realm of Scotland* (Edinburgh, 1566), sig. +2.

[40] See again the contribution to this volume by Andrew Simpson.

mentioned suggested a further connection with French experience.[41] Drawing attention to a chapter of François Hotman's *Francogallia*, he maintained that Buchanan's concern was to prevent the authority of the Scottish parliament from being undermined by recognition of the College of Justice as an institution comparable to the *parlement* of Paris, to which, according to Hotman, the name *parlamentum* had been misappropriated from ancient assemblies of the people.[42] In the histories written by Leslie and Chalmers, as well as the more general discourse of the lords of session, Buchanan would certainly have encountered references to the session as a *parlement* like the French court, together with a tendency to follow the French style in applying the term *senatus* to the supreme court, leaving to the legislature the term *comitia*.[43] It may well be that Buchanan regarded the session as a threat to parliament, for he was keen to confine the role of the judges to interpreting and applying the laws enacted there.[44] In his *Dialogus*, having agreed with Cicero that *leges*, like *reges*, were introduced to implement *aequitas* in society, Buchanan addressed several problems that his ancient sources recognised as inevitable when this method of government was adopted.[45] One was that the legislator, *qui leges ad praesentia et praeterita accommodat*, could not foresee all the cases that might arise for decision in the future.[46] Buchanan thought that much could be achieved if judges received advice on the application of general laws from jurists, *qui plurimum suae arti tribuunt, cuique se iustitiae sacerdotes haberi*

[41] T. M. Cooper, '*Regiam maiestatem* and the Auld Lawes', in ed. H. McKechnie *An Introductory Survey of the Sources and Literature of Scots Law* (Edinburgh, 1936), p. 70, at p. 72; Williamson, *Scottish National Consciousness in the Age of James VI*, p. 65; Cairns, Fergus and MacQueen, 'Legal Humanism and the History of Scots Law', p. 52.

[42] Buchanan, *Rerum Scoticarum historia*, Aberdeen edition, p. 409; Hotman, *Francogallia*, ed. R. E. Giesey, and trans. J. H. M. Salmon (Cambridge, 1972), pp. 496–525.

[43] Leslie, *De origine, moribus et rebus gestis Scotorum*, pp. 79, 300, 376, 434, 437–8, 524–5 and 573; Chalmers, *Histoire abbregée de tous les roys*, f. 206r, and *La recerche des singularitez plus remarquables*, ff. 7v and 23v; *The Acts of Sederunt of the Lords of Council and Session*, 2 vols. (Edinburgh, 1790–1811), vol. 1, pp. 23–4.

[44] If the third reading proposed here is correct, Buchanan would have regarded the Scottish parliament as a deliberative body equivalent to the Roman senate, with the people at large either granting or withholding their approval of statutes, though not in a formally constituted *comitia*, in their practice, which is what Julian declared to be equivalent in effect. As practice developed in the next century, the Scottish parliament did at times seem in danger of becoming no more than a *comitia* that approved legislation deliberated on elsewhere.

[45] *Dialogue on the Law of Kingship among the Scots*, pp. 38–9; Cicero, *De officiis*, trans. W. Miller (Cambridge, MA, 1913), 2.12.41–2.

[46] *Dialogue on the Law of Kingship among the Scots*, pp. 40–53.

volunt.[47] Another problem was that the strict application of laws set down in writing could lead to injustice, as cases debated in the ancient schools of rhetoric demonstrated.[48] Buchanan believed that injustice could mostly be avoided if, in interpreting laws, judges identified and gave effect to their underlying purpose, which ultimately had to be the promotion of *salus populi, suprema lex.*[49] Yet the problem persisted that the skilful application and purposive interpretation of laws could not provide solutions to all the issues that might be cast up by the infinite diversity of human life.[50] Buchanan's response was that when it proved beyond the *iudices ordinarii* to provide solutions by interpreting and applying the law, cases ought to be referred *ad consilium rege*, meaning to the parliament or the privy council. Far from attributing conciliar authority to the lords of session, Buchanan believed that when they dealt with 'things arbitrall', they were behaving like tyrants.[51] What they needed to remember was that *ex lege iudici, non e iudice legi auctoritatem est.*[52]

II. A juridical perspective

Near the end of the sixteenth century another account of the origins of law was written by an advocate who had been in practice before the lords of session when Buchanan's *Historia* and *Dialogus* were published.[53] In the opening chapter of his *Ius feudale*, Thomas Craig took the same line as Buchanan – as it happened, his wife's uncle – in agreeing with Cicero that in order to ensure the just settlement of their disputes people had introduced first kings and then laws.[54] Again like Buchanan and Cicero, he explained that kings had initially administered justice in accordance with *aequitas naturale*, or *ius naturale et gentium*, constrained *nulla lege* yet guided *instinctu naturae.* Alluding vaguely to Justin's history, Craig

47 *Digest*, 1.1.1. On the significance of Buchanan's allusion to this text see further below.

48 *Dialogue on the Law of Kingship among the Scots*, pp. 56–61; Cicero, *De oratore I–II*, trans. E. W. Sutton and H. Rackham (Cambridge, MA, 1942), 2.24.100; Quintilian, *Institutio oratoria*, 4 vols., trans. H. E. Butler (Cambridge, MA, 1920–22), 4.4.4 and 7.6.6–7.

49 Cicero, *De legibus*, trans. C. W. Keyes (Cambridge, MA, 1928), 3.3.8.

50 *Dialogue on the Law of Kingship among the Scots*, pp. 66–7.

51 Burns, *True Law of Kingship*, p. 202; Mason, 'Introduction', pp. liii–iv.

52 *Dialogue on the Law of Kingship among the Scots*, pp. 144–5.

53 J. Finlay, 'The Early Career of Thomas Craig, Advocate' (2004) 8 *Edinburgh Law Review* 298.

54 *Ius feudale* (Edinburgh, 1655), pp. 2–3. On the relationship between the thinking of Craig and Buchanan see too Cairns, Fergus and MacQueen, 'Legal Humanism and the History of Scots Law', pp. 61–2.

observed more precisely that Nimrod had been the first ruler who *rerum omnium arbitrium sibi arrogaret*, and he quoted Livy's comment that *apud barbaros regum imperia pro legibus sunt*, though he took both passages to refer to a particular type of ruler.[55] He did not accept that before *leges* were introduced there could be nothing but *arbitria principum*, believing not only that rulers who implemented natural equity correctly were true kings rather than tyrants, and that their equitable administration of justice could give rise to customary practices and institutions, but also that these customary practices and institutions would then have amounted to a kind of law. Apparently educated in the law schools of France, Craig was not prepared to deny authority to customary laws in the way Buchanan had done.[56] As well as Callistratus' observation that custom ought *vim legis optinere*, and Julian's remark that custom *pro lege non immerito custoditur*, the *Digest* also preserved Ulpian's opinion that custom was adhered to *pro iure et lege*, Hermogenian's explanation that it was understood to derive from *tacita civium conventio*, and other similar statements.[57] In the previous title of the *Digest*, a lengthy extract from a work by Pomponius had recounted how at first the government of Rome had been placed in the hands of kings, *sine lege certa, sine iure certo*, and how following the overthrow of the monarchy there had been a further period when Rome was regulated *incerto iure et consuetudine aliqua* rather than *per latam legem*.[58] While these statements resembled to some extent those that could be found in the works of historians like Justin and Livy, they were also subtly different, for they left open the prospect not only of *consuetudo* taking shape alongside *lex*, but also of *ius certum* emerging. That the jurists did not take the expression *pro lege* to mean 'instead of statute' is evident from Pomponius' observation that the enactments of the *concilium plebis* came to be treated *pro legibus*, or as it was put elsewhere, *non minus valere quam leges*.[59] In the second chapter of his treatise, Craig merged comments borrowed from Cicero and Livy into an account of Roman legal history primarily based on the one left by Pomponius, and in later chapters he noted that the feudal law with which

55 *Ius feudale*, pp. 3–5; Genesis, 10.9; Livy, *Ab urbe condita*, 37.54.

56 It is generally believed that Craig had studied law in France, though concrete evidence remains elusive.

57 *Digest*, 1.3.32–40. Of course, Craig would also have been familiar with *Code*, 8.52, and *Institutes*, 1.2.9 – both in the *Corpus iuris civilis* – together with *Decretum*, D. 1 cc. 4–5, *Liber extra*, 1.4, *Liber sextus*, 1.4, and *Extravagantes communes*, 1.4 – all in the *Corpus iuris canonici*, 2 vols., ed. A. Friedberg (Leipzig, 1879–81).

58 *Digest*, 1.2.2.1–3.

59 *Ibid.*, 1.2.2.8; *Institutes*, 1.2.4.

he was primarily concerned had taken shape as a body of customary law, before one variant of it was redacted in the *Libri feudorum*.[60] Later, still he insisted that *consuetudo apud omnes gentes iuris nomen sibi vendicet, iusque moribus constitutum dicatur*, reiterating that in all societies, before *leges scriberentur, consuetudo et tacitus civium consensus omnes dirimebat controversias*.[61]

At this point in his treatise, Craig spelled out the practical significance of his treatment of custom as a source of law. Following the example of Julian, he wrote that when lawyers in Scotland were faced with a legal question they would first look for an answer in *ius scriptum*, and then, if no assistance could be found there, would turn to *consuetudo*.[62] By written law he meant *acta parliamentorum*, and by custom *rerum perpetuo iudicatarum consuetudo*, referred to in Scotland as 'practick'. Callistratus had linked *consuetudo* with *rerum perpetuo similiter iudicatarum auctoritas*, and Craig evidently found forensic custom a more meaningful notion in his own time than popular custom. It has been suggested that he preferred to think in terms of forensic custom because it could be taken to involve the exercise of sovereign authority by a branch of the king's council.[63] This seems rather doubtful, however, for several reasons. In the first place, his stated position was that *ex frequentia rerum eo modo iudicatarum maiorem aut minorem authoritatem consuetudo capit*, which clearly emphasised the recurring conduct of the judges, and placed no stress on their status. In the second place, in the rest of his treatise, he did not refer very often to decided cases, and when he did, he showed more interest in what the lawyers involved had argued than in what the court had eventually decided, which he did not always trouble to mention.[64] While he clearly did attach significance to court decisions, it was as an especially potent form of opinion that he related them to the opinions expressed by lawyers elsewhere. In the third place, when he wrote about court cases, Craig tended to adopt the terminology Pomponius had used in explaining that the enactment of *leges* created a need for *interpretatio* and *disputatio fori*, that the need was satisfied by the exercise of *prudentium auctoritas*, and that it was through the exercise of juristic authority that *ius non scriptum* gradually took shape.[65] In these terms, the practick

[60] *Ius feudale*, pp. 7–11 and 18–23. [61] *Ibid.*, p. 39. [62] *Digest*, 1.3.32.pr.

[63] Cairns, Fergus and MacQueen, 'Legal Humanism and the History of Scots Law', p. 64.

[64] For more detail on this point see J. D. Ford, *Law and Opinion in Scotland during the Seventeenth Century* (Oxford, 2007), pp. 236–8.

[65] *Digest*, 1.2.2.5.

developed in the Scottish courts, while not dependent for its authority on the tacit consent of the people, was more dependent on the authority of expert lawyers than on the sovereignty of the king's judges. In the fourth place, when he wrote about the *auctoritas iuris aut rerum iudicatarum* of courts like the *parlement* of Paris, he attributed it to the learning of the judges, declaring firmly that decisions did not enjoy the same kind of authority as legislation.[66] Decisions were a species of opinion, and lines of decisions a species of common opinion. For Craig, the authority of a particular forensic custom depended on how often an opinion had been endorsed by learned judges.

To explain how this type of authority had come to operate in Scots law, Craig prefaced his treatment of feudal land tenure with an account of its history in which the lords of session played a crucial part. Adopting the conventional stance that the earliest legislator in the world had been Moses, *amanuensis Dei*, Craig maintained that the Israelites had probably influenced the Egyptians, from whom the Greeks were believed to have derived their customs and laws, and from whom in turn the Romans were believed to have derived the laws contained in their XII Tables.[67] As the XII Tables had been described by Livy as the basis of all the laws developed by the Romans, it followed that everything eventually incorporated into Justinian's books of law could be taken to have flowed down through various channels (*scaturgines sive rivulos*) from the divine fountainhead (*fons*) opened by Moses.[68] After explaining in more detail how Roman law had been developed, partly through further legislation and partly through juristic interpretation, Craig described how after Justinian's time it had been largely forgotten in the West, until its study was revived around the start of the twelfth century in the new universities.[69] By then, the papacy had established its predominance in the vacuum left by the Roman Empire and its law began to be studied in the universities too, as did the feudal law, after the *Libri feudorum* was added to the *Corpus iuris civilis*.[70] Several centuries of learned commentary on written sources had thus generated the civil and canon laws that were considered authoritative throughout Europe, though Craig was aware that the authority attributed to them differed from place to place. He recalled Baldus' distinction between the necessary authority the civil law enjoyed in Italy and the

[66] *Ius feudale*, p. 15. On this passage see too Ford, *Law and Opinion in Scotland*, pp. 224–5.

[67] *Ius feudale*, pp. 5–7; *Decretum*, D. 71 c. 1; *Digest*, 1.2.2.4.

[68] *Ius feudale*, p. 8; Livy, *Ab urbe condita*, 3.34.

[69] *Ius feudale*, pp. 7–10.

[70] *Ibid.*, pp. 11–29.

probable authority it enjoyed in France, explaining that although the civil law was studied in the French universities, it was only followed in the northern courts to the extent that it was found consistent with natural reason and equity.[71] Given that the learned laws were generally thought to be *aequitatis fontes purissimi*, even the probable authority that required a degree of expert reappraisal was highly significant, and it was this type of authority that Craig believed both the civil law (embracing the feudal law) and the canon law (following the Reformation) enjoyed in Scotland.[72] However, he admitted that there was a problem with this argument, for while the universities of Scotland were supposed to have taught the civil and canon laws, they did not in practice do so, which was why prospective advocates like Craig himself tended to complete their education in France. The Scots appeared to lack the centres of learning that would have enabled them to participate in the transfer of legal wisdom that had started with Moses. Craig believed he had a solution to this problem, though, which was that those appointed to serve as lords of session had always been men *in iure civili et pontificio egregie instructi*, and that the reinvention of their court as a College of Justice had been intended to ensure that cases would continue to be heard by men who were *docti et iuris utriusque periti*, and who would promote the learned development of the law through their decisions (*qui in iudicando ius civile sequentes, illud etiam posteritati commendarunt*).

Craig thus offered a significantly different perspective on the lords of session from the one offered by Buchanan. His reading of the important text attributed to Julian led him to agree with Buchanan that the first thing the judges should try to do in handling a case was interpret and apply a relevant act of parliament, for he also agreed that acts of parliament were the only *leges* in force in Scotland.[73] But he did not agree that where a relevant act could not be found, there could be no law to apply. Popular custom, quite apart from having the power to deprive acts of parliament of force by leaving then *in desuetudine*, could in principle at least amount to law, and how Craig believed forensic custom could develop becomes clearer if attention is paid to how he believed cases ought to be handled in the absence of either statute or custom. Still basing his account of the sources of Scots law on a reading of Julian's text, he remarked that in novel cases the lords of session were expected to search for answers to any questions raised in the civil, canon and feudal laws, which they would follow if the answers found there seemed consonant

[71] Baldus de Ubaldis, *Commentaria super Codicem*, 4 vols. (Venice, 1500), vol. 4, f. 44.
[72] *Ius feudale*, pp. 10–11. [73] *Ibid.*, pp. 38–40.

to natural law and right reason (*quatenus legibus naturae et rectae rationi congruunt*), for in doing so they would be drawing from the *scaturgines et fontes* from which almost all their *ius, usus et praxis* had been derived. The expert appraisal of the learned laws had to be undertaken locally, but account could be taken of how they had been appraised by expert lawyers elsewhere, and the opinion formed by the court could then be compared with the opinions formed elsewhere. Eventually, if the judges adhered to their opinion consistently in similar cases, it would become a customary law, but it was not at this stage alone that their decisions would be legally founded. The learned authority behind forensic custom came into play as soon as lawyers looked for answers to their questions in learned sources, and although only probable, it still had binding force, at least in the minds of lawyers like Craig. Buchanan seems to have held a different view. As already mentioned, he thought advice should be taken from *iurisprudentes* on the interpretation of statutes, but in identifying the *iurisconsultus* with the *orator*, and expecting forensic debates to be governed by *rhetorum praecepta*, he revealed that he was thinking more of court practitioners like Cicero than of jurists like Julian.[74] When he talked about lawyers, it was in disparaging terms as mercenary pettifoggers who were more interested in devising clever arguments than discovering the truth.[75] Hostile to the canon law, he regarded it as a body of legislation that had been entirely deprived of force at the Reformation, and in reproducing a document defending the deposition of the late queen, which in most respects involved arguments similar to his own, he carefully omitted the references it contained to the civil law, including the comment that the civil law was 'receaved in Scotland in all decisions wher there is no expresse municipall law wrytten'.[76] In a surprising number of passages in his *Historia*, Buchanan gave the impression that Scots law was unlike French law and more like English law.[77]

The similarity with French law that was especially significant for Craig was the place allotted to a *senatus* in which account could be taken of equity as well as law. As counsellors to the monarch in his own supreme court, the judges of the *parlement* of Paris were believed to have the

74 *Dialogue on the Law of Kingship among the Scots*, pp. 20–21 and 58–9.

75 *Rerum Scoticarum historia*, f. 73r; *History of Scotland*, vol. 1, p. 394.

76 *Rerum Scoticarum historia*, ff. 157v, 167v, 190–1r and 212v–13; *History of Scotland*, vol. 2, pp. 353, 400, 502, 505 and 601–7. For the document referred to see H. R. Trevor-Roper, 'George Buchanan and the Ancient Scottish Constitution' (1966) *English Historical Review*, Supplement 3, pp. 40–50.

77 *Rerum Scoticarum historia*, ff. 142v, 160r, 174r and 192v; *History of Scotland*, vol. 2, pp. 285, 365–6, 431 and 512.

authority to ground their decisions in deserving cases on equity, and it was this authority that enabled them, among other things, to find answers to questions that the statutory and customary laws of France left unanswered.[78] Apart from anything else, where the authority of the civil law was dependent on recognition of its equitable quality, reference had to be made to equity as a standard against which the learned sources could be measured by judges authorised to follow that standard. Believing that the lords of session had comparable authority to the judges of the *parlement*, Craig maintained that they too could base their decisions on learned sources when they were found to be equitable, and in his treatise he accordingly made reference to equity as the standard against which these sources were to be measured. In recommending adoption of the Roman heir's *beneficium abstinendi* from an insolvent estate, for example, he commented that the lords of session were likely to be moved by the *aequitas* of any case put to them, and in recommending adoption of Constantine's prohibition on *leges commissoriae* permitting the sale of property delivered as security, he commented that *cum aequitate convenire videtur.*[79] However, although it was the equitable quality of provisions like these that Craig hoped the lords of session would recognise, his understanding was that in giving effect to them in novel cases the court would not be turning from law to equity, but would be turning from one type of law to another. In civilian terms, the equity manifested in the Roman sources was *aequitas constituta*, an enacted form of equity, not *aequitas rudis*, or natural equity in a pure form.[80] It was the responsibility of the lords of session to decide whether or not to follow the civil law in cases to which acts of parliament or established customs could not be applied, but Craig maintained that when the civil law was found to be

[78] J. P. Dawson, 'The Equitable Remedies of the French Chancery before 1789', in H. Dölle, M. Rheinstein and K. Zweigert, eds., *Festschrift für Ernst Rabel*, 2 vols. (Tubingen, 1954), vol. 1, p. 99; G. Boyer, 'La notion d'équité et son rôle dans la jurisprudence des parlements', in *Mélanges Georges Boyer*, 2 vols. (Paris, 1962), vol. 1, p. 210; J.-L. Thireau, 'Le bon juge chez les juristes français du XVIe siècle', in J.-M. Carbasse and L. Depambour-Tarride, eds., *La conscience du juge dans la tradition juridique européenne* (Paris, 1999), p. 131.

[79] *Ius feudale*, pp. 173 and 257.

[80] E. M. Meijers, 'Le conflit entre l'équité et la loi chez les premiers glossateurs' (1941) 17 *Tijdschrift voor Rechtsgeschiedenis* 117 remains valuable, though see too H. F. Jolowicz, *Roman Foundations of Modern Law* (Oxford, 1957), pp. 56–8; H. E. Yntema, 'Equity in the Civil Law and the Common Law' (1966–7) 15 *American Journal of Comparative Law* 60, at pp. 75–8; I. Maclean, *Interpretation and Meaning in the Renaissance: The Case of Law* (Cambridge, 1992), pp. 175–7.

consistent with equity, the Scots were already bound by it (*obligamur*).[81] The *aequitas constituta* applied to novel cases was already law before its repeated observance transformed it into the forensic custom known as practick, and it was for this reason that it did not matter especially when such a transformation could be taken to have occurred. Craig typically made little effort to justify his assertions that provisions of the learned laws had been received into the customary law of Scotland, and it is notable that one occasion on which he did specify that a ruling of the court *iam pro consuetudine receptum est* was in dealing with a decision to follow *aequitas* instead of the civil law.[82] This was not the only indication that the equitable jurisdiction of the lords of session enabled them to do more than adopt the solutions to difficult problems found in the learned sources. Another way in which they were similar to the judges of the *parlement* was in their ability to mitigate the rigour of the law when its strict application would result in injustice.[83] Although authorised by statute or custom, certain types of remedy were considered to be of an equitable character, partly in the sense that they allowed for the normal operation of the law to be dispensed with, and partly in the sense that they required the judges to exercise discretion.

In talking about the exercise of judicial discretion, Craig tended to remark that matters were left *ad arbitrio iudicis*.[84] It was a principle of the canon law that *bonus iudex nihil ex arbitrio suo facit, sed iuxta leges et iura pronunciat*, but while it might be maintained that applicable *iura* were generally available even when *leges* were lacking, the problem remained that sometimes matters had to be left to the discretion of the judge.[85] Craig often used the word *arbitrium* in something like the sense favoured by Buchanan, as in writing that a superior *potest uti vel abuti pro arbitrio suis rebus*, whereas no vassal *alium pro suo arbitrio et sua electione substituere potest*.[86] He also noted, however, that the word had a different significance *in iure*.[87] Not only were judges expected to exercise their *arbitrium* as *boni*

81 *Ius feudale*, p. 11.

82 *Ibid.*, p. 171; *cf.* W. M. Morison, ed., *The Decisions of the Court of Session, from Its First Institution to the Present Time*, 22 vols. (Edinburgh, 1801–4), vol. 9, p. 7227.

83 *Ius feudale*, pp. 59, 144, 197–8, 253, 258 and 265.

84 *Ibid.*, pp. 34, 165, 195, 211–12, 219, 258, 299, 304–5, 331, 371 and 378.

85 *Decretum*, C. 2 q. 7 c. 4.

86 *Ius feudale*, pp. 18, 22, 30, 48, 63–4, 71–2, 75–6, 82, 89, 97, 100, 104, 128–30, 144, 157, 169, 171, 182, 192, 194, 196–8, 203, 213, 223–4, 240, 246, 256–7, 264–5, 268, 275, 287, 290, 294–7, 318, 327, 332, 339, 342, 346, 349, 369 and 371.

87 *Ibid.*, pp. 130, 202, 334, 369 and 371.

viri, striving to implement the requirements of *ius naturale et gentium*, but they were also expected to exercise any discretion left to them within the general context provided by the law they applied more strictly in other cases.[88] They were to pursue the purposes for which the discretion was left to them, were to reach their decisions *ex circumstantiis et praesumptionibus* and were to proceed wherever possible *a similibus ad similia*, making use of provisions of the law designed for other cases. In exercising discretion they were to follow, if not the letter, then at least the spirit of the law. It was this legal notion of *arbitrium*, it has recently been argued, that Dante had in mind when he wrote the passage in his *Purgatorio* in which he took his leave of Virgil, who advised him to follow *tuo arbitrio* and *suo senno*.[89] Contrary to the view that Dante was intent here on asserting his sovereignty as an artist, and thus laying claim to the status of a modern author over a century ahead of his time, it is now more plausibly argued that he was asserting his readiness to continue working in the way he had been taught without further instruction.[90] Having immersed himself in the literary tradition represented by Virgil, he was ready to contribute to its development through the composition of verse that might not adhere strictly to settled rules but would be faithful to the spirit of the tradition. It has been argued elsewhere that Craig both envisaged himself and was regarded by others as an author who contributed in essentially the same way to the development of a tradition of enquiry in the law.[91] As a member of the College of Justice, he contributed to the development of Scots law by writing about it in the style of the civilian and canonist doctors who taught in the continental law schools.

[88] B. Schnapper, 'Les peines arbitraires du XIIIe au XVIIIe siècle (doctrines savantes et usages français)' (1973) 41 *Tijdschrift voor Rechtsgeschiedenis* 237 and (1974) 42 *Tijdschrift voor Rechtsgeschiedenis* 81; J.-M. Carbasse, 'Le juge entre la loi et la justice: Approches médiévales', in Carbasse and Depambour-Tarride, *La conscience du juge*, p. 67; M. Meccarelli, 'Dimensions of Justice and Ordering Factors in Criminal Law from the Middle Ages till Juridical Modernity', in G. Martyn, et al., eds., *From the Judge's Arbitrium to the Legality Principle* (Berlin, 2013), p. 49.

[89] *The Divine Comedy of Dante Alighieri*, 2 vols., trans. R. M. Durling (Oxford, 1996), vol. 2, pp. 462–3.

[90] J. Steinberg, *Dante and the Limits of the Law* (New Haven, 2013), pp. 53–88, responding to E. H. Kantorowicz, 'The Sovereignty of the Artist: A Note on Legal Maxims and Renaissance Theories of Art', in M. Meiss, ed., *De artibus opuscula xl: Essays in Honor of Erwin Panofsky* (New York, 1961), p. 267, and A. R. Ascoli, *Dante and the Making of a Modern Author* (Cambridge, 2008).

[91] Ford, *Law and Opinion in Scotland*, pp. 46–52 and 222–33.

III. A theological perspective

In 1607, shortly before his death, Craig dedicated his *Ius feudale* to James VI, by then also James I of England.[92] Just days earlier, the king had said more about the lords of session in a speech he delivered before both houses of his parliament at Westminster in defence of his desire for a closer union between Scotland and England.[93] On the supposed 'Antipathy of the Lawes and Customes of these two Nations', he had attempted to put the minds of his listeners at rest by telling them a little about the legal system in operation north of the border, claiming to be speaking on the strength of advice received from 'the best Lawyers of Scotland'.[94] One piece of reassurance he felt able to offer was that when the Scots talked about preserving their 'fundamentall lawes', as they had done in appointing representatives to discuss a closer union three years earlier, they were not using the expression 'as you doe, of their Common Law, for they have none'.[95] After explaining that they meant only the constitutional laws sustaining the monarchy, he later modified his position by saying that they did not have 'any olde Common Law of their owne, but such as in effect is borrowed from yours'. He understood that James I of Scotland had introduced forms of action 'drawen out of the Chauncerie of England', with the result that much of the law there differed from English law only 'in certaine termes'. Had he read Craig's treatise, he would have found it vigorously insisted that the similarities between the two laws resulted from their shared origins in the learned tradition, not from any adoption by the Scots of English institutions.[96] It was James' impression that the Scots had not become involved in the learned tradition until his grandfather founded the College of Justice less than a century before, 'according to the forme of the Court of Parliament of Fraunce', and he was less interested here in celebrating the emergence of the session as a centre of learning

[92] National Archives at Kew, SP 14/27/1. [93] *Political Works of James I*, pp. 300–302.

[94] There is no more reason to believe that Craig was 'James's adviser in matters to do with the union and the law' than there is to believe that he was a 'judge of the Court of Session', as is erroneously stated in C. Russell, 'Topsy and the King: The English Common Law, King James VI and I, and the Union of the Crowns', in B. Sharp and M. C. Fissel, eds., *Law and Authority in Early Modern England* (Cranbury, NJ, 2007), p. 64, at p. 71. A more likely source of the king's ideas is the anonymous 'Relation of the Manner of Judicatores in Scotland', ed. J. D. Mackie and W. C. Dickinson (1922) 19 *Scottish Historical Review* 254.

[95] Records of the Parliament of Scotland, 1604/4/20; *Acts of the Parliaments of Scotland*, vol. 4, pp. 263–4.

[96] *Ius feudale*, pp. 29–40.

than in emphasising the limited use that was made of the learned laws. Since they were only used 'to supply such cases wherein the Municipall Law is defective' and not to supplant the common law borrowed from England, 'it is not so hard a matter as is thought, to reduce that Countrey to bee united with you under this Law'. As for the acts of the Scottish parliament, these could be altered 'as oft as occasion shall require', and the first task in moving towards a legal union would be 'to reconcile the Statute Lawes of both Kingdomes'. If this hinted after all at some alteration to English law, James made it clear that he did indeed have this in mind. 'For who can blame Scotland to say', he asked, 'if you will take away our owne Lawes, I pray you give us a better and cleerer in place thereof?' He believed the opportunity should be taken to enact 'standing Lawes' in parliament, so that the people of the whole of Britain would not live in future under 'an uncertaine and arbitrarie Law'.[97] Identifying the civil law with *ius gentium*, 'which in the point of conjunction of Nations should beare a great sway', James adopted from Justinian the related propositions that it was the sovereign's prerogative 'to supply the Law where the Law wants', and that *eius est explicare, cuius est condere.*[98]

That James was not entirely out of sympathy with the teaching of his former tutor was confirmed in another speech he delivered to both houses of the Westminster parliament three years later.[99] 'In the first originall of Kings', he remarked then, 'their wills at that time served for Law'. Only later were laws introduced, but once they had been, a king who did not rule in accordance with them would degenerate into a tyrant. Where James disagreed with Buchanan was in maintaining – as he had already done before leaving Scotland in his *Trew Law of Free Monarchies* – that it was kings who made laws for their people, not vice versa, and that kings were answerable for their conduct of government to God alone.[100] Again identifying the civil law with *ius gentium*, 'being most necessary for matters of Treatie with all forreine Nations', James also noted that it was followed in England in 'the Ecclesiasticall Courts, Court of Admiraltie, Court of Requests, and such like'. He emphasised once more, however, that there was no country in the world, 'not onely

[97] *Political Works of James I*, pp. 292–3.

[98] *Constitutio Tanta*, 21; *Code*, 1.14.12.

[99] *Political Works of James I*, pp. 309–12.

[100] J. P. Sommerville, 'James I and the Divine Right of Kings: English Politics and Continental Theory', in. L. Levy Peck, ed., *The Mental World of the Jacobean Court* (Cambridge, 1991), p. 55; Burns, *True Law of Kingship*, pp. 231–42; R. A. Mason, *Kingship and Commonweal: Political Thought in Renaissance and Reformation Scotland* (East Linton, 1998), pp. 215–41.

Scotland, but not France, nor Spaine nor any other Kingdome, governed meerely by the Civill Law', since each people had 'their owne municipall Lawes agreeable to their Customes, as this Kingdome hath the Common Law'. James had no wish to replace the common law with the civil law, but he did still hope to see it amended by legislation, 'for the King with his Parliament here are absolute (as I understand) in making or forming of any sort of Lawes'. He was aware that 'no Text of Law can be so certaine, wherein the circumstances will not make a variation in the Case', and that the civil law texts were themselves the subject of constant controversy and commentary in the schools. Nevertheless, he wished 'some more certaintie were set downe in this case by Parliament'. The common law, he understood, 'hath not a setled Text in all Cases, being chiefly grounded either upon old Customes, or else upon the Reports and Cases of Judges'. These reports were referred to as *responsa prudentum*, and were indeed like the 'Presidents' found in other countries, yet because they were 'not alwayes so binding, but that divers times Judges doe disclaime them, and recede from the judgment of their predecessors', people were effectively dependent 'upon the bare opinions of Judges, and uncertaine Reports'. Whatever respect James may have had for his judges, he had not entirely escaped the assumption that prescriptive legislation was the only reliable antidote to arbitrary adjudication.

The lords of session were mentioned again in a speech James delivered to a gathering of his English judges in the Star Chamber in 1616, through which he hoped to terminate a dispute that had been raging for some years over the relationship between the courts of common law and equity.[101] In all free kingdoms, he declared, kings not only made laws but also delegated responsibility for their enforcement to judges, though how this was done differed in detail in England, Scotland, France and other realms.[102] Just as kings were responsible to God for the administration of justice according to his laws, and must 'make conscience not to alter, but to declare and establish the will of God', so it was the responsibility of judges 'to interprete the Law of the King', without presuming 'to make Law'. In England, admittedly, judges had not only 'Statute Law' to interpret and implement, but also 'Common Law', which was 'the Law set downe in

[101] J. P. Dawson, 'Coke and Ellesmere Disinterred: The Attack on the Chancery in 1616' (1941) 36 *Illinois Law Review* 127; J. H. Baker, 'The Common Lawyers and the Chancery: 1616' (1969) 9 *Irish Jurist* 368; M. Fortier, 'Equity and Ideas: Coke, Ellesmere and James VI and I', in D. Fischlin and M. Fortier, eds., *Royal Subjects: Essays on the Writings of James VI and I* (Detroit, 2002), p. 265.

[102] *Political Works of James I*, pp. 326–35.

our forefathers time, expounded by learned men divers times after in declaratory Comments, called *Responsa Prudentum*'. James made it clear, however, that he did not regard these expository and declaratory opinions as a source of new law. 'You are no makers of Law, but Interpreters of Law', he reminded the judges again, 'for your Office is *Ius dicere*, and not *Ius dare*'. Although it might require great expertise to declare the law accurately and precisely as it applied to particular cases, and although the common law in particular might be 'a mystery and skill best knowen unto your selves', James insisted that it was not 'Sophistrie or straines of wit that must interprete, but either cleare Law, or solide reason', meaning 'common sense and reason, and trew Logicke'. He was evidently remembering here the occasion a few years earlier when Sir Edward Coke had enraged him by observing that while he was possessed of 'excellent science, and great endowments of nature', he nevertheless lacked the 'artificial reason and judgment of law' relied on by the judges in their decision of cases.[103] James now warned his judges that 'if your interpretation be such, as other men which have Logicke and common sense understand not the reason, I will never trust such an Interpretation'. His judges were to keep within the bounds of existing law and natural reason in their decisions, and also within the bounds of their separate jurisdictions, with those who sat in courts of common law respecting the authority of the court of chancery. A court of equity rather than law, 'called the dispenser of the Kings Conscience', the chancery did not subvert the law but did perform the king's function before God of 'mixing Mercie with Justice', in cases where 'the rigour of the Law' would 'undoe a Subject'. It was at this point that James mentioned the lords of session, who were judges of law yet had equitable jurisdiction 'mixed and incorporate in their Office'. In Scotland, it was the lords of session who exercised what he had described elsewhere as the king's prerogative to have general laws 'mitigated and suspended upon causes onely knowen to him'.[104]

It would be an obvious mistake to expect to find consistency throughout the treatises James wrote before leaving Scotland and the speeches he delivered on various occasions after he arrived in England.[105] On

[103] *English Reports*, 178 vols. (London, 1900–1932), vol. 77, p. 1343.

[104] *Political Works of James I*, p. 63.

[105] Q. Skinner, *Visions of Politics*, 3 vols. (Cambridge, 2002), vol. 1, pp. 67–72; and see too J. Wormald, 'James VI and I, *Basilikon doron* and *The Trew Law of Free Monarchies*: The Scottish Context and the English Translation', in Levy Peck, *Mental World of the Jacobean Court*, p. 36.

the other hand, it would be equally mistaken to neglect entirely the assistance his scattered remarks about the lords of session afford in construing the passage from his *Basilikon doron* with which this paper opened, provided the context in which each remark was made is kept in view. One part of the intellectual context in which he had written in his *Basilikon doron* about the equitable jurisdiction exercised in 'things arbitrall' was clearly provided by the humanist historiography in which he had been ably instructed by Buchanan. In this context, things ceased to be arbitral to the extent that they were regulated by laws, but James came to concur with civil lawyers like Craig and common lawyers like Coke that laws need not be enacted in statutory form. Whether he also shared their belief that the exercise of *prudentium auctoritas* could itself amount to a source of law is more doubtful, for he appears to have appreciated that while most lawyers would have accepted that the role of judges was *ius dicere, non ius dare*, and was limited to interpreting and applying existing law, there was a need to insist on the literal meaning of these commonplace propositions. When the English judges, gathered in the Exchequer Chamber in 1608, granted James' wish to have the Scottish *postnati* recognised as subjects of the English crown, Coke commented that 'before Judicial or Municipal Laws were made, Kings did decide cases according to natural equity, and were not tied to any rule or formality of Law, but did *dare iura*'.[106] By his own time, however, in view of the huge number of 'examples and precedents in like cases' available, the judges who heard cases on the king's behalf had no need to do anything more than *dicere ius*. In response to the argument advanced at the bar that judges ought to apply *lex scripta*, failing which *mos et consuetudo*, and failing that *recurrere ad rationem*, Coke remarked that this would only be consistent with Julian's advice in the *Digest* (to which allusion was being made), and with his own understanding of how English law worked, if *ratio* were taken to mean something other than 'natural reason'.[107] It would have to be taken to mean 'the legal and profound reason of such as by diligent study and long experience and observation are so learned in the Laws of this Realm, as out of the reason of the same they can rule the case in question'. Coke believed that the indigenous learning of the common lawyers would yield answers

[106] *The Reports of Sir Edward Coke*, 6 vols., ed. J. H. Thomas and J. F. Fraser (London, 1826), pt 7(1).

[107] J. W. Tubbs, *The Common Law Mind: Medieval and Early Modern Conceptions* (Baltimore, 2000), pp. 141–72; A. D. Boyer, *Sir Edward Coke and the Elizabethan Age* (Stanford, 2003), pp. 83–107; A. Cromartie, *The Constitutionalist Revolution: An Essay on the History of England, 1450–1642* (Cambridge, 2006), pp. 179–233.

to all the questions raised in the English courts, and that there was no need for recourse to the learning of the law schools, yet he was describing the same kind of tradition of enquiry as was found there, as he made clear by citing in support of his argument the Aristotelian principle that *cuilibet in sua arte perito est credendum*, which was fundamental to every claim to learned authority.[108] The chancellor, however, in responding to the same line of argument in the *postnati* case, adopted a significantly different position.[109] Lord Ellesmere agreed that when questions were raised to which answers were not provided by acts of parliament or settled rules of the common law, it was fitting to examine 'former Judgements given in like Cases', and that when no earlier case had similar facts, judges should 'guide themselves by discretion', both 'judging upon Presumptions' and reasoning *a similibus*. Thus far, he would have caused neither Coke nor for that matter Craig much concern, and they might have been reassured by his remark that novel cases had to be governed by the reason of expert lawyers, not ordinary people, 'drowned with drincke, or blowne away with a whiffe of Tobacco'.[110] But he added that when 'examples and arguments *a simili* doe fail, then it remaineth *Recurrere ad Rationem*'. Even when the reason implicit in the law had been pushed to its fullest extent, cases might arise in which '*Arbitrium Iudicum* is to seeke out the true and solide reason'.[111] In Ellesmere's opinion it would not be acceptable to tell the parties to these cases to 'stay for a Parliament', for the settled rules of the common law included the maxim *nullus recedat a Cancellaria sine remedio*.

In his judgment in the *postnati* case, Ellesmere repeatedly coupled the phrase *responsa prudentum* with the phrase *arbitria iudicum*, explaining that the *arbitria iudicum* delivered in novel cases became the *responsa prudentum* on which decisions in later cases could be based, either through their direct application as precedents or through analogous reasoning.[112] While this meant that judges could after all make law, Ellesmere stated

[108] Aristotle, *Topics*, 100b21–2, in J. Barnes, ed., *The Complete Works of Aristotle*, 2 vols. (Princeton, 1984).

[109] L. A. Knafla, *Law and Politics in Jacobean England: The Tracts of Lord Chancellor Ellesmere* (Cambridge, 1977), pp. 202–53.

[110] To support this point, he cited Ioachimus Hopperus, *Sedvardus, sive de vera iurisprudentia* (Antwerp, 1590), p. 118.

[111] Ellesmere did not believe that the *postnati* case was itself beyond the resources of the common law, but he could scarcely have made it clearer that he did believe these resources to be limited.

[112] Like James, and unlike most civil lawyers, Ellesmere always used the genitive form *prudentum*.

that *arbitria iudicum* were 'received, allowed and put in practice and execution by the Kings authoritie', and James may have been less troubled by the prospect of judicial innovation in his conciliar courts than in the common law courts. Although he declared during his speech in the Star Chamber that he had instructed Ellesmere 'to goe on in his Court according to Presidents, warranted by Law', he also spelled out his conviction that kings were bound in conscience to have justice administered equitably, and accepted the chancellor's claim to serve as keeper of the king's conscience.[113] Expressing concern that his English judges paid scant regard to the requirements of divine law, and were insufficiently respectful of the instruction provided by moral theologians, James based all his comments about human law on his conception of its connection with divine law.[114] In one of the most influential works in the theological branch of the *speculum principis* genre, to which James meant his *Basilikon doron* to form a contribution, Aegidius Romanus had contended that *quantum possibile est, sunt omnia legibus determinanda, et quam pauciora possunt, sunt arbitrio iudicum committenda.*[115] This was not to deny, however, that judgments might justly be delivered *per leges, aut per arbitrium, aut per utrunque*, and it was further maintained that *leges humanae*, whether written or unwritten, could never satisfy all the requirements of *leges evangelicae et divinae.*[116] While judges could found their decisions on human laws with clear consciences, there would be cases in which the particular dictates of conscience remained to be discerned, and it was here that moral theologians were able to offer advice.[117] In principle, moral theology was another discipline in which probable, if not necessarily certain, knowledge was available, and while its objectivity became more doubtful following the Reformation, the handling of cases of conscience continued to be viewed as a central task of practical divinity, in relation to which the exercise of equitable jurisdiction could be meaningfully discussed.[118]

[113] *Political Works of James I*, p. 334.

[114] L. A. Knafla, 'Britain's Solomon: King James and the Law', in Fischlin and Fortier, *Royal Subjects*, p. 235.

[115] *De regimine principum* (Rome, 1556), ff. 299r–301r. The requirements of sound adjudication stated at f. 302v are worth comparing with the passage Ellesmere cited from Hopperus' *Sedvardus*.

[116] *De regimine principum*, ff. 316r–17r.

[117] Thomas Aquinas, *Summa theologiae*, 60 vols., ed. T. Gilby (London, 1964–76), 2a2ae 60.5 and 67.4.

[118] A. Walsham, 'Ordeals of Conscience: Casuistry, Conformity and Confessional Identity in Post-Reformation England', in H. E. Braun and E. Vallance, eds., *Contexts of Conscience*

It is a surprising feature of Buchanan's *Historia* that while the word *conscientia* often appears there, it never seems to have been used in the theological sense of a process of moral appraisal, but always in the more general sense of awareness or consciousness, typical of the *literae humaniores.*[119] If anything, it is an even more surprising feature of Craig's *Ius feudale* that while the word is sometimes found there in its theological sense, it is far from prominent in his discussion of equity. He wrote about the tyranny the papacy had established in people's consciences, noted Christopher St German's interest in matters of conscience in his *Dialogus inter doctorem et studentem*, and occasionally mentioned the use of the concept in arguments, yet despite affirming at one point that the provisions of the civil law would normally be found *animo et conscientiae satisfacere*, he tended to base his assessment of their equity on remarks drawn from legal and literary sources.[120] Where the concept acquired greater prominence was in a treatise by one of several lawyers who were inspired to write about Scots law by the first printing of Craig's *Ius feudale* in 1655.[121] James Dalrymple, eventually elevated to the peerage as Viscount Stair after serving for many years as an ordinary lord, then president, of the session, began the book known as his *Institutions of the Law of Scotland* by exploring the relationship between divine and human law, examining in the process the concepts of equity and conscience.[122] In his treatment of Scots law, these terms were of vital importance because, while he agreed with Craig that a huge amount had been and might continue to be learned from the civil, canon and feudal laws, he denied that these laws could have binding authority until particular provisions were adopted from them into the statutory or customary laws of Scotland.[123] The learned laws offered no more than 'an example' of how natural equity might be effectively implemented, and the truth was that until statutory or customary laws

in Early-Modern Europe, 1500–1700 (Basingstoke, 2004), p. 32; D. R. Klinck, *Conscience, Equity and the Court of Chancery in Early Modern England* (Farnham, 2010); W. Decock, 'The Judge's Conscience and the Protection of the Criminal Defendant: Moral Safeguards against Judicial Arbitrariness', in G. Martyn, et al., *From the Judge's Arbitrium to the Legality Principle*, p. 69.

119 C. Lefebvre, *Les pouvoirs du juge en droit canonique* (Paris, 1938), pp. 84–6; C. S. Lewis, *Studies in Words* (Cambridge, 1967), pp. 181–213; J. Q. Whitman, *The Origins of Reasonable Doubt: Theological Roots of the Criminal Trial* (New Haven, 2008), p. 106.

120 *Ius feudale*, pp. 10, 13, 17, 161, 235, 248 and 383.

121 Ford, *Law and Opinion in Scotland*, pp. 73–89 and 215–22.

122 *Institutions of the Law of Scotland* (Edinburgh, 1681), 1.1–10.

123 Ford, *Law and Opinion in Scotland*, pp. 240–46, 254, 275–7, 279 and 417–21.

emerged, people had no option but to rely on 'their Judges Arbitriment'.[124] The lords of session, Stair maintained, 'did differ little from Arbiters, until they came to have fixed Customs and Statutes, clear and known', and no such law could 'come the length of a sufficient Rule for all Cases'.[125] In novel cases the judges would seek to find equitable solutions to the problems raised, and Stair aimed in writing his book to provide them with assistance in doing so, yet he recognised that the objectivity of their rulings would be contested. He was the first Scottish jurist to enunciate clearly the notion that all human laws derived their force from the exercise of sovereign authority, explaining in Hobbesian terms that to avoid living in a state of 'perpetual War', in which everyone 'should be a Judge to himself, and should take and hold by force, what he conceived to be his Right', each nation submitted 'to the Determination of their Soveraign', in much the same way as 'parties are understood to submit themselves to Arbiters'.[126] In some cases, the sovereign might exercise his authority by laying down general rules in the form of statutes, but Stair thought it preferable for customary laws to be allowed to emerge gradually from the determination of disputes in the courts. After stressing in the early versions of his book that the lords of session exercised authority derived from parliament, he came to place greater stress on their role as 'the Kings Council at law'.[127] As judges authorised to make 'final and irrevocable' decisions on the king's behalf, the lords of session were able to exercise in particular cases the sovereign authority from which in time 'Custome or Practique' might emerge.[128] In a revised and enlarged edition of his book, printed shortly before his death in 1695, Stair explained in considerable detail how the procedure followed in the session enabled a kind of customary law to emerge from a combination of the sovereign determination of disputes by the judges and the tacit acquiescence of the people in the creation of new forms of action.[129]

If it is correct that Buchanan understood popular approval to play a part in the making of law in Scotland, then there is some similarity between

[124] Stair, *Institutions of the Law of Scotland*, 1.14–15.

[125] *The Decisions of the Lords of Council and Session*, 2 vols. (Edinburgh, 1683–7), vol. 1, sig. A3v.

[126] *Institutions of the Law of Scotland*, 1.15.

[127] Ford, *Law and Opinion in Scotland*, pp. 316–17, 434, 437 and 504–5.

[128] *Institutions of the Law of Scotland*, 1.15.

[129] Ford, *Law and Opinion in Scotland*, pp. 507–39.

his understanding of how law related to authority and Stair's.[130] The similarity is, however, quite superficial, for any part assigned to the people by Buchanan was in the legislative process, on which he focused because his classical sources identified *leges* and *arbitria* as alternatives, and not because he subscribed to the theory of legislative sovereignty that was emerging in the later sixteenth century from a mode of historical enquiry rather different from his own.[131] Buchanan would surely have taken Stair to typify the lords of session he complained about, who opposed the enactment of legislation designed to limit their scope for arbitrary adjudication. Although Stair was actually involved in the promotion of several important enactments, his decision to send the first edition of his treatise through the press in 1681 seems to have formed part of an attempt to distract the king and parliament from their scheme, revived in that year, of enacting a comprehensive code of law 'to establish constant and clear rules for directing all his judges'.[132] It was no coincidence that it was during the later seventeenth century that Buchanan's complaint about the lords of session came to be treated as an almost oracular pronouncement, for it was a period in which people tried, as one member of the College of Justice put it, 'to make all whom they hate pass for such as love Arbitrary Government'.[133] Stair's contemporaries in the session seem mostly to have believed that the way for the judges to avoid the charge of arbitrariness was to base their decisions as far as possible on statutes or customs, and to search for answers to more difficult questions in the learning ultimately derived from the law schools and now developed further in the College of Justice itself.[134] Although it was maintained by learned lawyers that

[130] The political theory behind Stair's understanding that the authority of law both descended from the sovereign and ascended from the people is remarked on in J. D. Ford, 'Divine Right and Constitutional Settlement: Traces of Political Theory in Stair's *Institutions*' (1990) 11 *Journal of Legal History* 134. The intention is to return both to this particular topic and to the theological context in which Stair wrote his treatise more generally, in a book called *Law and Conscience in Scotland during the Seventeenth Century*.

[131] J. L. Brown, *The Methodus ad facilem historiarum cognitionem of Jean Bodin: A Critical Study* (Washington, 1939); J. H. Franklin, *Jean Bodin and the Sixteenth Century Revolution in the Methodology of Law and History* (New York, 1963); D. R. Kelley, 'The Development and Context of Bodin's Method', in H. Denzer, ed. *Jean Bodin: Proceedings of the International Conference on Bodin* (Munich, 1973), p. 123.

[132] Records of the Parliament of Scotland, 1681/7/52; *Acts of the Parliaments of Scotland*, vol. 8, p. 356.

[133] Sir George Mackenzie of Rosehaugh, *The Laws and Customs of Scotland in Matters Criminal* (Edinburgh, 1678), sig. A2v; and see again the sources cited in nn. 8–9 above.

[134] The views of Stair's contemporaries are discussed at length and contrasted with the position attributed to him here in Ford, *Law and Opinion in Scotland*.

arbitrary decisions could still be legal decisions, the connotations of the word 'arbitrary' were becoming so negative that even those who adopted Craig's perspective on the session tended to accept that 'things arbitrall' should be referred for decision to parliament or the privy council.[135] Their perspective would become more problematic after the closer union James VI and I had sought to promote between his realms was finally achieved in 1707, when Scotland lost both its own parliament and its own privy council, with the result, as one lord of session pointed out, 'that there can be nothing of Soveraignty left to reside among us but our Soveraign courts of Judicature'.[136] Stair's explanation of how the exercise of sovereign authority by the lords of session could combine with the acquiesence of the people to create a kind of customary law provided a more dynamic vision of how the law might continue to be developed in a country absorbed into a larger state. It is unlikely that James would have found Stair's views entirely agreeable, but fundamentally he was in agreement that laws did not have to be enacted in the form of statutes, that professional expertise could not as such be regarded as a source of legal authority and that it was appropriate for conciliar courts to fashion equitable solutions to any problems that remained arbitrary. Although decisions in these cases might gradually give rise to new laws, in first addressing the problems raised, the courts had no alternative but to think in ethical terms, which for both James and Stair meant thinking in terms of moral theology.

[135] Sir George Mackenzie of Rosehaugh, *Observations on the Acts of Parliament*, pp. 18–19, 75–6, 127, 132, 135 and 459, and *Laws and Customs of Scotland in Matters Criminal*, 2.25.4; Sir John Lauder of Fountainhall, *The Decisions of the Lords of Council and Session*, 2 vols. (Edinburgh, 1759–61), vol. 1, p. 320, and *Historical Notices of Scotish Affairs*, 2 vols. (Edinburgh, 1848), vol. 1, pp. 131–2; Sir John Nisbet of Dirleton, *Some Doubts and Questions in the Law, Especially of Scotland* (Edinburgh, 1698), pp. 78–9, 107 and 180.

[136] George Mackenzie, earl of Cromarty, *Letter to a Member of Parliament upon the 19th Article of the Treaty of Union* (n.p., 1706), pp. 4–6.

8

Legal authorities as instruments of conflict management

The long endgame of Anglo-Hanseatic relations (1474–1603)

ALAIN WIJFFELS

I. From the Peace of Utrecht (1474) to the Bremen Conference (1603)[1]

In 1474, the peace treaty signed at Utrecht between England and the Hanse was apparently a major diplomatic victory for the latter.[2] The

[1] Recent monographs on the Anglo-Hanseatic relations include: Terence Henry Lloyd, *England and the German Hanse, 1157–1611. A Study of their Trade and Commercial Diplomacy*, Cambridge, 1991; Stuart Jenks, *England, die Hanse und Preußen, Handel und Diplomatie 1377–1474* (Köln, Wien, 1992), 3 vols.; John D. Fudge, *Cargoes, Embargoes, and Emissaries. The Commercial and Political Interaction of England and the German Hanse 1450–1510*, Toronto, Buffalo, London, 1995; Nils Jörn, *"With Money and Bloode". Der Londoner Stalhof im Spannungsfeld der englisch-hansischen Beziehungen im 15. und 16. Jahrhundert*, Köln, Weimar, Wien, 2000. These works provide extensive bibliographies to previous literature. Shorter surveys are offered by Eleonora M. Carus-Wilson, 'Die Hanse und England', in *Hanse in Europa, Brücke zwischen den Märkten 12.-17. Jahrhundert, Ausstellung des Kölnischen Stadtmuseums 9. Juni-9. September 1973*, Cologne, 1973, pp. 85–106; idem, 'The German Hanse in the Economy of Medieval England', in Paul Kluke en Peter Alter (dir.), *Aspekte der deutsch-britischen Beziehungen im Laufe der Jahrhunderte. Ansprachen und Vorträge zur Eröffnung des Deutschen Historischen Instituts London, Aspects of Anglo-German Relations through the Centuries, Addresses and Papers given at the Opening of the German Historical Institute London*, Stuttgart, 1978, pp. 14–23; Stuart Jenks, 'Der Englandhandel: Erfolge und Rückschläge', in *Die Hanse, Lebenswirklichkeit und Mythos, Eine Ausstellung des Museums für Hamburgische Geschichte in Verbindung mit dem Vereins- und Westbank*, Hamburg, 1989, Bd. 1, pp. 68–73. For insights of the Anglo-Hanseatic relations in the general history of the Hanse: Philippe Dollinger, *Die Hanse* (Neu bearbeit von Volker Henn & Nils Jörn), Stuttgart, 2012, *passim* (cf. index *in fine, s.v.* 'England').

[2] The treaty is dealt with at length in the monographs by Lloyd, Jenks, Fudge and Jörn mentioned in the previous note. Among the articles discussing specifically the treaty see Stuart Jenks, 'Der Frieden von Utrecht 1474', in Stuart Jenks and Michael North (eds.), *Der Hansische Sonderweg?, Beiträge zur sozial- und Wirtschaftgeschichte der Hanse,*

treaty, however, failed to solve the underlying sources of conflict between the parties, some of which had been apparent for many decades before hostilities took a more violent form in 1468–1469.[3] Nevertheless, the English Crown perceived that its interest was to favour and protect the Hanseatic interests in England during the years that followed its conclusion. By the end of the century, the diplomatic conferences held by the parties[4] made it clear that the tensions between them were growing again and during the Bruges conferences of 1520–1521,[5] it seemed that the Utrecht settlement was on the brink of being abandoned by the English. During the later years of Henry VIII's reign, the position of the Hanse in England appeared to have regained greater stability, but under Edward VI, a new crisis prompted stronger diplomatic efforts from the Hanse to safeguard their commercial interests in English foreign trade. The illusion of a restoration of these interests under the reign of Mary was further eroded, and eventually vanished during the reign of Elizabeth. Towards the end of Elizabeth's reign, the Hanse had

Cologne-Weimar-Vienna, 1993, pp. 59–76; Terence Henry Lloyd, 'A Reconsideration of two Anglo-Hanseatic Treaties of the Fifteenth Century', *English Historical Review*, 1987, pp. 916–933; H.P.H. Jansen, De vrede van Utrecht, *Spiegel Historiael*, 1974, pp. 136–143; Walter Stark, 'Der Utrechter Frieden von 1474 zwischen der Hanse und England', *Zeitschrift für Geschichtswisssenschaft*, 1971, pp. 893–903; Alain Wijffels, 'De vrede van Utrecht (1474)', *Pro Memorie* 16/1 (2014), pp. 3–23. See also the proceedings of the conference held in London in commemoration of the 400th anniversary of the treaty, Klaus Friedland (ed.), *Frühformen Englisch-Deutscher Handelspartnerschaft. Referate und Diskussionen des Hansischen Symposions im Jahre der 500. Wiederkehr des Friedens von Utrecht in London vom 9. bis 11. September 1974.* [Quellen und Darstellungen zur Hansischen Geschichte, Neue Folge, vol. 23], Cologne, 1976. The text of the treaty (in Latin, 28 February 1474) is printed in. Thomas Rymer, *Foedera, Conventiones, Literae, Et cujuscunque generis acta publica inter reges Angliae, Et alios quosvis imperatores, reges, pontifices, principes, vel communitates ab ineunte saeculo duodecimo, viz. ab Anno 1101, Ad nostra usque tempora, habita aut tractata [...], Editio tertia*, T. V, *Pars III. et IV*, Hagae Comitis, Apud Joannem Neaulme, 1741, pp. 36–40; also in Goswin Frhr. von der Ropp, *Hanserecesse von 1431–1476*, Bd. 7, Leipzig, 1892, pp. 340–352.

3 Walther Stein, *Die Hanse und England. Ein hansisch-englischer Seekrieg im 15. Jahrhundert* [Pfingstblätter des Hansischen Geschichtsvereins, Blatt. 1], Leipzig, 1905; Erich Weise, 'Die Hanse, England und die Merchants Adventurers. Das Zusammenwirken von Köln und Danzig', *Jahrbuch des kölnischen Geschichtsvereins*, 1957, pp. 137–164.

4 For the Antwerp 1491 conference see Dietrich Schäfer, *Hanzerecesse von 1477–1530*, Bd. 2 (Leipzig, 1883), pp. 438–638; for the Antwerp 1497 conference: Dietrich Schäfer, *Hanserecesse von 1477–1530*, Bd. 4, Leipzig, 1890, pp. 7–36; for the Bruges 1499 conference: Schäfer, *Hanserecesse von 1477–1530*, Bd. 4, pp. 167–354.

5 The conference had been preceded by negotiations in London in 1519: Dietrich Schäfer, *Hanserecesse von 1477–1530*, Bd. 7, Leipzig, 1905, pp. 397–413; on the Bruges 1520–1521 conference itself: *ibid.*, pp. 574–902.

effectively lost its importance in English trade, without any prospect of recovery.

The conflict between opposing Hanseatic and English commercial interests was mainly one of competition for access to, and their respective share in, each other's foreign trade. The English Crown had a stake in the conflict because, during the sixteenth century, it became increasingly able to rely on its own merchants for ensuring English exports to and strategic imports from the Continent, thus increasingly becoming independent from the Hanse in order to support its foreign economic relations, whether in peacetime or during wars. The conflict originated therefore in international commercial competition and economic policies. In spite of the steady deterioration of Anglo-Hanseatic relations during the second half of the sixteenth century, the parties never went back to war against each other, probably due to the shifting balance of power. The English Crown grew in strength during the Tudor era, and the English merchant community became a much more autonomous player in Northern and Western European maritime trade. Conversely, the Hanse lost much of its coherence as a political entity in its own right in international relations, and its commercial role in the Baltic and the North Sea was much weakened. The Hanse could no longer afford to wage a war against England, while the English could see their position improving without going to war. Both parties found it more expedient to negotiate, or to keep up the appearance of negotiating, about general and specific issues on which they were opposed, rather than using armed force to press an advantage or to uphold their claims. Law was not at the forefront of those developments, for the conflict was essentially about trade. Attempts to settle issues were mainly pursued between the English and Hanseatic political authorities, at diplomatic conferences and through *ad hoc* embassies. Particular interest groups lobbied their own government or other political authorities which could foster and protect their interests. Recourse to legal proceedings could in that context be regarded as a strategy of lobbying. Legal arguments could nonetheless also extensively be used in the course of diplomatic and political negotiations. Law may not have been seen as offering a way out of the conflict, in the sense of a form of dispute resolution, but it did contribute by formalising the controversial issues and subjecting them to legal arguments supported by legal authorities, to secure some form of conflict management. Law, in that sense, supported the political and diplomatic means to avoid warfare. It offered an alternative and comparatively peaceful way of pursuing the exchange of opposing and controversial claims.

The German Hanse's origins may be traced to Westphalia, but it was during the twelfth century, when the territories adjacent to the South-western area of the Baltic Sea acquired greater weight in the affairs of the Holy Roman Empire, that the economic and commercial centres developed into a confederation of cities which became known, also internationally, as the Hanse. At the outskirts of the main Hanseatic heartlands, concentrated on the southern coasts of the Baltic Sea (with ports such as Lübeck, Wismar, Rostock, Stralsund, Danzig and others) and in the Rhineland (where Cologne played a major role), four important trading offices were usually referred to as the outer trading centres to which the Hanse's influence reached.[6] In the East, Novgorod was the Hanse's commercial outpost for trade with North-eastern Europe, but also indirectly with the trade routes which reached southwards to the Black Sea. In the North, Bergen was a centre mainly important for the fish trade. Bruges in Flanders had been in the Middle Ages the gateway to trade with the Low Countries, Western France and Southern Europe. In the sixteenth century, the office was moved to Antwerp in Brabant, which had taken over Bruges's role as the most important centre for maritime commercial exchanges between Northern and Southern Europe. Finally, London was the most Western outpost of the Hanse. It was the main export centre for English wool and cloth,[7] an industry which had traditionally close links with the economic centres of Flanders and Brabant, and from where a large proportion of maritime trade in the Channel and the North Sea could be controlled.[8]

By the end of the twelfth century, the first royal grants to German merchants in England are recorded.[9] By the beginning of the following

[6] Justyna Wubs-Mrozewicz, 'De Kantoren van de Hanze: Bergen, Brugge, Londen en Nowgorod', in Hanno Brand and Egge Knol (eds.), *Koggen, Kooplieden en Kantoren. De Hanze, een praktisch netwerk*, Hilversum/Groningen, 2010, pp. 90–107.

[7] Carsten Jahnke, 'De Hanze en de Europese economie in de middeleeuwen', in Brand en Knol, *Koggen, Kooplieden en Kantoren, o.c.*, 45–61: from the beginnnings until the second half of the sixteenth century, the cloth trade was the backbone of the Hanseatic economic interests (p. 55).

[8] Already during the fifteenth century the (German) distribution network passing through the London office was substantially altered: Stuart Jenks, 'The London Steelyard's Certifications of Membership 1463–1474 and the European Distribution Revolution', in Justyna Wubs-Mrozewicz and Stuart Jenks (eds.), *The Hanse in Medieval and Early Modern Europe*, Leiden-Boston, 2013, pp. 59–108.

[9] See (e.g.) the privilege granted by Henry II to Cologne merchants and the protection of their office in London in Rolf Sprandel (ed.), *Quellen zur Hanse-Geschichte*, Darmstadt, 1982, pp. 170–171; Natalie Fryde, 'Deutsche England-Kaufleute in früh-hansischer Zeit', *Hansische Geschichtsblätter* 1979, pp. 1–14.

century, the Guildhall, forerunner of the Steelyard, became the official trading post of the German merchants and the Hanse in London. It was governed at first by Cologne merchants. Even in later centuries, Cologne, though a prominent member of the Hanse, often pursued distinct commercial interests from those of its fellow members in Northern Germany.[10] The series of Hanseatic privileges (involving the particular administration and jurisdiction of the Steelyard,[11] the access of Hanse merchants to London and English trade,[12] the import and export of goods, and, not least, tax exemptions) starts in most late-medieval and early-modern collections of documents and records with grants by Edward I. It became usual to obtain a confirmation of the privileges at the beginning of each new reign.

The Anglo-Hanseatic conferences of the beginning of the fifteenth century reflected an increased assertiveness of growing English interests in the Hanse's traditional areas of influence around the North Sea and the Baltic.[13] The maritime conflicts of the late 1460s turned into open

[10] Frank R. Salter, 'The Hanse, Cologne and the Crisis of 1468', *The Economic History Review* 1931, pp. 93–101; Horst Buszelo, 'Köln und England (1468–1509)', in *Köln, das Reich und Europa. Abhandlungen Über weiträumige Verflechtungen der Stadt Köln in Politik, Recht und Wirtschaft im Mittelalter*, Cologne, 1971, pp. 431–467; Claudia Schnurmann, *Kommerz und Klüngel. Der Englandhandel Kölner Kaufleute im 16. Jahrhundert*, Göttingen, 1991; Stuart Jenks, 'Die Hanse in England. Die wirtschaftliche und politische Bedeutung ihres Handels (1380–1474) und ihre Versuche zur Bewältigung der Krise von 1468', in Volker Henn and Arnved Nedkvitne (eds.), *Norwegen und die Hanse, Wirtschafliche und kulturelle Aspekte im europäischen Vergleich*, Frankfurt am Main, 1994, pp. 109–159; Joachim Deeters, 'Köln auf Reichs- und Hansetagen 1396 bis 1604. Ein Vergleich', *Hansische Geschichtsblätter* 2001, pp. 102–127.

[11] On the Steelyard (in German: *Stalhof*) see especially Derek Keene, 'Ein Haus in London: Von der Guildhall zum Stalhof', in Jörgen Bracker, Volker Henn and Rainer Postel (eds.), *Die Hanse, Lebenswirklichkeit und Mythos*, Lübeck, 1989 (2nd revised edition), pp. 57–62, and Stuart Jenks, 'Leben im Stalhof', *ibid.*, pp. 210–216; Werner Kurzinna, 'Der Name "Stalhof"', *Hansische Geschichtsblätter* 18 (1912), pp. 429–461; Martin Weinbaum, 'Stalhof und Deutsche Gildhalle zu London', *Hansische Geschichtsblätter* 3 (1928 [1929]), pp. 45–65; Derek Keene, 'New Discoveries at the Hanseatic Steelyard in London', *Hansische Geschichtsblätter* 107 (1989), pp. 15–25. The map of London published by G. Braun and F. Hogenberg (1572) includes a panegyric of the Steelyard, which did no longer reflect the situation at the time of its publication; the map may have been based on a former version, from the mid-century, which had been commissioned by the Hanseatic merchants in London (for a reproduction see, for example, Rolf Hammel-Kiesow, Matthias Puhle and Siegfried Wittenburg, *Die Hanse*, Darmstadt, 2009, p. 55).

[12] The Hanseatic trade with England should of course not be reduced to the London Steelyard; Karl Engel, 'Die Organisation der deutsch hansischen Kaufleute in England im 14. und 15. Jahrhundert bis zum Utrechter Frieden von 1474', *Hansische Geschichtsblätter* 19 (1913), pp. 445–517 and *Hansische Geschichtsblätter* 20 (1914), pp. 173–225.

[13] On the political and economic context of fifteenth-century Anglo-Hanseatic relations see M. Postan, 'The Economic and Political Relations of England and the Hanse from 1400 to

warfare. A settlement was reached, partly through mediation by the Duke of Burgundy, with the Utrecht Peace Treaty of 1474.[14] The Treaty confirmed the Hanse's privileges in England, but it also recognised some of the English claims. Overall, it was a settlement which strongly upheld Hanseatic interests in England. More significantly, several of the Treaty's provisions failed to solve the controversies which had developed before the war. As a result, the same issues became a recurrent theme in later Anglo-Hanseatic conferences.

During the first half of the sixteenth century, the increasing competition between the Hanseatic merchants in England and the English merchant community was attenuated by the general upward trend of English export trade. A substantial part of that trade was directed to Antwerp and the Low Countries. The wealth of Hanseatic merchants in London at that time is illustrated by many commissions from members of the Steelyard to a painter such as Holbein the Younger.[15] For example, the way Holbein portrayed the young Danzig merchant George Gisze in 1532 gives an impression of the riches gathered through the German trade in London. It is a case where the history of art and economic history each provides its own corroboration. The figures of English cloth export from the time of the Utrecht Treaty until the mid-sixteenth century[16] show a substantial increase (by almost three-fold within three-quarters of a century) of the volume of cloth exports. The Hanse's part in that export trade fluctuated during the same period, between about 20 and 25 per cent – a market share the English merchants were keen to take over.[17] The figures for the period 1523–1532, when Gisze was trading at the London Steelyard, indicate that during those years, export levels were relatively high and that the Hanse's share still seemed settled around almost a quarter of all exports.

1475', in: Eileen Power and M.M. Postan (eds.), *Studies in English Trade in the Fifteenth Century* London, 1933, pp. 91–153, 373–380.

14 K.A. Fowler, 'English Diplomacy and the Peace of Utrecht', in Friedland, *Frühformen, o.c.*, 9–24.

15 Katrin Petter-Wahnschaffe, *Hans Holbein und der Stalhof in London* Berlin-München, Deutscher Kunstverlag, 2010.

16 The figures are quoted from Table 15 in Lloyd, *England and the German Hanse, o.c.*, p. 268 (export of English cloth from 1468 to 1546, including the share of the Hanse).

17 The competition between London and Hanseatic merchants was largely focused on the trade via the Low Countries, and the decline of Antwerp later during the sixteenth century caused much insecurity for both merchant communities and affected at the same time the balance of commercial influence between them: Georges Daniel Ramsay, *The City of London in International Politics at the Accession of Elizabeth Tudor* Manchester, 1973), in particular Chapter VII. For a case-study see Georges Daniel Ramsay (ed.), *The Politics of a Tudor Merchant Adventurer. A Letter to the Earls of East Friesland*, Manchester, 1979.

Around the mid-sixteenth century, that success story came abruptly almost to an end. The Hanse lost its privileges in England and in England, the Low Countries, Germany and even in the Baltic trade, they steadily lost ground to the Merchants Adventurers.[18] In 1552, the Privy Council was instrumental in issuing a royal decree 'resuming' (i.e., in practice, abolishing) the Hanseatic privileges. The immediate context was a complaint from English merchants, who claimed that some Hanseatic merchants (against whom proceedings were started before the Exchequer) had been misusing the privileges. In more general terms, the decree also referred to the prejudice the privileges were causing to the English Crown because of the tax exemptions enjoyed by the Hanse.

In 1553, the Hanse sent an embassy whose mission was to negotiate the restoration of their privileges. During the late Spring and early Summer of 1553, the embassy, on its way to England, stayed for several weeks in the Low Countries, probably on a fact-finding mission and in order to gather as much information as possible on the state of the trade with England. In early July, news of the King's death reached them in Antwerp. By the time it became clear that Mary Tudor was effectively in power, they crossed the Channel, perhaps in the hope that the new queen's politically fragile hold on the throne would offer them a more favourable position in the negotiations. The embassy ended in the early Autumn of 1553. The Queen reinstated the privileges, but the reinstatement was qualified and provisional, and was soon followed by new restrictions.

The Hanse's strategy, under Mary's reign, was an attempt to strengthen their position by lobbying Philip II after his marriage with the Queen.

[18] During the first half of the sixteenth century, the Company of Merchants Adventurers specialised in the export of English cloth, in particular to the Low Countries. During the second half of the sixteenth century, in spite of their successes against the German Hanse, they were increasingly facing competition in North European maritime trade from new English companies, especially the Muscovy Company (1555) and the Eastland Company (1579). For elements of the Company's documentary history see William Ezra Lingelbach, *The Merchant Adventurers of England: Their Laws and Ordinances with Other Documents*, *s.l.*, 1902. Ernst Pitz, 'Die Hanse und die Merchant Adventurers', in J. Bohmbach (ed.), *Fernhandel und Stadtentwicklung im Nord- und Ostseeraum in der hansischen Spätzeit (1550–1630). Symposion zum 14. Hansetag der Neuzeit in Stade am 8. und 9. April 1994*, Stade, 1995, pp. 44–66; Jan K. Fedorowicz, *England's Baltic Trade in the Early Seventeenth Century. A Study in Anglo-Polish Commercial Diplomacy*, Cambridge, 1980. Dutch merchants also succeeded in conquering a substantial part of Baltic trade: Wim P. Blockmans, 'Der Holländische Durchbruch in der Ostsee', in Jenks and North, *Der hansische Sonderweg?, o.c.*, 49–58; for earlier developments and networks in Norway see Justyna Wubs-Mrozewicz, *Traders, Ties and Tensions. The Interaction of Lübeckers, Overijsslers and Hollanders in Late Medieval Bergen*, Hilversum, 2008.

Whatever short-term advantages they may have gained during Mary's short reign, it was a strategy which would prove counter productive after her successor's accession to the throne. During Elizabeth's long reign, the Hanse found it difficult to obtain any firm and lasting confirmation of their privileges. Meanwhile, the German merchants were no longer a match for their English competitors. The Merchants Adventurers' more aggressive commercial policies enabled them to acquire footholds on the continent, even within the Holy Roman Empire. The privileges they obtained at Hamburg[19] were one of the many symptoms that, at that time, the Hanse struggled to maintain a degree of unity and a coherent front towards its commercial competitors and the increasing political influence of territorial rulers. From the 1580s onwards, the Hanse tried to counter more effectively the progress of the Merchants Adventurers in Germany. They lobbied the imperial court and the influential territorial princes of the Empire in order to put an end to the English trade in Germany.

After many delays, the Emperor finally issued in August 1597 an order (called 'mandate', *Mandat*)[20] which, if it had been effectively executed, would have barred the Merchants Adventurers' access to trade in the Holy Roman Empire. The formal prohibition, in a contemporary translation[21] of the German original, stated:

> Therefore wee forbid, proclaime, banishe and commaunde to departe the aforenamed English merchants (namely the whole company of Merchants Adventurers) togeather with theire Monopolish, highly hurtfull contracts, negotiations and advantageous trades, over all the Holie Empire. Also in the like sorte, that such hurtfull comerces and traffiques of the Englishe Adventurers and the contracts and bargaines yssewinge theare out, shalbee hence further forbidden and of noe valew and that heareafter noe mann, nether by him self nor by anie other, shall use or exercise them . . .

In the order's extensive justification (presumably derived from the arguments put forward by the Hanse in their complaints), the reference to the Merchants Adventurers' alleged monopolistic trade expresses a shift in the Hanseatic strategy, which until the 1580s had almost entirely emphasised the argument of the irrevocability of their privileges.

[19] Richard Ehrenberg, *Hamburg und England im Zeitalter der Königin Elisabeth*, Jena, 1896; on earlier commercial relations between the Hamburg merchants and England: Klaus Friedland, 'Hamburger Englandfahrer (1512–1557)', in *Mensch und Seefahrt zur Hansezeit*, Cologne, Weimar, Vienne, 1995, pp. 103–145.

[20] For an original printed broadsheet, sealed and signed see City Archives Lübeck, Hanseatica, Externa Anglicana 150.

[21] British Library, Add. Ms. 48126, f. 68r–71r.

Predictably, the Queen retaliated. The Steelyard was closed, and even though it would be reopened during James I's reign, it never recovered any of its former significance. The Hanseatic merchants had lost not only their privileges, but also their old and new competitors prevailed in international maritime trade, and the Hanse itself was no longer a cohesive and powerful actor on the international scene.[22]

During the last months of the Elizabeth's reign, a German-English conference convened in Bremen, without tangible results.[23] The Queen herself had expressed her reservations about any direct negotiations or dealings with the Hanse's delegates rather than with the representatives of the Emperor and of the territorial princes. James Stuart's accession to the English throne did not change the situation. By that time, the English government was no longer dependent on Hanseatic merchants for securing English international trade, whether in times of peace or war, and the city merchants had become too influential in English foreign trade policies to be ignored in favour of competing Hanseatic interests. The Steelyard remained in German hands until the Victorian times, when it was finally sold to make way for the London railway developments.

II. Legal arguments in support of the Hanse

Three documents which reflect the Hanse's legal arguments at three different stages during the sixteenth century may indirectly illustrate the shift in the balance of power between the Hanse and the English authorities and merchants. First, a document from probably 1552–1553, which addresses a preliminary issue raised by the English earlier during the reign of Henry VIII, viz. whether the English King had, in his controversy with the Hanse, to submit to civil law – a claim which the English authorities denied. Second, two legal consultations from 1553, following the conventional pattern of late-Medieval legal *consilia* in the *ius commune* tradition, show how civil lawyers discussed substantial controversies between the English government and the Hanse in the course of

[22] Heinz Duchhardt, 'Die Hanse und das europäische Mächtesystem des frühen 17. Jahrhunderts', in Antjekathrin Grassmann (ed.), *Niedergang oder Übergang? Zur Spätzeit der Hanse im 16. und 17. Jahrhundert*, Cologne, Weimar, Vienna, 1998, pp. 11–24.

[23] Richard Grassby, 'Die letzten Verhandlungen zwischen England und der Hanse 1603–1604', *Hansische Geschichtsblätter* 76 (1958), pp. 73–120; E.A. Beller, 'The Negotiations of Sir Stephen le Sieur, 1584–1613', *English Historical Review* 40 (1925), pp. 22–33; Benjamin Möller, *Verhandlungen der Hanse im Jahr 1604 über Handelsprivilegien in England (AHL, ASA Externa Anglicana 59)*, diss. Kiel, 2010.

diplomatic exchanges. Third, a document probably written shortly after the last, failed, conference of Bremen in the Spring of 1603. At that time, the conflict had been fought out and the Hanse had practically lost all its stakes in England, and it is unlikely that, at that stage of the endgame, they could hope to reverse the tendency by persuading their English opponents with civil law arguments. The extensive memorandum of 1603 was most likely intended to support the Hanse's political lobbying on their home front, within the Holy Roman Empire.

III. The King's subjection to civil law

The first document consists of two fragments (two sheets) which I found in different series of the Hanseatic archives in Gdańsk. So far, only those two sheets, that is, the first four pages, have been recovered.[24] The document does not give a date or indication of its author or addressee, but it clearly states the issue it deals with:

> Whether, in the controversy which arose [with] the Hanse cities with respect to their privileges, the King of England is bound to act with us according to the writtten law.[25]

A few elements of the document may suggest that the fragment can be dated within the narrow bracket of 1552–1553, but that depends on the interpretation of a few passages and the assumption that the use of the term 'Rex Angliae' in the title and in the text is not gender-neutral. If those dates are correct, the document may therefore address the issue of the applicability of civil law on the Anglo-Hanseatic controversy which arose from the suppression of the privileges under Edward VI. It follows a typical and fairly traditional line of argumentation along civil law principles, and it refers to several specific *ius commune* authorities. The central issue mentioned in the title had been prominently discussed during the unsuccessful conference of Bruges in 1520–1521, where the Hanseatic delegates had been confronted with Thomas More at his worst (or, if you are

[24] These fragments have been published; cf. Alain Wijffels, 'International Trade Disputes and ius commune: Legal Arguments on the "Gdańsk Issue" during the Hanseatic Embassy to London in 1553', in Albrecht Cordes and Serge Dauchy (eds.), *Eine Grenze in Bewegung: Öffentliche und private Justiz im Handels- und Seerecht. Une frontière mouvante: Justice privée et justice publique en matières commerciales et maritimes* [Schriften des Historischen Kollegs 81], München, 2012, pp. 65–89.

[25] 'An Rex Angliae oborta controversia inter civitates Anzae de privilegiis, ex iure scripto agere nobiscum teneatur?' (Gdańsk APG 300,28/117, f. 40r). *Ius scriptum* in this context refers to the civil law, possibly both Roman and canon law, but definitely the former.

an unconditional supporter of More, at his best – he certainly contributed effectively to scupper what had been in any case an unpromising conference, possibly under the influence of Cardinal Wolsey's less benevolent analysis of the Hanse's usefulness for English interests).[26]

The document, in a characteristic scholastic fashion of *pro* and *contra* considerations which pervaded many civil law arguments, starts off with grounds for admitting that the King of England could decide himself the Anglo-Hanseatic conflict without being bound by civil law rules. This initial part refers to the King as a sovereign (the term is not used as such, but the author uses the well-known phrase of 'a ruler who does not recognise any superior political authority'), it acknowledges that as a full sovereign, the King can adjudicate even in his own cause, and it also observes that the King would not recognise any superior authority of the pope.

The rest of the document, at least what has been preserved, provides an argument for the opposite thesis, and that is obviously the thesis the author wanted to put forward. The principle that the King can decide and adjudicate in favour of his own interests is qualified, especially when interests of non-subjects are at stake. Some emphasis is laid on an

[26] Schäfer, *Hanserezesse*, vol. 3.7, 397–413 (especially No. 203), and, *ibid.*, p. 584, No. 332, item 18 (where More opposed the Hanse's civil law arguments: '... verumtamen hoc constare, quod neque leges imperatoriae, quas tamen minime aspernaretur, neque decisiones doctorum juris neque canonice sanctiones in temporalibus et ubi de bono et tranquillo statu regni Anglie ageretur regem suum obstringerent, neque ipsum, qui regius orator esset'. The protestations of the Hanseatic delegates were still steeped in pre-Reformation reasoning: '... ad id, quod Anglicus presumptuose dixerat, regem Anglie legibus imperialibus non distringi nec canonibus in temporalibus subici, replicavimus, neutrum eorum indistincte, sicut ipse locutus esset, veritati fulciri. Nam quod de Romanis legibus dixisset, hoc eciam secundum eorum sentenciam, qui astruunt regem imperatori non esse subjectum, verum esse auctoritative, hoc est, quod leges naturali racione et equitate innituntur, eatenus ipsum et omnes alios non ut leges sed ut raciones et equitates naturales obstringunt, quod nec aliquis abnegaret. Quod vero de canonibus dixisset, sane accipiendum fore; expeditum enim et in confesso esse, quod, ubi de pactorum, conventionum, federum et promissorum fide et impletione agitur, eciam regem Anglie ac imperatorem ipsum, quo eo longe superior existit, sacris canonibus et Romani pontificis decretis subjectum fore, illorum quoque auctoritate convinci et damnari posse, prout ex multis textibus et sanctorum patrum ac theologorum dictis probari posset. Cui consequens esse diximus, quod cum inter regem ipsum et nostrates de impletione et observatione mutuorum federum, pactorum et conventionum, privilegiorumque nostrorum violatione et infractione ad presens disputetur et contendatur, ista allegatio et evasio, qua se tueri voluit impertinens, erronea et falsa habeatur'. During the 1521 discussions, More (following a line of argumentation which was also Wolsey's) stated that the Hanse had already lost its privileges a long time ago (because of various alleged infringements against their proper use), *ibid.*, pp. 818–824, No. 448, items 31 ss. (5 October) and item 48. Against the English attacks, the Hanse's first line of defence remained the Treaty of Utrecht, e.g. *ibid.*, p. 876, No. 457 (Bruges, September 1521).

individual's right to have a proper defence and legal protection, especially when proceeding before a court, and that would not be guaranteed in a case opposing (in a royal court in England) the King and the Hanse. (This was perhaps a reference to the case pending before the Exchequer shortly before the resumption of the Hanseatic privileges in 1552.)

Most of all those arguments *pro* and *contra* are buttressed by *ius commune* authorities (borrowed from both Roman and Canon laws). However, since the issue was precisely whether such authorities would apply or not in the Anglo-Hanseatic controversy (presented as a *lis*, a form of litigation), the author repeatedly highlights that the principles he relies upon stem from the law of nature, the law of nations, and even divine law. Those were more fundamental and superior rules, and the inference made by the author is that even when the King of England exercised his full regal powers (the *plenitudo potestatis* of late-medieval legal doctrine), those fundamental principles (of due process of law) could not be overruled.

Two short passages from the document may illustrate the author's argument. First,

> . . . that the Kings of England . . . are bound by the authority and determinations of imperial law . . . .[27].

In other words, it is not the authority of the Roman empire or of the Roman emperors which would prevail over the English kings, but the authority of the Roman law.

The second passage is somewhat more explicit on the same point:

> . . . It is only true as regards authority and supremacy that the Kings of England are not subordinate to the authority of the emperors. For in so far as the (Roman law) statutes proceed from the law of nature and the law of nations (ius gentium), rulers all over the whole world are bound by them. It follows therefore that the Kings of England, even though their power may not depend on the authority of the former emperors, are nevertheless bound by the common laws drawn from the law of nature and the law of nations. Throughout Greek and Latin history narratives, we find examples of this. . . . [28]

27 '. . . reges Angliae . . . ad iuris caesarii authoritatem decisionemque adstringi . . . ' (Gdańsk APG 300, 128/117, f. 40v).

28 '. . . tamen palam notum est hoc non nisi per modum authoritatis ac superioritatis verum esse ut scilicet authoritati imperatorum reges Angliae non subiiciantur. Nam quoad constitutiones ex nature et gentium iure profluxerunt, omnes totius orbis principes iis obligantur. Ex quo sequitur reges Angliae si non ob id, quod illorum potestas a divorum imperatorum authoritate dependet, saltem igitur communibus ex nature et gentium legibus depromt[is] obligari . . . ' (Gdańsk APG 300,128/130, f. 571v).

(At that point, we read the beginning of such an ancient illustration, but the text abruptly ends, as the following sheets are missing.)

Paraphrasing a famous formula, the central thesis in this document appears to be that, as regards the English kings, Roman law is not applicable *ratione imperii*. However, this is too early in time to state that it would apply *imperio rationis*. Instead, fundamental Roman law principles are said to be applicable by reason of their foundation in natural law and in the law of nations.

IV. 1553: consultations by Louvain jurists on behalf of Danzig and the Hanse

The second document can most probably be dated to the Summer of 1553, that is, when the Hanseatic embassy travelled to London shortly after Queen Mary's accession. It consists of two, largely overlapping legal consultations, co-signed by the Louvain law professor Gabriel van der Muyden (Mudaeus) and his junior colleague Elbert de Leeuw (Elbertus Leoninus).[29] The embassy's report, probably mostly written by the Danzig member of the embassy, himself a civil lawyer, informs us that shortly before leaving for England, a few members of the delegation travelled to Leuven where they met and conferred with Mudaeus. During the London embassy, the same Danzig delegate was prompted by the other delegates to justify his city's discriminatory policies towards English merchants, an issue which takes central stage in the Louvain legal consultations, and his line of argumentation and use of legal authorities show a striking resemblance with the written consultations of Mudaeus and Leoninus.

It is therefore unlikely that the consultations were written before the Hanseatic embassy had reached the Low Countries in the Spring of 1553 or after the embassy had finished its business by the end of the Summer. The consultations (of which I have found four copies: two in Danzig and two in London) also show that the authors had been briefed about specific local trade practices and policies in Danzig,[30] and those practices play an

[29] On Mudaeus and his contemporaries in Leuven see the catalogue by Jan Papy, *Recht uit Brecht. De Leuvense hoogleraar Gabriel Mudaeus (1500–1560) als Europees humanist en jurist. Catalogus van de tentoonstelling in het Kempisch Museum Brecht, 31 maart-15 mei 2011*, Brecht, 2011.

[30] Przemyslaw Smolarek, 'Gdansk, sein Handel und seine Schiffahrt vom 14. bis 17. Jahrhundert', in *Hanse in Europa, o.c.*, 233–250; on the development of Danzig (based on, in particular, archeological evidence): Aleksander Pluskowski, *The Archeology of the Prussian Crusade. Holy War and Colonisation*, London, New York, 2013, pp. 216–227.

essential role in the central argument developed by the Louvain jurists in favour of the Hanse – and more particularly, of the Danzig protectionist interests.[31]

The Louvain consultations discuss a variety of issues which were raised during the London conference, but which – apart from the question of the recent resumption of the Hanseatic privileges – had already been contentious and recurrently discussed for a long time. In the case of the Danzig treatment of English merchants, the issue can even be traced back to conferences held in the early fifteenth century.[32]

English merchants complained that Danzig restricted or prohibited their trade in Danzig with non-citizens and outside the city, apart from imposing all sorts of other vexatious regulations during their stays in the town. The English merchants and officials pointed out that this was against the agreements of reciprocity with regard to access to trade: whereas the English claimed that Hansards were allowed free access to the English market (a claim which the Germans would increasingly gainsay), they complained that Danzig in particular denied them such free access in Prussia.

The principal legal authority the English could refer to was the Utrecht Treaty of 1474, a convention which, during the sixteenth century, the weakened Hanse was ever more keen to rely upon for protecting its own legal position. Article 4 of the treaty appears to have guaranteed English merchants free access to Danzig and Prussia:

> All and single merchants and other subjects or lieges of the lord King of England while he reigns, whatever their status, could and can, whenever it is convenient to them and they wish to do so, have safe and secure access to the land of Prussia and other places of the Hanse, stay there and have intercourse, leave and return home, buy and sell with any persons whatsoever, freely, in such way and in such manner, as until now before the present time they have been able and have been accustomed to buy and sell, have access and leave, provided they have paid the customary and owed customs and duties on their commodities.[33]

[31] On the Danzig policy towards foreign merchant interests see E. Frankot, '*Of Law of Ships and Shipmen*'. *Medieval Maritime Law and its Practice in Urban Northern Europe*, Edinburgh, 2012, pp. 69–75, referring to older literature see Walter Stark, *Lübeck und Danzig in der zweiten Hälfte des 15. Jahrhunderts*, Weimar, 1973, gives an account of the respective positions of both towns in the relations with England, pp. 183–211.

[32] Johannes Schildhauer, 'Veränderungen in der Stellung der Hanse im Ost- und Nordseeraum vom Stralsunder Frieden 1370 bis zum Frieden von Utrecht 1474', in *Kultur und Politik im Ostseeraum und im Norden 1350–1450*, Visby, 1973, pp. 17–28.

[33] Here and below, my translations of the original Latin version of the treaty as published by Goswin Frhr. von der Ropp, *Hanserecesse von 1431–1476*, Bd. 7, *o.c.*, pp. 340–352.

The key passage, in the original Latin version, are the words 'cum quibuscumque personis' ('with any persons whatsoever') for they played a crucial role in the Louvain consultations. In addition, article 5 appeared to safeguard English merchants from new taxes which could have restricted their trade in Prussia:

> All and single merchants and other subjects and lieges of the lord King of England shall fully use and enjoy in the land of Prussia and other places of the Hanse all and every liberty and free usages, as they have reasonably used and enjoyed at any time before, and no new impositions, taxes or other duties shall be levied upon their persons or goods, other and otherwise than those which are and have been levied for 10, 20, 30, 40, 50 and even 100 years and more.

The ambivalence of the Treaty's provisions is obvious: they refer to earlier practices, but it was precisely those practices which had been controversial before the war. The English would argue in favour of a literal and extensive construction of the text, while the Hanse, especially Danzig, would qualify the general wording by construing the provisions restrictively in the light of what, they claimed, had been the actual practices in their city and Prussia. Inevitably, the diverging interpretations would fuel fresh animosity and conflicts, and would be argued over during later diplomatic exchanges and conferences.

In 1553, faced with the English merchants' protests that they were not allowed free access to trade in Danzig and Prussia (a claim which the English government in turn used in order to argue that the Hanse was not implementing their own obligations under the 1474 Treaty), the Hanseatic delegates relied on formal arguments, including legal arguments and authorities, to establish that in spite of the general phrasing of the Treaty, free access to trade in particular places and territories could legitimately be excluded. The consultations by Mudaeus and Leoninus were elaborate legal arguments which made precisely that point.

Whether such learned consultations made much of an impression on the Privy Councillors is doubtful. At an early stage of the 1553 negotiations, they bluntly told the Hanseatic embassy that they were not interested in 'scholastic disputations', but that they wished to clear their differences '*ex aequo et bono*', on a just and equitable footing – perhaps a sly ironic move, as in the civil law tradition, it was an established principle that controversies involving merchants had to be settled not according to strict law (the rigorous principles of civil law), but *ex aequo et bono*. The reference to equity in this context could only imply an adjustment to the changed balance of power and interests.

The consultations by Mudaeus and Leoninus faced the – at first sight – uphill task of arguing that the words 'with any persons whatsoever' excluded any non-citizens, and that, therefore, English merchants (though in fact, Danzig would claim, *any* merchant from outside Danzig) were only allowed to deal with Danzig citizens, and, moreover, according to local Danzig regulations.

The consultations are therefore typical examples of civil law arguments where a specific legal authority (in this case s. 4 of the Utrecht Treaty) is subjected to a restrictive interpretation. That purpose is achieved through conventional civil law rules of interpretation (based on logical arguments, grammatical arguments, on the theory of legal authorities . . .), but also by drawing into the discussion the fifteenth-century diplomatic history of the issue, referring to earlier treaties and their import, and to the constant position of Danzig on the same issue. Supported by those interpretative arguments, the main argument, however, appears to be drawn from the local practice, styled as custom or statute, which had allegedly prevailed at all times (before and after the Treaty of 1474) and which had retained the restrictive policy of excluding trade by foreign merchants with non-citizens. The consultants' argument was that the general terms of the Treaty had not intended to extend the faculty of trading to dealings with non-citizens, and that, as general terms, they could not be construed as carrying such an effect.

In the following passage, the consultants suggest that the particular usage in Danzig could prevail over a well-established *ius gentium* principle such as freedom of trade, and thus also over any free trade construction of the controversial provision in the Utrecht Treaty:

> However, especially those who are more strongly attached to free trade may question whether that same custom is valid. I am not undertaking at present such a line of argument, although there is no lack of arguments to sustain that this custom can rightly be upheld, both with reference to canon law and civil law authorities, and even more extensively if need be through the fundamental precepts and reasons of philosophy, which are not unrelated to natural law and the law of nations.[34]

Compared to the previous text, which raised the preliminary question whether civil law could be applied in discussing the Anglo-Hanseatic

[34] Quod vero illa ipsa consuetudo in dubium vocari possit an valeat presertim apud eos qui libertati commerciorum ex iure gentium forte sunt addictiores id equidem non suscepi nunc defendendum quamvis non desit quod ea consuetudo valide defendi possit tam ex iure pontificio [. . .] quam civili [. . .] ut latius si res ita postularet demonstrari posset ex intimis philosophie preceptis et rationibus a iure naturali et gentium non alienis (British Library, Lansdowne Ms. 170, f. 186v).

conflict, these consultations simply assume the authority of civil law, if only as an instrument of legal interpretation. But here again the need to refer to some higher legal authority is present, and it is significant that the possible objection to the Hanseatic position based on a principle of the law of nations is being refuted by referring to principles deemed to be founded in the law of nature and the law of nations.

V. 1603: lobbying at the imperial and princely courts

The third and last document[35] brings us to the last year of Elizabeth's reign, when the Steelyard's and the Hanse's former position in London and England was irredeemably lost. The document is an extensive memorandum of more than 400 pages. It is anonymous, but obviously written by a (German) civil lawyer, probably shortly after the Bremen conference in 1603. It was not printed, but more copies of this volume are to be found in other Hanseatic archives, which proves that it was circulated in Germany.[36]

To some extent, the memorandum is an elaborate refutation of a pamphlet published two years before by John Wheeler, secretary of the Company of Merchants Adventurers.[37] Wheeler's text is a merchant's policy document, which does not dwell on legal arguments.[38] Its main purpose is to advocate the Merchants Adventurers' usefulness for English

[35] I rely on Lübeck ASA, Hanseatica, Externa Anglicana 158 (one bound volume of 202 numbered folios and some unnumbered folios); the same text appears to be kept at the City Archives of Stralsund, Hans. Fach 10 No. 13, *Defensio iurium Hansae.*

[36] The memorandum is briefly discussed in Alain Wijffels, 'History and Law. The Case for the German Hanse against the English Merchants Adventurers (1603–1604)', in Ignazio Czeguhn (ed.), *Recht im Wandel – Wandel des Rechts. Festschrift für Jürgen Weitzel zum 70. Geburtstag*, Cologne-Vienna, 2014, pp. 427–452.

[37] Iohn Wheeler, *A Treatise of commerce, wherin are shewed the commodies arising by a well ordered, and ruled trade, Such as that of the Societie of Merchantes Adventurers is proved to bee, written principallie for the better information of those who doubt of the Necessarienes of the said Societie in the State of the Realme of England*, Middelburgh, By Richard Schilders, Printer to the States of Zeland, 1601; a reproduction of the original edition can be viewed on the internet, but I refer here to the reprint (with a useful historical introduction) by George Burton Hotchkiss (ed.), *A Treatise of Commerce by John Wheeler, Secretary of the Society of Merchants Adventurers of England 1601*, New York, 1931.

[38] Wheeler's pamphlet is of course only one example of a long string of various arguments developed during the earlier decades; see Nils Jörn, 'The Crocodile Creature Merchant: The Dutch Hansa. Die Widerspiegelung der english-hansischen Auseinandersetzungen in den Denkschriften englisher Kaufleute und Politiker in der zweiten Hälfte des 16. Jahrhunderts', in Antjekathrin Grassmann (ed.), *Niedergang oder Übergang? Zur Spätzeit der Hanse im 16. und 17. Jahrhundert*, Köln-Weimar-Wien, 1998, pp. 63–91.

commercial interests, and to dismiss accusations directed against the Company by the Hanse. It was written in English (and published, shortly after the first publication in Middelburg, Zeeland, in London), which suggests that it was not primarily intended to reach a German or even an international audience, but a readership and figures of influence in England itself. The Hanseatic memorandum refers on many occasions to Wheeler's text, but it follows its own structure. The two texts illustrate the point that both parties were no longer attempting to exchange arguments with each other, but were pursuing their own propaganda on their respective home fronts. The language and the register are in each case entirely different.

The 1603 memorandum can be divided into two parts. The first part (covering a little more than 100 pages) gives an historical overview of the Hanse's presence in England since the earliest times and of the development of Anglo-Hanseatic relations. The circumstances around the Utrecht Treaty of 1474 and the resumption of the privileges in 1552 and English policies during the second half of the sixteenth century receive the most attention. If one would compare this first part with a civil law-style consultation (a *consilium*), it could be compared to a very elaborate *species facti*, a statement of the relevant facts – presented by one party, and therefore biased, but nevertheless in a way which purports to remain objective.

The second part of the memorandum, which covers almost three-quarters of the more than 400 pages, consists of mainly legal argumentation, buttressed by several hundred marginal notes containing a great many references to a wide range of civil law authorities: texts of the *corpora iuris*, commentaries, *consilia*, *repetitiones*, legal treatises, drawn from a very rich library of late-medieval and sixteenth-century legal works. This second part, if one pursues the analogy with a very elaborate consultation, would be the equivalent of the *in iure* part, where the author argues specifically in favour of one party and against that party's opponent.

Part 2 is subdivided into twenty-two chapters. There is a clear progression and structure throughout the sequence of those chapters. The first fourteen chapters consider the 1552 decree and the reasons it stated for resuming the Hanseatic privileges. Each individual reason is then discussed separately and refuted through legal arguments. Chapters 15–18 consider, likewise, further restrictions of the Hanse's rights during the reigns of Mary and Elizabeth, referring to what has been set out in Part 1, but challenging here the lawfulness of the decisions under both queens. Finally, the reasons given in the imperial order of 1597 are given a formal justification through legal arguments and authorities in Chapters 19–22.

The memorandum's closing pages no doubt provide the best clue as regards the addressees of the whole argumentation and its purpose. The author asks the Emperor and the Estates to ensure that the 1597 Order be effectively executed, that no leeway should be granted to the Merchants Adventurers and that Hanseatic interests be better protected – demands which reflect complaints the Hanse had repeatedly expressed during the previous years. It makes sense that, if the addressees were the Emperor and the Estates, which implied that the memorandum would have to be read by the rulers' specialised councillors, the register of the memorandum would be that of a formal and technical civil law argument, a format that would appeal to such councillors who were mostly academic law graduates.

The technical characteristics of such a text remind us that because, in the imperial and territorial princes' councils (in the Holy Roman Empire), jurists were holding offices at the heart of public governance, the model of legal reasoning and the use of legal authorities were also part of the system of public governance itself. It is striking that, on the one hand, the methods in the memorandum (partly expressed through the use of authorities) remain on the whole fairly traditional. Sixteenth-century works are well represented, but mostly through those works which followed traditional legal thinking. Legal humanism, for example, is mostly absent. On the other hand, a recent work such as Gentili's *De iure belli*, which had been published only five years before, is quoted more than twenty times. (It was, of course, a book which provided highly relevant material for the issues at stake, and, moreover, which contained two passages where Gentili specifically discussed the position of the Hanse in England in his day.)[39]

The reliance on traditional methods meant that a great deal of the specific arguments are based on general legal concepts and principles, that analogies are still freely used and that rules of interpretation play a major role here, too, a major role. As an example, Chapter 12 of Part 2 shows how the author of the memorandum deals with one of the justifications given for the 1552 decree, namely the English objection that over the centuries, and particularly in recent times, the Hanseatic privileges had become excessively harmful to English interests. The issue is of particular interest, because, on the one hand, the principle that a privilege (or, more

[39] Alain Wijffels, 'Alberico Gentili and the Hanse: The Early Reception of De iure belli (1598)', in Pierre-Marie Dupuy and Vincent Chétail (eds.), *The Roots of International Law/Les fondements du droit international. Liber amicorum Peter Haggenmacher*, Leiden, 2014, pp. 181–209.

generally, a private right) could be ended by a ruler when its exercise was harmful to the commonwealth had already been established by late-medieval legal doctrines. However, in early-modern times, when a new concept of sovereignty was developed which often reflected a new balance of power in the polity in favour of the sovereign ruler, the practical importance of such a principle was that individuals' rights became *de facto* more vulnerable – whenever the ruler faced less effective checks and the rule of law could not rely on the backing of strong political and social actors.[40]

The Hanseatic memorandum offers a typical example of a corporation which had acquired rights and titles in bygone, more propitious times, when it enjoyed a relative position of power, but, when the balance of power had changed to its disadvantage, was forced to rely more heavily on what it saw as its vested rights. Thus, most of the legal arguments against the legitimacy of the King's resumption of their privileges brought forward the traditional legal grounds asserting that the king was strictly bound by the grants he had made and which had been confirmed by conventional and official acts. Those arguments drawn from late-medieval civil law doctrines were inevitably regarded as restrictions of the ruler's prerogative powers, and thus at odds with the early-modern concept of sovereignty which had since then been developed.

Perhaps, the most difficult issue for the Hanse was the need to argue that their privileges would remain valid and in force even if, as the English government and merchants claimed, they had become harmful to the realm with the passing of time. In this context, the arguments founded on the binding force of conventions were more difficult to reconcile with the higher principle of the commonwealth's overruling public interest, of which the early-modern sovereign had often become in practice the supreme judge. It is at that stage of the argument in Chapter 12 that the memorandum has to argue that the *rebus sic stantibus* principle would not apply. This part of the argument inevitably combines both legal arguments tending to qualify the applicability of the *rebus sic stantibus* principle and policy considerations.

The policy arguments of the Hanse are that their part in developing English foreign trade was not harmful to English economic interests, but that, conversely, the Adventurers' increasing monopolistic position

40 I have outlined that general argument in a different context; see Alain Wijffels, 'Early-Modern Consilia and Decisiones in the Low Countries. The Lost Legacy of the mos italicus', in P. Maffei and G.M. Varanini (eds.), *Honos alit artes. Studi per il settantesimo compleanno di Mario Ascheri*, Florence, 2014, 4 vols., vol. 1, pp. 125–137.

did have a negative economic and social impact within the Realm. They refer to riots in different parts of England, which, they claim, had been the consequence of the Adventurers' restrictive practices and price-fixing policies. As more often in civil law arguments at the time, these policy arguments are backed up with other authorities, both legal and religious or moral. The conclusion of Chapter 12 returns to its starting point: it says that if the use of lawful privileges becomes harmful in later times, that is not a legitimate reason for abolishing the privileges. Thus, another ground of the 1552 decree is said to fail.

The technical legal register of the memorandum does not prevent the occasional barbed comment, for example,

> No one is so stupid and ignorant of worldy affairs, that he would not recognise . . . that our opponents want to oust us, so that all commercial traffic of all nations and even of the subjects of the Realm themselves will be reserved to the exclusive benefit of the Adventurers – even though their private interests are the worst example of what ought to be in the general interest of the Realm.
>
> . . . It is therefore all too obvious, that, whatever the English may object against our privileges on the pretext of a serious prejudice (laesio enormis), their argument cannot provide a lawful or acceptable legal justification or even amount to a factual basis [viz. for the resumption of the privileges].[41]

Neither the general approach and register of the memorandum, nor such quips as the one just quoted, could have been helpful to reverse the English policies towards the Hanse. Nor was there any international forum acceptable to all parties where the arguments of such a memorandum could have been submitted. As already suggested, the purpose of the memorandum was to offer policy makers in the Empire (both the emperor's court and the courts of territorial princes) an elaborate justification for fully and strictly implementing the 1597 order and for supporting the Hanse in commercial policies and diplomatic exchanges, especially when dealing with English merchants or with the English government.

VI. Conclusion

Three texts over a period of more than half a century are insufficient to yield a legal history of the Anglo-Hanseatic relations during the sixteenth century. Nevertheless, they provide an insight into the use of civil law arguments in an essentially non-legal context, viz. the diplomatic and

[41] Freely translated from Lübeck SA, ASA, Hanseatica, Externa Anglicana 158 f. 129v.

political exchanges between the commercial and political actors involved in the conflict.

As regards the legal methods and the use of authorities, the chronological progression of the three documents shows a large degree of continuity, from late-medieval legal methods to a somewhat more systematic approach by 1603.

That internal continuity, however, cannot hide the fact that external factors affected the very purpose of the legal arguments, and that, appearances notwithstanding, by 1603, the legal arguments and authorities operated in a substantially different context which affected their significance. Whereas until the mid-sixteenth century the Hanse could still hope to rely on civil law as an instrument for formalising the discussion about their controversial commercial status, by the end of the century, they needed the civil law in order to legitimise their claim for protection by political actors on whom, both in domestic affairs and in international relations, the Hanse had become increasingly dependent.

9

History and the justification of governmental authority and individual rights in the age of John Locke and Samuel Pufendorf

ANDREAS THIER

I. Introduction

It is a typical narrative of medieval and early-modern explanations for individual rights and governmental power that society, legal order and statehood have a point of origin in a far, mythical or sacral past. The Fall, one or several social contracts and/or behavioural patterns of humans are typical manifestations of these origin narratives.[1] In the context of

[1] For the Fall of man see as a survey Peter Landau, "Der biblische Sündenfall und die Legitimität des Rechts", in *Die Begründung des Rechts als historisches Problem (Schriften des Historischen Kollegs, Kolloquien, 45*, ed. Dietmar Willoweit (Munich: Oldenbourg Verlag, 2000), pp. 203–214; in more detail see Wolfgang Stürner, *Peccatum und Potestas. Der Sündenfall und die Entstehung der herrscherlichen Gewalt im mittelalterlichen Staatsdenken* (Sigmaringen: Thorbecke, 1987), Bernhard Töpfer, *Urzustand und Sündenfall in der mittelalterlichen Gesellschafts- und Staatstheorie* (Stuttgart: Hiersemann, 1999); see also Kathleen M. Crowther, *Adam and Eve in the Protestant Reformation* (Cambridge: Cambridge University Press, 2010); Klaus Schreiner, "Adams und Evas Griff nach dem Apfel – Sündenfall oder Glücksfall?", in *Der Fehltritt. Vergehen und Versehen in der Frühmoderne*, ed. Peter von Moos (Köln/Weimar/Wien: Böhlau, 2001), pp. 151–176. On the tradition of social contract doctrine see as a survey Samuel Freeman, "Social Contract Approaches", in *The Oxford Handbook of Political Philosophy* (Oxford: Oxford University Press, 2012, accessed 18 June 2015, DOI: 10.1093/oxfordhb/9780195376692.013.0007), and Wolfgang Kersting, "The Classic Social Contract Tradition", in *Handbook of the Philosophical Foundations of Business Ethics*, ed. Christoph Luetge (Dordrecht/Heidelberg/New York/London: Springer, 2013), pp. 605–629; for more details see the contributions in *The Social Contract from Hobbes to Rawls*, eds. David Boucher and Paul Kelly (London: Routledge, 1994; repr. 2005), and *L'Idée contractuelle dans l'histoire de la pensée politique Actes du Colloque International de l'A.F.H.I.P., septembre 2007 (Collection d'histoire des idées politiques, vol. 19)* (Aix-en-Provence: Presses universitaires d'Aix-Marseille, 2008). For a recent historical contextualisation see the essays by Deborah Baumgold, in *Contract Theory in Historical Context. Essays on Grotius, Hobbes, and Locke* (London/Boston: Brill, 2010, accessed 18 June 2015, DOI: 10.1163/ej.9789004184251.i-190).

legal doctrine and legal philosophy, this kind of regression to a zero point of mankind and human existence can serve different purposes.[2] First and foremost, it justifies the existence and, as a consequence, the binding power of legal rules and governmental dominion. Isidor of Seville (560–636),[3] for instance, explained the loss of human liberty to law and governmental power by the "sin of the first man" as the "penalty of slavery" handed out by God.[4] And, as a matter of fact, later on the contract as a device of individual liberty and formation of statehood would come to the fore as, for instance, in Thomas Hobbes' (1588–1679)[5] famous definition of the commonwealth as "One person, of whose Acts a great Multitude, by mutuall covenants one with another, have made themselves every one the Author, to the end he may use the strength and means of them all, as he shall think expedient, for their Peace and Common Defence".[6]

But there is another important function of narratives about the origins of mankind and law. The evolution from an origin somewhere in the abyss of an early past to the present – the idea of the history of mankind – offers the analytical means to explain and justify different types of legal

[2] For a survey see Andreas Thier, "Heilsgeschichte und naturrechtliche Ordnung: Naturrecht vor und nach dem Sündenfall", in *Naturrecht in Antike und früher Neuzeit. Symposion aus Anlass des 75. Geburtstags von Klaus Luig*, eds. Matthias Armgardt and Tilman Repgen (Tübingen: Mohr Siebeck, 2014), pp. 151–172, 151–152.

[3] Survey: Michel Banniard, "Isidore of Seville (570–636)", in *Encyclopedia of the Middle Ages, vol. 1*, eds. Andre Vauchez, Harrie Dobson and Michael Lapidge (Cambridge: James Clarke & Co, 2000), pp. 740–741. For a deeper account see John Henderson, *The Medieval World of Isidore of Seville: Truth from Words* (Cambridge: Cambridge University Press, 2007).

[4] Isidore of Seville, Sententiae III.47, 1: *Propter peccatum primi hominis humano generi poena divinitus inlata est servitutis*, cf. *Isidorus Hispalensis Sententiae (Corpus Christianorum, Series latina, 111)*, ed. Pierre Cazier (Turnhout: Brepols, 1998), p. 225; see Thier, "Heilsgeschichte" (n. 2), pp. 151–152 with n. 4, and in more detail Töpfer, *Urzustand* (n. 1), pp. 86–91.

[5] *The Cambridge Companion to Thomas Hobbes*, ed. Tom Sorrel (Cambridge: Cambridge University Press, 1996, online 2006, accessed 4 March 2015, http://dx.doi.org/10.1017/CCOL0521410193).

[6] Thomas Hobbes, *Leviathan or The Matter, Forme and Power of a Common Wealth Ecclesiasticall and Civill* (London: Andrew Crooke, 1651), used here as in *Thomas Hobbes. Leviathan, vol. 2 (Clarendon Edition of the Works of Thomas Hobbes)*, vol. 4, ed. Noel Malcolm (Oxford: Oxford University Press, 2012), ch. 17, pp. 260–261 (p. 88 in the 1st edition). On this definition and its epistemical context see the contributions in *The Cambridge Companion to Hobbes's Leviathan*, ed. Patricia Springborg (Cambridge: Cambridge University Press, 2007, online 2007, accessed 18 June 2015, http://dx.doi.org/10.1017/CCOL0521836670), in particular Kinch Hoekstra, "Hobbes on the Natural Condition of Mankind", *ibid.*, pp. 109–127, Quentin Skinner, "Hobbes on Persons, Authors, and Representatives", *ibid.*, pp. 157–180, and Luc Foisneau, "Omnipotence, Necessity and Sovereignty. Hobbes and the Absolute and Ordinary Powers of God and King", *ibid.*, pp. 271–290.

normativity. This applies in particular to the idea of natural law. Gratian,[7] the famous "father of the science of canon law",[8] explained in his *Decretum*[9] around 1140 the particular normative importance of natural law by the argument, "natural law receives first place among all others [i.e. other laws] because of its time [*tempore*] and dignity".[10] Here, the temporal character of natural law as eternal was one of the reasons for its normative power.[11] But the idea of a chronological sequence of different types of legal rules coming into existence could also be used in order to resolve normative tensions between different legal ideas. A typical example of this approach was the legitimisation of individual property as opposed to the early Christian ideal of common property and poverty,[12] which might be illustrated by another example taken from medieval canon law: Gratian discussed the idea of common property,[13] stating that "by natural law all things are common for all" (*iure naturae sunt omnia communia omnibus*); individual property, however, had, in Gratian's view, been created by human law (*iure vero consuetudinis vel constitutionis hoc meum est, illud vero alterius*).[14] This posed a serious problem for medieval canonists:

[7] See as one of the most recent contributions on Gratian's biography Anders Winroth, "Where Gratian Slept: the Life and Death of the Father of Canon Law", *Zeitschrift für Rechtsgeschichte, Kanonistische Abteilung* 130 (2013): pp. 105–128.

[8] Stephan Kuttner, "The Father of the Science of Canon Law", *Jurist. Studies in Church Law and Ministry* 1 (1941): pp. 2–19.

[9] Peter Landau, "Gratian and the Decretum Gratiani", in *The History of Medieval Canon Law in the Classical Period, 1140–1234. From Gratian to the Decretals of Pope Gregory IX*, eds. Wilfried Hartmann and Kenneth Pennington (Washington, DC: The Catholic University of America Press, Washington DC, 2008), pp. 22–54 with further reference; for a continuously updated survey see Kenneth Pennington, entry "Gratian", in ibid., *Medieval Canonists. A Bio-Bibliographical Listing*, online, accessed 4 March 2015 (URL: http://faculty.cua.edu/pennington/1140a-z.htm#Gratian).

[10] Gratian, Decretum, Dict. ante D. 5 c. 1 § 1, quoted from the edition *Decretum Magistri Gratiani*, ed. Aemilius Friedberg (Leipzig: Tauchnitz, 1879, repr. Graz: Akademische Druck- und Verlagsanstalt, 1995), col. 7: *Naturale ius inter omnia primatum obtinet et tempore et dignitate*; the translation in English follows Augustine Thompson in ibid., James Gordley and Katherine Christensen, *Gratian. The Treatise on Laws (Decretum DD. 1–20) with the Ordinary Gloss (Studies in Medieval and Early Modern Canon Law, 2)* (Washington, DC: The Catholic University of America Press, 1993), p. 16.

[11] For a deeper discussion of Gratian's argument see Thier, "Heilsgeschichte" (n. 2), p. 154.

[12] For a survey see Eric Francis Osborn, Art. "Eigentum IV. Alte Kirche", *Theologische Realenzyklopädie* 9 (1982), pp. 414–417.

[13] For a survey on Gratian's property doctrine see Janet Coleman, "Property and Poverty", in *The Cambridge History of Medieval Political Thought, c. 350 –c. 1450*, ed. J. H. Burns (Cambridge: Cambridge University Press, 1988), pp. 607–648, 617–618.

[14] Gratian, Decretum, Dict. ante D. 8, c. 1, quoted from the edition by Friedberg, *Decretum* (n. 10), col. 12.

Gratian described common property as established by natural law, while individual property was granted by the rules of positive law, with both rules contradicting each other.

This contradiction meant a serious threat for the realisation of the canonists' claim to create "Harmony from Dissonance", to quote Stephan Kuttner's famous formula for the intention underlying medieval canonists' efforts to order the vast material of legal texts.[15] Alanus, a canonist teaching in Bologna around 1200,[16] brought this problem to the formula *duo contraria* [*scil. iura*] *sunt iusta*: two contradictory legal rules were apparently just.[17] One way out from this dilemma[18] was the regression to the history of the fall of Adam and Eve. Laurentius Hispanus,[19] for example, distinguished a *ius naturale primaevum* and a postlapsarian natural law: while common property existed in the period before Adam's and Eve's expulsion from paradise as rule of divine natural law, individual property came to existence by divine decree and thus divine law when God ordered Adam "By the sweat of your brow you will eat your food" (Genesis 3:19).[20] Here, the course of events since the creation of Adam was understood as the course of divine creation of different kinds of property, which made it possible to harmonise two opposing ideas of proprietary orders both as natural law.

The last mentioned example demonstrates, however, also the importance of the conception of history for the validity of these narratives of origin and their justification of legal rules: the idea of the divine creation

15 Stephan Kuttner, *Harmony from Dissonance. An Interpretation of Medieval Canon Law* (Latrobe, PA: Archabbey Press, 1961) reprinted in ibid., *The History of Ideas and Doctrines of Canon Law in the Middle Ages* (London: Variorum 1992), pp. 1–16.

16 Kenneth Pennington, "The Decretalists 1190 – 1234", in *The History of Medieval Canon Law in the Classical Period, 1140–1234. From Gratian to the Decretals of Pope Gregory IX*, eds. Wilfried Hartmann and Kenneth Pennington (Washington, DC: The Catholic University of America Press, 2008), pp. 211–245, 219–220 with further reference.

17 Alanus, second recension of his gloss on the *decretum Gratiani*, ed in Rudolf Weigand, *Die Naturrechtslehre der Legisten von Irnerius bis Accursius und von Gratian bis Johannes Teutonicus* (München: Max Hueber, 1967), p. 317, § 535; on Alanus' gloss see the survey in Pennington, "Decretalists" (n. 16), p. 219.

18 For a survey see Landau, "Sündenfall" (n. 1), 211–213, and Thier, "Heilsgeschichte" (n. 2), pp. 159–160; for a discussion in deeper detail Weigand, *Naturrechtslehre* (n. 17), pp. 319–336.

19 Survey: Pennington, "Decretalists" (n. 16), pp. 228–230 with further reference.

20 Laurentius Hispanus, Gloss ad D. 1 c. 1, ad v. *per agrum alienum fas est*, edited in Weigand, *Naturrechtslehre* (n. 17), p. 251, § 428: *De iure naturali primevo omnia sunt communia . . . set de iure diuino aliquid est proprium etian ueteri testamento; nam et Abel de suis et Caym de suis frugibus optulit et dictum est Ade: 'In sudore uultus tui uesceris pane tuo'.*

of individual property shortly after Adam's fall only made sense for the legitimisation of present individual proprietary rights if the present was actually conceived in continuity with sacred history, as embedded in a universal divine order of past, present and future. If, however, another idea of history formed the reference for the interpretation of the present legal rules, for instance, the idea of an abstract state of nature, the idea of individual property as part of natural law had to be explained another way. In fact, as will be argued in what follows, by the seventeenth and early eighteenth centuries, such a transition in the conception of history occurred. In this perspective, as demonstrated in the following section of this paper (Part II), John Locke's ideas on the state of nature (and individual property rights) represented a more conservative tradition of narratives of origin, which was basically rooted in continuities with medieval traditions. In Samuel Pufendorf, however, a new approach emerged, which would result in the separation between sacred history and legal reasoning (Part III). The rise of this perspective indicated more or less a transition in conceptualising history during the sixteenth to eighteenth centuries, as it shall be tentatively argued in conclusion (Part IV).

II. Sacred history and governmental power

As indicated above, the idea of a divinely ordered course of history had a deep impact on the justification of individual rights and, to a lesser extent, dominion. The controversy on Apostolic poverty in the thirteenth and fourteenth centuries[21] is a typical example of this kind of reasoning: in arguing about the legitimacy of property rights, advocates on both sides relied heavily on the biblical account of paradise and fall.[22] William of Ockham (1287–1347),[23] for example, tried to disprove the idea of natural law-based property with the argument that "the first parents after their sin

[21] For a magisterial survey see Coleman, "Property" (n. 13), pp. 631–648, and Jürgen Miethke, *Politiktheorie im Mittelalter: von Thomas von Aquin bis Wilhelm von Ockham* (Tübingen: Mohr Siebeck, 2008), pp. 248–271; for a recent account of the debates on this controversy on property in particular see Jonathan Robinson, *William of Ockham's Early Theory of Property Rights in Context (Studies in Medieval and Reformation Traditions, vol. 166)* (Leiden: Brill, 2013), pass., for a previous, but still indispensable analysis of the ideas surrounding this controversy see Töpfer, *Urzustand* (n. 1), pp. 417–495.

[22] On this aspect see Thier, "Heilsgeschichte" (n. 2), pp. 163–165.

[23] Paul Vincent Spade, ed., *The Cambridge Companion to Ockham* (Cambridge: Cambridge University Press, 1999).

did not own property... but they had only the power (*potestas*) to make things their own".[24] As a consequence, he could claim that property rights could not be derived from divine order and thus attack the position of Pope John XXII (1316–1334),[25] who had claimed that individual property had been created by divine will.[26]

These approaches were still strongly present in the discourses of the sixteenth and seventeenth centuries.[27] Adrian Saravia (c. 1531–1612),[28] a Flemish theologian active since 1587 in England, was a prominent representative for this kind of reasoning on statehood and law, which might be called "patriarchalism".[29] In his treatise *De imperandi authoritate, et Christiana obedientia, libri quatuor* (1593),[30] he argued that "from sacred history the true origin of dominion is taught", and claimed "that the first dominion has been paternal".[31] The dominion of Adam over Eve

[24] William of Ockham, *Opus nonaginta dierum*, c. 14, in *Guillemi de Ockham, Opera Politica*, vol. 2, eds. Ralph F. Bennet and Hilary S. Offler (Manchester: Manchester University Press, 1963), p. 435: *...quod primi parentes post peccatum non habuerunt dominium commune... sed habebant potestatem appropriandi sibi.* For a deeper discussion of this argument see Miethke, *Politiktheorie* (n. 21), pp. 281–285, and Brian Tierney, *The Idea of Natural Rights. Studies on Natural Rights, Natural Law, and Church Law 1150–1625 (Emory University, Studies in Law and Religion, no. 5)* (Grand Rapids: Eerdmans, 2001 [repr. of 1st edition 1997]), pp. 157–168.

[25] Hans-Joachim Schmidt and Martin Rohde, eds., *Papst Johannes XXII. Konzepte und Verfahren seines Pontifikats: Freiburger Colloquium 2012 (Scrinium Friburgense, vol. 32)* (Berlin/Boston: De Gruyter 2014).

[26] For a reconstruction of John's argument see Tierney, *Natural Rights* (n. 24), pp. 154–157, and a short account in Thier, "Heilsgeschichte" (n. 2), pp. 163–164.

[27] See in particular Janet Coleman, "Dominium in Thirteenth- and Fourteenth-Century Political Thought and its Seventeenth-Century Heirs: John of Paris and Locke", *Political Studies* 33 (1985), pp. 73–100, here pp. 85–89, 97–100 with further reference; in general Tierney, *Natural Rights* (n. 24), pp. 167–168.

[28] For a survey see Johann P. Sommerville, "Saravia, Hadrian (or Adrian, Adrianus, Hadrianus: c.1532–1613)", *The Continuum Encyclopedia of British Philosophy*, ed. A.C. Grayling, Naomi Goulder and Andrew Pyle, online 2010 (www.oxfordreference.com/view/10.1093/acref/9780199754694.001.0001/acref-9780199754694-e-1845?rskey=UWfCZw&result=1, accessed 4 March 2015) with further references; Willem Nijenhuis, *Adrianus Saravia (ca. 1532–1613): Dutch Calvinist, First Reformend Defender of the English Episcopal Church Order on the Basis of the Ius Divinum* (Leiden: Brill, 1980).

[29] Cf. Johann P. Sommerville, *Royalists and Patriots: Politics and Ideology in England, 1603–1640*, 2nd edition (London: Longman, 1999, repr. 2014), p. 29.

[30] On this treatise in general and its historical context see Nijenhuis, *Adrianus Saravia* (n. 29), pp. 244–255.

[31] Adrian(us) Saravia, *De imperandi authoritate, et Christiana obedientia, libri quatuor* (London, 1593), II.9, p. 62 (http://gateway.proquest.com/openurl?ctx_ver=Z39.88-2003&res_id=xri:eebo&rft_id=xri:eebo:image:17242:41, accessed 4 March 2015): *Ex sacra historia docetur vera imperii origo, et quod... prima imperii fuisse paternal.*

was understood as the archetype of political order, and later kings like Noah, Sem or Iapeth were successors in this kind of royal kingship, which thus formed a part of divinely ordained history and, as a consequence, of the present.[32] Another, and it may be said notorious, author using this kind of argument was Robert Filmer (1588–1653).[33] In his treatise *Patriarcha*, written around 1630 and published in 1680,[34] he intensified the thesis of paternal royal authority stating, "And indeed not only Adam but the succeeding patriarchs had, by the right of fatherhood, royal authority over their children".[35] This combination of sacred history, political conceptions and legal reasoning[36] became even more distinct in Filmer's criticism of Hobbes's social contract theory,[37] which was published in 1652. Here, Filmer combined the idea of Adam's creation and power, paternal dominion, sacred history and property rights: "if also God gave to Adam not only the dominion over the woman and the children that should issue from them, but also the whole earth to subdue it, and over all the creatures on it, so that as long as Adam lived no man could claim or enjoy anything but by donation, assignation or permission from him".[38] It was telling for this kind of merging of sacred history and legal thinking

32 For a deeper discussion of these conceptions see Sommerville, *Royalists* (n. 29), pp. 31–37; (for Saravia see *ibid.*, pp. 34–35).

33 Cesare Cuttica, *Sir Robert Filmer (1588–1653) and the Patriotic Monarch: Patriarchalism in Seventeenth-Century Political Thought* (Manchester: Manchester University Press, 2012); James Daly, *Sir Robert Filmer and English Political Thought* (Toronto: University of Toronto Press, 1979).

34 Johann P. Sommerville, "The Authorship and Date of Some Works Attributed to Filmer", *Filmer. Patriarcha and other Writings*, ed. Johann P. Sommerville (Cambridge: Cambridge University Press, 1991, repr. 2001, online 2012), pp. XXXII–XXXVII, XXXII–IV with further reference (http://dx.doi.org/10.1017/CBO9780511812644.005, last accessed 4 March 2015).

35 Robert Filmer, "Patriarcha" (1680), I.3, in *Filmer. Patriarcha and other Writings*, ed. Johann P. Sommerville (Cambridge: Cambridge University Press, 1991, repr. 2001, online 2012), pp. XXXII–XXXVII, XXXII–IV with further reference (http://dx.doi.org/10.1017/CBO9780511812644.005, last accessed 4 March 2015), 6.

36 On this aspect see also Thier, "Heilsgeschichte" (n. 2), pp. 166–167.

37 For a survey see Alan Ryan, "Hobbes's Political Philosophy", in *Cambridge Companion to Hobbes* (n. 5), pp. 208–245, here pp. 216–241 (http://dx.doi.org/10.1017/CCOL0521410193.010, accessed 22 October 2014). For a deeper discussion see Jean Hampton, *Hobbes and the Social Contract Tradition* (Cambridge: Cambridge University Press, 1986, online 2012), pp. 132–188. See also Baumgold, *Contract Theory* (n. 1), passim.

38 Robert Filmer, "Observations concerning the Originall of Government, upon Mr Hobs Leviathan, Mr Milton against Salmasius, H. Grotius De Jure Belli" (1652), 1.1, in *Filmer. Patriarcha and other Writings*, ed. Johann P. Sommerville (Cambridge: Cambridge University Press, 1991, repr. 2001, online 2012), pp. 184–234, 187 (http://dx.doi.org/10.1017/CBO9780511812644.011, accessed 4 March 2015).

that Filmer referred to the bible as absolute authority for his narrative stating "We must not deny the truth of the history of the creation".[39]

Filmer and Saravia were not alone with these interpretations of sacred history. There were, however, other, different perspectives on creation, the fall and government. Already Richard Hooker (1554–1600)[40] had laid out another understanding of the origins of government in his famous treatise *Of the Lawes of Ecclesiastical Polity* (1593/97). Here, he discussed the idea of original paternal dominion and actually conceded, "To fathers within their private families Nature hath given a supreme power; for which cause we see throughout the world even from the foundation thereof, all men have ever been taken as lords and lawful kings in their own houses". Moreover, Hooker accepted the idea that possibly "when numbers of households joined themselves in civil society together, kings were the first kind of governors amongst them".[41] Contrary to Saravia (and later Filmer), however, this kind of paternal monarchy was not the only possible type of political order. In this regard, the theologian Hooker understood history more as an open process, governed also by the people's rational decisions: "Howbeit not this [sic] the only kind of regiment that hath been received in the world.... So that in a word all public regiment of what kind soever seemeth evidently to have risen from deliberate advice, consultation, and composition between men, judging it convenient and behoveful".[42] On this view, the history of mankind was not a determined sequence of paternal monarchies, but it remained open to autonomous human arrangement, including the choice of other types of dominion than paternal monarchy.

In this denial in particular of paternal monarchies as the only possible government, Hooker was in agreement with John Locke (1632–1704).[43]

[39] Filmer, "Observations" I.3., in *Filmer* (n. 38), p. 188.

[40] William John Torrence Kirby, "Hooker, Richard (1554–1600)", *The Continuum Encyclopedia of British Philosophy*, ed. A.C. Grayling, Naomi Goulder and Andrew Pyle, online 2010 (www.oxfordreference.com/view/10.1093/acref/9780199754694.001.0001/acref-9780199754694-e-1021?rskey=XCX1d1&result=1, accessed 4 March 2015); *A Companion to Richard Hooker (Brill's Companions to the Christian Tradition, vol. 8)*, eds. William John and Torrence Kirby (Leiden: Brill, 2008); Richard Kirby, *The Theology of Richard Hooker in the context of the Magisterial Reformation* (Princeton: Princeton Theological Seminary, 2000), pp. 1–22 and passim.

[41] Richard Hooker, *Of the Laws of Ecclesiastical Polity, book 1* (1593), chapter 10.4, ed. Arthur Stephen McGrade, vol. 1 (Oxford: Oxford University Press, 2013), pp. 72–73.

[42] Hooker, *Laws I* (n. 41), chapter 10.4, ed. McGrade, 73.

[43] *The Cambridge Companion to Locke*, ed. Vere Chappell (Cambridge: Cambridge University Press, 1994); *The Continuum Companion to Locke*, ed. S.-J. Savonius-Wroth, Paul Schuurman, Jonathan Walmsley (London/New York: Bloomsbury 2010). Manfred Brocker, *Die Grundlegung des liberalen Verfassungsstaates. Von den Levellern zu John Locke* (Freiburg i.

And so it was not by coincidence that Locke frequently referred to the "judicious Hooker", in his *Two Treatises on Government* (1689).[44] The relation between Hooker and Locke has been the subject of debate.[45] Alexander Rosenthal, for instance, has recently argued that Locke's constitutional ideas were strongly influenced by Hooker's doctrines, which for their part translated medieval scholastic traditions into early-modern political ideas.[46] This topic cannot be discussed here in further detail. But it is true that Locke adopted the former traditions of sacred history and in particular the importance of Adam and the Fall in creating his famous concept of political power. This becomes clear already in Locke's first treatise, which was nothing less than a merciless dismantlement of Filmer's argument on paternal dominion as established by divine order.[47] In doing so, Locke always referred to biblical sources, thus, like Filmer, using sacred history as his main argument. Filmer's idea of Adam's original royal authority, for instance, was dismissed by Locke with the prosaic argument that Adam could not have acted as a king because he lived "at a time when there was actually no government, no subjects to be governed".[48] But Locke's use of the former, medieval, tradition reached further and was also part of his famous labour theory of property.[49] The initial point was basically similar to Filmer's idea of Adam as first ruler of

Br.: Karl Alber 1995); Walter Euchner, *Naturrecht und Politik bei John Locke* (Frankfurt a. M.: Suhrkamp, 1979); Wolfgang Kersting, *Die politische Philosophie des Gesellschaftsvertrags* (Darmstadt: Wissenschaftliche Buchgesellschaft, 1996), pp. 109–139.

44 Cf. George Bull, " What Did Locke Borrow from Hooker?", *Thought* 7 (1932), pp. 122–135.

45 For a survey see William John Torrence Kirby, *Richard Hooker's Doctrine of the Royal Supremacy* (Leiden: Brill, 1990), pp. 11–13 with further reference.

46 Alexander S. Rosenthal, *Crown under Law: Richard Hooker, John Locke, and the Ascent of Modern Constitutionalism* (Lanham, MD: Lexington Books, 2008), pp. 83–139, 203–243 and passim.

47 Kim Ian Parker, *The Biblical Politics of John Locke* (Waterloo, Ontario: Wilfried Laurier University Press, 2004), pp. 103–119.

48 John Locke, *Two Treatises of Government: In the Former, The False Principles and Foundation of Sir Robert Filmer, And His Followers, are Detected and Overthrown. The Latter is an Essay Concerning The True Original, Extent, and End of Civil-Government*, book 1, chapter 1, § 16, edition used here Peter Laslett, *John Locke. Two Treatises of Government. Edition with an Introduction and Notes* (Cambridge: Cambridge University Press, 1988/2012), p. 166.

49 James Tully, *A Discourse on Property. John Locke and his Adversaries* (Cambridge: Cambridge University Press, 1980); ibid., *An Approach to Political Philosophy: Locke in Context* (Cambridge: Cambridge University Press, 1993), pp. 71–136; Manfred Brocker, *Arbeit und Eigentum. Der Paradigmenwechsel in der neuzeitlichen Eigentumstheorie* (Darmstadt: Wissenschaftliche Buchgesellschaft, 1992), pp. 125–291 and passim; for an impressive analytical account see A. John Simmons, *The Lockean Theory of Rights* (Princeton: Princeton University Press, 1992), pp. 222–306.

the world. But Locke understood the creation account in another way, by the idea of a divine order to mankind to make economic progress: "God gave the world to men in common; but since he gave it them for their benefit, and the greatest conveniences of life they were capable to draw from it, it cannot be supposed he meant it should always remain common and uncultivated".[50] This kind of cultivation, based on human *labour*, was therefore rooted in a divine command: "God, when he gave the world in common to all mankind, commanded man also to labour, and the penury of his condition required it of him."[51] So far, Locke's property conception came quite close to the former narratives of individual property as, for instance, those in Laurentius Hispanus.[52] But there was an essential normative innovation in Locke's argument,[53] which was the connection between individual freedom and individual property: "Though the earth, and all inferiour creatures, be common to all men, yet every man has a property in his own person: this no Body has any right to but himself."[54] Here, individual freedom was expressed as a property right adhering to each person. And it was this property to herself or himself which provided the basis for the acquisition of property in general: "The labour of his body, and the work of his hands, we may say, are properly his. Whatsoever then he removes out of the state that nature hath provided, and left it in, he hath mixed his labour with, and joined to it something that is his own, and thereby makes it his property."[55] At this point, Locke clearly took a new path of reasoning compared to former ideas on property and natural law. But the fact remains that in essence he justified the idea of individual property using the traditional narrative of origin in the Fall. This was also true for Locke's idea of economic progress by human labour and acquisition of private property. In an unpublished text of 1693 on *Homo ante et post lapsem*, Locke claimed that it was the Fall which caused Adam's mortality the need for "private possessions and labour", and resulted in "a distinction of conditions",[56] or, to use modern terms, in the rise of differentiated societies.

[50] Locke, *Two Treatises* (n. 48), book 2, chapter 5, § 34, p. 287.
[51] Locke, *Two Treatises* (n. 48), book 2, chapter 5, § 32, pp. 285–286.
[52] See above at n. 20.
[53] On this ambivalence between medieval tradition and innovation in Locke see Thier, "Heilsgeschichte" (n. 2), pp. 168–170.
[54] Locke, *Two Treatises* (n. 48), book 2, chapter 5, § 27, p. 284.
[55] Locke, *Two Treatises* (n. 48), book 2, chapter 5, § 27, pp. 284–285.
[56] John Locke, "Homo ante et post lapsem" (1693), in *Locke. Political Essays*, ed. Mark Goldie (Cambridge: Cambridge University Press, 1997), pp. 320–321, 321.

III. The eroding impact of the biblical past and the rise of the natural state concept

It is well known that Hobbes's theory of social contract represented a new kind of origin narrative in conceptualising the legitimation of governmental power using the idea of an abstract state of nature[57] and thus turning away from sacred history.[58] The definitive starting point for a new more ahistorical concept of the origins of law and government, however, was marked by Samuel Pufendorf (1623–1694).[59] At the beginning of his treatise *De statu hominum naturali* (1675),[60] he stressed the fact that he understood the state of nature as "abstraction of all forms" (*ab omnibus particularibus formis abstracta*).[61] This statement already indicated a certain distance from the traditional conceptions.[62] In fact, Pufendorf later in his book appealed to his readers, "let us abstract from the knowledge about humankind's origins that we have drawn from the Divine

[57] For a reconstruction see Hoekstra, "Hobbes on the Natural Condition" (n. 5), passim. For a recent detailed account see Daniel Eggers, *Die Naturzustandstheorie des Thomas Hobbes: Eine vergleichende Analyse von 'The elements of law', 'De Cive' und den englischen und lateinischen Fassungen des 'Leviathan'* (Berlin: Walter de Gruyter, 2008, online 2008, accessed 23 February 2015, www.degruyter.com/view/product/178844).

[58] On Hobbes's mixed relationship to history see the essays in G. A. J. Rogers and Tom Sorell, *Hobbes and History* (London/New York: Routledge, 2000), especially Karl Schuhmann, "Hobbes's Concept of History", pp. 3–23, in particular pp. 16–17 (on sacred history).

[59] For a survey see Alfred Dufour, "Pufendorf", in *The Cambridge History of Political Thought 1450–1700*, eds. J. H. Burns and Mark Goldie (Cambridge: Cambridge University Press, 1991, online 2008, accessed 4 March 2015, http://dx.doi.org/10.1017/CHOL9780521247160), pp. 559–588; in more detail Thomas Behme, *Samuel von Pufendorf: Naturrecht und Staat. Eine Analyse und Interpretation seiner Theorie, ihrer Grundlagen und Probleme* (Göttingen: Vandenhoeck & Ruprecht, 1995); *Naturrecht und Staatstheorie bei Samuel Pufendorf*, ed. Dieter Hüning (Baden-Baden: Nomos Verlag, 2009); see also Michael Seidler, "Pufendorf's Moral and Political Philosophy", *The Stanford Encyclopedia of Philosophy* (Spring 2013 Edition), ed. Edward N. Zalta, http://plato.stanford.edu/archives/spr2013/entries/pufendorf-moral/ accessed 26 February 2015.

[60] Edition and translation of the print of 1678 (Frankfurt/Main) by Michael Seidler, *Samuel Pufendorf's on the Natural State of Men: The 1678 Latin Edition and English Translation* (Lewiston/Queenston/Lampeter: E. Mellen Press, 1990). *Ibid.*, pp. 77–78 bibliographical references on the first publication (as in *Samuelis Pufendorfii, Dissertationes academicae selectiores*, Lund 1675, 582–632). For a short discussion of this treatise see also Thier, "Heilsgeschichte" (n. 2), pp. 171–172. For a detailed account see Helmut Zedelmaier, *Der Anfang der Geschichte: Studien zur Ursprungsdebatte im 18. Jahrhundert* (Hamburg: Meiner, 2003), pp. 26–30.

[61] Pufendorf, *De statu hominum*, § 1, in Seidler, *Pufendorf's On the natural state* (n. 60), p. 83.

[62] On Pufendorf's conception of the state of nature see in more detail Behme, *Samuel von Pufendorf* (n. 59), pp. 57–73.

Scriptures and remain within the limits of reason alone".[63] As indicated in this statement, Pufendorf was fully aware of the traditional rationale of sacred history. And, moreover, it was his firm belief that Adam had actually existed and hence that "we actually find its existence described in the Divine scriptures".[64] In the view of the Lutheran Pufendorf,[65] it was to the "scriptures, no doubt that we owe whatever knowledge we now have concerning the first man's state, from which he was ejected because of his own sin"[66] and based on that knowledge "we can infer quite clearly that humankind has not always existed but had a beginning sometime in the past".[67] But this knowledge was, in Pufendorf's view, not really helpful for *legal* reasoning. Pufendorf expressed serious doubts about "how useful it might be in the science of the state to imagine men in that primeval integrity".[68] This perspective was not compatible with the epistemological interests of jurisprudence and political science, "for that happy situation is inconsistent with the ends for which our current states have been established".[69] Here, the present was losing its connection to the biblical past, and in this process sacred history began to lose its overall importance

[63] Pufendorf, *De statu hominum*, § 4, in Seidler, *Pufendorf's On the natural state* (n. 60), 86: ... *age abstrahamus ab illa cognitione, quam super originibus humani generis ex divinis literis hausimus, ac intra limites rationis sibi jam soli relictae maneamus*. For the translation used here see Seidler, *ibid.*, 112.

[64] Samuel Pufendorf, *Specimen controversiarum circa ius naturale ipsi nuper motarum* (Uppsala/Osnabrück, 1678), III § 4 in ibid., *Eris Scandica und andere polemische Schriften über das Naturrecht*, ed. Fiammetta Palladini (Samuel Pufendorf, *Gesammelte Werke*, vol. 5) (Berlin: Akademie Verlag, 2002), pp. 114–197, 135: *quem (scil. statum Adami) revera existentem in divinis literis descriptum reperimus*; see also below, at and in n. 73.

[65] On the entanglement of religious and non-religious elements in Pufendorf's works see Detlef Döring, "Säkularisierung und Moraltheologie bei Samuel von Pufendorf", *Zeitschrift für Theologie und Kirche* 90 (1993), pp. 156–174, repr. in iibd., *Samuel Pufendorf in der Welt des 17. Jahrhunderts* (Frankfurt/M.: Vittorio Klostermann, 2012), pp. 273–292, 280–292.

[66] Pufendorf, *De statu hominum*, § 3, in Seidler, *Pufendorf's On the natural state* (n. 60), 85: *Sane enim quae de statu primi hominis, ex quo ipse peccato suo evolutis est, jam novimus, eam cognitionem divinis literis debemus*. For the translation used here see Seidler, *ibid.*, 111.

[67] Pufendorf, *De statu hominum*, § 4, in Seidler, *Pufendorf's On the natural state* (n. 60), 86: ... *satis liquid colligere videmur posse, humanum genus non extitisse ab aeterno, sed aliquando initium cepisse*. For the translation, used here see Seidler, *ibid.*, 112.

[68] Pufendorf, *De statu hominum*, § 3, in Seidler, *Pufendorf's On the natural state* (n. 60), 86: ... *quem magnopere usum in doctrina civili habeat, homines in primaeva illa integritate constitutos contemplari*. The translation, used here, in Seidler, *ibid.*, p. 112.

[69] Pufendorf, *De statu hominum*, § 3, in Seidler, *Pufendorf's On the natural state* (n. 60), p. 86: *Nam ea felicitas cum istis finibus, ob quos nostrae civitates jam sunt constitutae, stare nequit*. For the English translation see Seidler, *ibid.*, p. 112.

for legal doctrine. This was a consequence of Pufendorf's methodological approach[70] *in disciplina iuris naturalis universali*, the discipline of universal natural law.[71] Here, conclusions on law and government were possible only by rational deduction from the nature of man, which were the subject of analysis by using the category of the *status naturalis* as the state of humans "beyond any subsidy and human accomplishments". In that "hypothesis it is not necessary to inquire in the conditions of the first man, because also today human life outside of fellowship is extremely miserable. And how the first humans lived, is a question of facts, which can be understood only from the Scriptures".[72] So, the unity between the past, as reported in the Bible, and the present governed by reason only, split apart. Even though Pufendorf also described a *status naturalis qui revera existit*, a state of nature actually existing,[73] this reference to the early history of mankind leading to the early founding of *societas civiles*[74] had no normative quality.[75] Universal sacred history and universal natural law took different directions,[76] it might be said, even though they remained at some points connected.

[70] For an analysis see Andreas Thier, "Hierarchie und Dogmatik. Die Vernunftrechtslehre", in *Dogmatisierungsprozesse in Recht und Religion*, eds. Nils Jansen and Georg Essen (Tübingen: Mohr Siebeck, 2011), pp. 217–238.

[71] Pufendorf, *Specimen*, IV § 16, in *Eris Scandica* (n. 64), p. 157.

[72] Samuel Pufendorf, *Spicilegium controversiarum circa jus naturae ipsi motarum* (Frankfurt 1680), in ibid., *Eris Scandica* (n. 64), pp. 199–238, 229: ... *nec in nostra hypothesi necessarium est super primaeva hominum conditione inquirere, cum etiam hodie vita huma citra socialitatem sit miserrima. Et qualem vitam primi homini egerint, quaestio facti est, quae nisi ex S. Scripturis cognosci potest.* On this statement see also Behme, *Samuel von Pufendorf* (n. 59), pp. 59–61 with n. 16 and further reference.

[73] See, for example, Pufendorf, *De statu hominum*, § 7, in Seidler, *Pufendorf's On the natural state* (n. 60), 91: *Qui ipse status vel per fictionem concipitur, vel revera existit.* For a reconstruction see Behme, *Samuel von Pufendorf* (n. 59), pp. 69–71.

[74] Pufendorf, *De statu hominum*, § 6, in Seidler, *Pufendorf's On the natural state* (n. 60), p. 90.

[75] Similar assessment in Behme, *Samuel von Pufendorf* (n. 59), p. 70.

[76] Similar approach in Behme, *Samuel von Pufendorf* (n. 59), pp. 59–61 with n. 16; see also Hans Medick, *Naturzustand und Naturgeschichte der bürgerlichen Gesellschaft. Die Ursprünge der bürgerlichen Sozialtheorie als Geschichtsphilosophie und Sozialwissenschaft bei Samuel Pufendorf, John Locke und Adam Smith* (Göttingen: Vandenhoeck & Ruprecht, 1973), pp. 40–49; for a slightly different direction, however, see the argument in Zedelmaier, *Anfang* (n. 60), pp. 29–30, who argues that, in general, Pufendorf's conception was intended to present the Fall and the natural state as "models of the begin of history throwing light on each other" ("sich gegenseitig beleuchtende Modelle des Anfangs der Geschichte", *ibid.*, 30). In our perspective, this kind of correspondence lost its importance in Pufendorf at least in the field of reasoning about government, statehood, and law.

Similar transitions occurred also in the works of Christian Thomasius (1655–1728).[77] In his *Institutiones Jurisprudentiae Divinae* (1688), he raised the question, if "there was individual property or common property in the first state of humans" (*in primaevo hominum statu fuerit dominium aut communio*) and elaborated a conception of a *communio negativa* ("negative common property"), which changed to individual property after the lapse.[78] And in doing so, he claimed that it would be possible to draw "historical assertions also in unfolding discussion of natural law from sacred history without confusion of disciplines".[79] While here history and natural law reasoning were closely connected, Thomasius apparently moved a certain distance away from this approach in 1705. In his treatise about *Fundamenta juris naturae*, Thomasius announced to his readers, "I will abstract from the holy Scriptures and the status integritatis . . . because the state of integrity is not only completely gone, but it can also not be acquired again in this life".[80] And, in commenting on his earlier deductions from sacred history, Thomasius declared these arguments to be a means to pacify all those "extending to theology or sacred history", who might be offended by his reluctance to include the idea of the status integritatis in his argument.[81] Here, an initial close connection

[77] Ian Hunter, *The Secularisation of the Confessional State: The Political Thought of Christian Thomasius* (Cambridge: Cambridge University Press, 2007); *Christian Thomasius (1655–1728): Wegbereiter moderner Rechtskultur und Juristenausbildung: rechtswissenschaftliches Symposium zu seinem 350. Geburtstag an der Juristischen Fakultät der Martin-Luther-Universität Halle-Wittenberg*, ed. Heiner Lück (Hildesheim: Olms, 2006); *Christian Thomasius 1655–1728: Interpretationen zu Werk und Wirkung*, ed. Werner Schneiders (Hamburg: Meiner, 1989).

[78] Christian Thomasius, *Institutionum Jurisprudentiae Divinae libri tres*, II, cap. 10, §§ 58–119 (for the first time published in 1688, 7th edition Halle 1730, repr. Aalen: Scientia, 1963); the quote *ibid.*, § 58, 64, p. 189.

[79] Thomasius, *Institutionum Jurisprudentiae libri tres*, II 10, § 60 (n. 78), p. 189: . . . *assertiones historicas etiam in evolvendis discpetationibus juris naturalis ex historia sacra desumi posse. . . .*

[80] Christian Thomasius, *Fundamenta juris naturae et gentium: ex sensu communi deducta, in quibus ubique secernuntur principia honesti, iusti ac decori, cum adiuncta emendatione ad ista fundamenta, Institutionum iurisprudentiae divinae*, praefatio, § 19 (for the first time published in 1705 used here edition Halle/Leipzig 1718), p. 17: . . . *a sanctis literis & a statu integritatis plane abstraham, praeprimi, quia . . . status integritatis non solum est plane amissus, sed & non potest in hac vita rursus acquiri.* On this statement see also Thier, "Heilsgeschichte" (n. 2), p. 172, and on Thomasius's perspective in this regard in more detail Frank Grunert, *Normbegründung und politische Legitimität. Zur Rechts- und Staatsphilosophie der deutschen Frühaufklärung* (Tübingen: Niemeyer, 2000), pp. 248–250.

[81] Thomasius, *Fundamenta juris*, II 10 (n. 80), p. 234: *hic seponendi* (referring to the statement quoted at n. 79) *tanquam pertinentes ad Theologiam vel historiam sacram, vel librum de religione.*

between sacred history and legal reasoning was loosened by a more or less strict separation of the present from its biblical past. But in Thomasius's approach, a theological element came into play: Adam's situation before the fall, his proximity to God, was beyond all mundane experience and perceptibility; hence, even though it formed a part of human history, it was so unique and so far away from the present that it could no longer be used for concepts of law and legal evolution.

IV. The biblical past and universal history

The approaches and perspectives in Locke, Pufendorf and Thomasius reveal transitions in conceptualising history and its importance for law and legal ideas. It might be said that these phenomena mirrored a secular change of perspectives on history, which has often been highlighted[82]: in this view, the change from Adam and the Fall to the state of nature within the limits of reason would reflect the transition from a deeply religious conception of the world to its rationalistic understanding. In terms of historiographical conceptions, this would mean that God as creator and subject of history would have been substituted by man; in other words, sacred history would have been replaced by a universal history of mankind.[83] In fact, there are indications of this kind of development, if we compare two accounts from the sixteenth and the late seventeenth centuries. In 1532, Johann Carion (1499–1537)[84] published his survey

[82] Zedelmaier, *Anfang* (n. 60), pass.; summarising ibid., "Der Beginn der Geschichte. Überlegungen zur Auflösung des alteuropäischen Modells der Universalgeschichte", *Storia della Storiografia* 39 (2001), pp. 87–92; see also the groundbreaking contribution in Arno Seifert, "Von der heiligen zur philosophischen Geschichte. Die Rationalisierung der universalhistorischen Erkenntnis im Zeitalter der Aufklärung", *Archiv für Kulturgeschichte* 68 (1986), pp. 81–117; see also Adalbert Klempt, *Die Säkularisierung der universalhistorischen Auffassung. Zum Wandel des Geschichtsdenkens im 16. und 17. Jahrhundert* (Göttingen: Musterschmidt, 1960); Paolo Rossi, *The Dark Abyss of Time: the History of the Earth & the History of Nations from Hooke to Vico* (Chicago/London: The University of Chicago Press, 1984), pass.

[83] For this transitional process see Reinhart Koselleck, "Geschichte V.–VII.", in *Geschichtliche Grundbegriffe*, vol. 2, eds. ibid., Otto Brunner and Werner Conze (Stuttgart: Klett-Cotta 1975, repr. 2004), pp. 647–717, 682–691.

[84] For a short survey see Frank Ulriech Prietz, "Carion, Johannes", *Killy Literaturlexikon – Autoren und Werke des deutschsprachigen Kulturraumes*, vol. 2, ed. Wilhelm Kühlmann (Berlin/New York: De Gruyter, 2008), www.degruyter.com/view/VDBO/vdbo.killy.0910, accessed 3 March 2015; Karl-Reinhart Trauner, "Carion, Johannes (1499–1537)", *Biographisch-Bibliographisches Kirchenlexikon*, 28 (2007), pp. 285–300 (www.bbkl.de/lexikon/bbkl-artikel.php?art=./C/Ca/carion_j.art, accessed 2 March 2015).

Chronica, a history of the world, which would later become the subject of fundamental revision by his academic mentor Philipp Melanchthon.[85] Like some later treatises in this protestant tradition of historiography,[86] such as Johannes Sleidanus' (1506–1556)[87] influential book *De quattuor summis imperiis*,[88] history was put strictly in biblical perspective in Carion's book,[89] with, for example, "the first age that is two thousand years from Adam to Abraham".[90] Here, biblical history and the history of mankind merged into one inseparable horizon in time.

One hundred and fifty years later, in 1682, Samuel Pufendorf published his treatise *Einleitung zu der Historie der Vornehmsten Reiche und Staaten so itziger Zeit in Europa sich befinden*,[91] which was also published in an English version under the title *An Introduction to the History of the Principal Kingdoms and States of Europe*.[92] This book included a short reference to the early beginnings of mankind, which combined biblical

[85] Frank Ulrich Prietz, *Das Mittelalter im Dienst der Reformation: die Chronica Carions und Melanchthons von 1532. Zur Vermittlung mittelalterlicher Geschichtskonzeptionen in die protestantische Historiographie* (Stuttgart: Kohlhammer, 2014) with further reference.

[86] Matthias Pohlig, *Zwischen Gelehrsamkeit und konfessioneller Identitätsstiftung: Lutherische Kirchen- und Universalgeschichtsschreibung 1546–1617* (Tübingen: Mohr Siebeck, 2007).

[87] Gustav Adolf Benrath, "Sleidanus, Johannes", *Killy Literaturlexikon – Autoren und Werke des deutschsprachigen Kulturraumes*, vol. 11, ed. Wilhelm Kühlmann (Berlin/New York: De Gruyter, 2011), www.degruyter.com/view/VDBO/vdbo.killy.6250, accessed 3 March 2015. Donald R. Kelly, "Johann Sleidan and the Origins of History as a Profession", *The Journal of Modern History* 52 (1980), pp. 573–598; Alexandra Kess, *Johann Sleidan and the Protestant Vision of History* (Aldershot: Ashgate, 2008).

[88] Johannes Sleidanus, *De quatuor (sic) summis imperiis libri tres* (Strassburg: Riheli, 1556). Copy of the Bavarian State Library, call-nr.: 962252 A.gr.a. 1985#Beibd.2 962252 A.gr.a. 1985#Beibd.2, online available: www.mdz-nbn-resolving.de/urn/resolver.pl?urn=urn:nbn:de:bvb:12-bsb10169439-5.

[89] On this aspect as a defining mark of German-speaking protestant historiography in the seventeenth century see the survey in Seifert, "Von der heiligen zur philosophischen Geschichte" (n. 82), pp. 99–102.

[90] Cf. Johannes Carion, *Chronica, Gemert vnd gebessert* (edition Augsburg 1540), copy of the Bavarian State Library online, call-nr.: Rar. 1993, urn:nbn:de:bvb:12-bsb00069937-4, online: http://daten.digitale-sammlungen.de/~db/bsb00004647/images/, with the description of the "first book", *darinn das erst alter, das ist zwey tausent Jar, vonn Adam biß auf Abraham gefasset wird.*

[91] A copy of the second edition (Frankfurt/Main, Knoche) of 1683 in the Bavarian State Library, call-nr.: 12886481 Eur. 612 12886481 Eur. 612, is at www.mdz-nbn-resolving.de/urn/resolver.pl?urn=urn:nbn:de:bvb:12-bsb10618375-2, accessed 3 March 2015.

[92] Samuel von Pufendorf, *An Introduction to the History of the Principal Kingdoms and States of Europe*, translated by Jodocus Crull (1695), edited and with an Introduction by Michael J. Seidler (Indianapolis: Liberty Fund, 2013), http://oll.libertyfund.org/titles/2594, accessed, 3 March 2015. On the publication history see *ibid.*, Appendices 1–4, 603–640, http://oll.libertyfund.org/titles/2594#Pufendorf_1618_1033.

and Aristotelian perspectives: "To the time of the deluge", Pufendorf suggested, there was no magistracy, but "the Government was lodged only in each Father of his Family, a Paternal Government", which might have continued "for a considerable time after the deluge".[93] Here, the biblical account was combined with a more or less ethnographic approach. But this period was not at the centre of Pufendorf's interest, since, as the title of his book already indicated, he focused on the development of modern states and societies.[94] For his purposes, for the analysis of present political and legal developments, biblical history was nothing more than a vague reference point.

One reason for this reluctance was the distance between present historians and the biblical past, as Johann Peter Ludewig's (1668–1743)[95] *Historia sine parente* (History without procreator) demonstrates. While Ludewig fully accepted that human history began with the lapse, even though "people were simple fools and each and everyone by nature unskilled in the fine arts" at that time,[96] nevertheless all accounts about this period were unreliable, because even the Mosaic account "deals only with the essential parts and is very short for the first thousand years".[97] Therefore, it was nearly impossible to draw conclusions from a far distant historical past for the legal situation of the present: it was "for so much ages of centuries... unknown, by which concept a state was organized and the world was governed".[98] Against this background Ludewig was very

[93] Pufendorf, *Introduction*, ed. Seidler (n. 92), 13, http://oll.libertyfund.org/titles/2594#lf1618_label_144, accessed 3 March 2015.

[94] For a detailed discussion see Zedelmaier, *Anfang* (n. 60), pp. 30–34.

[95] For a short account see Walther Ludwig, "Ludewig, Johann Peter (von)", *Killy Literaturlexikon – Autoren und Werke des deutschsprachigen Kulturraumes, vol. 7*, ed. Wilhelm Kühlemann (Berlin, New York: De Gruyter, 2010), www.degruyter.com/view/VDBO/vdbo.killy.4001, accessed 3 March 2015; in greater detail: Notker Hammerstein, *Jus und Historie: ein Beitrag zur Geschichte des historischen Denkens an deutschen Universitäten im späten 17. und im 18. Jahrhundert* (Göttingen: Vandenhoeck & Ruprecht, 1972), pp. 169–204, where, however, Ludewig's treatise *Historia sine parentes* is not discussed; on this treatise see Zedelmaier, *Anfang* (n. 60), pp. 34–47.

[96] Johann Peter Ludewig, *Historia sine parente, de causis fabularum circa gentium origines* (Halle 1693), § 1: ... *homines post lapsum stipites plane ac rudes in bonibus artibus, omnibus ac singulis natura fuisset*; copy of the Bavarian State Library, call-nr.: 2136864 4 Diss. 3379,17 2136864 4 Diss. 3379,17, www.mdz-nbn-resolving.de/urn/resolver.pl?urn=urn:nbn:de:bvb:12-bsb10962889-8, accessed 3 March 2015; see on this text also Zedelmaier, *Anfang* (n. 60), p. 39.

[97] Ludewig, *Historia* (n. 96), § 3: ... *is (scil. Moses) vero cum summa tantum rerum capita tractet, & in primis mille annis concisus admodum ac brevis sit.* See also Zedelmaier, *Anfang* (n. 60), pp. 41–43.

[98] Ludewig, *Historia* (n. 96), § 2: ... *per tot seculorum aetates... qua ratione gesta respublica, & gubernatus orbis sit, notatum non est.* See also Zedelmaier, *Anfang* (n. 60), p. 40.

critical of those who "used to argue with the age of the root of a people or a kingdom", when "controversies on the claims on kingdoms and dignities arise".[99] In this perspective, the past in general and the biblical past in particular lost their relevance for law and legal reasoning, again as in Thomasius,[100] due to the distance between the past and present. The lapse kept its status as part of universal human history, but it also became more and more isolated.[101]

It corresponded to this development that influential accounts of universal history like Christoph Cellarius's (1608–1637)[102] *Historia universalis* completely omitted biblical history.[103] And it might even be said that this line of development pointed towards the great concepts of historically different stages of society: Adam Smith's idea of a *Natural History of Society* with its four stages of hunting, pasturing, farming and commerce[104] would certainly fit into this kind of development. In the same direction pointed the idea of the Pre-Adamites, of the existence of humans before Adam, which, even though referring to the creation story, entailed in consequence nothing less than questioning the full authenticity of the biblical narrative.[105] The monumental *Universal history from the earliest*

99 Ludewig, *Historia* (n. 96), § 10, note t: ... *cum enim de praetensionibus in Regna, ac dignitates controversiae oriuntur, e gentis ac Regiae stirpis antiquitate argumentari solent.* See also Zedelmaier, *Anfang* (n. 60), p. 45.

100 See above, at n. 81.

101 For a similar argument see Arno Seifert, *Der Rückzug der biblischen Prophetie von der neueren Geschichte: Studien zur Geschichte der Reichstheologie des frühneuzeitlichen deutschen Protestantismus* (Köln: Böhlau, 1990), and Zedelmaier, *Anfang* (n. 60), p. 55.

102 For a survey see Herbert Jaumann, "Cellarius, Christoph", in *Killy Literaturlexikon – Autoren und Werke des deutschsprachigen Kulturraumes*, vol. 2, ed. Wilhelm Kühlmann (Berlin/New York: De Gruyter, 2008), www.degruyter.com/view/VDBO/vdbo.killy.0931, accessed 4 March 2015. On Cellarius's importance for periodisation see Uwe Neddermeyer, *Das Mittelalter in der deutschen Historiographie vom 15. bis zum 18. Jahrhundert. Geschichtsgliederung und Epochenverständnis in der frühen Neuzeit* (Köln/Wien: Böhlau, 1988), pass.

103 Christoph Cellarius, *Historia Universalis. Breviter Ac Perspicue Exposita, In Antiquam, Et Medii Aevi Ac Novam Divisa* (1685, used here 8th edition, Jena 1730), a copy of the Bavarian State Library, call-nr.: 10215339 H.un. 723 m 10215339 H.un. 723 m, www.mdz-nbn-resolving.de/urn/resolver.pl?urn=urn:nbn:de:bvb:12-bsb10034862-7, accessed 4 March 2015: Cellarius began his account with the *prima orbis imperia minora*, cf. *ibid.*, 1 (title of § 1).

104 For surveys see J. G. A Pocock, "Adam Smith and History", in *The Cambridge Companion to Adam Smith*, ed. Knud Haakonssen (Cambridge: Cambridge University Press, 2006), pp. 270–287; for the context of the Scottish enlightenment see Murray G. H. Pittock, "Historiography", in *The Cambridge Companion to the Scottish Enlightenment*, ed. Alexander Broadie (Cambridge: Cambridge University Press, 2006), pp. 258–279.

105 David N. Livingstone, *Adam's Ancestors: Race, Religion, and the Politics of Human Origins* (Baltimore, MD: Johns Hopkins University Press, 2008); ibid., Preadamites: The History

account of time, however, which was published from 1730,[106] appeared to follow the biblical creation account closely. It devoted large parts of its first volume to topics like *The General History to the Flood*, comprising subchapters like *The Fall of Man – The Chronology from the Creation to the Deluge stated and the history of the antediluvian patriarchs.*[107]

In the field of law and legal philosophy, however, the erosion of sacred and biblical history as justification for governmental power, statehood and individual rights would evolve towards an unbroken continuity, as the rise of the Historical School[108] proves. From this perspective, as elaborated programmatically in 1814 by Friedrich Carl von Savigny (1779–1861), "all law is . . . first developed by custom and popular faith, next by jurisprudence – everywhere, therefore, by internal silently-operating powers, not by the arbitrary will of a law-giver".[109] Here, law is defined by its continuous evolution throughout history and by its "organic connection . . . with the being and character of the people"[110] as "a fixed character, peculiar to the people".[111] With this kind of cultural historicity as an essential mark of law, the relation between the origin of law and its present lost its importance. The question "how these peculiar attributes of nations . . . originated", and the idea "that all lived at first a sort of animal life, advancing gradually to a more passable state",[112] possessed very little

of an Idea from Heresy to Orthodoxy, *Scottish Journal of Theology* 40/1 (1987), 41–66, doi: 10.1017/S0036930600017312, accessed 4 March 2015; Andreas Pietsch, *Isaac La Peyrère: Bibelkritik, Philosemitismus und Patronage in der Gelehrtenrepublik des 17. Jahrhunderts* (Berlin: De Gruyter, 2012).

106 Guido Abbatista, "The Business of Paternoster Row: Towards a Publishing History of the 'Universal History'", *Publishing History* 17 (1985), pp. 5–50; for a survey see Zedelmaier, *Anfang* (n. 60), pp. 143–144 with further reference.

107 *An Universal History From The Earliest Account of Time, Compiled from Original Authors And Illustrated with Maps, Cuts, Notes etc. With a General Index to the Whole*, vol. 1 (London, 1747), pp. 121, 142, 149.

108 For a survey see Donald R. Kelley, *The Human Measure: Social Thought in the Western Legal Tradition* (Cambridge, MA: Harvard University Press, 1990), pp. 243–246; In general see Horst Heinrich Jakobs, *Die Begründung der geschichtlichen Rechtswissenschaft* (Paderborn: Schöningh, 1992); Jan Schröder, *Recht als Wissenschaft. Geschichte der juristischen Methodenlehre in der Neuzeit (1500–1933)* (München: C. H. Beck, 2012), pp. 193–200 with further reference; for a recent account from an American perspective see David M. Rabban, *Law's History: American Legal Thought and the Transatlantic Turn to History* (Cambridge: Cambridge University Press, 2013).

109 Friedrich Carl von Savigny, *Vom Beruf unserer Zeit für Gesetzgebung und Rechtswissenschaft*, English translation as *The Vocation of Our Age for Legislation and Jurisprudence* by Abraham Hayward (2nd edition, London: Littlewood & Co., 1831), p. 30.

110 Savigny, *Vocation* (n. 109), p. 27.

111 Savigny, *Vocation* (n. 109), p. 24.

112 Savigny, *Vocation* (n. 109), p. 25.

relevance to Savigny. And so his conclusion on the natural state doctrine marked in a certain way the decline of this narrative:[113] "We may leave this theory alone".[114]

[113] On the eroding impact of the natural state concept in nineteenth-century German-speaking jurisprudence see Jan Rolin, *Der Ursprung des Staates: die naturrechtlich-rechtsphilosophische Legitimation von Staat und Staatsgewalt im Deutschland des 18. und 19. Jahrhunderts* (Tübingen: Mohr Siebeck, 2005), pp. 97–151 with further reference.

[114] Savigny, *Vocation* (n. 109), p. 25.

10

The commissioners for claims on France and the case of the Baron de Bode, 1815–1861

MICHAEL LOBBAN

In October 1793, as the reign of terror deepened in revolutionary France, Charles Auguste Louis Frederick, Baron de Bode, fled east, taking refuge first with the advancing Austrian army, and then heading to Russia. For much of his life, Charles had enjoyed little wealth and had often been in debt. These debts had led him and his wife Mary – the daughter of Thomas Kynnersley of Loxley Park – to leave their home in Staffordshire and settle in the Franco-German borderlands, where he entered the service of Louis XVI's German regiments. It was here that fortune finally seemed to smile on them in December 1788, when he acquired extensive estates in the fief of Soultz-sous-Forêts in Alsace from the Archbishop of Cologne. As Mary (who had just given birth to their ninth child) put it, ''Tis a land flowing with corn and wine... If God has sent us a quantity of children, He has also sent us plentifully to provide for them!'[1] Thanks to the revolutionary events which commenced a mere seven months later, their happy life at Soultz was to be short-lived; but the family's attempts to recover compensation under a treaty between Britain and France for the value of the estates seized by the French authorities were to last nearly seventy years after Charles had fled.

The family's campaign was led not by Charles – who died in Crimea in 1797 – but by his son, Clement, born in Uttoxeter in 1777. After the family left Soultz, Clement entered the Russian military service, becoming a Colonel in a cavalry regiment which joined in the allied march on Paris. But when the war ended, he returned to England to pursue his claim for compensation from the French government for the confiscated lands. For

This essay was written in memory of my friend and former colleague Professor Kaiyan Homi Kaikobad.

[1] W.S. Childe-Pemberton, *The Baroness de Bode, 1775–1803* (London: Longmans, 1900) p. 68.

over thirty years, Clement pursued the claim through courts, parliament and the press.[2] In the words of *The Times*, 'He gave up his brilliant prospects in Russia to prosecute his claim, and thus doomed himself to a life of hope deferred and pecuniary difficulty'.[3] Since he had to borrow considerably to finance his long campaign he remained in debt all his life, constantly fleeing his creditors and living in the hope of getting a fortune. In 1834, while heavily in debt, he drafted his will, in which he left his widow an annuity of £2,000 a year, his daughters and illegitimate sons £10,000 each, and his eldest son the residue of what he confidently expected to be an estate worth in excess of a quarter of a million pounds.[4] In the event, he received no compensation, and his estate was worth only £450 on his death.

He died at the age of 69 in October 1846, just after having lost yet another round in his battle. After his death, his son (also named Clement) continued to pursue the matter for the family. Born in 1806, young Clement made his career in Russia, the land of his birth, becoming a councillor of state and chief secretary of the Russian embassy at Teheran. He might have become an ambassador, but gave that up after his father's death to pursue the claim. Like his father, he suffered a series of disappointments, and gave up the struggle in 1861, retiring to Russia, where he finally died in 1887.[5]

The Baron's was one of a series of Victorian cases, where impoverished outsiders made claims to recover their lost natural inheritance.[6] De Bode's was unusual in so far as he did not attract mass popular support (as the Tichborne claimant had), but he did persuade many influential figures in the political and judicial world of the justice of his cause. The Baron's case was also unusual in that it involved more complex legal questions than other more popular claimants' cases. These questions raised knotty

[2] The Baron himself wrote numerous pamphlets setting out his claims: *A Short Statement of the Case of the Baron de Bode* (London: T. Denham, 1828), *French Claims: A Few Words in Relation to the Funds Paid by the French to the British Government* (London: Mills, Jowett & Mills, 1830), *French Claims: an Address to the Honorable Members of the House of Commons* (London: T. Brettell, 1833), *French Claims. Appeal of the Baron de Bode to the Honorable Members of the House of Commons* (London: John Hearne, 1836), *French Claims in the Case of the Baron de Bode* (London: T. Brettell, 1837). See also John Hodgkin, *Case of the Baron de Bode in its Present Aspects* (London: W. Clowes, 1860).

[3] *The Times*, 18 June 1887, col. 7d.

[4] TNA PROB 11/2054/85. A codicil increased the sums to the illegitimate sons to £15,000.

[5] *The Times*, 18 June 1887, col. 7d.

[6] The most famous of the cases was the Tichborne case, for which see R. McWilliam, *The Tichborne Claimant: a Victorian Sensation* (London: Continuum, 2007).

problems of how individuals could assert rights they claimed to have as a result of treaties giving post-war reparation for wrongful expropriation of property. The case raised questions of how far the authority of law could be used by a private individual who sought to force reluctant political authorities to pay over money claimed.

I. The claim before the commissioners

1. The commissioners for claims on France

In the Treaty of Paris of 1814, France agreed not only to pay an indemnity to the Allies and to pay the debts it owed to private citizens in those countries, but she also entered into separate articles with the British to pay compensation for the value of her subjects' property 'illegally confiscated' [*'induement confisqués'*] after 1792.[7] On 10 October 1793, the revolutionary government had issued a decree confiscating the property of British subjects. This decree violated a Treaty of Commerce signed by the two countries in 1786, which provided that in case of war, each country's subjects were to be allowed to remain and trade in the other's territory, or (if their conduct rendered them suspect) were to be given a year to 'remove, with their effects and property'.[8] The arrangements made in 1814 were confirmed by another Treaty of Paris, signed on 20 November 1815 by Viscount Castlereagh and the Duke of Wellington for the British, and the Duke de Richelieu for the French. This treaty annexed two conventions, which fleshed out the stipulations made in 1814.[9] 'Convention No. 7', which was relevant to the Baron's claim, dealt with claims relating to losses within the territory of France, and made specific reference to the Treaty of 1786. 'Convention No. 13', which did not mention that treaty, related to claims outside the territory of France.[10] The French government agreed to pay a capital sum producing 3.5 million francs annual interest to pay the Convention No. 7 claims (plus interest at a rate of 4 per cent per annum).[11] A separate fund was created for the Convention No. 13

[7] R. Lewis Hertslet, *A Complete Collection of the Treaties and Conventions at Present Subsisting between Great Britain and Foreign Powers, So Far As They Relate to Commerce and Navigation*, 2 vols. (London: T. Egerton, 1820), vol. 1, p. 263.

[8] George Chalmers, *A Collection of Treaties between Great Britain and Other Powers* (London: John Stockdale, 1790), vol. I, p. 517.

[9] Hertslet, *Treaties and Conventions*, pp. 273ff.

[10] These conventions were drawn up since the commissioners were at first unclear which claims could be dealt with: TNA TS 25/2045, f. 81.

[11] The capital sum was worth £2.8 million in English money, or £217,540,157 at 2013 values.

claims. Claimants were given limited times to submit their claims: those living in Europe had to make claims within three months; those in the 'western colonies' had six months; those in the East Indies twelve months. Claims were to be liquidated by four commissioners, two French and two English, who had power to call witnesses and examine on oath.

A number of similar 'mixed' commissions met in Paris after 1815, dealing with claims involving various countries. Practical problems with this arrangement – and the potentially open-ended liabilities it suggested – led the French government to ask Wellington to negotiate a new solution. He proposed that the French should pay a sum calculated to cover their liabilities to each country in final settlement of the claims, which would then be liquidated locally.[12] As a result, another convention was entered into on 25 April 1818, under which the French made over an additional annuity of 3 million francs to commissioners who would be appointed solely by the King of England. In 1819, three commissioners were appointed under a statute,[13] which gave dissatisfied parties an appeal against the decision to the Privy Council within three months.[14] Under the statute, the Privy Council was forbidden from considering any new evidence, but had to determine on the same evidence as that considered by the commissioners. For the government, the claims were to be dealt with as quickly as possible as an administrative matter, which required limiting the nature of any possible appeal. The statute also provided for any surplus to be paid to the Treasury.[15]

The commissioners dealt with a large number of claims. Before 1818, the mixed commissioners had liquidated 308 claims and rejected eleven. By 1821, the British commissioners had liquidated a further 265 claims, rejecting 49.[16] At this point, there remained 373 unadjudicated claims. The largest claims to have been settled came from a bank, Boyd, Ker & Co., which submitted claims worth 4,655,713 francs to the joint commissioners and a further 8,092,338 francs to the British commissioners. They were awarded 2,373,081 francs (in *rentes*) from the joint commissioners and

[12] *Parl. Debs.*, 1st ser. 39: 515 (19 February 1819).

[13] C.A. Mackenzie, G.L. Newnham Collingwood and George Hammond. The method of proceeding by commissioners appointed under statute was not new. A mixed commission had been set up under a treaty of 1794 between the British and American governments to settle the claims of Britons owed debts in America before the end of the War of American Independence, which had given way in 1803 to an entirely British commission set up under statute to distribute funds paid by the Americans in final settlement of any claims: see PP 1812 (134) II. 137.

[14] 59 Geo. 3, c. 91. [15] 59 Geo. II c. 31. [16] PP 1821 (728) XXIII 411, pp. 12–13.

a further 6,307,414 francs from the British.[17] The bank was of course claiming not only on behalf of itself, but of its clients. One of the largest private claims was put in by the heirs of Sir Elijah Impey, chief justice of Bengal, who claimed 2,933,851 francs from the joint commissioners and a further 1,309,591 from the British.[18] But this claim was dwarfed by that submitted by the Baron de Bode, who claimed 13,529,062 francs in principal and arrears. This claim, which exceeded even that put in by the bankers, amounted to over half a million pounds sterling.[19] His own claim was outstripped only by that of the British Catholic establishments in France, whose claims ran to 19,391,295 francs.

2. *Clement's claim*

Clement was not seeking to claim compensation for the loss of his father's land, but for the loss of his own. The estates in question comprised the lordship of Soultz in Lower Alsace, as well as estates in Bergzabern in the duchy of Deux Ponts in the Rhineland. The estates had been granted to the family by the Archbishop of Cologne. They were held as a *fief d'oblation*, a form of tenure which descended only to the male heirs of the grantee, on whose failure it reverted to the Archbishop to regrant. When the male line of the previous grantee failed in 1788, Charles had paid the Archbishop a sweetener of £14,600, raised from his wife's family,[20] and had been formally invested – along with his son and heir – in December.[21] The Alsatian properties were the most valuable. Besides a chateau, which Charles had built and furnished lavishly, there were mines for salt, coal, tar and asphalt. Once installed, the family invested in the mines, incurring more debts (amounting to 300,000 francs, or nearly £13,000), which were charged on the estate in Bergzabern. As a result of these improvements, the mines yielded an annual profit of more than £7,500 per annum.[22]

[17] The sums added up to £347,219 (or £29,282,135 in 2013 values). The firm appealed against some rejected claims: see e.g. *Genesse's Case* (1823) 2 Knapp 345.

[18] They were awarded 1,382,577 francs for the first claim, while the second was rejected.

[19] The sum in English money as £541,162, or £40,451,859 in 2013 values.

[20] The Baron claimed to have paid a smaller sum than a rival had offered, but was granted it because of his family's connections with the Habsburgs. For details see 'Baron de Bode: Case Respecting His Claim on the Funds for Liquidating British Claims on France' [Law Officers' Opinion, 30 August 1832], The National Archives (henceforth cited as TNA) TS 25/2045, ff. 64, 85; 'The Baron's Replies' [to the commissioners award], TNA T 1/3760, f. 27.

[21] 'Baron de Bode: Case Respecting His Claim on the Funds for Liquidating British Claims on France', TNA TS 25/2045, f. 64.

[22] 'The Baron's Replies', TNA T 1/3760, f. 28.

According to Clement, in 1791, the elder Baron – 'being alarmed at the disturbances which had broken out in France' – made a public cession of the land to the son in order to protect it from being confiscated. Charles calculated that it was safer in the hands of his son, 'who was a British Subject, England being at that time highly popular with the Revolutionary party in France'.[23] Moreover, since Clement was only fourteen, he 'would not be bound by any abandonment of any part of his rights as owner of the said Lordship'. Meanwhile, Charles would run the property on behalf of his son. The ruse did not work: in October 1793, after the two men joined the Austrian army, the land was confiscated, with the 'Bode' family in general declared to be émigrés whose land could be taken (pursuant to a decree earlier that year).[24] When the family left Soultz, the contents of the house were emptied and eventually sold.[25] The mineral mines fell into disuse, while the salt mines were leased (in 1806) by the government to the Compagnie des Salines de l'Est for a period of ninety-nine years. The French government at first appropriated all the revenues of the Bergzabern estate, and then sold it off.[26] At the end of the war some of the Alsatian property remained unsold – including the salt mine, the manor house and some coal pits.[27] Clement told the commissioners that the family had been offered restoration of these properties, but that he had to abandon them to his father's creditors, since they had been charged with the Bergzabern debts.

The deadline for claims to be submitted was 20 February 1815. On 13 January, Clement gave the Russian ambassador in Paris details of his claim to pass on to the commissioners. He gave them to Richelieu (then the French Prime Minister), who thought that the Baron was not eligible, since he did not appear to be a British subject. Clement – who spoke hardly a word of English – then went to see the British ambassador in Paris, who assured him that he was British by virtue of his birth. Clement tried on several occasions to see the chief British commissioner, but only got hold of him the day after the deadline had passed. However,

[23] TNA TS 25/2045, f. 65. See also John Fonblanque's explanation to the 1834 select committee: PP 1834 (583) XVIII 855, p. 59.

[24] This decree was issued coincidentally on the same day as the decree confiscating the property of Britons in France.

[25] Clement's lawyer later claimed that his father's prized libraries were left on the streets for three days, but that the family was so revered by the community that no book was taken: TNA TS 11/528: Petition of Right hearing (1st day [15 June 1842]), f. 6.

[26] TNA TS 25/2045, f. 66.

[27] TNA TS 11 535: 'In the Privy Council: Case in support of the award of the commissioners', pp. 2–3 at Soultz there remained the salt mine, the coal pit, the mansion house and a few pieces of ground.

he was told that if he obtained a certificate from Richelieu to confirm that he had preferred his claims before him, then his claim would be considered. The letters were eventually forthcoming in 1816, when the French commissioners expressed their view in December that no difficulty would be made respecting the Soultz claim, provided that the Baron's nationality was established. In the meantime, the commissioners made it clear to Clement that he would need to answer three questions: whether he was British, whether the properties were in France and whether they were in his possession when they were seized.[28]

Clement conceded early on that he could not be indemnified for the loss of the Bergzabern property, since it was not within the borders of France.[29] To settle the nationality question, he obtained an opinion from Sir Samuel Romilly in March 1817. The case submitted to Romilly stated that Clement had been was born at Loxley, the son of a German nobleman, whose property at Soultz 'was confiscated by the Government under the pretence of its being the property of an emigrant although the Baron was a German & owed no other allegiance to France than that due from him as Commander of one of the German Regiments in the French service'.[30] Romilly's opinion, which drew on *Calvin's Case*, [31] was that Clement was a natural-born subject entitled to all the rights and privileges of all subjects, and that he could never shake off this allegiance.[32]

Clement met the commissioners in London on 31 March 1819, when he was first told in detail of what information they required.[33] What he did not then know was that his name had not yet been included on the register, but that the commissioners were still seeking the Law Officers' opinion whether the steps he had taken early in 1815 were sufficient to allow his name to be entered.[34] Having been satisfied on that score, the Board outlined the proofs required once more in a formal letter of 23 August 1821. Regarding the Soultz property, he was required to show that it had been formally ceded to him by his father before 10 October 1793, as evidenced by a notarial act (or a notarial act proving the loss of the

[28] 'The Baron's Replies', TNA T 1/3760.

[29] Letter dated 29 October 1816, TNA TS 11/535. He added that the French government had profited from the sale of the property.

[30] PP 1834 (583) XVIII 855, p. 17; the full case is also to be found in TNA C 206/90: the Baron's petition of right, f. 8.

[31] *Calvin's Case* (1601) 7 Co Rep 1.

[32] 'Pleas before the Lady the Queen in Her High Court of Chancery on the 2nd day of Febry AD 1839', TNA C 206/90, ff. 9–10.

[33] 'The Baron's Replies', f. 19.

[34] PP 1834 (583) XVIII 855, p. 10.

formal act of cession). He had to prove that he was known to the French authorities at that time to be the sole and *bona fide* owner of the property, and that it was confiscated on account of his being a British subject, by virtue of the decrees of confiscation.[35] The evidence required was detailed and comprehensive, and Clement complained repeatedly that the commissioners – having delayed in telling him what was needed – were setting impossibly tight timetables. However, the commissioners were unsympathetic to his requests for more time, and in April 1822 told him that unless he produced the necessary documentation within a fortnight, his claim would be rejected.[36] The commissioners' sympathy for the Baron had been seriously damaged by his habit of referring potential creditors to them and even giving promissory notes payable at their offices.[37]

They drew up their award rejecting the claim on 26 April. It contained two main conclusions. First, his claim relating to the mines was rejected, since a law of 12 July 1791 had placed all minerals at the disposition of the state, and there was no proof that either the father or the son had been granted the right to operate the mines. Second, his claims relating to the other property were rejected since there was no proof that the cession 'was admitted and recognised by the French authorities as valid and legal'. On the contrary, they concluded that it was his father who was in possession of the estates, which were seized on the grounds that the elder Baron was an émigré.[38] The commissioners felt that Clement's own case appeared to concede that the property had remained in the hands of his father: for as they read it, the wording both of the case submitted to Romilly and of a covenant drawn up by one of Clement's creditors, Thomas Richmond (to whom he had assigned part of the expected proceeds of the case), suggested that the land was confiscated as that of his émigré father. Although the Baron had struck out the passage in the covenant with Richmond, its presence alone was said to be 'fatal to the claim'. All this seemed to make it clear that the son was only entitled to inherit after the death of his

35 PP 1834 (583) XVIII 855, p. 11.

36 In February 1822, Clement's agent agreed to abandon part of his claim amounting to 3,023,306 francs, which represented the Bergzabern property, and feudal rights which had been abolished in 1789. The capital claim now valued at 3,903,600 francs. Letter from J.M. Brackenbury, 21 February 1822 TNA TS 11/535. The claim is broken down in the 'Case in support of the award of the commissioners' before the Privy Council in TNA TS 11/535.

37 Letter 15 July 1819, TNA TS 11/535; Letter 14 September 1820, TNA TS 11/535, cf. PP 1834 (583) XVIII 855, p. 42.

38 The award is given in 'Case in support of the award of the commissioners' before the Privy Council in TNA TS 11/535, p. 6.

father. The commissioners did not consider the question of the Baron's nationality in this award, although in an abstract drawn up five years later (which may have reflected considerations in their minds arising in other cases at that time),[39] they noted that 'although born in England, [he] was not such a British subject as was in any way contemplated by the Treaty of Commerce between England and France'.[40]

Clement appealed to the Privy Council in June. He reiterated his claim that the land had been ceded to him in 1791, and argued that while the documentary evidence of the cession had been lost in the revolution, he could offer additional evidence from witnesses. The Baron felt that he had been given an impossibly short timetable by the commissioners in which to obtain evidence from Alsace, which was a sixteen-day journey from London. However, the Privy Council upheld the award, refusing (as they were bound under the statute) to admit any new evidence. Lord Stowell held 'that the claimant had completely failed in regard to the ownership of the property': for the cession, while by no means an improper 'contrivance originating in the mind of the father' had 'proved ineffectual'.[41] In effect, there was no question of law for the Privy Council to consider in this case – since the commissioners' decision was based on questions of fact – but only matters of fact on which no new evidence could be admitted. The Privy Council, therefore, did not express a view on legal questions which would be debated in future in regard to his claim, namely, whether the Baron was English for the purposes of the treaty, and whether his property had been taken under the laws sequestering English property.

If the Privy Council did not pronounce on the legal aspects of Clement's claim, it did discuss legal issues in the few other cases which came before it. In a number of cases it took a more liberal view of how the treaty was to be applied than the commissioners had.[42] For instance, in *Pilkington's Case*, Sir William Grant MR noted that compensation under the treaty was for

39 It was at this time that they rejected the claim of the heirs of the Count de Wall, discussed below.

40 PP 1834 (583) XVIII 855, pp. 42–44. In this document, they added (five years after their award) that Clement could have had no rights since '*we are informed* that no minor can be invested with a German fief' (emphasis in original).

41 PP 1834 (583) XVIII 855, p. 106. Stowell was later quoted as having said 'that the claimant, who, no doubt, has been much excited by this engrossing object, seems to labour under some strange delusion'. Quoted in *Parl. Debs.*, new ser., vol. 19, col. 1574.

42 Only eighteen appeals were heard, brought by only eleven sets of appellants: PP 1826–1827 (428) XXII.637.

property seized 'unjustifiably', rather than property taken 'illegally', since a sovereign's actions within his own domain could not be illegal. Grant consequently felt that 'property may be said to be indument confisqué with reference to the Treaty of 1786, with reference to the modern usages of nations at war, or with reference to the conduct of this country towards the subjects of France'.[43] The Privy Council also seemed to take a less strict view than the commissioners on the question of nationality. In September 1820, it heard the appeal of the heirs of the Comte de Fanning, an Irishman who had settled in France and whose estates had been confiscated in 1792, after his return to Britain. The commissioners had rejected their claim on the grounds that Fanning was a naturalised Frenchman, whose property was seized as that of an émigré. However, the Privy Council held that it had not been proven that he had been naturalised and in the absence of proof, he was to be taken as a British subject whose property was seized after the decree of confiscation.[44] The Privy Council also took a generous approach when it came to French women who had married Englishmen.[45]

However, the Privy Council confirmed the commissioners' rejection of the largest claim of all, that of the Catholic colleges which had been set up in France after the Reformation to educate the children of English, Scottish and Irish Catholics. They had been treated under the revolution as distinct from French ecclesiastical houses and their property had been seized under decrees against British property. Although these claims attracted some sympathy from the British commissioners,[46] they were rejected on the ground that the property confiscated belonged not to individuals, but to bodies incorporated in France. In the Privy Council, Lord Gifford upheld this decision, holding that the parties to the treaty could not have intended 'that the British Government should demand, or

[43] *The Rev Charles Pilkington, William Thomas Williams, and J Newland* v. *Commissioners for the Claims on France* (1821) 2 Knapp 7, at 13.

[44] *Hill* v. *Reardon* (1826, 1827) 2 Russell 608. By contrast, the commissioners refused the claim of Count O'Mahoney for property seized in Nancy (under laws against émigrés and sold in January 1793), since it was seized under laws passed long before the decrees of confiscation and sequestration of British subjects' property, and before war broke out between Britain and France. PP 1861 (502) XI 513, at p. 175.

[45] The French-born Marie Girardot, who had married a naturalised Englishman, and the Marchioness of Wellesley, who had long been resident in England, but only married the Marquis after her property was confiscated, were both compensated, the first after an appeal to the Privy Council, the second after an opinion from the King's Advocate based on that decision: See *The Marquis du Bouchet, Executor of the Comtesse de Conway :The Award of the Commissioners for Liquidating British Claims on France* (1834) 2 Knapp 365; PP 1861 (502) XI 513, at p. 171.

[46] Note from C.A. Mackenzie, 19 December 1822; TNA FO 27/278.

the French Government grant, compensation for property held in trust for establishments in France, and for purposes inconsistent with British laws, and which were subject to the control of the French Government'.[47]

When the Catholic claims were rejected, it became clear that there would be a surplus in the funds paid by France, amounting to nearly half a million pounds.[48] With this in mind, the Treasury decided that the commissioners should now consider the claims of those who had failed to register their claims in time in 1816, but that they should not reopen closed cases.[49] Under these circumstances, the Baron wrote to the commissioners asking them to retain in their hands a sum sufficient to satisfy his claims; and in April he returned to the Privy Council. However, this appeal failed, for Lord Gifford held that the statute gave only one final appeal.[50] When the last appeal to the Privy Council was handed down in July 1826, the commission announced that it had completed its existing business and turned to the new cases.[51]

II. Political pressure

Having failed to persuade the Privy Council to reopen his case, Clement turned to France, which had passed a law in April 1825 to indemnify those who had lost lands in the law confiscating émigré property. However, he was told that he could not claim, since British subjects were excluded by the law of 1825: since he had been a registered claimant under the conventions, his claim had been included in the money paid over to satisfy the British claims.[52] With the French claims blocked – and with an opinion of Launcelot Shadwell that 'although his case has miscarried before the Commissioners and upon the Appeal, the Baron is entitled, in the view of moral justice, to indemnification for the loss of his property'[53] – he set about reviving his claims in England in the wider political realm. There were three prongs to his attack. The first was to attempt to get

[47] *Rev John Daniel, Rev John Beu, Rev Francis Tuite, Rev John Yates and Thomas Cleghorn* v. *Commissioners for the Claims on France* (1825) 2 Knapp 23, at 49.

[48] PP 1828 (417) XVI 573 gives the figure of £482,752. The figure of £455,319 is suggested by calculation from the figures in PP 1830–1 (320) XIV.5.

[49] Treasury Minute, 2 May 1826, PP 1834 (76) XLI.497.

[50] TNA T 1/3760. He followed this up with a petition to the House of Commons on 8 May, which was ordered to lie on the table. Gifford's judgment is in PP 1834 (583) XVIII 855, p. 136.

[51] Besides the 308 cases settled by the mixed commission, the second commission had settled 439 cases.

[52] PP 1860 (482) XXII 151, pp. 33–34.

[53] TNA T 1/3760.

the government to use its discretionary power over the remaining funds to pay his claim on the grounds that the commissioners had treated him unjustly. The second was to obtain a parliamentary investigation. The third was to keep the matter before the public mind through the production of pamphlets.

1. *Pressuring the Treasury*

In May 1827, Clement submitted his case once again to the Treasury, in the hope that it would pay him his claim out of the surplus. However, the Treasury simply referred it back to the commissioners, who reiterated the view they had taken in 1822. Rejected once more, the Baron submitted a lengthy response, which he also forwarded to his parliamentary supporters. In this reply, he pointed out that the commissioners had never considered that he had a vested right to the reversion of the property, which gave him an interest even if the cession had not been valid (as he continued to insist it was). He also reminded his readers that other cases before the Privy Council had settled that British subjects could obtain compensation for land seized as émigré property: it did not (as the commissioners had said) have to have been taken solely by virtue of the decree confiscating British property. He also sought to answer some of the commissioners' other suspicions. They had pointed out that he had claimed £540,000 for a property for which his family had recently paid only £14,000, by way of a 'bribe' to the Archbishop of Cologne. Answering this, he retorted that the douceur 'has nothing to do with the point in discussion', but was simply 'proof of the misrepresentation and malice' of the commissioners. Even if his father had bought the estate for so small a sum, he said, 'it would not be a reason why the Estate should not be worth the sum I claim'.[54] In Clement's view, the commissioners were biased against him, and their report was a 'tissue of misrepresentations'.[55] '[T]hey are the party I complain of', he wrote to Edward Littleton MP, 'and can therefore hardly be called upon to give an opinion in their own

[54] 'The Baron's Replies', TNA 1/3760. In his proceedings before the Privy Council, the Baron had also submitted a sworn statement from Richmond admitting the error in the document and asserting that Clement had always claimed the property as his own: 'Report from the Select Committee of the House of Lords appointed to inquire into the allegations of the Baron de Bode's Petition', Parliamentary Papers (House of Lords) 1852 (194), p. 32 (TNA TS 11/535).

[55] Letter to the Duke of Wellington, dated 2 May 1828, TNA 1/3760.

case'.[56] They looked for any technical reason to reject his name, to enable them to allocate his money to others. Where he was held to an impossibly strict timetable, 'how different were their proceedings in other cases, amongst others Mr Boyd the Father in law of Mr Baldwin the Secretary of the Commission', who was given time after the rejection of an award to obtain fresh evidence.[57]

In the meantime, the commissioners had progressed with settling the late-registered claims (distributing a further £191,589),[58] and determined to close the commission in March 1828.[59] Anticipating another surplus, Sir Robert Inglis sought a mandamus from the King's Bench to compel the commissioners to consider the case of claimants under Convention No. 13, who wanted the surplus funds received for Convention No. 7 claims to be used to pay theirs.[60] Alarmed by this, Clement immediately urged the Treasury not to pay any surplus out until all the claims under Convention No. 7 had been satisfied, and he added that his own case could not be regarded as having been decided 'until it has been investigated afresh with the additional evidence, which he was so arbitrarily prevented by the Commissioners from laying before them'.[61] In his correspondence with the Treasury, the Baron once again stressed the injustice done to him, the fact that a surplus remained and the legal point that the Treasury had discretion over the fund.[62]

However, the question whether a surplus still existed was in doubt in June 1828, when a parliamentary return revealed that £250,000 of the funds had been paid to the Commissioners of Woods and Forests, to help pay for the exorbitant cost of refitting and extending Buckingham Palace.[63] M.A. Taylor had followed this up with a motion condemning this as a 'misapplication of public money'. The motion failed, but it led to many petitions from various claimants on the funds. It also generated much publicity, and much sympathy, for the Baron's cause. *The Times*, for instance, printed Clement's, commenting that it revealed 'that unsightly palaces are to absorb immense sums, while just creditors go unpaid'.[64] Clement's petition was presented to parliament on 1 July by E.G. Stanley, who also moved that it be referred to a select committee. His motion was

[56] Letter, 7 June 1827, TNA 1/3760. [57] 'The Baron's Replies', TNA 1/3760.
[58] PP 1830–1 (320) XIV.5. [59] PP 1828 (417) XVI 573.
[60] *Morning Chronicle*, 6 May 1828. [61] Petition 7 May 1828, TNA T 1/3760.
[62] Petition 19 May 1828, TNA T 1/3760.
[63] PP 1828 (444) XVI 575.This disposed of all but £5,240 of the original money.
[64] *The Times*, 23 June 1828, col. 6c. For Taylor's motion see *Parl. Debs.*, new ser. 19: 1476. Numerous other claimants also presented petitions to be paid out of the surplus. See *Journals of the House of Commons*, 25 July 1828.

lost, however, in the face of the opposition of MPs who felt that this was not a matter for parliament, since it had already been determined by a court of law.[65]

The outcry compelled the government to restore the money advanced to the Commissioners of Woods and Forests. With the fund standing at £278,336, the government began in 1830 to consider once more how to dispose of the money.[66] Those staking claims on the fund now included some of the original claimants (including the Catholic establishments), as well as claimants under Convention No. 13, whose funds had run out. This alarmed Clement. When he saw the return of unsettled claims made by Charles Baldwin in March 1830,[67] which omitted his name but included the Irish Colleges, he suspected the government of including unsustainable claims to give the appearance of doing justice, while secretly planning to keep the money. 'The only legal and equitable unsettled claim existing, and which ought to have been on that return, was *mine*', he fulminated, 'and that was *omitted*!!'[68] Having held back from publishing another pamphlet in 1829 (anticipating a helpful attitude from the government), he now rushed into print with a response.[69] He was also alarmed by the fact that the Irish colleges might be allowed to appeal to the Privy Council, since success on their part would sweep away the fund, and asked Stanley to present another petition in the Commons.[70] In June, a Treasury Minute clarified the government's intentions. The original claimants whose cases had been rejected (such as the Irish) were not to be allowed to reopen their cases; and those who had not registered their claims before May 1826 were not to be allowed to claim. However, the late claimants admitted under the May 1826 Minute were to be allowed to appeal to the Privy Council in cases of rejection; while those who had claims under Convention No. 13 should also be allowed to claim.[71] This would exclude the Baron's claim.

65 *Parl. Debs.*, new ser., vol. 19 (1828), cols. 1563–1588. The Baron later claimed that the government had secured the victory by making false statements of fact: Memorial of 28 November 1830, TNA T 1/3760. Over the summer, Clement continued to write to Duke of Wellington, asking him to intervene: TNA T1/3760. He also published *A Short Statement of the Case of the Baron de Bode* (London, 1828).

66 *Parl. Debs.*, n.s. 24: 453 (6 May 1830). This had been discussed in 1829: in the debate on 28 May of that year, Dr Phillimore had asked the Chancellor of the Exchequer whether the Baron was to be included among those for whom the surplus was intended, but no answer was given. See letter from de Bode to G.R. Dawson, 8 June 182, TNA T 1/3760.

67 PP 1830 (200) XXIX 457.

68 Memorial 28 November 1830, TNA T 1/3760.

69 Baron de Bode, *French Claims* (London, 1830). He also paid for advertisements in newspapers detailing his claims: e.g. *The Times*, 11 March 1830, 6 c.

70 *Parl. Debs.*, ns 23: 1277. Sir James Graham and Dr Phillimore also spoke in the Baron's favour.

71 PP 1834 (76) XLI 497.

In the event, no new commission was issued in 1830, and the arrival of a new government in November gave Clement brief hope that his claims would be more favourably viewed.[72] Once again, he submitted a case to the Treasury arguing for his right to compensation, which expanded in a new way on the legal nature of his rights. The lordship of Soultz, he said, was an inalienable male *fief de protection*, regulated by the feudal law of the Empire rather than the law of France; for when Alsace became a part of France in 1648, the rights of the Alsatian nobility had been reserved in the Treaty of Münster.[73] Moreover, the decrees of 1789 and 1790 relating to feudalism had reserved the rights of the Alsatian nobles. Having been formally invested in the property with his father in 1788, and been ceded his father's rights in 1791, he was the legal owner of this feudal property. Moreover, the decree confiscating the property had simply listed the proprietor as 'Bode', omitting both the forename and the profession of the owner: it was not at all evident from the decree that the French had regarded it as his father's property, rather than as his.

Given these new arguments, the Treasury referred the question back once more to Charles Baldwin, the secretary of the commission. In a detailed report refuting the claims with far more detailed legal arguments than had been presented before, Baldwin noted that the agreement with France contemplated granting an indemnity for losses resulting from breaches of the 1786 treaty. The Baron's property was clearly not commercial property. It consisted largely of feudal and seigneurial rights, which were abolished in 1790, without any reservation for Alsatian rights. But even if such rights had been reserved, he asserted (referring to Philippe Antoine Merlin's *Repertoire de Jurisprudence*) that no British subject could hold such estates.[74] Even if the Baron was British by birth, he could therefore not be considered as British for the purposes of the treaty. As to the cession, it was void both for failing to comply with formalities required by an ordonnance of 1731 and for purporting to be a transfer to a minor lacking contractual capacity. The property consequently remained that

[72] Memorial of 25 November 1830, TNA T1/3760.

[73] 'The effect of the treaty upon the possessions of the immediate Nobility of the Empire situate in Alsace was to unite these possessions politically with France and at the same time to reserve their connection with Germany in respect of all the feudal incidents of tenure', TNA TS 25/2045, f 63.

[74] Under the title 'Droit d'Aubaine', Merlin had said that those born outside France were treated harshly by seigneurs: 'dans plusieurs provinces du Royaume, il était d'usage que les Seigneurs les reduissent à l'état de Serfs'. TNA TS 25/2045, ff. 87–8. However, a convention between the French crown and the Archbishop of Cologne in 1769 had abolished the Droit d'Aubaine in those areas: PP 1834 (583) XVIII 855, p. 154.

of the elder Baron when it was seized as émigré property. He concluded, '[s]hould their Lordships consent to reopen the case it would produce most serious circumstances as every claimant who has not been successful in his appeal to the Privy Council would naturally expect the same indulgence'. In a separate letter to Thomas Spring Rice (secretary of the Treasury), Baldwin wrote, 'I trust that I have completely shewn the Baron has not even the shadow of a claim'.[75] The report was sent to the Law Officers, who opined in August that 'no sufficient proof of mistake is given to authorize their Lordships to unravel the judgment that has been pronounced',[76] while adding that the government could compensate the Baron by an exercise of their equity, if they were clearly convinced that the decision had been wrong. They were not.

At the end of 1832, with doubts over Clement's case finally settled, the Treasury decided to appoint a new commission, to dispose of the remaining money, and in January three new commissioners were appointed: Dr Joseph Phillimore (who had been one of Clement's supporters), William Empson and Andrew Martin. A Treasury Minute in March reiterated the government's view that there should be no reopening of old cases, particularly when (as in Clement's case and that of the Catholics) the decision had been confirmed by the Privy Council. The Treasury was also now prepared to allow wholly new cases, provided that the delay had not arisen from circumstances over which the claimant had had any control.[77] Appeals would be allowed to go to the Privy Council, using an informal process.[78] The three commissioners would later acquire more powers to settle claims under different conventions: a Treasury Minute of November 1834 authorised them to examine the claims of British subjects whose property was confiscated by the Danish government in 1807, and another Minute of June 1837 directed them to examine the claims of subjects trading with Spain whose commercial property was sequestered by the Spanish government after 1804.[79]

2. *Hill's select committee*

With the government resolute on not exercising any discretionary power in Clement's favour, and with a new commission looking to dispose of the surplus, he returned to the parliamentary route. The Baron's

[75] Letter dated 19 July 1832, TNA T 1/3760. [76] TNA TS 25/2045, f. 93.

[77] PP 1834 (76) XLI 497. [78] PP 1861 (502) XI 513, at p. 119.

[79] PP 1861 (257) XXXIV. 393; PP 1842 (449) XXVI 373, p. 9. For the background to these claims see *Parl. Debs.*, 3rd ser. 24: 408 (12 June 1834).

continuing publicity campaign – which included placing large advertisements in the daily press, detailing the 'misappropriated' money received from France[80] – finally bore fruit in 1834, when a select committee of the House of Commons was appointed on the motion of Matthew Davenport Hill to investigate his claims.[81] The news of this committee being appointed was soon met by petitions from claimants under the other conventions, who feared that the Baron might sweep away all the remaining money, and who wanted to be allowed to be represented by counsel before the select committee, to oppose the Baron. Two representative claimants from other classes – Arthur Rondeau and James Bourdieu – were selected to oppose the claim.[82] The government clearly had a hand in this, for it agreed to pay the legal costs of these claimants (one of whose claims was rejected by the Privy Council while the select committee was sitting).[83] Moreover, their arguments (presented by Sir William Follett, soon to be Solicitor-General) reflected the position of the government. Although the committee never issued a final report with conclusions, it produced an interim report in August of over 150 pages, which gathered together much of the documentation which had been discussed over the years. It was before this committee that the most sophisticated legal arguments pertaining to the claim were to be heard.

Two arguments dominated the discussion, neither of which had been regarded as particularly important before the commissioners. The first concerned Clement's nationality. The issue of nationality had recently been debated once more in the Privy Council in cases arising from the late claims, where the issue had been explored in greater detail than previously. In April, the Privy Council heard the appeal brought by the siblings of James Drummond, whose claim amounted to 1,041,200 francs (£41,648). Born in Avignon, Drummond was the great-grandson of the Earl of Melfort, who had fled Britain with James II after the Glorious

[80] For example, *The Times*, 25 April 1834, col. 2e, 29 April 1834, col. 6d.

[81] *Parl. Debs.*, 3rd ser., vol. 23 (1834), col. 397. In 1832, Clement convinced a new MP, Thomas Wilde, to take up the matter in 1832, with a view to getting a select committee to investigate, though none had been appointed. Letter, 7 May 1832, TNA T 1/ 3760; *The Times*, 13 August 1832, col. 3f.

[82] *Journal of the House of Commons*, 89 (1834), p. 286 (13 May), 290 (14 May), 321 (22–23 May). *Parl. Debs.*, 3rd ser. 12: 1248 (22 May 1834). See also the Baron's claims regarding the Treasury's part in this: *Baron de Bode* v. *The Queen*, Appendix to the case of the plaintiff in error [House of Lords], TNA TS 11/528, p. 47.

[83] Rondeau's lawyer, Edward Richardson, was paid £1,584.3.8 by the Treasury: letter from George Maule, 18 March 1836, TNA T 1/3760; *Bourdieu's Case* (1834) 2 Knapp 353.

Revolution. He inherited the title of Duke of Melfort from his father, and an estate in Languedoc from his French mother. This estate was sequestered by the French government in October 1792 as the land of a French émigré, and subsequently sold. The commissioners had rejected the claim in 1827 on the grounds that he was not British, and the loss was hence not in consequence of the decrees against British property.[84] His family challenged this conclusion. Although he was born in France and had never lived in Great Britain, Drummond was claimed to be British by virtue of a series of eighteenth-century statutes, which enacted that the grandchildren of natural-born British subjects were themselves such subjects 'to all intents, constructions and purposes whatsoever'.[85] In the Privy Council, the King's Advocate, Sir Herbert Jenner, argued that even if Drummond were technically British by statute, he could not qualify under the conventions. When 'a treaty speaks of the subjects of any nation', he noted, 'it must mean those who are actually and effectually under its rule and government, not those, who although living out of its dominions, and never having been subject to its government, it may choose to designate its subjects, in its own municipal laws and statutes'.[86] Sir Launcelot Shadwell, giving the judgment of the Judicial Committee, upheld the commissioners' decision. Although 'formally and literally' British, Drummond was also French, according to the definition in Pothier's *Treatise on Persons*.[87] Since he was a French subject in French law by virtue of his birth, 'no act done towards him by the Government of France could be considered an illegal act, within the meaning of the treaty'.[88] This case seemed to provide a clear precedent for the Baron's opponents, in that it suggested that a person who was both French and English could not claim.

However, the question of nationality was also raised in June[89] in *Count de Wall's Case*. This case was brought by the heirs of an Irishman, who had

[84] *Drummond's Case* (1834) 2 Knapp 295.

[85] The Acts were 7 Anne, c. 5, 4 Geo. 2, c. 21, and 13 Geo. 3, c. 21.

[86] *Drummond's Case* (1834) 2 Knapp 295, at 305.

[87] 'Les Citoyens, les vrais & naturels François, suivant la définition de Bacquet, sont ceux qui sont nés dans l'étendue de la domination Françoise', R.J. Pothier, *Traité des Personnes et des Choses*, Book 1, tit. ii, sect. 1, in *Oeuvres Posthumes de M. Pothier*, vol. 2 (Orleans: J. J. Massot, 1777) p. 573.

[88] *Drummond's Case* (1834) 2 Knapp 295, at 311–312.

[89] In the same month, the Privy Council held that the foreign-born wife of a British subject could not obtain compensation for the loss of her property, unless she could be shown to have been domiciled in Britain. *The Marquis du Bouchet, Executor of the Comtesse de Conway: The Award of the Commissioners for Liquidating British Claims on France* (13 June 1834) 2 Knapp 522.

settled and married in France, and acquired properties which were seized in the revolution as that of an émigré. There were strong parallels with the position of the Baron's case, since he had joined the Irish Brigade in the French army, and had been made a Knight of the Order of St Louis. Arguing for the family, Dr Lushington insisted that members of the Irish Brigade had never been regarded as French nationals. Indeed, he added that the commissioners had in three other cases not regarded membership of the Irish brigade as fatal to a claim to compensation. Jenner countered that the Count had acquired French nationality by joining the order, and argued that the court should not be swayed by the fact that the commissioners may have given awards in similar claims, 'for they are the decisions of a tribunal determining without legal discussion, and most probably unappealed against, only because by the Act of Parliament no appeal lies where the determination has been in favour of the claimant'. However, in this case Shadwell held that there was no evidence that the Irish-born Count had ever lost his British nationality and assumed a French character.[90] This case seemed to confirm that compensation could be granted for the seizure of émigré property, which was more helpful to Clement's case.

As a result of these recent cases, when Hill's select committee sat the question of Clement's nationality became a crucial question for discussion. John Fonblanque sought to answer the doubts raised by *Drummond's Case* by distinguishing between natural-born subjects of the king and those (like Drummond) who were by statute allowed to enjoy the rights and privileges of a natural-born subject, such as inheriting property, but who would not, for instance, be regarded as a traitor if he fought for his native country in a war against Britain. Against this, Follett argued that the fact that 'a party born in England may, by the maxims of the old feudal law, owe allegiance to the sovereign of this state' did not mean that 'he is a British subject within the meaning of the contracting parties to this convention'. Had the Baron been domiciled in England, but had his French properties confiscated, he might have claimed: but the mere fact of his birth did not entitle him to claim.[91] This was simply the case of a French citizen having his property confiscated by a French law.

[90] *Count Wall's Case* (1834) 3 Knapp 13. The claim was for 1,119,050 francs (£44,762). Litigation in this case continued, insofar as the heirs sought to obtain compensation for the confiscated properties which had belonged to thier mother. In this they failed: *The Case of the Representatives of Angelique Michael Joseph Wall* (1848) 6 Moo PC 216.

[91] PP 1834 (583) XVIII 855, pp. 76, 85.

The second argument turned on the nature of the Baron's property. Fonblanque's main argument was that Clement had a vested interest in the property, since it was an inalienable male fief, with which neither his father nor the French state could interfere. He rejected the commissioners' argument that all feudal rights had been abolished before 1793, arguing that because of the provisions of the Treaty of Münster, the French revolutionary government had no power to abolish his feudal rights under Imperial law.[92] The power to break the feudal succession was only acquired by the French state under the Treaty of Lunéville of 1801, which ceded the Rhineland to France, but this was something which had occurred well after the confiscation. In short, although the French revolutionary state was free to abolish all feudal rights in France, thanks to the rules of international law, it could not abolish them in Alsace.[93] 'To state that a breach of the Treaty of Westphalia shall be an answer to a claim founded on a breach of the Commercial Treaty', Fonblanque declared, 'seems to me so monstrous a proposition, that no ingenuity can sustain it'.[94] Follett dismissed these international law claims. In his view, the idea that a country to which land was ceded could have no right to alter the laws of that land was in his view 'an absurd proposition'. While foreign states might complain about the breach of a treaty, and might even go to war over it, they could not prevent the new law in acquired territories taking effect.[95] In his view, the sovereign power of a state within its borders could not be limited by treaty. This did not settle the matter for the committee's chairman, Matthew Davenport Hill, who pointed out that the compensation commission's task was to establish whether property was taken in violation of international law, not whether it was taken in breach of domestic law. '[W]e are', he said, 'considering treaties as something above laws'.[96] Follett's answer to this was that the commission was concerned only with any breaches of treaties with Great Britain. Since she was not a party to the treaty between France and Austria in 1648, she had no standing to complain about it, and certainly could

[92] In his view, this gave the Baron a claim, even if the cession was not proved. This issue had not been raised in the original claim. However, it was raised before the Privy Council in the Baron's second appeal by Henry Brougham (see the letter of 'A Constant Reader', in *The Times*, 10 April 1830, col. 3c). The Baron, in his petition to Parliament in 1828, stated that he had not put his case properly initially, thanks to errors by his lawyers.

[93] He conceded that the French state could abolish feudalism within the rest of France, since those feudal rights derived from original French grants. This explained the Duke of Richmond's case: PP 1834 (583) XVIII 855, p. 52.

[94] *Ibid.*, p. 53. [95] *Ibid.*, p. 87. [96] PP 1834 (583) XVIII 855, pp. 89–90.

not use it to show a domestic French law was invalid. Quoting Vattel, he argued that if two contracting parties to a treaty broke their contract, a third party could not complain. The British could only complain about breaches of the 1786 treaty, not of wider breaches. The Barons's case thus raised complex issues over whether international obligations should have more authority in a tribunal deciding whether property had been taken 'unjustifiably' (in Sir William Grant's phrase) than domestic laws within a sovereign (if revolutionary) state.

Considering the Baron's property rights also involved looking into the question of the cession. Fonblanque argued that although there was no formal documentary evidence of the cession, there was sufficient evidence from witnesses to raise a moral presumption that it had occurred, and he argued that the commissioners were entitled under the treaty to use their discretion over such matters of evidence. Follett countered that only a formal cession could transfer property in French law. He sought support for this point from the French litigation Clement had been involved in regarding the unsold properties, notably the salt mines at Soultz. Follett argued that Clement had originally claimed these unsold properties (under a French law of 1814 reinstating confiscated émigré property) in his capacity as heir rather than as owner, suggesting that his father was owner until his death. He added that Clement had only obtained standing in the French courts in his capacity as a Frenchman, and that the French courts had rejected his subsequent claims to be the owner of the lands by virtue of a cession,[97] since the purported cession had not complied with the requirements of the 1731 ordonnance. In Follett's view, this did not only dispose of Hill's claim (when moving for the select committee) that the French had recognised his feudal rights in 1815 in restoring the unsold properties to him (prior to the Baron's having to abandon them to his father's creditors). It also showed there were no foundations to his claims to be owner by virtue of the cession.[98] His conclusion (like the Privy Council's) was that the purported cession was simply a ruse to convince the French authorities that there had been a transfer of property, when there had not. The Baron's lawyers challenged this version of events, but argued that they needed more time to get documentation to prove their claims, including the restoration of the unsold properties and the cession. In fact, at the time of the select committee's sittings, the litigation over

[97] Clement argued that the agent who submitted the first claim in 1816 had erred in describing him as heir.

[98] PP 1834 (583) XVIII 855, p. 104. The documentation pertaining to the mines is at pp. 109ff.

these properties was still ongoing in France, between Clement, his father's court-appointed administrator and the heirs of his father's creditors. It was not a settled question.[99]

With the hearings interrupted, Clement set out to gather new evidence, spending £3,000 in obtaining 132 new documents to support his claim. However, the select committee was not reappointed in 1835, after Hill lost his parliamentary seat. When Thomas Gisborne moved for a reappointment of the committee to consider this evidence,[100] it was opposed by Thomas Spring Rice (now Chancellor of the Exchequer), who said that the Baron had had quite enough time hitherto to establish his claim and that it would be unfair on other claimants not to distribute what remained of the fund. The Solicitor-General, Sir Robert Rolfe, described the Baron's claim as 'the most Quixotic that ever came before the House', and the motion was heavily defeated.[101] But Clement did not feel defeated: he pressed on with more explanations in the newspapers, and persuaded Daniel O'Connell to present yet another petition.[102] That the House of Commons had had enough of this claim can be seen clearly from the reception of O'Connell's announcement of two motions he was bringing:

> Mr. O'CONNELL gave notice, that on the 21st of June he would move for leave to bring in a bill to reform the House of Lords (laughter), and to make the constitution of that body elective; and that on the 23d of that month he would bring before the house the case of the Baron de Bode (Great laughter).[103]

99 In 1836, Clement obtained a judgment in his favour in Wissembourg, though on grounds not helpful to his English claims. Answering his adversaries' argument that he could only inherit as a French citizen (whereas he was British), the court held that the registration of his birth in Soultz had shown his father's intention to recognise his status as a Frenchman. On the issue of the cession of the property to an English subject, the court held that this cession was simply effected 'for the needs of the moment' and (in light of the registration of his birth at Soultz) did not disprove his French citizenship. TNA TS 11/535, 'Extrait des minutes du greffe du Tribunal civil de première instance de l'arrondissement de Wissembourg', sitting of 3 June 1836. Clement's success was short lived: having failed to pay his father's debts, he lost the estate in 1837 when his father's creditors (the heirs of Thomas Schwendt) successfully pressed their claims. TNA TS 11/535, 'Extrait des minutes du greffe du Tribunal civil de première instance de l'arrondissement de Wissembourg', sitting of 23 June 1837.

100 *Parl. Debs.*, third ser., vol. 29 (1835), col. 581.

101 *Parl. Debs.*, 3rd ser. 29: 582 (14 July 1835). Hill later compared the decision not to reappoint his committee with a decree of the Committee of Public Safety in Robespierre's era: *The Times*, 25 June 1844, col. 7a.

102 *The Times*, 17 August 1835, col. 3c, 20 August col. 3e, 12 September 1835, col. 1f.

103 *The Times*, 21 May 1836, col. 4a.

When another Radical, Henry Warburton, sought to have the select committee reappointed in 1838, setting out various aspects in which the commissioners had acted in harsh if not underhand ways, his opponents did not mince their words. One MP said the Baron had pursued his claims with 'a pertinacity approaching to monomania', while the Chancellor (Spring Rice) accused the Baron of making false statements about his dealing with the Treasury, suggesting that 'from rumination on one point for twenty years he had become insane'.[104] The motion was lost, with the Baron only getting support from the Radicals.

3. *Debts and desperation*

As he told the Duke of Wellington, Clement had, by the late 1820s, been 'reduced to a state of destitution, and absolute beggary'.[105] In October 1831, the barrister Robert Langslow implored the Prime Minister, Earl Grey, to 'make some allowance to him from the Treasury to enable him to support himself till his case can be brought before Parliament'.[106] The government was not minded to help out, however, and in 1833, he was imprisoned for debt. After 1835, he lived 'within the rules' of the King's Bench prison, and thereby was able to avoid paying his creditors,[107] surviving largely through the help of the Russian community in London.[108] Eventually, his friends paid his debts to secure his release, after a creditor sought a vesting order against him in 1842, which threatened to upset legal proceedings which at that moment promised to give the Baron the compensation he sought.[109] During this period, he continued to seek to raise credit, protesting to the Treasury in 1834 that potential creditors were being told by them that he had no claim, and that 'I am not the person I describe myself to be'.[110] Clement was happy to give bonds far

[104] *Parl. Debs.*, third ser., vol. 41 (1838), cols. 27, 31 (22 February 1838). The Baron protested against Rice's aspersions: *The Morning Post*, 1 March 1838.

[105] Petition, 9 July 1828, TNA T1/3760.

[106] Letter from Robert Langslow to Earl, 27 October 1831, TNA T1/3760. Langslow, later Attorney General at Malta, was a long-time friend and supporter of the Baron, who was to be left £10,000 in the Baron's will (in which Clement wrote that 'no one knows my case so well as he and sees it in the same light I do it myself').

[107] For a case against one of his guarantors see *Hodges* v. *Pritchard*, *The Times*, 1 December 1834, col. 3d.

[108] Letter from Count Nesselrode, 5 November 1836, TNA T 1/3760.

[109] See *Liverpool Mercury*, 1 July 1842; *The Standard*, 28 July 1842.

[110] Letter from de Bode to the Lords of the Treasury, 16 September 1834, TNA T 1/3760. For litigation giving an insight into his finances see *Hodges* v. *Pritchard*, in *The Times*,

in excess of the money he actually received, in order to keep his case afloat. Many others found their own financial well-being tied up with Clement's. In 1836, his younger brother William, another Russian army officer, who had interrupted his military career in 1831 to help Clement, petitioned the Insolvent Debtor's Court to be freed from his imprisonment for debts amounting to nearly £31,000.[111] Clement's own creditors repeatedly wrote to the Treasury, asking it not to pay the Baron until their debts had been paid. One of these was Edward Willies,[112] who had to petition the Insolvent Debtors' Court himself in 1838.[113] Despite such tales, the Baron continued to be able to raise credit from lenders who felt confident that one day their claims would be paid, but who in the meantime pestered the Treasury not to pay out the Baron first.[114]

By the late 1830s, Clement's behaviour appeared increasingly erratic. When, in 1836, an actuary friend of one of his creditors offered to intercede with the government, Clement took the approach as an admission by the government that there was a large surplus out of which they were prepared to pay a compromised sum. When questioned by the government about it, the actuary, John Finlaison, corrected the mixture of truth and falsehood which had come from Clement and raised the suggestion (soon to be repeated by Spring Rice in the debate) that he had gone mad.[115] With both the government and parliament deaf to his cries, Clement wrote to the Queen,[116] complaining that Spring Rice's 'base and scandalous calumnies on my character imputing to me falsehood, fraud or insanity'

1 December 1834, col 3 d; *Brunskill* v. *De Bode*, in *The Times*, 4 February 1835, col. 4b; *Toone and Halton* v. *The Baron de Bode*, in *The Times*, 25 January 1836, col. 4a. See also *The Times*, 31 July 1838, col. 7a.

111 See *Morning Chronicle*, 5 January 1836, and the letter from William de Bode in *The Standard*, 7 January 1836, p. 1. See also *The Times*, 5 January 1836, 4c; *The Times*, 7 January 1836, col. 4b. The case revealed that Clement had actually received far smaller sums than the value of the bills given for them.

112 See letter from Charles Baldwin to J. Stewart, 23 January 1829, TNA T1/3760, and letter from De Bode to the Treasury 2 November 1833, TNA T 1/3760.

113 *The Times*, 31 July 1838, 7a; cf the letter from Francis Thomas Champneys in *The Times*, 10 August 1838.

114 For instance, between 1841 and 1842, Clement raised £58,846 from John Wade, who on 9 May 1842 requested the Treasury not to pay Clement until he had been paid: TNA TS 11/534. For further evidence of continuing confidence in the Baron's debts see *Reay and Reay's Bankruptcy*, *The Times*, 27 November 1845, col. 7f.

115 PP 1837–1838 (163) XXXVII.305, p. 5. Finlason's wording was 'that this miserable man, by the mere circumstance of ruminating on one idea for a period of 20 years, has become finally insane'.

116 This was not the first time he had written a personal letter to the sovereign. See his memorial to the King, 22 October 1830, TNA T 1/3760.

had prevented the reappointment of Hill's committee. Not only had there been a defalcation in the funds amounting to £2 million, but rumour had it 'that the disappearance of these funds is attributable to Your Royal predecessor King George the forth through the agency of those who were then entrusted with the care of them!!!' Having insulted the Queen's uncle, he turned to constitutional theory. 'If I have formed a correct idea of the origin of the Prerogative as to appointing or dissolving an administration at the Royal pleasure; – it was intended for the purpose of watching and acting as a check of superior power over the proceedings of Ministers . . . to protect the subject from the malpractice of an administration in cases where redress is difficult or cannot, from being beyond the jurisdiction of courts of Law, be obtained in the ordinary way'. While the sovereign could, according to the maxim, do no wrong, she was morally responsible for good government, 'And we learn from history that the non observance of this moral Royal obligation has but too often sown the seeds of deep rooted discontent ending in the overturn of the then existing form of government'.[117] If only the Queen would sack the ministry and refer his case to a competent body, all would be well. Victoria's response was to pass the letter over to Lord Melbourne. In the following decade, Clement would once again attempt to get redress from the sovereign, but in a more formal way.

III. The claim in the Common Law courts

With the parliamentary route apparently blocked, Clement turned for the first time to the common law at the end of the 1830s. He was to find these courts far more receptive to his arguments relating to the validity of his claim. However, they ultimately proved of little practical help, for he found himself frustrated by the rules of English public law, which prevented him from getting the crown to disgorge money to which he was held to be entitled under the treaty. As time passed, the amount remaining in the hands of the commissioners steadily diminished. The new commissioners had continued to examine French claims (as well as Danish and Spanish) in the 1830s. In 1839, £150,379 remained in the hands of the Treasury,[118] which now ordered that the claimants who had only received a proportion of their claims hitherto should be paid in full. The government was clearly intent on winding down this operation. In March 1841, the number of commissioners was reduced to one –

[117] Letter to the Queen, 28 February 1838, TNA T 1/3760. [118] PP 1841-I (362) XIII.369.

Phillimore. By then, £56,855 had been awarded by the commission to eighty-two 'Spanish' claimants for whom no fund existed: in their case, the money to cover these claims had been voted specifically by parliament. Five years later, a sum short of £40,000 remained, waiting to be distributed following the final settlement of Privy Council cases.[119] By 1848, the sum remaining had diminished to £16,067.[120] If the Baron was finally to be paid, it would have to be from new money, voted by parliament.

1. *Seeking a mandamus*

The tone was set in his first foray into Queen's Bench, where in June 1838 he sought a mandamus to compel the Lords of the Treasury to pay the claim. In order to claim that the court had jurisdiction to hear a case which had already been rejected by the Privy Council in what the statute said was a final appeal, the Baron's counsel, Matthew Davenport Hill, put forward a new argument. The 1819 statute which gave power to the commissioners to settle the claims was premised (he argued) on the assumption that all claims which had been submitted on time had been registered; and the act only gave the commissioners (and the Privy Council) power to decide on registered claims. However, the Baron's claim had only been formally registered on 21 June 1819. According to Hill, Clement's claim was a *casus omissus*, and while all the registered claimants had a statutory preference over those who were not registered, the commissioners had no jurisdiction over his claim. However, the Baron had a claim on any surplus which remained, which derived from his 'original rights as created by the convention itself'.[121] The surplus money which had come (under the statute) to the Treasury had to be regarded as being held for his benefit, and the only remedy he had to obtain it was by a mandamus. Coleridge was not convinced that he had a case on the merits,[122] but held that, even assuming all his claims were true, he could give no remedy. To begin with, it was not clear that Clement had a *legal* right against the government, for although the government was fulfilling a duty owed to its people in negotiating with France for compensation of their property,

[119] PP 1846 (187) XXV.299. [120] PP 1849 (597) XXX.283.

[121] *In the matter of Clement De Bode, Baron de Bode* (1838) 6 Dowling Practice Cases 776, at 785.

[122] Attempting to convince him, Hill reiterated the point that the Baron did not claim to be a French citizen, and observed that thirteen claimants had been compensated by the commission, all of whom had had their land seized as émigrés, and all but one of whom had been naturalised in France. *The Times*, 30 May 1838, 6f, 11 June 1838, col. 6d.

this was not the kind of obligation which a court could enforce. Moreover, the statute had left the surplus absolutely at the discretion of the Lords of the Treasury, and consequently no individual could complain about how they used it. But even on the assumption that money had found its way from France into the Treasury 'charged with a solemn trust', there were two obstacles to Clement's recovery. The first was that his claim had never been liquidated – the Baron was in effect asking the Treasury to calculate what was due to him. The second was that the Lords of the Treasury took the money as mere servants of the crown, and it was settled law that mandamus did not lie against the crown. Coleridge 'entertained great regret at being obliged to come to this conclusion', but felt the law was clear.[123]

2. *The petition of right*

The Baron's next step was to seek a procedure which could give him a remedy against the crown. The procedure he alighted on was that of a petition of right, which he presented on 2 February 1839. Although writs could not be brought against the sovereign in his own courts, subjects had long been allowed to bring petitions of right, which allowed claims against the crown to be discussed in court. At the time the Baron sought to use this procedure, it was seen primarily as a restitutionary remedy, requiring the king to restore lands or goods which he had no right to retain. In showing a better title to the property in question, the suppliant prayed that the king should remove his hands – *amoveas manus* – from the property.[124] It was also settled that the remedy could be used to recover financial debts and annuities.[125] However, petitions of right were rarely used, and the ambit of the remedy remained very unclear. The Baron's case – a pioneering one in reviving its use[126] – would explore how far it could be used.

The procedure used was that a petition was made to the crown, which endorsed it with the words, 'Let right be done'. On this being done, the petition was sent to the Lord Chancellor, who would issue a commission

[123] *In the matter of Clement De Bode, Baron de Bode* (1838) 6 Dowling Practice Cases 776, at 790–793, *The Times*, 15 June 1838, col. 7b.

[124] J. Chitty, *The Prerogatives of the Crown* (London: J. Butterworth, 1820), p. 353.

[125] See *The Bankers Case* (1690–1700), in *A Complete Collection of State Trials*, ed. T.B. Howell, vol. 14 (London: Longman, 1812), 1 ff.

[126] Shortly thereafter it was also unsuccessfully used by Viscount Canterbury, speaker of the Commons, seeking compensation for property lost in the fire which destroyed the Houses of Parliament. *Viscount Canterbury* v. *Attorney-General* (1843) 1 Phillips 306.

to report on the facts alleged. In the Baron's case, the crown opposed the use of this remedy at the very first stage,[127] arguing that no commission should issue, since he was in effect seeking damages, and there was no fund from which the claim could be paid. However, Lord Cottenham LC ruled that he had no authority to inquire on the merits at this stage, and so a commission issued.[128] With the crown always seeking to put obstacles his path, it was not until June 1842 that a three-man commission, sitting with a special jury, sat to inquire into the truth of his allegations.

The crown was not represented at the proceedings and did not challenge the Baron's evidence. According to the crown's lawyers, the hearing before the commission was a purely *ex parte* proceeding necessary to establish a title to assert against the crown, which had to be done before he could compel the crown to defend its rights.[129] By now, the Baron and his supporters had gathered more and more expert and documentary evidence from France to sustain the claim. Evidence was given by Alfred de Bonard, a French advocate, on the law of Alsace, to establish Clement's legal rights to the fiefdom. The jury also heard evidence from the 82-year-old G.C.H. Rosentritt, who had known the family since 1787 and who had managed the mines until 1793. It also heard 81-year-old Matthew Hummel testify to having seen the cession at a public meeting in 1791, where a notary had set down in writing that the cession had been made.[130] When the jury was asked to consider whether the Baron's case had been made out, it confirmed that there had been a cession by the father to the son, and that there had been a balance of over £250,000 paid to the government after the commission had closed its work. The jury ended with a finding that the value of the Baron's property was £179,474 and that the accrued interest came to £161,208.[131]

[127] The law officers noted on 16 February 1839 that 'there is no ground whatever for this petition of right and that it ought not to be allowed to proceed further', TNA TS 11/532.

[128] *The Standard*, 2 May 1839, 15 July 1840; *In the matter of Baron de Bode* (1840) 2 Phillips 85.

[129] '[T]he Crown cannot be in a situation to defend itself until the Commissioners have found and recorded the Title of the Plaintiff'. Opinion of Robert Wray, 30 May 1842: TNA TS 11/530. The Treasury Solicitor did attend, however, to take notes of the proceedings.

[130] A transcript of the four days' evidence can be found in TNA TS 11/528. See also *The Morning Chronicle*, 16 June 1842, 17 June 1842, 20 June 1842.

[131] The total sum due (including additional interest for the period 1816–1819) was £364,266. The exact calculation is reproduced in 'Report from the Select Committee of the House of Lords appointed to inquire into the allegations of the Baron de Bode's Petition', Parliamentary Papers (House of Lords) 1852 (194), p. 112 (TNA TS 11/535). This sum is equivalent to £34,882,112 in 2012 values.

If the Baron thought he had finally hit the jackpot, the crown's lawyers had other ideas. According to H. Waddington, '[t]his Case is so entirely unlike those which are to be found in the Books that it is impossible to derive the slightest aid from precedents in dealing with it'. He advised a traverse of the entire inquisition, which would require another trial, the legal effect would have to be debated later. He also advised pleading the statute of limitations.[132] In the meantime, the crown's lawyers objected to the Baron's attempt to obtain a commission to take the evidence of the very elderly witnesses who were about to leave the country to return to eastern France.[133] It also undertook its own researches on the French law relating to Alsatian feudalism, the formalities required for a cession of property, and on the effect of the Treaty of Münster.[134]

The case was finally reheard in a trial at the bar of the Queen's Bench in June 1844. Once again, the crown opted not to offer evidence to counter the Baron's claims, but to dispute whether there was a remedy. According to the Solicitor-General, Sir Frederick Thesiger, this was a claim, in effect, that the Queen was his debtor for money had and received to his use; yet all the money had been paid into the Bank of England under statutory authority, and the monarch had no greater control of that money than over any part of the consolidated fund.[135] Summing up to the jury, Lord Denman told them that it was for them to determine what the French law was on the basis of the evidence given. He pointed out that the account of the law given by Clement's lawyers had not been contradicted for the crown had not offered any evidence on this, though he added that some might consider 'the improbability of such a law existing in all respects'. The question whether there was an undue confiscation under the treaty was also for the jury, which involved considering whether (as the lawyers claimed) the French state was bound by its Westphalian

[132] Opinion of 21 October 1842, TNA TS 11/530. Waddington was the Attorney General's Devil, who drew pleadings for the crown: *The Times*, 21 June 1844, 7c.

[133] TNA TS 11/529. See also *The Times*, 20 July 1842, col. 7a, 30 July 1842, col. 7e. The crown later asked for time to prepare its own case: 1 February 1843, col. 6e.

[134] TNA TS 11/534.

[135] Rough notes drawn up by the crown set out an argument that a petition of right could not lie for money or unliquidated damages, since that would allow any soldier or sailor to sue the Queen for his pay. But even if a petition of right lay, 'What form of action? assumpsit? indebitatus? or special assumpsit? or case? Money had & rec^{d}? Supposes the money paid into Q's hands for use of Plt But here no specific payment for his use. The paym^{t} for all claims indefinite in No. And amount. If one could being money had and receiv^{d} so c^{d} all. Then if claims amount to more than fund What is to be done that cannot be': TNA TS 11/534.

treaty obligations.[136] However, he noted that the main fact for the jury to consider was whether the cession – the fact of which had not been disputed by the crown – had been *bona fide* or not. Once again, a jury again found that there had been a valid cession of the land to the Baron from his father, at a time when the transmission of fiefs was still regulated by the old law of Alsace.[137] However, they were directed to find for the crown on the other two issues – that the issue had not arisen within the previous six years or in the reign of the present Queen. They also found (after prompting from the crown's lawyers) that there was no evidence that the sum given by the French in 1818 had been expressly augmented to provide for the Baron's claims.[138]

Once again the jury's verdict did not settle the matter. Nothing was done by the crown on this for another five months, until Hill moved to have a verdict entered for the Baron on the substantive merits.[139] This prompted the law officers to make their own motion, calling on him to show the cause why judgment should not be entered for the crown.[140] The case was argued in the Queen's Bench at the beginning of 1845, and judgment was handed down in December. Giving the judgment of the court, Lord Denman rejected the Baron's claim on three grounds. First, while the jury had certainly established the fact that his property had been confiscated, the Baron had not shown that as a matter of law the confiscation was 'undue'. It was not shown that the confiscation was caused by the rupture of relations between France and Britain; rather, it seemed to have followed from some violation of French law, as determined by a French tribunal. In Denman's view, the court could not pronounce the French law against émigrés to be void. 'Whatever we may know historically of the conduct of the Courts during the Revolution', he ruled, 'we certainly should not

[136] Denman's own summing up indicated that his own view was that the French state was not internally bound by these obligations, and that there was no evidence to show that its confiscation had been improper. For the text see 'Report from the Select Committee of the House of Lords appointed to inquire into the allegations of the Baron de Bode's Petition', Parliamentary Papers (House of Lords) 1852 (194), 113 ff. (Appendix I) (TNA TS 11/535).

[137] *The Times*, 25 June 1844, col. 7b.

[138] The crown's lawyers appear to have accepted that the Baron had established his right, even if there was no remedy: see the note by Frederick Thesiger in TNA TS11/534.

[139] *The Times*, 6 November 1844, col. 6g.

[140] *The Times*, 28 January 1846, col. 6e. The grounds of the crown's case were the statute of limitations; that no specific money had been paid over by the French for his claim (something found by the jury); that he was not within the meaning of the treaties; that a petition of right would not lie for unliquidated damages; and that he was barred by the statute under which the surplus had been paid to the treasury.

be justified in pronouncing their judgment wrong in any particular case without, at least, some direct proof'.[141] This was perhaps an odd position to take, for as the Baron's lawyers pointed out in challenging this decision, the Treasury (and Privy Council) had accepted in many other cases where émigré property had been confiscated that it was 'undue'.

Second, even if his property had been unduly confiscated, he had not made out any legal or equitable claim to any surplus remaining after the claimants registered under the 1819 act had been paid. Like Coleridge, he held that the sum claimed had never been ascertained, and that the Treasury had in any event complete discretion over the surplus. There was nothing to show that the surplus had been received to his use by anyone. Clement's lawyers were once more nonplussed by this finding: 'A claim is, of course, not to be paid, until it has been shown to be legitimate, and the amount ascertained', they argued, 'but it can be no serious answer to a claimant to say . . . that before he can be heard to urge his claim . . . he must be able to show that the very claim which he urges, has been already proved and ascertained'.[142] Finally, even if the sum had been ascertained, it was not shown that Her Majesty had received the money. It did not follow from the fact that Coleridge had held that the Lords of the Treasury could not be reached by a mandamus since they were mere servants of the Crown that the money was in the hands of the sovereign: it had further to be shown 'that the Sovereign has or has had a personal benefit from that which is sought to be received'.[143] Responding to this, Clement's lawyers argued that the court was taking too technical a view of the matter: the real question was not whether an action for money had and received could lie against the Queen for this money, but 'whether it does not establish a case of a claim of *justice* against the Crown'.[144]

The press was outraged by the decision. 'We do not impugn the correctness of Lord DENMAN's judgment', *The Times* thundered, 'but we believe that in all the annals of all time there cannot be found an example where the forms of justice have been so grossly and palpably perverted'.[145] Clement determined to press on, obtaining a writ of error to challenge

[141] *Baron de Bode's Case* (1845) 8 QB 208, at 280.

[142] *Baron de Bode* v. *The Queen*, Case of the Plaintiff in Error [in the House of Lords], TNA TS 11/528, p. 31.

[143] *Baron de Bode's Case* (1845) 8 QB 208, at 285.

[144] *Baron de Bode* v. *The Queen*, Case of the Plaintiff in Error [in the House of Lords], TNA TS 11/528, p. 37.

[145] *The Times*, 13 December 1845, col. 4d.

the decision.[146] However, six weeks after obtaining the writ, he died of a heart attack – 'Or from the cruelty of Government', as one of the inquest jury puts it.[147] Sympathetic notices of his death were published in the press, with one journal predicting that his executors would imitate his 'constancy and unflinching resolution' in the pursuit of the justice which everyone who had investigated his case agreed to be on his side.[148] His son Clement now took on the case, first to the Exchequer Chamber and then to the Lords. Once again, the crown attempted to put obstacles in the path of the claim,[149] but in February 1847, the case was argued again in the Exchequer Chamber. The younger Clement was soon to find the courts no more receptive to his arguments than to those of his father. Delivering the judgment of the court for the crown, Parke B focused exclusively on the statute. He held that the court did not have to decide on the question of the crown's obligations as a potential trustee of money paid by the French, for parliament had the right to dispose of the entire fund as it sought fit, and had in fact done so by the statutory arrangement put in place in 1819. His reading of the statute was that it did give the commissioners some discretion to hear claims registered late (which would have given them the jurisdiction to hear the Baron's claim); but even if they had not, parliament had given the Treasury absolute discretion to deal with the surplus.[150]

The new Baron appealed to the House of Lords in 1851. In this forum, the crown sought to reopen a number of old issues, which it had not focused on hitherto in this phase of the proceedings, including the question of his nationality. However, the only question which was referred to seven judges to advise on was the remedial one of whether a claimant for funds under the convention had any other remedy than that set out by the 1819 statute. The judges' answer was in essence the same as that given by the Exchequer Chamber[151]: the statute disposed of the whole fund, and the matter of the crown's liability simply did not arise. The Baron's claim had in effect been trumped by parliamentary sovereignty. Yet it was notable that, in argument, the Lord Chancellor, Lord Truro, formerly Thomas

[146] On three days before his death, he gave details of recent proceedings in a letter to *The Times*, 29 September 1846, col. 3e.

[147] *The Times*, 6 October 1846, col. 8d. [148] *Ipswich Journal*, 10 October 1846.

[149] *Baron de Bode* v. *The Queen* (1848) 13 QB 364.

[150] *Baron de Bode* v. *The Queen* (1848) 13 QB 364, at 381ff.

[151] Pollock CB's wording at *Baron de Bode* v. *The Queen* (1851) 3 HLC 449, at 468–469 is identical to Parke B's in *Baron de Bode* v. *The Queen* (1848) 13 QB 364, at 384–385.

Wilde, who had first raised Clement's case in the Commons in 1832, and who only handed it over to Hill in 1834 because he was so busy with the mammoth case of *Atwood* v. *Small*, observed that it was 'admitted law, that if the subject of a country is spoliated by a foreign Government, he is entitled to obtain redress from the foreign Government through the means of his own Government. But if, from weakness, timidity, or any other cause on the part of his won Government, no redress is obtained from the foreigner, then he has a claim against his own country'.[152] It remained evident to many that the Baron had a substantial claim in justice, which was being hampered by technicalities in domestic law.

3. *Return to parliament*

The fact that the family retained significant public support became manifest in the following year when Lord Lyndhurst secured the appointment of a select committee in the House of Lords to investigate the claims. Lyndhurst had been present in the Lords when the decision was made against the Baron, and while he agreed with the view of the law taken there, he felt the injustice of the case to be so strong that he undertook to bring the case before the chamber.[153] In the course of a speech relating the prior history of the claim, the ex-Chancellor indicated his incredulity at the crown's argument that any money remaining was in the hands of the Lords Commissioners of the Treasury and not the crown; he added that even if the money had been spent for public purposes, the public had reaped the benefit of it and should restore it. He wanted a committee to be set up to confirm the facts he had related with a view to asking the government for redress. The select committee – whose members included Lord Brougham (who had represented the Baron in his first case before the Privy Council) and Lord Truro – in effect provided another opportunity for the Baron to state his claim in detail, reprinting a great deal of the evidence which had been amassed over the years, and which had been rehearsed before two juries. Once again, his opponents did not participate. Unsurprisingly, the committee's report was a ringing endorsement of the claim: the cession, it reported, was *bona fide* and in every respect legal and valid. His property was unduly confiscated; he had presented his claim in time, and even after the other registered claims had been paid, a surplus sufficient to pay him had remained. The commissioners had

[152] *Baron de Bode* v. *The Queen* (1851) 3 HLC 449, at 465.
[153] *Parl. Debs.*, 3rd ser. 122: 478 (11 June 1852).

erred in requiring him to show that his property had been confiscated under the laws sequestrating British property, and in closing the inquiry before the Baron could bring all his proofs. The committee reported that this was a case of great hardship and injustice.

The Lords' report attracted much public attention, for it seemed to settle that the Baron had a legitimate claim and that parliament had a duty to respond.[154] In August 1853, Lyndhurst raised the case again in the Lords, after having unsuccessfully raised the case with the prime minister. However, the government continued to resist, Lord Cranworth setting out the objections to the claim, including that 'to all intents and purposes [the Baron] was practically a foreigner' and that the cession (notwithstanding the jury's finding) was 'invalid and fraudulent'.[155] In any event, even admitting that tribunals might err, he did not think disappointed claimants could ask parliament decades later to vote money to make good the error – particularly in a case where the sum to be voted would amount to £1.5 million. The Lords' debate of 1853 in effect revisited the parliamentary squabbles of 1835, as Lords Monteagle and Cranworth (formerly Spring Rice and Rolfe) were pitted against Truro (formerly Wilde) who now berated the Lord Chancellor for the unfounded allegations he had made nearly twenty years previously in the Commons, which prevented the reappointment of Hill's select committee.[156] Once again, the motion was lost, but the Baron's supporters had once more appealed to the court of public opinion. As *The Standard* reported, 'The case is a foul opprobrium upon the British character – a flagrant violation of the promise of Magna Charter'.[157]

Ten months later it was the turn of the Commons to reject another motion, brought this time by Montagu Chambers, who regarded the question as one of 'national honours'.[158] Once again, the government resisted, with the Attorney-General (Cockburn) setting out the oldest of grounds: that Clement had not been British within the terms of the 1786 treaty, nor had his property been confiscated as the property of an

[154] *The Times*, 7 August 1852, col. 4c. The newspaper pointed out that 'as if to crown the poor Baron's misfortunes, the Parliament in which his claims were at last recognised has become extinct before redress could be made'.

[155] *Parl. Debs.*, 3rd ser., 129: 1063 (1 August 1853). At 1072, he said, 'he doubted very much the competency of any jury, in 1844, to decide whether a transaction which had a great appearance of fraud in 1791 was fraudulent or not'.

[156] *Parl. Debs.*, 3rd ser., 129: 1075 (1 August 1853). Rolfe (as Cranworth then was) had been responding to Wilde (as Truro then was).

[157] *The Standard*, 2 August 1853.

[158] *Parl. Debs.*, 3rd ser., 134: 400 (20 June 1854).

Englishman, but because he had violated the laws of France.[159] Once again, the motion was lost. However, when George Denman brought the matter back to parliament in 1861, asking for an inquiry (rather than a vote of money), the Baron's supporters won the vote. A select committee was appointed, hearing legal argument in July 1861. By now, the government was well prepared to argue the case, having amassed a great deal of evidence with respect to the Baron's French claims, and also much detail on the cases which had gone to the Privy Council. Vernon Harcourt, for the crown, put together an argument which challenged the conclusions come to by the Lords committee. The question of Clement's nationality came to the fore once again: for the purposes of international law – which was what they were dealing with here – the Baron was (Harcourt argued) to be regarded as the same nationality as his father. The English rule – 'a remnant of feudal barbarism' – was irrelevant in that context.[160] He also argued that the commissioners had followed the policy of awarding compensation only to those whose land had been seized because they were English, an assertion which required him to argue that some of the reports of cases in the Privy Council had misrepresented what had been decided. Harcourt also argued that the very notion of a cession had been concocted by the Baron around 1821; and that the French courts had never recognised his right to the unsold properties of his father.[161] By the early 1860s, the government was clearly keen to set the heavy guns out to destroy the Baron's arguments. Indeed, in 1862, the Treasury commissioned an opinion from two Parisian advocates on the French law relating to the claims, which claimed not only that the cession had not complied with the necessary formalities, but that the very grant by the Archbishop had been void in the first place.[162] But if the government was now seeking to put together a case on the law of France, and the feudal rules pertaining in Alsace, to challenge the version presented by Clement for the first time, they were never called on to make the argument. Like its predecessor of 1834, the work of this select committee was interrupted by

[159] These grounds were supported by Sir Frederick Thesiger, who had argued the case for the crown in the trial at the bar of the Queen's Bench: *Parl. Debs.*, 3rd ser., 134: 408 (20 June 1854). Thesiger stressed the precedent of *Drummond's Case* as barring Clement's claim.

[160] PP 1861 (502) XI 513, at p. 73. [161] PP 1861 (502) XI 513, at p. 80.

[162] *La Trésorerie Anglaise contre M. Le Baron de Bode* (Paris, 1862), pp. 10–18 (in TNA TS 11/535). The argument was that later treaties had vested the feudal rights of the Archbishop in the French crown. Indeed, the French lawyers wrote that 'cet acte de 1788 constituait encore *l'entreprise la plus audacieuse* de la part d'un prélat étranger, contre l'autorité et la souveraineté du roi de France' (29).

the end of the parliamentary session; and when George Denman was asked in 1862 whether he would move for a reappointment of the committee, he declined to proceed, since the younger Clement had been away in Russia for some time and had not yet signalled his desire for the inquiry to continue.[163] In effect, he had given up the fight. Despite the strong and continued public support for his case, and the endless arguments which had been deployed to establish validity of his claim, the younger Clement realised that he would never persuade the government to reopen a case involving so much money, the result of which would surely lead to a flood of other claims being revived. Politics triumphed. The Baron's family would never get their inheritance.[164]

The demise of the Baron's claim did not immediately end interest in the fate of the commission's funds. The younger Clement's researches in Paris in 1861 had caught the attention of local politicians, who began to ask about what had happened to the money paid over in 1815 and 1818. In 1868, the French press again raised questions about this money, claiming that any surplus should be repaid to France. Now that the Baron's claim had died, they wondered whether this money should now be returned.[165] Within three years, the question of these funds was raised again in England by the Irish colleges, who called for a select committee to look at their claims, on the precedent set by the Baron's case. The government was forced to publish returns to show there was almost no money left,[166] but still had to resist continued pressure from the Irish interest into the mid-1870s to appoint a select committee.[167]

IV. Conclusion

For nearly half a century, the Baron de Bode and his son strove to force the British authorities, who had received a capital sum of £5.6m[168] to settle French claims, to pay compensation for the losses his family suffered by the confiscation of their properties. There was no doubt that the family had

[163] *Parl. Debs.*, 3rd ser. 166: 1127 (2 May 1862).

[164] Some other members of the family did continued to ply a living on the prospect of the fortune coming their way: Clement's illegitimate half-brother, Augustus Wilkins, continued to give creditors post-obit bonds, secured on the £15,000 he expected to receive under his father's will. See *Willis* v. *Clegg*, *The Times*, 8 June 1875 col. 11a, and the case of James Schneider in *Reynolds Newspaper*, 9 March 1884.

[165] *Glasgow Herald*, 25 July 1868.

[166] PP 1871 [C. 376] LXXI. 483.

[167] See PP 1872 (239) XLVI.713, *Parl. Debs.* 3rd ser, 223: 1916 (30 April 1875).

[168] Or £422,248,818 in 2012 values.

lost its assets, and that the French government had refused to consider his claims relating to the properties which had been sold off, on the grounds that the British should pay. The Baron was wrong to claim that his specific claim had been provided for in calculating that sum,[169] but he was correct to claim that his case was well known to those negotiating the sums to be paid over in 1818. Nor was he wrong to assert that numerous other Britons, whose property had been confiscated as émigré property, had been given compensation. Certainly, over four decades, the family obtained the support of a large number of eminent lawyers, as well as politicians and aristocrats, who felt that he had a just claim on this fund. Moreover, two English juries had agreed.

The Baron sought to assert his claim by invoking the authority of law, yet he found that the law which he hoped would secure his fortune was far more indeterminate than he hoped. The law relating to his nationality, which seemed so unambiguous in *Calvin's Case*, appeared far more unsettled when debated by government lawyers. The rules of feudal and Alsatian law on which his property rights were based were also hotly contested, as was the question whether English tribunals, settling claims arising from an international treaty, should determine his rights according to France's international law obligations, or her domestic law. Finally, when it came to holding the government to account, the Baron found that the rule of law did not reach the highest authority in the state at all. Even the issue of which questions had to be answered to settle his claim was not a stable or settled one, but shifted over time and according to venue.

The one constant feature in the Baron's long dispute was his persistent failure, and the dogged determination of various governments that he should not receive the enormous sum he was claiming. Far less constancy is to be found in the law which was argued or held to apply. In the first stage of his claim before the commissioners the crucial decision was one of fact regarding the ownership of the estates, which was determined by a body of lay commissioners, an administrative body which did not hear legal argument. It was only later, at the second 'political' stage, that more sophisticated legal arguments were made about his nationality, the nature of his rights to the property and the powers of the French state over the estates in question. The most intricate legal questions pertaining to the nature of his claim were set out before a political body, the select

[169] The sum was described by Castlereagh as a 'compromise' between the parties regarding French liabilities, which 'might not go to the full extent of the claims': *Parl. Debs.*, 1st ser. 39: 531 (19 February 1819).

committee of 1834, where the goal was to procure parliament to vote a sum to compensate the Baron. After all the legal arguments, it was politics which defeated the Baron in this venue. The third stage in his battle was that before the courts, where Clement appeared to have established his legal claim to the conviction of two juries. Yet his vision was not challenged in court by the crown, even though behind the scenes crown lawyers were gathering as much evidence as they could to challenge his version. Instead, the crown allowed the Baron to establish his right, and rather challenged whether he had a remedy. Their simple argument was that all the money had been appropriated by parliament under a statute, and that none of it came into the hands of the crown. Parliamentary sovereignty triumphed, for it gave the Treasury – not the Queen – compete discretion over the funds. But such a judgment could hardly persuade public opinion that all was well. If parliament had appropriated money which should in justice have been destined to the Baron, why could it not – as it had in the Spanish claims – simply vote him compensation? From the government's point of view, the obvious answer lay in the size of the claim (and the other claims, such as the Catholic ones, which might follow). However, from a constitutional point of view, the notion that the crown might be regarded as a trustee of sums received from former enemies to pay to her subjects, but whose trust had been displaced by act of parliament, was not a very comfortable one. By 1876, crown lawyers had developed a more secure argument as to why people in the Baron's position could not use a petition of right to recover foreign compensation: such exchanges between sovereigns were to be seen as acts of state, simply beyond the power of any court.[170]

[170] *Rustomjee* v. *R.* (1876) 2 QBD 69.

11

The authority of law in a bureaucratic framework

The nineteenth-century medicine stamp duty

CHANTAL STEBBINGS

I. Introduction

Bureaucratic law-making, namely the interpretation of legislation and the making of rules by members of the executive which in practice if not in theory bind the actions of the public, has always characterised tax in the modern era. It reached its zenith in the taxation system of nineteenth-century Britain, when the rapidly increasing sophistication of tax law, the growth of the civil service and the relative inexperience of the taxpaying public combined to create a new dynamic of conflicting fiscal, constitutional and practical imperatives. Bureaucratic law-making was found in varying degrees in all the principal taxes of the nineteenth century – customs and excise duties, the land tax, income tax and the assessed taxes. In no tax was it more prevalent, or its extremes more starkly revealed, than in the medicine stamp duty. This tax, which, in its existence of nearly 160 years from 1783 to 1941, spanned the formative period of modern British taxation, was unique in that it united all those characteristics which gave rise to a fertile breeding ground for bureaucratic law-making. The object of this paper is to investigate the process of such law-making by civil servants in the context of this tax, to identify the reasons for its proliferation, and to examine the problems of authority which emerged from it. It assesses how far pragmatic necessities led to a practice of taxation by administrative act that was constitutionally unsound, threatened the integrity of the authority of the law, and which resulted in a body of law directly applicable to chemists and druggists and yet vague and essentially inaccessible to them. It reveals how this practice reflected tax law and administration as a closed and inward-looking

This work was supported by the Wellcome Trust [WT095723MA].

institution, concerned with its own operation, setting its own criteria for success within an operational culture which excluded both the taxpayer and the orthodox conception of the authority of the law.

II. The statutory framework

The Bill of Rights 1689 stated in unequivocal terms that no one could be taxed without his or her consent. That consent was parliamentary in nature, meaning that all taxes had to adopt the statutory form, ensuring that no one could be taxed other than by express words in a statute. A tax could, therefore, be imposed only by legislation. That meant that tax was law, and that brought with it all the norms and conventions of the English legal system. The authority of Parliament was paramount. The officers of the executive who administered the tax were bound to adhere to the words of the statute, to tax where the statute instructed and not to relieve from tax where the statute did not allow it. Tax law permitted no discretion. Furthermore, only the judges of the regular courts could legitimately and authoritatively interpret the statutory language and assign it a meaning – that meaning reflecting the intention of Parliament. Once a judicial decision had been pronounced on the meaning of a tax provision, that was its definitive meaning and was to be applied by the tax authorities and relied upon by the taxpaying public. There was no reason or principle in English law which suggested that tax law was in any way different from any other branch of law. Indeed, such was the importance of the control of tax-raising powers in the struggle for democratic rights, it was all the more crucial to ensure that the authority of Parliament and of the judiciary was maintained as paramount and inviolable.

The primary objective of all eighteenth- and nineteenth-century taxation was to raise public revenue, and it was the thriving trade in shop-bought 'quack' medicines that caught the attention of the Treasury as an activity ripe for an impost. This trade, which was physically dangerous in that many such medicines contained poisonous or addictive substances, and morally dangerous in that it exploited the fears of the ill and desperate, was nevertheless flourishing in the late eighteenth century and throughout the nineteenth century.[1] The tax was first introduced in 1783[2] when

1 See generally Roy Porter, *Health for Sale, Quackery in England 1650–1850* (Manchester, 1989).

2 23 Geo. III c. 62 (1783). The tax was revised by William Pitt to adopt its modern form in 25 Geo. III c. 79 (1785).

the need for public revenue in the wake of a century of expensive warfare was acute, and formed part of a raft of new taxes all directed to this end.

Like every tax, the medicine stamp duty necessarily adopted statutory form. The Act of Parliament in force for most of the nineteenth century and until the abolition of the tax in 1941 was the Medicine Stamp Act 1812.[3] As it was inherent in the constitutional principle of consent to taxation that an individual could be taxed only by express and absolutely clear words, never by implication, and that in an ambiguous or uncertain Act the taxpayer would be given the benefit of the doubt, the draftsmen had to be precise and explicit. This made all tax Acts exceptionally long, detailed, complex and frequently lacking in any coherence. What was immediately clear in the case of the medicine stamp duty was that the legislators faced exceptional problems of statutory definition. The intention of Parliament was undoubtedly to tax quack medicines, but although the term 'quack' was familiar and one that most people thought they understood, it was a slang term that was too loose for use in something as formal as an Act of Parliament. As a result of this intractability legislators and draftsmen had to turn to description rather than definition. The characteristics of quack medicines were easily identified. These were medicines invented and aggressively promoted for sale to the general public by unqualified entrepreneurs, who kept their compositions secret, claimed ownership of them and made wildly exaggerated claims as to their powers to cure or relieve.

These features of quack medicines were accordingly cast in statutory language and incorporated into a general charging clause which essentially taxed every preparation used internally or externally as a medicine to prevent, cure or relieve any human ailment, if it was patented, secret, proprietary or recommended to the public as an effective remedy. Furthermore, the Act contained a schedule of some 550 of the most common quack medicines at the time, each one being specifically brought into charge. The Act also allowed three exemptions aimed primarily at protecting regular medical practitioners and medicines, namely for some imported medicines already paying customs duties, for pure drugs sold by qualified chemists or licensed individuals, and for mixed drugs which were 'known, admitted and approved remedies' and sold by medically qualified individuals.

These legislative provisions were inherently unsatisfactory from their inception. The difficulty stemmed from the challenges of definition, but

[3] 52 Geo. III c. 150 (1812).

also from the need to bring all quack medicines within the charge while ensuring that regular medicines and practitioners were not inadvertently caught. The legislation was consequently excessively complicated in its structure, with its list of expressly charged medicines, a comprehensive general charge on all medicines, a refinement of the meaning of medicines in order to impose the general charge on quack medicines only, and the exemptions to mitigate the impact of the tax in the interests of regular medicines. Furthermore, the express repetition of some clauses in order to emphasise the exclusion of some regular medicines added another element of impenetrability. The drafting was not helped by the practice inherent in all Stamp Acts of using standard form, catch-all clauses and applying them to a range of different articles from newspapers to gloves to medicines. Moreover, and crucially, key terms such as 'medicine', 'preparation', 'recommended', 'ailment' and 'known, admitted and approved remedies' were left undefined in the Act itself.

As the years passed with minimal legislative revision,[4] the problems of complexity, uncertainty and ambiguity became more acute as the statutory regime became out of date and antiquated. In terms of medicines brought into charge in the first half of the nineteenth century, most were those expressly named in the schedule, but as those medicines fell into disuse and new ones were introduced with no revision of the schedule, the general charging provision came into prominence. Similarly, the exemptions were unsatisfactory. That for imported medicines already paying customs duties and named in the Book of Rates quickly became obsolete and was described as 'absolutely useless', while that for pure drugs was very wide.[5] Almost from its inception, therefore, and increasingly so throughout its life, the legislation imposing and regulating the medicine stamp duty was chaotic, impossibly wide,[6] repetitive, overlapping, vague, uncertain and persistently out of date. While much of nineteenth-century tax law came within this description to some degree, the medicine stamp duty fell squarely within it and as such constituted the most extreme example of an unsound statutory framework in British tax.

[4] The only legislative revisions occurred in 1815 and 1833 with respect to confectionary and artificial mineral waters respectively: 55 Geo. III c. 184, s. 54; 3 & 4 Will. IV c. 97, s. 20.

[5] Minutes of Evidence before the Select Committee on Patent Medicines, *House of Commons Parliamentary Papers* [hereafter *HCPP*] (1914) (414) ix 1, q. 193 *per* Sir Nathaniel Highmore, solicitor to Customs and Excise [hereafter S.C. Patent Medicines 1914].

[6] *Parliamentary Debates*, vol. 25, ser. 2, col. 89, 8 June 1830 (HC).

III. Administrative action

The overall responsibility for the administration of the medicine stamp duty lay in the hands of the revenue board having charge of the tax. Until 1834 that was in the Board of Stamps, and in that year it was merged with the Board of Taxes. This process of consolidation continued, and in 1849 the Board of Stamps and Taxes merged with the Board of Excise to form the Board of Inland Revenue which managed the duty until 1909 when it followed the Excise in its merger with the Board of Customs. The patent appointing the Stamp Commissioners for England in 1819 placed all the stamp duties under their 'care and management'.[7] They were empowered to do everything necessary to execute the stamp duty legislation and administer the tax. All formal decisions were made by the six or so commissioners who made up the revenue board, and were salaried civil servants[8] drawn from public life. As such they had no specific tax or legal expertise other than that acquired through their experience as members of the board or, rarely, because they had been appointed from the ranks of revenue officials. However, to assist them in their implementation of the tax, they had legal and scientific expertise of quality to call upon. Legal expertise was provided by the solicitor to the board. He was formally the board's legal adviser, but the evidence reveals that he had considerable influence. When any question of law arose, his view was almost invariably adopted.[9] It is clear that most of the board's interpretation of key terms and the development of concessions came from the solicitor.[10] And where scientific advice was called for, the board could call upon the Inland Revenue Laboratory, founded in 1842.[11] Throughout the nineteenth century, and until the abolition of the tax in 1941, samples were sent to the laboratory for analysis to decide, for

[7] Thirteenth Report of the Commissioners of Inquiry into the Collection and Management of the Revenue arising in Ireland, Scotland; etc. Board of Stamps, London, *HCPP* (1826) (435) x 1, p. 17.

[8] *Ibid.*, pp. 17, 19.

[9] Fourteenth Report of the Commissioners of Inquiry into the Collection and Management of the Revenue arising in Ireland, Scotland; etc. Board of Stamps, London, *HCPP* (1826) (436) x 69, p. 756.

[10] For example, the concession for asthma cigarettes, below, was based on advice given to the board in 1876 by Sir William Melvill, Solicitor to the Inland Revenue: S.C. Patent Medicines 1914, q. 40.

[11] For a comprehensive and insightful history of the Laboratory see P.W. Hammond and Harold Egan, *Weighed in the Balance, A History of the Laboratory of the Government Chemist* (London, 1992). See too John St Clair Cholmondeley, *The Government Laboratory* (London, 1902).

example, whether a drug was indeed pure or mixed for the purpose of the exemption, or whether a wine was sufficiently medicated to be taxable as a medicine rather than a beverage.[12]

With the assistance of its solicitor and of the laboratory, the board interpreted the vague and uncertain provisions in the Act and assigned them a meaning. The schedule was the most straightforward part of the legislation in that a medicine expressly included in it was clearly taxable. It was the general charge which was full of words and phrases that needed to be assigned a meaning in order to decide whether a particular medicine was dutiable or not. The board did this on a daily basis, in order to keep up with the thriving trade in quack medicines and the constant invention of new products. The words and phrases the commissioners had to interpret were fundamental to the tax. The charge applied only to 'preparations', and that was taken to mean that some active processing had to have taken place. For this reason, simple unmedicated and unprepared herbs were held not to be within the charge.[13] A medicine was only chargeable if it was used as such. The commissioners had to decide whether certain articles which were recommended for an ailment but were used as a food, or confectionary or a beverage were chargeable or not. There were a number of borderline preparations, notably Guinness, Bovril and Ovaltine, which were all advertised as beneficial to general health and as preventing colds and influenza. The commissioners took the view that these were used as beverages rather than medicines, and so escaped the charge.

Another phrase in the general charge which the commissioners interpreted was that providing that for a preparation to be chargeable it had to be 'used or applied internally or externally'. In the context of asthma cigarettes, preparations which were burnt and the fumes inhaled to treat respiratory diseases, the commissioners decided that that requirement was not satisfied because it was not the preparations themselves that were 'used' but the product of their burning.[14]

The provision charging medicines if they were 'recommended' for the relief of human ailments was one with respect to which the interpretation of the commissioners was of particular importance, if only because most

12 See, for example, The National Archives [hereafter, TNA] DSIR 26/138 (1892).

13 TNA IR 83/61.

14 TNA IR 83/61. This was not extended to products such as smelling salts, which were themselves inhaled as such: Board of Customs and Excise and Predecessor: Private Office Papers, The Medicine Stamp Duties 1783–1936, TNA CUST 118/366, p. 36 [hereafter Private Office Papers].

commercially sold medicines were chargeable within it. It was a long-established commercial practice to sell a medicine with a reference either to the ailment it purported to relieve or prevent, or to the organ of the body it maintained it would benefit. Cough mixtures, fever powders, eye lotions, antibilious pills, liver pills and stomach tinctures were ubiquitous. If such medicines were neither proprietary nor expressly recommended, which was unusual, the revenue authorities tacitly agreed not to charge them on the basis that such names were mere descriptions of the medicines, not recommendations. This was embodied in the Board of Stamps and Taxes' instructions to its officers in 1848.[15] In 1903, in response to a decision of the court, the practice was modified. Since the recommendation had to be for the relief of a human ailment, the revenue authorities took the view that if no ailment was mentioned, then the recommendation was not a dutiable one. It followed that if a medicine was described by its general operation, for example, as 'a good, general tonic', 'beneficial for improving the health generally', 'astringent mixture' or 'aperient pills', it would not be chargeable under this head.[16] As before, the mere mention of the organ of the body did not bring the medicine into charge, but if the medicine's effect on the organ was mentioned, as in 'blood purifier' or 'liver invigorator', it would amount to a recommendation and be taxable.[17]

Once a recommendation was established, it had to be for the relief of an 'ailment' for the charge to attach. In the absence of any guidance in the Act itself, the board decided as a matter of practice that afflictions such as baldness, dandruff, freckles or chapped lips were not 'medical' enough. In the light of this, hairdressers and perfumers were permitted to sell hair lotions and skin creams free of duty, even though they were recommended for the relief of such minor conditions.[18]

The revenue authorities went much further in their practice than merely interpreting vague or uncertain key words and phrases in the statutory charging provisions, and instances abound where they decided where the charge should attach with no statutory foundation whatever.[19] In many instances, such decisions were specific and relatively narrow in their effect. For example, the legislation expressly provided that if at any point since a medicine's invention a proprietary right had been claimed in it–perhaps by selling it with a proprietary name–thereby rendering it

[15] *Ibid.*, pp. 150–156. [16] *Ibid.*, p. 47. [17] TNA IR 78/289.

[18] Private Office Papers, p. 48.

[19] *Parliamentary Debates*, vol. 25, ser. 2, col. 89, 8 June 1830 (HC).

liable to the tax, then that liability endured even after the medicine had become common property and its formula widely known and open to anyone to manufacture.[20] In other words, once taxed, forever taxed. The practice of the board, however, was to ignore this requirement and regard such medicines, even though named, as non-dutiable. In 1936, the Board of Customs and Excise named twenty-one such preparations, including Gregory's Powders and Hamilton's Pills.[21] A further example is found in the board's treatment of lozenges prior to their exclusion from the tax in 1815.[22] These were essentially confectionary in nature, but as they were expressly included in the schedule strictly they were taxable. The practice, however, was to tax named lozenges, such as the famous Ching's Worm Lozenges, as proprietary medicines, but to allow unnamed ones, such as simple Peppermint Lozenges, to escape the charge. The only condition the board added was that such lozenges should be sold in small amounts with no printed recommendation.[23]

In other instances, the board's practice of relieving certain products while taxing others and doing so on its own initiative and entirely outside the statute – a practice that today is recognised as that of extra-statutory concession – was of far wider scope and significance. Three were of particular importance.

The first was the board's practice in relation to the trade custom of breaking up bulk purchases of medicines. Shopkeepers and retail chemists usually purchased their medicines in bulk from a manufacturer or wholesaler. The latter – the original vendor – paid the duty according to the value of the medicine.[24] It was common practice for the retailer subsequently to open the stamped box and sell the individual contents either as two or three pills, or in penny doses of powders in a twist or cone of paper. Despite the legislative provision that duty was to be paid on every inclosure containing a dutiable medicine,[25] the board took the view that no further stamp duty needed to be paid.[26] The board reasoned that the duty had already been paid, and that the mode of retail was not such as to involve any inclosure within the meaning of the Act. But while two or

20 See the general charge in 52 Geo. III c. 150 (1812).

21 Private Office Papers, p. 41. 22 55 Geo. III c. 184, s. 54.

23 William Chamberlaine, *History of the Proceedings of the Committee appointed by the General Meeting of Apothecaries, Chemists, and Druggists, in London, for the Purpose of obtaining Relief form the Hardships imposed on the Dealers in Medicine, by certain Clauses and Provisions contained in the new Medicine Act, passed June 3, 1802 etc* (London, 1804), pp. 31–32.

24 42 Geo. III c. 56, s. 3 (1802). 25 *Ibid.* 26 Private Office Papers, p. 57.

three pills in the hand were clearly not in any kind of inclosure, powders sold in twists of paper clearly were. Nevertheless, the board decided that as long as the paper containers were not sealed in any way, with wax, string or glue, they were not inclosures within the statute and so did not have to pay the tax. This concession resulted in the practice of selling medicines in penny twists very common, notably Beecham's Pills, a popular laxative, and Stedman's Powders, widely used teething powders. It became increasingly attractive after 1915 when the rates of medicine stamp duty doubled. Furthermore, while the paper twists originally had to be completely plain, after 1910, it seems that they were allowed to bear a recommendation or advertisement and as such were almost identical to normal inclosures which bore the medicine stamp.[27]

The second example of the board's practice reaching far beyond the letter of the law is the dispensing concession. The schedule provided that 'all foreign medicines except drugs' were taxable.[28] Not only did the board unilaterally decide in 1885 that it would tax foreign medicines according to the criteria that it applied to British medicines[29] rather than to tax all foreign medicines indiscriminately as the Act directed, but it decided to permit foreign medicines to be free of tax if they were sold by a British wholesaler to a retail chemist for dispensing purposes, namely to make up prescriptions. This had been provoked by a scheme conceived by Irish medicine manufacturers in 1884. Since the legislation did not apply in Ireland, they sold their medicines in Ireland to British chemists free of the stamp duty. When the British chemists used these medicines for the purpose of making up medical prescriptions, the revenue authorities demanded no duty. Although the Act itself made no distinction between the sale of a medicine and its use for dispensing, the board took the view that dispensing was not a 'sale' within the meaning of the Act and accordingly created a concession.[30] The board even chose subsequently to extend this dispensing concession to all British medicines, so that any dutiable medicine could be supplied free of duty to a retail chemist for use as a component in making up a prescription medicine.[31] This extra-statutory concession was unprinted and not to be found in any official instructions. The board allowed it on an individual case-by-case basis.

[27] *Ibid.*, p. 60. [28] 52 Geo. III c. 150 (1812).

[29] Namely, if they were secret, proprietary, patented or recommended: S.C. Patent Medicines 1914, qq. 174–177, 4811.

[30] See E. N. Alpe, *Handy Book of Medicine Stamp Duty* (London, 1888), p. 110.

[31] Private Office Papers, pp. 68–69.

The third example of a board practice which transcended the words of the statute was one of particular significance: it began as an instance of the board disregarding a statutory provision and became one of ignoring a judicial decision. The practice in question was the board's approach to the statutory exemption for 'known, admitted and approved remedies' sold by a qualified surgeon, apothecary, chemist or druggist.[32] Throughout the nineteenth century, the board discounted this exemption, maintaining that because it was implicit in the charging provision, it was merely declaratory in nature and had no separate effect.[33] It did not take out of the charge a medicine that would otherwise be within it. It had been included in order to make it absolutely clear that established remedies which formed the stock of qualified practitioners were not within the very wide general charge to the tax as long as they were not secret, patent, proprietary or recommended to the public.[34]

This understanding of the statutory exemption as a dead letter of no practical importance continued throughout the nineteenth century. In 1903, however, the pharmaceutical profession challenged its validity through a deliberate test case. William Glyn-Jones, the Secretary of the Chemists' Defence Association and himself a qualified chemist and barrister, was prosecuted for selling unstamped a bottle of medicine with a label bearing the words: 'TINCTURE OF QUININE B.P.' A well-known and highly recommended remedy for INFLUENZA AND COLDS. Dose – One teaspoonful in water every four hours until relieved'. There was no doubt that the medicine had been 'recommended' by Glyn-Jones as a remedy for a human ailment, the label saying as much, and this appeared to breach the words of the exemption, which said that a known, admitted and approved medicine sold by a qualified person would escape the charge as long as it was not secret, proprietary, patent or recommended by the 'owners, proprietors, makers, compounders, original or first vendors thereof'.[35] As the other conditions were clearly satisfied, the point at issue was whether Glyn-Jones was the 'original or first vendor'. The court accepted his argument that the 'original or first vendor' was the person who first made up and sold the medicine from his original prescription. Glyn-Jones had purchased the medicine from a manufacturing chemist without any label recommending the medicine. The only

[32] 52 Geo. III c. 150 (1812). [33] S.C. Patent Medicines 1914, q. 19.

[34] Private Office Papers, p. 56; Stephen Dowell, *A History of Taxation and Taxes* (London, 1884), vol. 4, p. 367.

[35] 52 Geo. III c. 150 (1812).

recommendation had been made by Glyn-Jones at the retail stage. It followed that the tincture came within the exemption and was not dutiable.[36]

The decision of the Divisional Court to the effect that the exemption was material was received by the board with dismay, primarily because it reversed the revenue practice of over one hundred years, a practice which was well settled and understood. The board was obliged to implement the exemption, but proceeded to give it the widest possible scope. Under its revised practice, it laid down only two conditions for claiming the exemption: professional pharmaceutical qualification and a disclosure of the ingredients.[37] This, however, ignored two important issues. First, the practice ignored the key point in the decision itself to the effect that the chemist who claimed the exemption had to establish that the original or first vendor had never recommended it. Second, it did not insist on the other conditions in the statutory provision. It allowed the medicine to be recommended; it did not limit the exemption to chemists qualified by apprenticeship and allowed those qualified by examination to claim it; and eventually it even allowed corporate bodies to claim it even though they could clearly not have undergone an apprenticeship. Having therefore disregarded the statutory provision for over a hundred years, the board proceeded to treat this first definitive interpretation of the provision by the regular courts in 1903 with equal indifference. As a result, the method of the exemption's implementation by the revenue authorities bore little relation to the words of the provision in the statute.

The reasons for the board's interpretation of the wording of all the legislative provisions relating to the tax were clear and were founded in necessity. It has been seen that the statutory expression of the medicine stamp duty was flawed in that it was antiquated, obscure, full of lacunae and in many instances impossibly uncertain. Nevertheless, the board was under a statutory duty to implement the tax, and in order to do so it had no choice but to undertake the interpretation of the Act itself.[38] The trade in quack medicines was so large and dynamic that a rapid and operationally definitive interpretation of key terms was essential if the tax were not to collapse completely. With the slowness, unpredictability and paucity of judicial decisions, it inevitably fell on the executive to undertake the construction of the legislation.

[36] *Farmer* v. *Glyn-Jones* [1903] 2 K.B. 6.

[37] TNA IR 83/61; Private Office Papers, pp. 84–86; S.C. Patent Medicines 1914, qq. 19–34.

[38] See Sir Maurice Sheldon Amos, "The Interpretation of Statutes", 5 *Cambridge Law Journal*, p. 163 (1934).

Less evident were the reasons for the board's practice of ignoring some parts of a statutory provision or a judicial decision and thereby granting relief from the tax to certain individuals. Four can be identified: pragmatism, fairness, the convenience of the public and ideology, all of which were underpinned by the essential element of yield. Yield was the motive force of nineteenth-century taxation, and the medicine tax duty was no exception. Although it was not overtly presented as a reason for any kind of administrative action, without the practices of the board the tax would have been inoperative and there would have been a loss to the public revenue.

The first and principal reason for the board's actions was entirely practical, namely to ensure the antiquated tax worked in practice in order to collect the revenue.[39] For example, the provision to the effect that if a preparation had ever been subject to tax as a proprietary article, it would continue to be so was ignored for the simple reason that it was generally impossible for chemists or the board retrospectively to prove the existence or non-existence of a proprietary claim made perhaps many decades before.[40] Similarly, the extraordinary interpretation of the 'known, admitted and approved remedies' exemption was adopted in order to circumvent the administrative difficulties resulting from the court's attempt to revive an out-of-date and hitherto inoperative provision in *Farmer* v. *Glyn-Jones.* The burden of proof imposed by that decision on a chemist claiming the exemption, namely that the original or first vendor had never recommended the medicine, was instantly understood by the board to be unrealistic and unworkable in practice.[41] Again, the 'breaking bulk' concession was introduced on the grounds of administrative convenience in the face of an outdated provision.[42] It was clear that the legislation assumed that packets of medicines would be stamped by the makers or original vendors and sold, thus stamped, to the public, and never contemplated the breaking up of bulk purchases. Similarly, it was pragmatic considerations that led to a strong reluctance to abolish any practice once it was established, for it would disrupt the administrative process of tax. The upsetting of a practice was regarded as sufficient reason to ignore a judicial ruling or statutory provision.[43] For example, the board carefully balanced the advantages and disadvantages of the

[39] S.C. Patent Medicines 1914, qq. 90, 209. [40] Private Office Papers, p. 41.

[41] *Ibid.*, pp. 82, 87. [42] S.C. Patent Medicines 1914, q. 245.

[43] See, for example, the Bradley Haverstoe decision in 1851 where a decision of the Court of Queen's Bench in relation to the land tax was ignored on pragmatic grounds: Letters relative to Judgment of Court of Queen's Bench in Case of *Queen v Commissioners of Land Tax for Bradley Haverstoe, HCPP* (1851) (528) xxxi 329.

'breaking bulk' concession, and though accepting that the revenue advantage was not clear, decided in 1906 not to interfere with the long-established practice.[44]

Second, the revenue authorities acted in the interests of fairness, though not always entirely altruistically. Only if a tax was perceived by the tax-paying public as fundamentally fair would compliance be ensured. For example, the practice not to tax peppermint lozenges even though they were named in the earliest schedules was to mitigate what the board saw as a clear unfairness in the law, and similarly it did not tax some scheduled perfumes because they had already paid customs duty on perfumed spirits[45] nor some beverages containing medicinal drugs, such as dandelion coffee if the excise duty on coffee substitutes was payable.[46] Commercial fairness was equally valued. The reason for the dispensing concession was to put British manufacturers on the same commercial footing as foreign manufacturers. Similarly, the board felt it was unjust to deny the 'known, admitted and approved remedies' exemption to limited companies where a qualified chemist was employed, though the legislation forbade it.[47]

Third, some revenue practices were introduced in order to help the general public. For example, the concession for medicines that were described according to the ailment they purported to relieve was introduced in order to enable the public to distinguish medicines from each other according to their needs.[48]

Fourth, there is some evidence of ideological motivation behind the board's practice. The reason why foreign medicines were treated more favourably than the statute dictated, namely by the practice of taxing them exactly as British medicines were taxed and therefore more leniently than the law required, was in the interests of free trade.[49] Indeed, even this concession was objected to in the late nineteenth century as being contrary to the accepted policies of free trade in that it impeded the importation of foreign medicines. This was one of the reasons underlying the call of the British Medical Association for the repeal of the Medicine Stamp Acts in 1884.[50]

[44] Private Office Papers, p. 61.

[45] Unless held out as a medicine or beneficial for some human ailment: S.C. Patent Medicines 1914, q. 37 *per* Sir Nathaniel Highmore, solicitor of Customs and Excise.

[46] Private Office Papers, p. 37. [47] *Ibid.*, pp. 83, 89.

[48] 7 *Pharmaceutical Journal* 453 (1848); S.C. Patent Medicines 1914, q. 4709.

[49] S.C. Patent Medicines 1914, q. 4797.

[50] "The Stamp Act and Proprietary Medicines", *British Medical Journal* 328 (1884).

IV. The legality of revenue practice

The board conceived and implemented its practices with confidence. As far as the interpretation of the statutory language was concerned, it had been closely involved in drafting the legislation[51] and felt it understood precisely the intention underlying it and, therefore, what the 'correct' interpretation was. Indeed, the decision in *Farmer* v. *Glyn-Jones* provoked the board's wry observation that 'it might appear that an interpretation of a statute sanctioned by a century of practice was that intended by Parliament'.[52] And with regard to the introduction of concessions, the board argued that its actions were legitimately in fulfilment of its overarching statutory duty of the care and management of the tax for which it was given the widest powers under the Inland Revenue's parent Act of 1849.[53] The board was expressly given all necessary powers to execute the taxing Acts, including those powers which had been in the hands of the old boards, and confirmed the validity of all rules, orders and regulations the old boards had made and the new board would make. And the board topped this all by saying that in all its practices it was not imposing tax, but legally relieving individuals of it in cases of hardship or injustice on the margins of the tax code.[54]

Whatever its motivations and justifications, the actions of the board were illegal. Whether it believed it understood Parliament's intention underlying the legislation was irrelevant: constitutionally, the meaning of a statute could be drawn only from the written words and only the judges were permitted to interpret the statutory language upon which the public could legitimately depend and act. It was not a function which the constitution gave to the executive. And yet every time the board interpreted vague or uncertain key words and phrases in the statutory charging provisions – and it had a monopoly on the initial interpretation of the legislation – it was acting exactly as the judges of the regular courts would. Revenue practice involving the wide interpretation of a charging section or the narrow interpretation of an exemption, though potentially imposing a fiscal burden on the taxpayer, was not subject to the scrutiny of Parliament. It thereby constituted taxation by the executive and, as such, was contrary to the fundamental constitutional principles of law and taxation. Similarly, when the board chose not to tax certain

[51] See, for example, Stamp Office: Observations upon the Present Medicine Act and Proposals for an Improvement of that Duty, TNA T1/624/514–19, 21 May 1785.

[52] Private Office Papers, p. 77. [53] 12 & 13 Vict. c. 1, s. 1.

[54] The same justification is used today: www.hmrc.gov.uk/specialist/esc.pdf.

individuals or groups by granting the various concessions, it was taking upon itself the right to decide on the chargeability of an individual which was strictly the right only of Parliament.[55] It is true that in relieving some individuals from tax the board was not imposing a charge on any other taxpayer directly so as to infringe the fundamental constitutional principle of taxation only by parliamentary consent, and the concessions were subject to some, albeit weak, scrutiny by Parliament through the Public Accounts Committee.[56] However, those distinctions were fine ones and the board's concessions were already recognised in the nineteenth century as dangerous and fundamentally illegal.[57]

While it was true that the powers the authorities were given in their parent Act to execute the tax legislation covered virtually any act in the administration of the taxes within their remit, the overarching statutory duty of care and management imposed on them was undefined. That term, well known within the tax authorities, had never been defined in the parent Acts of the various revenue boards, and neither had it been considered by the courts. As its precise meaning was unclear, so the authority it conferred on the board was not legally robust. It could not permit it to disregard statutory provisions and judicial decisions in the interests of practicality, common sense or even perceived fairness. Furthermore, it was arguable that the board was using its express powers illegally. Only the board or the Attorney-General was legally permitted to institute proceedings for the recovery of penalties for selling dutiable medicines unstamped. It was the board's decision whether to prosecute or to come to terms with the offender.[58] If proceedings were begun, the board could also stay those proceedings or even mitigate the penalties as it saw fit. Although the board maintained that these wide powers were 'carefully administered',[59] they were never intended to be used so as to enable the board to grant exemption from taxes at its pleasure. And yet, for example, the board determined the scope of the 'known, admitted and approved remedies'

[55] Bill of Rights 1689 (1 Will. & M. sess. 2 c. 2), s. 4.

[56] "A Hundred Years of Inland Revenue Extra-Statutory Concessions", *Inland Revenue Tax Bulletins Archive/Tax Bulletin* 32 (December 1997).

[57] Second Report and Minutes of Evidence before Committee of Public Accounts, *HCPP* (1897) (196) viii 5, pp. 5–12, qq. 359–463, 878–1006. They would become of particular importance in the twentieth century: see generally Sir Alexander Johnston, *The Inland Revenue* (London, 1965), pp. 67–68; David W. Williams, "Extra-Statutory Concessions", *British Tax Review* (1979), p. 137.

[58] 43 Geo. III c. 73 s. 4 (1803); S.C. Patent Medicines 1914, q. 205.

[59] *Ibid.*, q. 205 *per* Sir Nathaniel Highmore, solicitor to Customs and Excise.

exemption by deciding whether or not to prosecute, thereby granting the exemption to some bodies or individuals, and not to others. In 1935, counsel's opinion was that this wide discretion as to the instigation and management of prosecutions amounted to taxation at the discretion of the board and the assumption of a power to exempt individuals from tax whom Parliament had decreed should be taxed.[60] The board adopted a similar practice of refraining from prosecuting in relation to foreign medicines unstamped by a British manufacturer or wholesaler to a retail chemist for the purposes of dispensing legitimate prescriptions.[61]

The board fully appreciated the illegality of its practices and the undesirability of dealing with flawed legislation through concessions.[62] In some instances, it acknowledged that the strict rules were not always observed, as where in relation to the provision which required that once a medicine had been subject to the tax, it would always be subject to it, it admitted that this was 'one of several instances where the rule is relaxed in practice'.[63] On occasion, it acknowledged that it had strayed even beyond this. For example, the official interpretation of the 'known, admitted and approved remedies' exemption following the Glyn-Jones decision was clearly far wider than either the legislation or the interpretative case law warranted, unambiguously ignoring the words of both. The board allowed the exemption to certain corporate bodies even though the provision did not apply to them, and when it allowed the exemption to medicines recommended as beneficial for a human ailment, it did so directly contrary to the Act. When the board sought counsel's opinion in 1935 about its practice in relation to the exemption, it received an uncompromising reply condemning its actions as illegal and unconstitutional. The board ensured this was not made public. Indeed, its internal papers show that it privately admitted that it 'might be represented as a glaring instance of legislation by Executive action and an unauthorised assumption, or usurpation, of the functions of Parliament'.[64] Successive solicitors to the board knew it could not stand in a court of law.[65] Similarly, the board admitted, again only internally, that the 'breaking bulk' concession was a 'legal and administrative' interpretation,[66] namely one only partly based on the statutory provision and significantly affected by pragmatic considerations of revenue yield and collection. Here too the board's solicitor in 1904 understood that the concession contravened the statute, as did the

[60] Private Office Papers, p. 181. [61] *Ibid.*, pp. 67–68; S.C. Patent Medicines 1914, q. 4715.
[62] S.C. Patent Medicines 1914, q. 252. [63] Private Office Papers, p. 41.
[64] *Ibid.*, p. 86. [65] TNA T 172/1844. [66] Private Office Papers, p. 60.

professional bodies who pressed for its abolition on those grounds.[67] One of the rare public admissions of the illegality of its practice by the board was in relation to its concession for asthma cigarettes which its solicitor acknowledged in 1914 was 'not quite legal'.[68]

Just as the board itself was conscious of the doubtful legitimacy of its actions, so were the chemists and other medicine vendors. They perfectly understood that the board interpreted the legislation itself and introduced concessions as it thought fit. And as far as they were concerned, the revenue authorities were making law. In the early nineteenth century, *The Lancet* condemned this practice by the board as the 'whims and caprices of the senseless and heartless creatures, who may be appointed to carry its provisions, or rather its *no*-provisions, into effect'.[69] By the mid-nineteenth century, however, professional and commercial objections were fewer for a number of reasons, including the acceptance that such interpretation was necessary in view of the nature of the legislation and a wider understanding of the practice as it became established and as the burgeoning professional press explained it to its readers.[70] And by the middle of the twentieth century, when the obsolescence of the legislation was universally recognised[71] and the need for a code of practice fully appreciated, while the illegality of bureaucratic law-making was understood,[72] the board was regularly praised for its 'extreme fairness and courtesy' in dealing with borderline cases and its adherence to 'the dictates of common sense'.[73]

V. The consequences of bureaucratic law-making

The administrative actions of the revenue departments of the executive in interpreting the obscure medicine stamp duty legislation and the few judicial decisions for use in the daily context of implementing the tax amounted, for practical purposes, to law-making. As the central board

[67] *Ibid.*, p. 61. However, counsel's opinion in 1926 on the legality of the concession was inconclusive: *ibid.*, pp. 61–62.

[68] S.C. Patent Medicines 1914, q. 38 *per* Sir Nathaniel Highmore.

[69] 13 *The Lancet*, 377–81, at 379–80 (12 December 1829).

[70] See, for example, the explanation of the board's understanding of 'recommendations', in 7 *Pharmaceutical Journal* 453 (1st series) (1848).

[71] Including by the board itself: S.C. Patent Medicines 1914, q. 90.

[72] 68 *Pharmaceutical Journal* 247 (1902).

[73] Minutes of Evidence before the Select Committee on Medicine Stamp Duties, *HCPP* (936–37) (54) viii 129, p. 220.

in London arrived at its decisions on every new situation or commercial development, prompted by inquiries from the trade and their own officers, so it disseminated them throughout the national network of its officers through its published regulations, instructions and circulars.[74] The board insisted on uniform and complete adherence by its staff to these numerous official communications. On a point of law, the board's opinion – whether in a formal circular or expressed in individual correspondence – was conclusive for its officers. This created a robust policy of statutory implementation that left no room for any local or individual divergence.

The rulings of the board were thus binding in every practical way until taxpayers challenged them. They could and did do so unofficially by writing to or waiting upon the members of the board, and there is abundant evidence of this kind of informal appeal.[75] Despite the considerable discretion the board possessed, applicants found little flexibility there where the dominant concerns were for a uniform and unambiguous implementation of the law. Neither was there much realistic scope for official challenge. While appeals were permitted from the magistrates' decisions to the High Court on a point of law by way of case stated under the Summary Jurisdiction Acts 1857 and 1879,[76] most individuals drawn into the criminal process through a breach of the legislation were concerned above all with negotiating the reduction of any penalty imposed upon them. This they did informally and directly with the board, which had the power to mitigate or even waive the penalties imposed by the magistrates on a successful conviction for breach of the medicine stamp duty legislation. Even if their circumstances allowed it, and despite the active encouragement of the board to appeal whenever a taxpayer disagreed with its interpretation,[77] nearly all taxpayers decided not to pursue a formal challenge. To do so in the superior courts was inconvenient, expensive and stressful for individual taxpayers. Furthermore, they were well aware of the determination and resources of the board to pursue appeals to the highest court, and indeed it was generally the board which would appeal in this way, as, for example, in *Farmer* v. *Glyn-Jones*.

[74] See, for example, Precedents and Instructions, TNA IR 78/289 (1903); TNA IR 78/60.

[75] See, for example, Board of Inland Revenue decisions on medicine stamp duty, TNA DSIR 26/138 (1892).

[76] 20 & 21 Vict. c. 43; 42 & 43 Vict. c. 49.

[77] See, for example, letter published in 18 *Pharmaceutical Journal* 760 (3rd series) 1888.

As a result, the administrative decisions as to the meaning of the legislation and the granting of concessions were not short-lived rulings amended on a case-by-case basis as the merits of each instance required. Rather, no matter how mistaken, illegal or unfair they might be, they remained in place as definitive interpretations until overturned by the courts. In the first half of the nineteenth century, the medicine stamp duty was almost invariably charged on the medicines expressly mentioned in the schedule, and indeed the evidence suggests that at first tax officials rarely looked beyond it.[78] And although there were some problems of drafting in the schedule, it was by its very nature generally relatively straightforward and unambiguous. This, and the practical limitations on the right of appeal, resulted in no interpretative case law emerging from the courts of law. As the century progressed, however, the medicines listed in the schedule were discontinued or less popular, and as the schedule remained unamended, so medicines increasingly fell to be taxed under the general charge.[79] The general charge being so loosely worded, recourse to the courts was inevitable and necessary to determine its precise scope. The first judicial decision was in 1878,[80] but they were few in number – by 1910 there were only six.

This extensive bureaucratic law-making had a number of disturbing consequences. Since the eighteenth century, taxpayers had been unable to understand the statutory law with its multiple enactments, obscure language, overlapping and superfluous provisions, express contradictions and incompatible clauses. The observation in *The Lancet* of 1829 that the legislation was 'loose and vilely written', 'defective' and a 'piece of tom-foolery'[81] remained true for the entire life of the tax. Nearly one hundred years later, a judge described it as a 'mass of confused and obsolete verbiage'.[82] The considerable body of largely unpublished revenue practice regulating the implementation of the medicine stamp duty increased the inaccessibility of the law relating to the tax considerably. While in general terms, the trade came more or less to understand it, its underlying principles and precise application were sufficiently obscure to prevent

78 Fourteenth Report of the Commissioners of Inquiry into the Collection and Management of the Revenue arising in Ireland, Scotland, etc. Board of Stamps, London, *HCPP* (1826) (436) x 69, p. 561, Appendix 138, *per* Louis Legoux, Registrar and Distributor of Medicine Licences and Labels.

79 S.C. Patent Medicines 1914, q. 9; Private Office Papers, pp. 30, 34.

80 *AG* v. *Lamplough* (1878) L. R. 3 Ex. D. 214.

81 13 *The Lancet*, pp. 377–381, at pp. 379–380 (12 December 1829).

82 *AG* v. *Lewis and Burrows Ltd.* [1932] K.B.D. 538, at 543 *per* Rowlatt J.

vendors from approaching it with confidence. For example, the bafflingly fine nature of the distinctions the board drew when deciding on the chargeability of medicines described by reference to the ailment or the organ of the body during the nineteenth century gave rise to considerable problems of certainty in the law for vendors of such medicines.[83] In allowing their concessions, the board was being 'lenient' and 'indulgent' in the interpretation of the letter of the law, but it was alive to any taxpayer taking advantage of this and thereby evading the spirit of the legislation. Were this to happen, the board would 'act as might seem advisable in accordance with the power it possesses'.[84] Chemists and grocers were thus in a constant state of uncertainty. Whether an item was dutiable or not was not a question of whether it was legally dutiable, but whether the members of the board regarded it as such. Vendors never knew whether the medicines they were selling had to be stamped or not, or how far they could rely on the board's practice, and the consequences for them if they sold dutiable medicines unstamped were severe: a criminal prosecution in the form of an information brought usually by a tax official and heard by a magistrate, followed by financial penalties if found guilty.[85]

Principally, bureaucratic law-making had a profound effect on the tax itself. The breadth and pervasiveness of the revenue practice evolved to implement it was such that it brought about the very demise of the tax. Ultimately, it made it untenable. The catalyst was the judicial ruling in *Farmer* v. *Glyn-Jones* in 1903. The practical administrative difficulties resulting from the decision led to the board drawing the concession for 'known, admitted and approved remedies' so widely that its use was virtually unrestricted. The intention of the eighteenth-century legislature had been to exempt individual qualified retail chemists from the burden of the tax in selling common remedies without any quackery. By the early years of the twentieth century, any retail chemist could claim it as long as he disclosed the formula of his particular medicine, something he could do with ease, and the concession was also being exploited by the large manufacturing chemists for popular products such as Beecham's Powders, Listerine, Veno's cough mixture, Vick Vapor-Rub and Aspro.[86] The outcome was that the tax yield began to fall and had halved by the

83 Private Office Papers, pp. 50–51; S.C. Patent Medicines 1914, qq. 4709–4714.

84 7 *Pharmaceutical Journal* 453 (1st series) (1848).

85 £10 per article sold unstamped: 52 Geo. III c. 150, s. 2 (1812).

86 See generally Private Office Papers, pp. 103–116.

mid-1930s. The decisive development was the challenge of the board's interpretation of the exemption in 1935 by Woolworths, who wanted to sell proprietary medicines but, not being a chemist, could not compete with the duty-free status of Boots and Timothy Whites.[87] The Law Officers knew that the board's practice would not stand up in a court of law.[88] It was as a result of the impossibility of the government's situation that a select committee was appointed in 1936 to see how the tax could be put on 'a modern and defensible basis'[89] and which resulted, five years later, in its abolition.

VI. Conclusion

The board thus paid the price for undermining the authority of Parliament and the function of the judiciary. The consequences were fatal in the specific case of the medicine stamp duty because there the exceptionally flawed legal framework and the remarkable dynamism of the trade in medicines resulted in the tax being almost entirely dominated by highly internalised bureaucratic law-making. Within this intersection of formal law, a framework of bureaucratic application and the demands of the taxpayers' field of activity emerges the driving force of a fiscal imperative: the overriding need to ensure the inadequately drafted and antiquated law could be implemented so as to bring in the public revenue.[90] The board adopted a pragmatic perspective and balanced a variety of factors in developing its practice, including illegality and compliance. The need to raise the public revenue was allowed to dominate even the illegality of the board's behaviour. It has been seen that this illegality went further than the 'administrative elasticity'[91] that the revenue departments were well known to enjoy, but the case of the medicine stamp duty reveals not only that there was a limit to bureaucratic law-making in tax, but also where this limit lay.

It might be thought that in view of the illegality of bureaucratic law-making, any limit to it would emerge from self-regulation by the board itself, by the Law Officers of the Crown, by Parliament or indeed by the

[87] *Ibid.*, pp. 117–122. [88] TNA T 172/1844.

[89] *Ibid.* At this point, the Woolworths proceedings were withdrawn.

[90] Thirty-sixth Report of the Commissioners of Customs and Excise, *HCPP* (1945–46) (6703) xi 1, p. 20.

[91] Private Office Papers, p. 121.

Treasury. It has been seen that the board was precisely aware of the extent of the illegality of its own practice and on a number of occasions sought counsel's opinion to determine it, but felt that it acted out of necessity and a legal obligation to fulfil its own statutory duty to implement the tax. The Treasury, ultimately responsible for the mechanism of tax administration, exerted a weak and ineffectual control largely due to the semi-autonomous status of the members of the board resulting from their appointment by the Crown.[92] Parliament did control the activities of the revenue boards through the Public Accounts Committee, but could have done far more by overhauling the legislation and insisting on new and better statutory provision. It has been seen that when the tax was abolished in 1941 the language of the legislation was that of 1783, the governing Act was that of 1812 and only two minor statutory amendments for confectionary and artificial mineral waters had ever been made to that Act. Parliament felt overwhelmed by the difficulties in attempting to revise the legislation, and accordingly the statutory law governing the medicine stamp duty was allowed to stagnate. The courts tried to set a limit by providing legitimate clarification of the legislation, and indeed judicial decisions were badly needed. The courts, however, were necessarily reactive and were entirely dependent on the initiative of taxpayers, an initiative that was rarely exercised.

It was therefore no official or legal limit that was put on bureaucratic law-making in the context of the medicine stamp duty. It was a practical one which resulted from the fact that administering a tax through reliance on extensive administrative practice was not sustainable and ultimately failed in its objective of rendering the tax viable. Left to the executive department, and without the controls of considered and up-to-date legislation and the scrutiny of the courts, the law became even more uncertain, more inconsistent and more inaccessible. It was said to bristle with anomalies.[93] In short, it became chaotic with no possibility of coherent development. That in turn led not only to the opportunity for widespread avoidance, but also to the undermining of taxpayer confidence and trust, upon which compliance – and therefore enforcement – depended. It was bureaucratic law-making that ultimately led to the unravelling of the tax and its abolition in 1941. It went too far and eventually turned on itself

[92] Twentieth Report of the Commissioners of Inquiry (Excise Establishment), *HCPP* (1836) (22) xxvi 181, pp. 303–306.

[93] Private Office Papers, p. 122.

so as to diminish the yield to such an extent that it was no longer viable. So the same fiscal imperative that led to illegal bureaucratic law-making in the first place was ultimately the one that drew it to a close.

Despite the eventual failure of bureaucratic law-making in the context of the medicine stamp duty, its intensity, pervasiveness and overt illegality were such that it undoubtedly revealed the authority of the law as fragile, as essentially unable or unwilling to assert itself to prevent its undermining in this way. The response of the legal establishment was virtually non-existent in the face of a potentially serious threat to its authority. It is suggested that the reason for that apparent indifference was a view that the manifest undermining of the authority of law was regarded by the legal establishment as entirely confined to the sphere of taxation, an exceptional occurrence in English law resulting from the unique nature of tax law. As such it was not considered to reflect a wider undermining of the law by the executive, nor any kind of generalised reluctance of the law to engage with it. It did not threaten the integrity of the authority of law as a whole and was, accordingly, acceptable.

Tax law, though indubitably formal law, possessed characteristics that set it apart from other branches of English law, and it is this isolation which lies at the heart of the law's passive response to an activity which would, in any other area of law, have been regarded as a challenge to its authority. In varying degrees, tax law stood outside the norms of the legal system in the key elements of that structure. Not only did it have a rare and very prominent constitutional underpinning, in terms of its statutory expression, tax legislation had its own special parliamentary process characterised by its confinement to the Lower House and, in the nineteenth century, scarcely any informed discussion. In terms of its judge-made law, it had remarkably little. Whereas the definitive interpretation of Parliament's legislation by expert judges rigorously trained in the law and entirely independent of the executive built the substance of most of English law, and did so rationally, pragmatically and robustly, tax law was denied the full benefit of this safeguard. The dominance of the board through its power to mitigate judicial penalties served effectively to bypass the orthodox appeals process. Taxpayers understood that the real power, the immediate and practical authority, lay with the board and not the courts of law, and they acted accordingly. Tax law was equally distinct in terms of its administration, which was intricate, with pressing political and economic demands. With its complexity of expression in the statutory provisions and its highly specialised nature, it inevitably came to be dominated by the civil servants responsible for its implementation. This exceptionally high degree of bureaucratic involvement became its leading characteristic and one which was unique. As a result of the combination of these factors, tax law came to be regarded by both lawyers and the public as distinct from other branches of English law and, accordingly, from legal norms.

12

The authority of treatises in English law (1800–1936)

STEPHEN WADDAMS

I. Introduction

Were legal treatises authorities in nineteenth-century English law? This question is not so easy to answer as might at first be supposed, because of the shifting meanings of the word 'authority'. At least four meanings must be disentangled: an authority might mean a decree commanding obedience, as where a judge might say, 'whatever might be my own opinion, I am bound by authority to decide in favour of the claimant;' judicial decisions sometimes had this effect, and by extension, the word came, second, to mean any prior judicial decision that had not been overruled, whether strictly binding on the later court or not, as where, in overruling a prior case, a court might say that it was 'no longer' to be treated as an authority; third, authority might mean an opinion tending to support an argument, as where a judge might say, 'I asked for some authority – even a passage from a text-book . . . but no such authority has been produced'[1]; fourth, authoritative, in relation to a book, may mean commanding respect because of its inherent merit. Evidently a treatise, written by any author, however eminent, living or dead, can never be authoritative in the strict sense of actually commanding the obedience of a judge: the judge cannot give effect to an opinion in a treatise that the judge, on due consideration, considers erroneous. Thus, Erle CJ said in 1865, 'I am well aware of the authority of *Sugden's Vendors and Purchasers*, but I think his opinion is not supported by the cases'.[2] Where a judge had decided against his own opinion because he thought that he was bound by a passage in a treatise (Lindley on *Partnership*), Vaughan Williams J said, 'To my mind, that view of the county court judge was altogether

[1] North J in *Re Ebsworth and Tidy's Contract* (1889) 42 Ch D 23, 35.
[2] *Edgell* v. *Day* (1865) LR 1 CP 80, 84–85.

wrong in principle. He was bound to exercise his own judgment, and in doing so could only be controlled by decided cases'.[3] But a treatise may be authoritative in either the third or the fourth sense, and, as Erle CJ's statement indicates, may be called an authority even though its conclusions are rejected. It is one thing to say that a treatise is not strictly binding; it is quite another thing to say that reference to a treatise is not admissible in argument. The four senses of the word have often been confused – a confusion that is itself significant in that it has rhetorical overtones, and reflects differing views, on the part of judges and commentators, of the legal process itself.

II. The supposed rule or convention that living authors may not be cited as authority

The confusion of these meanings has the consequence that it is quite difficult to determine whether there was, in the nineteenth century, any rule or convention prohibiting or restricting the citation of treatise writers, and, if so, what precisely it was. Lord Eldon said, in 1814, referring to Serjeant John Williams (1757–1810), that 'though one who had held no judicial situation could not regularly be mentioned as an authority, yet he might say that to any one in a judicial situation it would be sufficiently flattering to have it said of him that he was as good a common lawyer as Mr Serjeant Williams. . . . There was, however, no judicial decision on the point'. The thrust of this passage, as Sir John Baker points out,[4] is to draw a distinction between judicial and non-judicial opinion. No author, living or dead, could be an 'authority' in the same sense in which a judicial opinion might sometimes be an authority, i.e., in the sense of commanding obedience. Lord Eldon is not here saying that Williams' highly regarded annotations should never be referred to, but only that they cannot have the same force as judicial decisions, and, perhaps, that it would be preferable to avoid the word 'authority' in connection with treatise writers and annotators (living or dead).

The first reference to a possible distinction between living and dead authors seems to be in *Turner* v. *Turner* (1819), where Sir Thomas Plumer MR is reported as saying:

[3] *Dibb* v. *Brooke & Sons* [1894] 2 QB 338, 342.

[4] J H Baker, *The Law's Two Bodies: Some Evidentiary Problems in English Legal History*, Oxford University Press, 2001, p. 66.

> I called for authorities in support of the objection, but in all the books on the duties of executors, and in all the cases on the subject, not a solitary instance is to be found. There is indeed a hint in general terms in the work of a living author [Toller on Executors, 426][5]; but it is no authority. There may be cases of actual loss or destruction of the property, where, legatees, as well as creditors, may sue; but it is nowhere said, that an executor is bound, for the sake of the legatees, to postpone the payment of debts not carrying interest.[6]

The opening words of this quotation indicate that, in Plumer's opinion, treatises might be 'authorities' in the sense of tending to support an argument. If this passage were truncated so as to end with the words 'but it is no authority', it might be supposed that reference to Toller was excluded because he was a living author. But the context suggests that what Toller had written was rejected, not because Toller was living, but because what he had to say was not cogent in relation to the point in issue (whether residuary legatees could complain if executors promptly paid the non-interest-bearing debts of an estate).[7] It is evident that Plumer had in fact considered what Toller had written, and rejected it because it was not in point. If he had not read it, he could scarcely have called it 'a hint in general terms'.

Three years later, in *Cox* v. *Troy*,[8] the question was whether the drawee of a bill of exchange was liable, having first written an acceptance on the bill, but having subsequently deleted the acceptance before delivering the bill to the plaintiff. There was a decision of Lord Ellenborough[9] precisely on point in favour of the plaintiff, and counsel for the plaintiff naturally relied on this and on a work by a contemporary French author, Jean Pardessus (1772–1853). The court rejected the plaintiff's argument not even calling on opposing counsel, but citing an earlier French writer, Robert Joseph Pothier (1699–1772). Abbott CJ (later Lord Tenterden, and himself the author of a treatise on shipping) said:

> In a case like the present, which depends on the law merchant, the opinions of learned lawyers and the practice of foreign and commercial nations, though they cannot, strictly speaking, be quoted as authorities here, yet are entitled to very great weight and attention. When I find, therefore, that it is laid down in Pothier's treatise, that a party who has given an

[5] Reporters' footnote. [6] *Turner* v. *Turner* (1819) 1 Jac & W 39, 44.

[7] Toller had written that an executor might be liable for unreasonably postponing payment of debts carrying interest, so as to cause the estate to incur unnecessary interest charges: Samuel Toller, *The Law of Executors and Administrators*, 3rd edition, London, 1814, p. 426.

[8] (1822) 5 B & A 474. [9] *Thornton* v. *Dick* (1804) 4 Esp 270.

> acceptance may erase it before the bill goes out of his hands, it affords a strong argument in support of the view which I take of the question. I think the rule there laid down is far better than the one contended for by the plaintiff.[10]

Best J also relied on Pothier, and explained the passage from Pardessus, after a brief (five lines) consideration of it in its context, as not applicable.[11] It is clear that Pardessus' opinion was given consideration, and that Pothier was preferred, not because Pardessus was living, but because Pothier's opinion was thought to be the better, and in accordance with 'common sense'.[12] One of the other judges, Bayley J, also relied on 'the principles of common sense'.[13] It is notable also in the present context that, though neither of the French writers could 'strictly speaking' be quoted as an authority, yet both were 'entitled to great weight and attention', one being actually preferred to what certainly was (until then) an 'authority', namely the decision of Lord Ellenborough in *Thornton* v. *Dick*. The usage here well illustrates the shifting meanings of the word and shows that, on occasion, often under the influence of practical considerations and what is called common sense, the non-authoritative may displace the authoritative.[14]

In *Lodge* v. *Lysely*,[15] counsel referred to 'what is said by an eminent living author', referring to Sugden, later Lord St Leonards, who was actually counsel for the opposite side in the same case. The reporter added a note with a case reference and the words, 'In the statement of this case in Sugd Vend 8th edit 476, the author adds that the purchaser had paid off the mortgage, and taken a surrender of the term'. There is no suggestion here that a living author (if eminent) should not be cited, though it may fairly be said that the fact that it was thought right to mention that the author was living suggests that this had some sort of significance.

In attempting to assess the actual practice in this period, it should not be overlooked that in very many cases, not usually noticed in this context because nothing was expressly said about the propriety of citation, and which it would scarcely be feasible to enumerate, authors, living and dead, were freely cited. Sometimes (where they tended to support counsel's argument), writers, living and dead, were called authorities, or writers of

[10] 5 B & A 477–478. [11] *Ibid.*, at 481. [12] *Ibid.* [13] *Ibid.*, at 478.

[14] *Thornton* v. *Dick* was said to be weakened by indications in subsequent cases that Lord Ellenborough had changed his mind on the point, but allowing weight to such indications itself detracts from the notion of the unshakeable authority of judicial decisions.

[15] (1832) 4 Sim 69.

authority. In *Withy* v. *Mangles* (1843),[16] for instance, a case in the House of Lords on a point of intestate succession, counsel cited Godolphin, Toller, Blackstone, the current edition of Burn's *Ecclesiastical Law*, by a living editor,[17] and two books by living authors, Thomas Jarman (died 1860), and William Burge (died 1849).[18] He summarised them all by saying:

> Thus it appears that there is a wonderful concurrence, if not an identity, of opinion among all commentators and text-writers of authority that [a child should be preferred to a parent on an intestacy].[19]

No adverse comment by the court is recorded.

In *Knight* v. *Boughton*,[20] also in the House of Lords in the following year, counsel is reported as saying (again referring to Thomas Jarman), 'if it were not irregular to cite the opinions of a living author, as has been done on the other side [Roper on Legacies], enough might be found in Mr Jarman's notes to Powell on Devises, to dispose of this question'. The Lord Chancellor (Lyndhurst) is then reported as interrupting: 'However eminent a living author may be, we cannot act on his opinions, but we attend to the authorities to which he refers us'.[21] Subsequently, counsel on both sides referred to Jarman's work. The opening words of this exchange suggest that it was thought to be of some significance that the author was still living and might be quoted to support the idea that it was considered 'irregular to cite the opinions of a living author', perhaps echoing Lord Eldon's use of the word 'regularly' quoted above. But all that Lord Eldon had condemned was mention of a writer 'as an authority'. The context shows that counsel were not constrained in 1843 in citing living authors as part of their argument. The very reference to the supposed irregularity is slightly facetious and itself demonstrates the lack of constraint ('if it were not irregular for me to do so, I would say the following . . . ' – an instance of the rhetorical device of apophasis), and the intervention of Lord Lyndhurst, as well as the subsequent citations, shows that there was no constraint recognised by either judge or counsel. Lyndhurst said, 'we cannot act on his opinions'. In the sense that the opinions cannot be strictly binding, this is obviously true of any author, living or dead. Lyndhurst's next words show that it was considered perfectly proper, and indeed desirable, for counsel to cite living authors in argument: 'we attend to the authorities to which he [the author] refers us'.

16 (1843) 10 C & F 215. 17 Ninth edition, 1842, by Robert Phillimore (died 1885).
18 *Commentaries on Colonial and Foreign Laws*, 1838. 19 10 C & F 224.
20 (1844) 11 C & F 513. 21 *Ibid.*, at 539.

In a criminal case, *R* v. *Ion*,[22] the following exchange took place:

Counsel: In the eleventh edition of a work, formerly edited by one of your Lordships [Lord CJ Jervis][23] Arch Crim Pl by Welsby, Mr Welsby, who may be cited as authority, comments on the words 'utter or publish'.

Pollock CB: Not yet an *authority*

Counsel: It is no doubt a rule that a writer on law is not to be considered an authority in his lifetime. [Reporter's note: This rule seems 'more honoured in the breach than in the observance'. The annotations of Mr Greaves, Russ on Crimes, and the learned work of Mr Pitt Taylor on Evidence, are constantly cited in the Crown cases.] The only exception to the rule, perhaps, is the case of Justice Story.

Coleridge J: Story is dead.

Cresswell J: No doubt the cases are carefully abstracted by Mr Welsby in the passage you refer to.

Lord Campbell CJ: It is scarcely necessary to say that my opinion of Mr Welsby is one of sincere respect.

This exchange shows that by the middle of the century the notion that there was a distinction in the deference due to living and dead writers had attained a degree of currency, but the illuminating comment of the reporter (Denison) shows that in practice there was no effective constraint, except perhaps that the word 'authority' was to be avoided. The interventions of Cresswell and Campbell indicate a desire to correct the impression that Welsby's opinion could not be considered, and suggest some difference of opinion among the judges.

Hundreds of references were made to the books by Sugden, Lindley and Fry, and to many other authors, during their lifetimes, often with high praise for the value of the work, and without any suggestion that citation might be improper.[24] In 1913, Vaughan Williams LJ said that 'counsel are not entitled to quote living authors as authorities for a proposition they are putting forward, but they may adopt the author's statements as part of their argument'.[25] This formulation permits the most ample freedom that any counsel, or indeed any author, could properly expect.

22 (152) 2 Den 475. 23 Reporter's note.

24 Edward Burtenshaw Sugden (later Lord St Leonards), *Concise and Practical Treatise on the Law of Vendors and Purchasers of Estates* ('to which we are all in the habit of referring on such subjects', Malins V-C, in *Aberaman Ironworks* v. *Wickens* (1868) LR 5 Eq. 485, 513), Nathaniel Lindley, *Treatise on the Law of Partnership* ('one of the most valuable contributions ever made by a learned writer to the law and practice of the Court', Bacon V-C in *Helmore* v. *Smith* (1887) 35 Ch D 436, 440), Edward Fry, *Treatise on the Specific Performance of Contracts*. A search of the Justis database indicates about 228 references to Sugden, 315 to Lindley, and 116 to Fry. To these must be added references not noted by the reporter, and references in cases reported in other series, and unreported cases.

25 *Greenlands* v. *Wilmhurst* (1913) 29 TLR 685, 687.

The net effect was that counsel were perfectly free to cite living authors in support of their argument, but might be well advised, particularly before certain judges, to avoid use of the ambiguous word 'authority'. In the case of multiple successive editions of a well-known work continuing after the death of the original author, as, for example, Sugden on *Vendors and Purchasers*, it would scarcely be practicable to permit citation of old editions, on the ground that the original author was dead, while excluding reference to the current edition on the ground that the current editor was still living.

Different judges took different views on the propriety of citing living authors. Kekewich J said, in 1887:

> It is to my mind much to be regretted, and it is a regret which I believe every judge on the bench shares, that text-books are more and more quoted in court – I mean of course text-books by living authors – and some judges have gone so far as to say that they shall not be quoted.[26]

As Neil Duxbury has pointed out,[27] this statement itself indicates that practice at the time was not consistent: 'some judges have gone so far as to say' that treatises shall not be cited indicates that the practice of citation was widespread (though apparently disapproved by Kekewich). But Kekewich himself was scarcely consistent. Earlier in the same year he had quoted and relied on a passage from Pollock's *Principles of Contract*,[28] and, a few years later, he said:

> I have . . . been referred to what I may now regard as a work of undoubted authority – I mean the present edition of Sir Edward Fry's work on Specific Performance – and to a passage in it which is well worth attention. The learned author says this . . . [29]

And in *In re Wellborne* in 1900 he said, 'before turning to the decided cases I will refer to the book before me, which, though a modern work, and that of a living author, and therefore not entitled to the same respect as we pay, for instance, to the works of Lord St Leonards [1781–1875], has been well known to the profession for many years and is an extremely valuable work'.[30]

26 *Union Bank* v. *Munster* (1887) 37 Ch D 51, 54.
27 N Duxbury, *Jurists and Judges: an Essay on Influence*, Oxford, Hart, 2001, 63.
28 *Foster* v. *Wheeler* (1887) 36 Ch D 695, 698.
29 *Fortescue* v. *Lostwithiel and Fowey Railway Co.* [1894] 3 Ch 621, 638
30 [1900] 1 Ch 857, 863. The author's opinion (Cordery on *Solicitors*) was rejected.

Occasional expressions of disapproval of the practice of citing living authors do not establish that there was a general convention or rule on the matter, though they suggest that some judges wished that there were such a convention, and did what they could to help to establish one. In a case in 1880 Lindley J, who was himself the author of a widely cited treatise on partnership, referred to three living authors (Pollock, Leake and Benjamin), specifically adopting Pollock's argument on the point in issue and calling his book the 'excellent work on *Principles of Contract*'.[31] Pollock's book had been dedicated to Lindley, and in the third edition (1881) Pollock expanded the dedication to include very high praise – verging on the fulsome – of Lindley. It is possible that this mutual admiration of author and judge might not have struck all the judges, or all members of the practising bar, as entirely desirable, though I have no direct evidence on this point. Lindley's decision shows that some judges welcomed citation of living authors. It does not establish that other judges did not hold a contrary opinion. The opinions of the judges on such a matter would be known to practising barristers, and, of course, self-interest would usually be sufficient to induce counsel to avoid putting arguments in a form likely to alienate the judge.

III. Reasons for judicial caution in the use of treatises

A related, but separate, question from the ability of counsel to cite treatises is the question of what use should properly be made of them by judges. Lord Esher said, in 1889, 'I will refer to Chitty's Archbold's Practice 12th ed, vol. i, 498, as a specimen of the way in which the case has been treated in text-books, and that shews, I think, how careful we ought to be in adopting statements in text-books'.[32] This is a plea for caution in judicial use of all textbooks, and is not confined to those by living authors. Neil Duxbury, in his discussion of the question, identified eight possible reasons for excluding consideration of treatises by living authors.[33] These were the growth of law reporting (making judicial decisions more accessible), the declaratory theory of law, the fear of causing offence to those whose works were not cited, the avoidance of immature or unreflective commentary, the Laconic style of English judgments, an impoverished academic environment, the possibility that a living author

[31] *Byrne & Co.* v. *Leon van Tienhoven & Co.* (1880) 5 CPD 344, 347.

[32] *Stumm* v. *Dixon & Co.* (1889) 22 QBD 529.

[33] Duxbury, *Jurists and Judges: An Essay on Influence*, n. 27, above, pp. 66–74.

will have a change of opinion, and the distinct task of judges (as opposed to academics).

Duxbury considers these reasons insufficient to preclude citation of treatises in argument, and his conclusion is persuasive, but this does not establish that the reasons have no force: they are relevant to the question of what weight judges should give to treatises, whether cited by counsel or not. Some of the reasons apply to works by all authors, living or dead. Cumulatively, the reasons suggest the need, not for a rule precluding citation by counsel, but for judicial caution in the use to be made of the citations. To Duxbury's reasons may be added another, related to Duxbury's third reason (fear of causing offence), namely, that many writers of treatises were practising barristers, and judges may have thought it improper to confer on some barristers (but not on others) a kind of favoured status, or seal of approval: to praise a work explicitly, as Lindley did Pollock's book, might have seemed awkward, especially in the light of Pollock's extravagant dedication in praise of Lindley, and especially if Pollock were likely to be appearing the next day before Lindley in an unrelated case.

This consideration probably explains the apparently puzzling reference in some statements of the supposed rule to the effect that it applied only to works by practising barristers: 'text-books written by practising barristers are not quoted in the courts'.[34] Pollock rarely appeared in court,[35] and in the case of authors who had been appointed to the bench, as had Lindley himself, and Blackburn, Sugden and Fry, the danger of favouritism to practising barristers was absent. This may partly explain the comparative frequency with which these authors were cited. Another reason might be the added credibility lent to the work by the judicial appointment. In 1876, Sir George Jessel said, 'I may cite further from . . . Mr Lindley's book, considering that learned gentleman is now a judge'.[36] In one case, Denman J referred to a passage in Lindley's book, and rather surprisingly added, Lindley having been recently appointed to the bench, that 'the learned judge himself, having read this judgment, has authorised us to give this explanation of the passage in question'.[37] The appointment to

[34] *Tichborne* v. *Weir* (1892) 67 LT 735, 736 (Lord Esher MR). Precisely the opposite rule was suggested in *Re Thompson* [1936] Ch 676, i.e., that *only* works written by barristers should be cited.

[35] N Duxbury, *Frederick Pollock and the English Juristic Tradition*, Oxford, Oxford University Press, 2004, p. 29.

[36] *Pooley* v. *Driver* (1876) 5 Ch D 458, 481.

[37] *Yorkshire Banking Co.* v. *Beatson* (1879) 4 CPD 204, 210–11 (Div Ct).

the bench of an author could not, as Sir John Baker pointed out, endow his writings (even those after appointment) with judicial status.[38] On this point, Sir Edward Fry, in the preface to the second edition of his book, remarked that:

> There is one notion often expressed with regard to works written or revised by authors on the Bench, which seems to me in part at last erroneous – the notion, I mean, that they possess a quasi-judicial authority. It is hardly enough remembered how different are the circumstances under which a book is written and a judgment pronounced, or how much the weight and value of the latter are due to the discussions at the bar which precede the judgment.[39]

The fact that Fry found it necessary to warn against too great a deference on this account shows that such deference, or the appearance of it, occurred sufficiently often to attract his attention.[40] This passage was mentioned by Kekewich J in support of the first of his opinions quoted above (that works by living authors should not be cited), but it should be noted that Fry's statement was made specifically in reference to authors *who had been appointed to the bench*, and he did not say that their works should not be cited; he said merely that they should not be afforded a quasi-judicial authority.

IV. The writer's perspective

An aspect of the question that is also worth examining is the attitude and style of writing of the treatise writers themselves. On the whole, the nineteenth-century English writers did not usually make a priori assertions on their own authority; the preferred style was a mixture of description, prescription, prediction and advocacy, inviting the reader (and, indirectly, the court) to adopt the 'better' view of a disputed question in the light of past judicial decisions as 'properly understood'. But there was an important and interesting exception, which probably influenced the style of subsequent writing not by its success, but by its failure. This was the *Treatise on Obligations and Contracts, Part 1*, by Henry Colebrooke,

[38] J Baker, *The Law's Two Bodies*, 2001, p. 66.

[39] E. Fry, *Specific Performance of Contracts* 2nd edition, 1881, Preface. Fry was appointed to the bench in 1877.

[40] The Justis database indicates that judicial references to the works of Lindley, Fry, Sugden, and Blackburn all increased in frequency after the appointment of those authors to the bench.

privately printed in 1818. Colebrooke was an eminent Sanskrit scholar who had spent most of his career in India, where he had held judicial office. His treatise contains many assertions of abstract conceptual divisions, with no attempt to relate the divisions to any practical consequences, or to actual English law, past or present. Over fifty years later his son made the revealing comment that 'the law of England, he [Henry Colebrooke] considered, was law in disguise; it must be stripped of its technicalities before it could be made the subject of study'.[41] This was the approach of a grammarian seeking to discover an ancient and universal language, partly lost, partly corrupted by modern usages. It was not a starting point likely to lead to a legal treatise agreeable to English readers. So, for example, Colebrooke wrote, near the beginning of the treatise, that:

> Obligations are either *natural* or *adventitious*... Obligations are *perfect* or *imperfect*. They are both *natural* and *civil*; or merely *natural*, or purely *civil*.... Both are *imperfect obligations*.... *Mixt obligations*, being both natural and civil, are full and perfect... Obligations are either *pure* and *simple* or *conditional*: and with or without a *term* or day... An obligation is for a thing *certain*, or one *uncertain*, or for an *indeterminate* thing *of a kind certain*.... Obligations are either *alternative*, or *single*... An obligation may be *joint*; or it may be *several*; or it may be *joint* and *several* relatively either to parties promising or to those stipulating.... Obligations are *divisible* or *indivisible*.... .Obligations are *principal* or *accessory*.... Obligations are *primary* or *secondary*... *Secondary obligations* are also subdivided as succeeding or acceding to the primary one.... Obligations are either *conventional* or *obediential*... Obligations are *mutual* and *reciprocal*, or *non-reciprocal*... Mutual obligations are *entirely* or *unequally* reciprocal.[42]

These distinctions are accompanied by very brief sidenotes referring (by short abbreviations, some of them rather mysterious to the modern reader, and probably also to many of Colebrooke's contemporaries) to civilian sources: Puf. (Pufendorf), Poth. (Pothier), Ersk. (Erskine), Barb. (Barbeyrac), C.C. (the Code Civil), Dig. (the Digest), P.F. (the *Pandectes Françaises*),[43] Molin. (Dumoulin), and Vinn. (Vinnius). There is no reference in this passage to any English decided case, and the only reference to an English writer is to Ev. on Poth., i.e., Evans's notes to his translation of Pothier's treatise on Obligations. This might be called an authoritative style of writing: Colebrooke demands of his readers their assent to

[41] Sir T E Colebrooke, *Miscellaneous Essays, with the Life of the Author by his Son*, London, Teubner, 1873, p. 280 (footnote).

[42] Colebrooke, *Treatise*, pp. 4–9 (emphases in original).

[43] J.B.D[elaport], and P. N. R[iffé]-C[aubray], *Les Pandectes Françaises*, Paris, 1803–1809.

and understanding of a complex set of distinctions, and the multiplication of conceptual entities, without explanation of how they relate to practical consequences or to English law, and he makes this demand on his own authority. The sources mentioned in the sidenotes, even if they were carefully studied, would not persuade an English reader that this set of distinctions was a part of English law, nor would they explain why they were supposed to be fundamental. Other parts of the work refer to the Hindu Digest,[44] and there are a few references to English writers, including Blackstone, Powell, Comyn and Newland, but an abbreviated reference to one of these writers would not strike an English reader as sufficient support for the assertions made in the text. There is scarcely a reference in the whole book to a decided English case.[45]

Colebrooke's style of writing was authoritative, but it could not be persuasive to English readers. The work was privately printed, and the projected second part (together with a projected 'preface with other preliminary and introductory matter', which would presumably have included a table of references) never appeared. 'The second portion', his son later wrote, 'was considerably advanced; but he received little encouragement to pursue his task'. His son said of the treatise, 'I think it was a matter of some disappointment to its author that it was not more generally appreciated'.[46] He suggested, as a reason for the failure, that 'the work is perhaps too succinct, and it is wanting in practical examples and illustrations', a comment that probably reflects tactful attempts by judges and lawyers to explain to the author why such a book could not succeed.

Subsequent English treatise writers[47] all gave prominence to decided English cases, adopting a persuasive, rather than authoritative, style, and inviting the reader to join with the author in complimenting the judges or, where necessary, in respectful remonstrance. This style enabled the author to carry on a kind of dialogue with the courts. An illustration may be found in Pollock's treatment of the simple question of whether an offer could

[44] Probably Jaganatha Tarkapanchanana, *A Digest of Hindu Law on Contracts and Successions* . . . translated by H T Colebrooke, Calcutta, 1798 [D.N.B., and B.L. catalogue].

[45] One only occurs in the first sixty-nine pages, '7 Term Rep 350', that is, *Rann* v. *Hughes*, supporting the proposition that written contracts not under seal are denominated contracts by *parol*.

[46] Colebrooke, *Miscellaneous Essays*, 279. See Waddams, 'Nineteenth-Century Treatises on English Contract Law', in Angela Fernandez and Martin D Dubber (eds.), *Law Books in Action*, Hart, Oxford, 2012, p. 127.

[47] Addison's preface appeared to foreshadow a universalist approach similar to Colebrooke's, but the body of the work did not follow through: C Addison, *A Treatise of the Law of Contracts*, London, 1847.

be effectively withdrawn without communication to the offeree. If there were a stringent rule that contractual obligation depended on intention, or on mutual consent, or concurrence of wills, it would follow that there ought to be no liability where the offeror had demonstrably intended to withdraw the offer before acceptance. A much discussed test case was that of an offer sent by mail, with a subsequent retraction also sent by mail; the legal issue was whether the offeror was bound if the offeree purported to accept the offer without notice of the offeror's change of mind. On this issue, Pothier had expressly said that there could be no contractual liability because 'there is not that consent, or concurrence of . . . wills, which is necessary to constitute the contract of sale'.[48]

Pollock (1876), following Benjamin and Leake, rejected Pothier's approach, Pollock commenting on 'the manifestly unjust consequences' of permitting the offeror to retract after reliance by the 'offeree', and rejecting a non-contractual solution proposed by Pothier as 'cumbrous and inelegant'. Pollock then asserted that 'the declaration of an *animus contrahendi* [intention of contracting] . . . when once made must be regarded as continuing so long as no revocation of it is communicated to the other party. A revocation not communicated is in point of law no revocation at all'. Pollock added: 'These principles, it seems to us, are entirely right if tested by common sense and convenience, and are in accordance with the authorities of the common law when rightly understood'.[49]

This last sentence is of interest in the present context. Pollock, having set out two rather specific propositions ('an offeror's declaration of intention must be regarded as continuing' and 'a revocation not communicated is no revocation'), evidently newly formulated by himself to support the conclusion he favoured on the point in issue, then called these propositions principles (these principles), while Pothier's idea of concurrence of wills, which might more naturally be considered a general or fundamental principle, but the apparent consequences of which Pollock was in the process of rejecting, was not here called a 'principle'. Pollock's conclusion was based primarily on general considerations of justice and policy ('common sense and convenience', and avoidance of 'manifest injustice'). It is

[48] R J Pothier, *Treatise on the Contract of Sale* [1817], trans. L S Cushing, Boston, Little, Brown, 1839. For a fuller discussion see Waddams, 'What *were* the principles of nineteenth-century contract law?', in Andrew Lewis, Paul Brand and Paul Mitchell (eds.), *Law in the City: Proceedings of the Seventeenth British Legal History Conference, London, 2005*, Dublin, Four Courts Press, 2007, p. 305.

[49] Pollock, *Principles of Contract*, 1st edition, 1876, p. 11.

significant that principles were to be 'tested' by common sense and convenience: in case of conflict, it would seem, it was the principles (or apparent principles) that must give way. These considerations were then made to conform to the convention that Pollock was describing the actual state of English law (in accordance with the authorities of the common law). But it is evident from the next three words (when rightly understood) that the search for authorities was neither a technical nor primarily a historical enquiry. 'Right understanding' impliedly imported the author's own opinion, primarily informed, as the context shows, by considerations of common sense, convenience and avoidance of injustice. The awkward use of the editorial plural (it seems to us) shows that Pollock was conscious of reliance on his own opinion, and, at the same time, embarrassed by it and reluctant to make it too plain.

Pollock's approach to this question was rewarded with almost immediate success, for, in 1880, in *Byrne* v. *Leon van Tienhoven & Co.*, Mr. Justice Lindley, to whom, as mentioned above, Pollock's book had been dedicated, expressly rejected Pothier's view and adopted Pollock's.[50] In 1822, an English judge had said that 'the authority of Pothier is . . . as high as can be found, next to a decision of a Court of Justice in this country'.[51] But Lindley J said:

> I am aware that Pothier and some other writers of celebrity are of opinion that there can be no contract if an offer is withdrawn before it is accepted, although the withdrawal is not communicated to the person to whom the offer has been made. The reason for this opinion is that there is not in fact any such consent by both parties as is essential to constitute a contract between them. Against this view, however, it has been urged that a state of mind not notified cannot be regarded in dealings between man and man; and that an uncommunicated revocation is for all practical purposes and in point of law no revocation at all. This is the view taken in the United States . . . and it was adopted by Mr Benjamin. The same view is taken by Mr Pollock in his excellent work on *Principles of Contract*, 2nd ed . . . and by Mr Leake in his *Digest of the Law of Contracts*. . . . This view, moreover appears to me much more in accordance with the general principles of English law than the view maintained by Pothier.[52]

Treatises by authors, dead and living, were here treated respectfully, but with deference not so much to the writers as 'authorities', as to their opinions insofar (and only insofar) they were found to be persuasive. Pothier's opinon (on acceptance of a bill of exchange) had been welcomed in 1822

[50] *Byrne & Co.* v. *Leon van Tienhoven & Co.* (1880) 5 CPD 344 (6 March).

[51] *Cox* v. *Troy* (1822) 5 B & A 474, 480 (Best J).

[52] n. 50, above, at p. 347.

because it was perceived to be in accordance with 'the practice of foreign and commercial nations' and with 'common sense'.[53] His opinion (on contract formation) was rejected in 1880 because it was perceived not to be in accord with 'practical convenience': Lindley J went on 'to point out the extreme injustice and inconvenience which any other conclusion would produce', adding that 'both legal principles and practical convenience require that a person who has accepted an offer not known to him to have been revoked shall be in a position safely to act upon the footing that the offer and acceptance constitute a contract binding on both parties'.[54] Shortly afterwards, in *Stevenson* v. *McLean*,[55] Lindley J was expressly followed on the same point by another judge. Pothier's treatise on obligations was certainly influential in helping to form a nineteenth-century English vision of contract law, but his opinions on particular points, though readily cited by judges who happened to agree with those opinions, as in *Cox* v. *Troy*, were equally readily rejected by judges who disagreed with them, as in *Byrne* v. *van Tienhoven*. Bernard Rudden has said, 'Pothier comme autorité en *Common law* se révéla á la fois influent et impuissant', adding that 'Pothier, ayant joué son rôle d'aide á la formation d'un certain esprit de généralization, la doctrine pouvait désormais s'en émanciper'.[56]

In Pollock's third edition (1881) the dedication was expanded, as mentioned, to include extravagant praise of Lindley, and Pollock was able to cite the two decisions of 1880 as authoritatively settling the question, omitting the awkward phrasing of his first edition and substituting a much smoother formulation: 'In the earlier editions of this book the question was treated as practically settled, but only in 1880 was it actually decided... [citing the two cases]'.[57] Thus, the dialogue between writer and judge enabled each to disclaim an unmediated appeal to such very general considerations as common sense, convenience, justice and practicality, though each was strongly influenced by those considerations.

Pollock valued his close connection with the profession and with the judiciary, and carried on the dialogue in many forums. He was the editor of the *Law Reports* and of the *Law Quarterly Review*, which gave him

53 See nn. 10–13, above.

54 *Ibid.* 55 (1880) 5 QBD 357 (Lush J, 25 May).

56 Bernard Rudden, 'Pothier et la Common Law', in Joël Monéger, Jean-Louis Sourioux and Aline Terrasson de Fougères (eds.), *Robert-Joseph Pothier, d'hier ā aujourd'hui*, Economica, 2001, pp. 91, 100–101.

57 Pollock, *Principles of Contract*, 3rd edition, pp. 25–26.

power both to select the cases reported and to comment on them.[58] He maintained informal contacts with the judges, writing to Holmes in 1914, with evident pride in his informal influence on and privileged access to the judges:

> Haldane asked me last week to a tobacco talk of *Derry v. Peek*, and the possibility of minimizing its consequences. The Lords are going to hold that it does not apply to the situation created by a positive fiduciary duty such as a solicitor's, in other words, go as near as they dare to saying it was wrong, as all Lincoln's Inn thought at the time.[59]

Pollock continued to be cited in the courts throughout his long life. In the very important Scottish case of *Donoghue* v. *Stevenson*,[60] Lord Macmillan quoted a lengthy passage from Pollock's book on torts directly relevant to the crucial question of the relation of contractual obligation to tortious liability. Alan Rodger, later Baron Rodger of Earlsferry, has drawn attention to a draft final speech,[61] which Lord Macmillan subsequently revised, probably, as Rodger convincingly argues, in order to ensure that the decision would constitute a definitive ruling not only on Scots law but also on English law in the face of the two dissenting English law lords. As Rodger points out, the whole structure of Macmillan's speech was fundamentally altered to this effect. In the draft version, the passage from Pollock was quoted, but the final version was changed[62] to add the following introductory words: 'I may be permitted to adopt as my own the language of a very distinguished English writer on this subject'.[63] The deliberate alteration of the draft to include these words shows that this formulation was no casual courtesy: the words are significant both in their acknowledgement of Pollock's influence, and in the phrase 'adopt as my own'. This addition supports Rodger's thesis that the object of the revisions was to establish that Macmillan's speech applied directly to English law. Lord Buckmaster, dissenting, said pointedly, and a little peevishly, that 'the law books give no assistance, because the work of living authors, however deservedly eminent, cannot be used as authority, though the opinions they express may demand attention';[64] this remark

58 See N Duxbury, *Frederick Pollock and the English Juristic Tradition*, Oxford, 2004.

59 Pollock to Holmes, 20 May, 1914, M Howe (ed.), *Holmes Pollock Letters*, Harvard, University Press, Cambridge, MA, 1941 (2 vols.) i, 215. The pending case was *Nocton* v. *Ashburton* [1914] AC 932 (19 June).

60 [1932] AC 562 (HL – Sc).

61 See Alan Rodger, 'Lord Macmillan's Speech in Donoghue v. Stevenson' (1992) 108 LQR, p. 236.

62 See appendix to Rodger's article, 108 LQR at p. 253.

63 [1932] AC at p. 610.

64 *Ibid.*, at p. 567.

must be read in the context of the majority speeches, which contradict the assertion that the law books 'give no assistance'. Lord Macmillan's speech shows the influence of Pollock on a crucial question, vital to English as well as to Scottish law, that could easily have been decided the other way, or, as Rodger shows, left in a state of uncertainty in relation to English law, and other systems based on English law. Lord Atkin (with whom Lord Thankerton agreed with respect to English law)[65] did not mention Pollock's name, but his conclusion was in close accord with Pollock's opinion, of which Lord Atkin must certainly, having read Lord Macmillan's draft speech, have been aware. It has also been suggested[66] that Lord Atkin was influenced by another living writer, Percy Winfield. Pollock had been cited in argument, but, so far as the Law Reports indicate, only by (unsuccessful) counsel for the respondent.[67]

A few years later, when Pollock was ninety, Lord Wright quoted his book on torts, saying that it was 'fortunately not a work of authority'.[68] This courteous and gently humorous compliment was misunderstood by two reporters, who misreported it as 'unfortunately'.[69] This incident also shows that by the 1930s, the supposed convention that living authors should not be cited as authority had ceased to be (if it ever had been) a definite part of common legal understanding: Lord Wright, in citing Pollock's book with high approval ('the words apply exactly to the present case, and I accept them as part of my judgment'), while taking the opportunity to convey an elegant compliment, was simultaneously flouting and mocking the supposed convention, while the reporters were apparently wholly unaware of it.

Pollock was said to have been charmed by Lord Wright's humorous allusion,[70] and after Pollock's death in the following year Wright wrote a substantial obituary in the *Law Quarterly Review* in which he said that 'Pollock has vindicated to this generation the vital importance of extra-judicial writing in law . . . The writings of a lawyer like Pollock, constantly

[65] *Ibid.*, at p. 604. [66] Duxbury, *Jurists and Judges*, n. 27, above, p. 65 (footnote).

[67] [1932] AC 566, presumably citing Pollock for his assessment of the actual state of English law, rather than for his criticism of it. Pollock had written, somewhat tentatively (*The Law of Torts*, 13th edition (1929), 570), 'From all this it appears that there has been (though perhaps there is no longer) a certain tendency to hold that facts which constitute a contract cannot have any other legal effect'.

[68] *Nicholls* v. *Ely Beet Sugar Factory Ltd* [1936] Ch 343, 349 (CA).

[69] 105 LJ Ch 279, 282, 154 LT 531, 533 (emphasis added). See R Megarry, *Miscellany at Law*, London, Stevens, 1955, p. 328.

[70] Wright, *In Memoriam Right Hon Sir Frederick Pollock* (1937) 53 LQR 151,152, rep. in Lord Wright of Durley, *Legal Essays and Addresses*, Cambridge University Press, 1939, pp. 411, 412.

cited in the Courts and quoted by the judges, are entitled to claim a place under [the] category of unwritten law even in a system like ours which does not usually seek its law from institutional writers'.[71] This was high praise, and Pollock would probably have been more than satisfied with it, though it did not include the word 'authority'.

V. Conclusion

The variation in the meaning of the word 'authority' in the present context is itself a significant phenomenon, and not mere accidental or linguistic oversight. It springs from a static and rigid view of the judge's function, and belief in a very restricted judicial role in effecting legal change. Lord Romilly said, in 1870:

> It is a great scandal to the public and the profession generally that there should be a case in which a court of law is not able to determine what the law is. I admit that the law is very difficult to determine, but I hope that, by means of improvements, the law will ultimately be reduced into a state that a man of ability, who has devoted his whole life to the subject, may be able to tell a person what the law really is on any one point. That state of things, I hope, may be arrived at; but it is not so now, and will not be so in my time.[72]

This formalistic ideal of law as fixed and determinable tends towards the reduction, and ultimately to the elimination of the authority of treatises, for, if the law on every conceivable question could truly be deduced by any 'man of ability' from prior decided cases, a treatise could be little more than a sophisticated index. Romilly's view, though certainly prominent in the late nineteenth century, was not universally held, even by judges. Sir George Jessel MR said, in 1880:

> Now, I have often said, and I repeat it, that the only thing in a judge's decision binding as an authority upon a subsequent judge is the principle upon which the case was decided: but it is not sufficient that the case should have been decided upon a principle if that principle is not itself a right principle, or one not applicable to the case; and it is for a subsequent judge to say whether or not it is a right principle, and, if not, he may himself lay down the true principle. In that case the prior decision ceases to be an authority or guide for any subsequent judge, for the second judge who lays down the true principle in effect reverses the decision.[73]

[71] 53 LQR, at 152. [72] *Mullings* v. *Trinder* (1870) LR 10 Eq 449, 455.
[73] *Osborne to Rowlatt* (1880) 13 Ch D 774, 785–786.

This comment is not compatible with a static view of the law, nor with a passive role for the judge, because it applies also to the second judge whose opinion will be, in turn, liable to be in effect reversed by a later judge. An appreciation of the mutability of law in the light of practical considerations and changing social circumstances tends to be accompanied, on the one hand, by a loss of unwavering reverence for past judicial decisions, which come more rarely to be treated as authoritative in the sense of commanding obedience, and, on the other hand, by a willingness to consider, in addition to past judicial decisions, a wider variety of kinds of argument, including those advanced by writers of treatises.[74]

[74] I am grateful to Fidelia Ho and to Patrick Healy for valuable assistance in preparing this article.

13

Maitland and Austin

Legal history and legal thought in the late nineteenth century

JOHN HUDSON

'J.A. = 0'.[1] So wrote F. W. Maitland to Sir Frederick Pollock on 4 December 1899. The object of his contempt was John Austin. This paper examines Maitland's view of Austin, asking why the most famous and influential nineteenth-century historian of law reacted in so negative a fashion to the most famous and influential nineteenth-century philosopher of law. Whilst it is a contribution to study of the reception of Austin,[2] its focus is upon Maitland, asking how his reaction to Austin may help us to understand his own work.

Although Austin was writing the *Province of Jurisprudence Determined* and his other lectures about twenty years before Maitland was born, the re-publication of the former in 1861 and the first publication of the latter in 1863 meant that Austin's ideas were particularly prominent at the time of Maitland's intellectual formation.[3] The thoroughness with which Maitland read Austin's corpus is not clear, his mentions of Austin being

[1] *The Letters of Frederic William Maitland*, i., ed. C. H. S. Fifoot (Selden Society, Supplementary Series, i, London, 1965), no. 253.

[2] See especially W. E. Rumble, *Doing Austin Justice: The Reception of John Austin's Philosophy of Law in Nineteenth-Century England* (London, 2005). Rumble's index contains only references to Maitland, at pp. 184 and 250; in both places he cites Maitland's 'J.A. = 0'. In the former he quotes Buckland's comment on Maitland's reaction to Austin (see below, 326), in the latter he describes Maitland and Bryce as 'extreme examples' of those who reacted negatively to Austin.

[3] See, for example, Rumble, *Doing Austin Justice*, 106, for Austin's reputation being at its zenith in the period 1863–85; also see, for example, M. Lobban, 'Legal Theory and Judge-made Law in England, 1850–1920', *Quaderni Fiorentini* 40 (2011), 553–94, at 593–4; Lobban in W. Cornish, et al., *The Oxford History of the Laws of England. XI 1820–1914: English Legal System*, 124–5.

determined by his own interests, but he did refer explicitly to the *Province* and to the 'Outline' of the lectures, allusively to other portions of them.[4]

Before looking at Maitland's response, we must sketch the essential points of Austin's arguments. He states that his is a general jurisprudence, rather than a particular one relating to a single country or system.[5] His special concern is 'positive law': he states that 'the aggregate of the rules, established by political superiors, is frequently styled *positive* law, or law existing *by position*'.[6] The adjective 'positive' indicates that such law 'flow[s] from human sources'.[7] His science of jurisprudence treats positive law as it is, not positive law as it ought to be, the latter being the focus of what he calls the science of legislation.[8] He distinguishes between positive law and morals, although noting the close links between the two.[9] The defining characteristic of positive law is that it rests on the command of the sovereign: 'Every positive law or every law simply and strictly so called, is set by a sovereign person, or a sovereign body of persons, to a member or members of the independent political society wherein that person or body is sovereign or supreme'.[10] Regarding sovereignty, he states that 'if a *determinate* human superior, *not* in the habit of obedience to a like superior, receive *habitual* obedience from the *bulk* of a given society, that determinate superior is sovereign in that society, and the society (including the superior) is a society political and independent';[11] by definition 'sovereign or supreme power is incapable of

[4] F. W. Maitland, *The Constitutional History of England* (Cambridge, 1908), 528–33 (the footnotes giving references in Austin were supplied by the volume's editor, H. A. L. Fisher – see *Constitutional History*, vii); see below, 324–6, for concern with issues of rights. Maitland's reference to Austin as 'at times an acute dissector of confused thought', below, 296, may well be to the *Lectures* as a whole.

[5] See especially J. Austin, *Lectures on Jurisprudence, or the Philosophy of Positive Law* (5th edition, 2 vols., London, 1885), 1072. Note also W. L. Morison, *John Austin* (London, 1982).

[6] J. Austin, *The Province of Jurisprudence Determined*, ed. W. E. Rumble (Cambridge, 1995), 19.

[7] *Province*, ed. Rumble, 110.

[8] See, for example, *Province*, ed. Rumble, 14.

[9] For the complexity of this issue, note, for example, Rumble, *Doing Austin Justice*, 113, 215–16.

[10] *Province*, ed. Rumble, 16. Cf., for example, Sir Frederick Pollock, *A First Book of Jurisprudence for Students of the Common Law* (London, 1896), 14: 'In English we use the word Law in a concrete sense to mean any particular rule, having the nature of law in the abstract sense, which is expressly prescribed by the supreme power in the State, or by some person or body having authority for that purpose, though not generally supreme'; note in particular the opening words.

[11] *Province*, ed. Rumble, 166. Austin's treatment of the habit of obedience seems often to be quite culture-specific and therefore difficult to apply historically; see, for example, *Province*, ed. Rumble, 248. On sovereignty see generally *Province*, Lecture VI.

legal limitation'.[12] Many other arguments might be added to this sketch, and it is important to point out that a very significant proportion of the *Lectures* is devoted to the refinement of definitions of legal concepts such as right and duty.[13]

It should, furthermore, be noted that a summary in this form may mislead when considering responses to Austin. In the first place, there are at least arguably internal inconsistencies within Austin's central arguments.[14] Second, even when arguments are not internally inconsistent, individual points may allow for multiple readings, despite Austin's stated emphasis on clarity and definition.[15] Third, different readers have privileged different elements within Austin's work,[16] sometimes by privileging the *Province* over Austin's other writings.[17]

I. Maitland and Austin

Maitland is widely and correctly regarded as generous spirited towards those with whom he disagreed. In particular, he sought to avoid being critical in print, except about works that he considered particularly poor and possibly about authors who were known for the harshness of their views.[18] The degree of criticism of Austin suggests the strength of Maitland's disagreement.

[12] *Province*, ed. Rumble, 188. [13] Note Morison, *John Austin*, esp. 57, 66–7, 142.

[14] Note, for example, M. Lobban, *The Common Law and English Jurisprudence, 1760–1850* (Oxford, 1991), 241–2: 'There is an obvious clash between Austin's positivist conception of law and his acknowledgement that the law could grow through the decisions of judges, a contradiction that appears to be resolved only by seeing judges as subordinate legislators whose powers came from the sovereign'. See also below, 311, 314–15.

[15] For conflicting interpretations of Austin see, for example, the discussion in Lobban, *Common Law*, 224–7.

[16] See, for example, Lobban, *Common Law*, 246: 'Austin created confusion by spending much time in the *Province of Jurisprudence Determined* discussing utilitarian theory. Yet this was irrelevant to *jurisprudence*; jurisprudence was a realm of pure theory and abstract concepts, whereas utilitarian theory addressed the question of what should be the content of law.... The *Province* should therefore not be seen as separate and distinct from the *Lectures* it precedes: what should be seen as distinct are the chapters on utilitarianism'.

[17] Note Lobban, *Common Law*, 246 and n. 83, 251–3.

[18] See Maitland, *Letters*, i. no. 224, concerning Round. Maitland eventually did attack Round's willingness to castigate, in his review of Round's *Commune of London*, in *The Athenæum* 3756 (1899), 547–8; see further *Letters*, i. nos. 252, 264. Cf. *Letters*, i. no. 225, for Maitland being unhappy at the possibility of having upset Stubbs; also i. no. 115: 'Such is my admiration for Palgrave that I do not like saying anything that anybody, however perverse, could twist into blame'. For Austin's asperity of expression see below, 305.

Let us start with some of Maitland's letters to those intellectuals for whom he felt particular respect. To Sidgwick he wrote in 1888 that 'your dealings with Austin are very delightful to me, for the formal jurisprudent sits heavy upon us and you will deprive him of his terrors', and in 1899 that 'You once proposed to put the Austinian doctrine on the back of a postcard; and now will you not have to put that postcard behind the fire?'[19] To Leslie Stephen he wrote in 1900:

> I congratulate you heartily on coming out at the other end of the *Utilitarians*.... Especially I want to see what you say of Austin. Since I was here I wrote an article 'Hist. Engl. Law' for the *Encyclop. Britan.* and risked about Austin a couple of sentences which are not in accordance with common repute – and now I feel a little frightened. I don't want to be unjust, but I cannot see exactly where the greatness comes in.[20]

In *The English Utilitarians*, Stephen was critical of Austin, for example, regarding his definition of law and his failure to explain historical change.[21] Stephen's tone in general was less sharp than Maitland's, although he did write of Austin's London lectures that 'Austin thought it a duty to be as dry as Bentham, and discharged that duty scrupulously'.[22]

Most famous is a letter to Pollock about Maitland's proposed *Encyclopaedia Britannica* article, a letter already mentioned at the start of this paper: 'Qu. whether editor will suffer the few lines given to J. Austin: they amount to J. A. = 0'.[23] The editor did suffer the lines that Maitland gave to Austin, thereby providing a very public platform for his criticisms:

> Some credit for rousing an interest in law, in definitions of legal terms, and in schemes of codification, is due to John Austin (d. 1859) who was regarded as the jurist of the reforming and utilitarian group. But, though he was at times an acute dissector of confused thought, he was too ignorant of the English, the Roman and every other system of law to make any considerable addition to the sum of knowledge; and when Savigny, the herald of evolution, was already in the field, the day for a 'Nature-Right' – and Austin's projected 'general jurisprudence' would have

[19] *Letters*, i. no. 38 (quoted further, below, 324), 239.

[20] *Letters*, i. no. 258. *The Letters of Frederic William Maitland*, ii., ed. P. N. R. Zutshi (Selden Society, Supplementary Series, xi, London, 1995), no. 346, to C. S. Kenny: 'You have, I think, just the right amount of belief (a little more than I have) in Austin's methods to write a book that would be just what English people want and in a way you might save Austin's fame while you supplanted his book'. Note the mention here of concern with Austin's methods, as opposed to his learning.

[21] L. Stephen, *The English Utilitarians* (3 vols., London, 1900), iii. 322, 325–6, and more generally 317–34.

[22] Stephen, *English Utilitarians*, iii. 318.

[23] *Letters*, i. no. 253.

> been a Nature-Right – was past beyond recall. The obsolescence of the map of law which Blackstone had inherited from Hale, and in which many outlines were drawn by medieval formulas, left intelligent English lawyers without a guide, and they were willing to listen for a while to what in their insularity they thought to be the voice of cosmopolitan science. Little came of it all. The revived study of Germanic law in Germany, which was just beginning in Austin's day, seems to be showing that the scheme of Roman jurisprudence is not the scheme into which English law will run without distortion.[24]

Austin is occasionally mentioned by name elsewhere in Maitland's works, although there is very little extended discussion and the issues raised are limited. At times, it may be Maitland's silences that are telling, for example, the absence of reference to Austin in his 'Survey of the Century: Law'.[25] He mentioned Austin in his early dissertation on liberty and equality, but the remarks prompt no significant conclusions and it must be remembered that Maitland later wrote that his dissertation should have been 'wiped out'.[26] His most extended discussion of Austin comes in the lectures published posthumously as *The Constitutional History of England*. Unsurprisingly, given its subject, this discussion concentrates mainly on summarising and questioning Austin's view of sovereignty, but the implied criticisms extend more broadly.[27] Elsewhere, a passage in the *History of English Law* with a footnote to Austin is quite playful in the

[24] 'English Law (History)', in *Encyclopaedia Britannica* (11th edition, Cambridge, 1910), ix. 600–607, at 606.

[25] *The Collected Papers of Frederic William Maitland*, ed. H. A. L. Fisher (3 vols., Cambridge, 1911), iii. 432–9.

[26] 'A historical sketch of liberty and equality as ideals of English political philosophy from the time of Hobbes to the time of Coleridge', in *Collected Papers*, i. 1–161, at 4, 34; *Letters*, i. no. 255. I do not discuss statements in the Introduction to Pollock and Maitland, as most but 'not quite all' of it was Pollock's work; *The Pollock–Holmes Letters*, ed. M. DeWolfe Howe (2 vols., Cambridge, 1942), i. 60.

[27] *Constitutional History*, 526–7: 'I hope that I do not undervalue that study of general jurisprudence which holds the first place in the programme of the law tripos; still you will by this time have learnt enough to know that a classification of legal rules which suits the law of one country and one age will not necessarily suit the law of another country or of another age. One may perhaps force the rules into the scheme that we have prepared for them, but the scheme is not natural or convenient. Only those who know a great deal of English law are really entitled to have any opinion as to the limits of that part of the law which it is convenient to call constitutional'. Note also *Constitutional History*, 526: 'it seems to me that we cannot profitably define a department of law until we already know a good deal of its contents'; cf. below, 322, on 'comparative jurisprudence'. See *Collected Papers*, iii. 427–9, for Maitland's views on the stage of the Law degree at which 'general jurisprudence' might best be taught.

tone of its criticism: 'The theory urged by a modern writer, that "public law" is but a department of the "law of persons," however inapplicable to modern states, may sometimes be applied with advantage to the middle ages'.[28]

Further allusions, without explicit footnotes, are quite obviously to Austin, his writings or their influence. They mention 'general jurisprudence' or 'a speculative jurist's mind'. Some, for example in Maitland's Introduction to his translation of Gierke, are to the lack of historical dimension in Austin's work[29] or to the inapplicability of his classifications to the law of the past.[30] Others are to his definitions of terms such as 'right', 'positive morality' or 'law properly so called'.[31] And to Bigelow Maitland wrote in 1887:

> I send you a list of the Law Lectures delivered in this University. I am sorry to say that at present we have a great deal of Roman Law and of what is called General Jurisprudence in our scheme – but I hope that a projected alteration may give English law a fairer chance.[32]

The prominence of the teaching of 'General Jurisprudence' helps to explain Maitland's worries about the dominance of Austinian thought in the minds of the students to whom he lectured on constitutional history.

Were space more extensive, this might be the place to ask whether Maitland's interpretations of Austin were correct, whether his frustration

[28] Sir Frederick Pollock and F. W. Maitland, *The History of English Law before the Time of Edward I* (2nd edition; 2 vols., Cambridge, 1898; reissued with a new introduction by S. F. C. Milsom, Cambridge, 1968), i. 230.

[29] O. Gierke, *Political Theories of the Middle Age*, trans. with an introduction by F. W. Maitland (Cambridge, 1900), xi: 'to shew that our popular English *Staatslehre* if, instead of analysing the contents of a speculative jurist's mind, it seriously grasped the facts of English history, would shew some inclination to become a *Korporationslehre* also'.

[30] See, for example, F. W. Maitland, *The Forms of Action at Common Law*, eds. A. H. Chaytor and W. J. Whittaker (Cambridge, 1936), 62: 'to call an action based on covenant, or contractual right, a real or mixed action must of course seem very strange to students of "general jurisprudence"; but it was the logical result of making the distinction turn on the answer to the question whether the plaintiff demands land or damages or both'. At Pollock and Maitland, ii. 572, making the same point, he refers to 'the impatient student who looks down upon medieval law from the sublime heights of "general jurisprudence"'.

[31] See Pollock and Maitland, i. 361, quoted below, 325.

[32] *Letters*, i. no. 27. A further reason for Maitland being so critical of Austin may have been his concerns about pedagogical problems regarding 'general jurisprudence', and his wider worries about the standing of law as an academic subject in universities; see, for example, *Collected Papers*, iii. 419–31, and note S. Collini, *Public Moralists: Political and Intellectual Life in Britain 1850–1930* (Oxford, 1991), ch. 7.

with Austin led him into misinterpretation. Certainly, Austin has been defended up to the present day on issues such as his knowledge of Roman law and his sympathy for and understanding of Common Law.[33] However, I here limit myself to asking what were Maitland's criticisms of Austin and what these reveal about Maitland.

There were some elements in Austin which Maitland accepted, or which were common views accepted by both writers, or which became common views after Austin and were accepted by Maitland who would not have seen them as peculiarly Austinian. Although he raised some difficulties with aspects of Austin's distinction between law and morality, Maitland like other writers made full use of such a distinction. In the *Constitutional History*, he stated with regard to rules of governmental organisation that 'we must carefully distinguish between rules of law and rules which, however binding they may be considered, are not rules of law and could not be enforced by any legal proceedings'.[34] He also may have admired some of Austin's work on the clarification and classification of terms; as we have seen, in the *Encyclopaedia Britannica* article, he called Austin 'an acute dissector of confused thought'.[35]

Such praise was very much the exception. In assessing Maitland's hostility, I examine first his stated reasons, and then other possible explanations. Let us begin with the *Encyclopaedia Britannica*, where we find that the two main issues are Austin's lack of a historical perspective and his failings on matters of detail.

Mentions of history are not entirely absent from Austin's writings. He commented that 'the advantage of the study . . . of history considered as a preparative for the study of one's own particular system, is fully appreciated in Prussia'.[36] His *Lectures* included lengthy passages on the development of equity in Roman and, more briefly, in Common Law.[37] He very occasionally made more general statements about legal development, for example, that 'in almost all rude societies, the domain of Criminal Law is extremely narrow: and, for reasons which I shall shew hereafter, it generally enlarges as society advances'.[38] He even writes of 'the *historical* school of jurisprudence', but in a very revealing fashion:

[33] See below, 305–7.

[34] *Constitutional History*, 400. Note also, for example, Pollock and Maitland, i. 264, 297.

[35] See above, 296.

[36] *Lectures*, 1083; such study was to go along with that 'of common principles and distinctions'.

[37] *Lectures*, 576–620.

[38] *Lectures*, 405. On Austin and history, note also Rumble, *Doing Austin Justice*, 165–7.

> Bentham belongs strictly to the *historical* school of jurisprudence. The proper sense of that term as used by the Germans is, that the jurists so designated think that a body of law cannot be spun out from a few general principles assumed *à priori*, but must be founded on experience of the subjects and objects with which law is conversant. Bentham therefore manifestly belongs to this school. . . . The character of the historical school of jurisprudence in Germany is commonly misconceived. . . . The meaning of their being called the historical school is simply this, that they agree with Bentham in thinking that law should be founded on an experimental view of the subjects and objects of law, and should be determined by general utility, not drawn out from a few arbitrary assumptions *à priori* called the law of nature. A fitter name for them would be the *inductive* and *utilitarian* school.[39]

As well as affecting the way in which we pose questions about the relative influence upon Austin of his English and German predecessors[40] – and casting doubt upon Austin's open-mindedness in his reading the works of others – the passage suggests how limited was Austin's interest in historical law and in historical processes of legal development.[41]

This absence of the historical dimension is central to Maitland's critique. He mentions it in the *Encyclopaedia Britannica*: 'when Savigny, the herald of evolution, was already in the field, the day for a "Nature-Right" – and Austin's projected "general jurisprudence" would have been a Nature-Right – was past beyond recall'. Although not named, Austin is also the target in Maitland's Introduction to Gierke, where the influence of German writers is joined by that of Darwin:

> Let it be allowed that the State is a highly peculiar group-unit; still, it may be asked whether we ourselves are not the slaves of a jurist's theory and a little behind the age of Darwin if between the State and all other groups we fix an immeasurable gulf and ask ourselves no questions about the origin of species.[42]

39 *Lectures*, 679; note Morison, *John Austin*, 20, 92. See J. A. Burrow, *Evolution and Society: A Study in Victorian Social Theory* (Cambridge, 1966), 65, for J. S. Mill commenting in his autobiography that Austin returned from Germany and 'professed great disrespect for what he called the "universal principles of human nature of the political economists" and insisted on the evidence which history and daily experience afford of the "extraordinary pliability of human nature"'.

40 See M. Lobban, 'Austin and the Germans', in *The Legacy of John Austin's Jurisprudence*, eds. M. Freeman and P. Mindus (Dordrecht, 2013), 255–70; also Lobban, *Common Law*, 223, 229.

41 See also below, 314–15, for the issue of how general was Austin's 'general jurisprudence'.

42 Introduction to Gierke, *Political Theories*, ix; note also xviii on the German approach to concepts: 'in this work there was sometimes shewn a delicacy of touch and a subtlety of

From the mid-nineteenth century, as John Burrow and others have shown, across a wide range of areas of thought, greater emphasis was laid on history.[43] In some but not all cases, this involved focus on the particularities of historical periods, the examination of each for its own sake.[44] Such a focus was – or perhaps became – particularly clear in Maitland. In his early and highly entertaining essay on 'The Law of Real Property', published in the *Westminster Review* in 1879, he had examined the results of the past for the purposes of present reform:

> the question . . . for those who would limit the rights of property in land is, whether they would rather work in the dark or in the light; whether they would rather deal with a modern and reasonable system, capable of further improvement, or with a mass of old theories – once, perhaps, an organized whole, but long since fallen into decay.[45]

The same essay shows Maitland distinguishing his own approach and interests from those who in his eyes misused history:

> To any reader trained in the historical school now fashionable our arguments may savour of a narrow and frigid Utilitarianism long since abandoned by all enlightened persons. The law of real property is, we shall be told, an historical institution – the product of social evolution, of national life – and as such it must be criticised; nor must it be rashly condemned if it fail to conform to our notions of practical convenience. Now, it is but too probable that we are sadly deficient in the historic sense which it is the pride of this generation to have discovered in itself. It is not unlikely that we are behind an age whose chief ambition is to be behind itself.[46]

Anyone familiar with Maitland's use of irony will recognise that he is here fighting multiple distortions of history; proper knowledge of history might free the present generation from reverence for inherited law, allowing urgently needed reform.[47]

historical perception, of which in this country we, having no pressing need for comparisons, can know little, especially if our notion of an analytical jurisprudence is gathered from Austin's very "natural" exploits'.

43 See Burrow, *Evolution and Society*; also D. M. Rabban, *Law's History: American Legal Thought and the Transatlantic Turn to History* (Cambridge, 2013).

44 See Burrow, *Evolution and Society*, 67.

45 *Collected Papers*, i. 196–7.

46 *Collected Papers*, i. 194–5.

47 See *Collected Papers*, i. 189; 'a history, however interesting, is not a reason'. Note also esp. *Collected Papers*, iii. 439: 'Now-a-days we may see the office of historical research as that of explaining, and therefore lightening, the pressure that the past must exercise upon the present, and the present upon the future. To-day we study the day before yesterday, in order that yesterday may not paralyse to-day, and to-day may not paralyse to-morrow'.

Judgements on the influence of past legal developments are not absent from Maitland's later writings, including the *History of English Law*.[48] He continued to seek to uncover how inherited concepts, rules and procedures might either have changed from their original purpose or be no longer fit for any purpose, save perhaps obfuscation and lawyerly profit. However, such judgements ceased to predominate as they had in the *Westminster Review* article. The difference in part arises from the nature and purpose of that essay, but Maitland's way of thinking and writing about history may also have shifted, a development connected to his work on medieval sources and then his move from practice back to academic life in Cambridge. His desire to replace the false history assumed by lawyers only reinforced his main focus from *c.* 1880 onwards, to seek to understand his particular periods of study in themselves, and to show how developments in one period may explain later situations. The latter purpose is clear in his posthumously published lectures on the *Forms of Action*:

> What was a form of action? Already owing to modern reforms it is impossible to assume that every law student must have heard or read or discovered for himself an answer to that question, but it is still one which must be answered if he is to have more than a very superficial knowledge of our law as it stands even at the present day. The forms of action we have buried, but they still rule us from their graves.
>
> We have constantly to remember this, that an action instituted for one purpose in one age comes to be used for another purpose in another age.[49]

Survival could involve evolution as well as fossilisation.

[48] See, for example, Pollock and Maitland, ii. 1 'Our interest in the land law of Henry III's day, when we regard it as private law, will lie in this, that it is capable of becoming the land law of the England, the America, the Australia of the twentieth century'. Events and developments are praised or condemned: see, for example, ii. 363; 389 'when we weigh the merits of the medieval church and have remembered all her good deeds, we have to put into the other scale as a weighty counterpoise the incalculable harm done by a marriage law which was a maze of flighty fancies and misapplied logic'.); 407 ('lamentable'); 432 ('unfortunately'); 447; 453 ('the worst cruelties belong to a politer time'); 489 ('our law, if it had once been too severe, became much too mild'); 490 ('to our regret'); 534 ('defects in our nascent "law of torts"').

[49] *Forms of Action*, 1, 27. Note also, for example, *Forms of Action*, 13, 'the point now to be seized is that the history of the forms of action presupposes the background of ancient courts with their unprofessional judges, their formal, supernatural modes of proof'; 42, 'The king's courts had come to be regarded as omnicompetent courts, they had to do all the important civil justice of the realm and to do it with the limited supply of forms of action which had been gradually accumulated in the days when feudal justice and ecclesiastical justice were serious competitors with royal justice'.

Three related points can be identified in Maitland's attack on Austin's ahistoricism: Austin's general jurisprudence failed in describing and explaining the law of the past; it failed in describing and explaining legal development; and it therefore failed even in describing and explaining the law of the present.[50]

Austin's categorisations and definitions, according to Maitland, failed to fit the facts of the past.[51] In the thirteenth century, the law book known as *Bracton* stated that the king was to obey the law, but if he broke it, his punishment was to be left to God. 'Now', says Maitland in his *Constitutional History*:

> to a student fresh from Austin's jurisprudence this may seem an absurd statement. You put the dilemma, either the king is sovereign or no; if he be sovereign then he is not legally below the law, his obligation to obey the law is at most a moral obligation; on the other hand if he is below the law, then he is not sovereign, he is below some man or some body of men, he is bound for example to obey the commands of king and parliament, the true sovereign of the realm. This may be a legitimate conclusion if in Austin's way we regard all law as command; but it is very necessary for us to remember that the men of the thirteenth century had no such notion of sovereignty, had not clearly marked off legal as distinct from moral and religious duties, had not therefore conceived that in every state there must be some man or some body of men above all law.[52]

Austin did occasionally mention the need of historical knowledge for the understanding of past law: 'Feuds [i.e. fiefs] and the feudal system are really an exceedingly specific and purely historical notion, not to be got at by scientific speculation, but by diligent reading of the history of the middle ages'.[53] However, as this sentence suggests, he treated the historical specificity of such law as a reason to exclude it from his 'general

[50] Others attacked Austin on similar grounds; see, for example, H. Sidgwick, *The Elements of Politics* (2nd edition, London, 1897), Appendix (A); note his criticism of Austin on the grounds that his ideas did not work for societies of the past and are flawed and sometimes internally contradictory on contemporary societies; see also below, n. 82. Note also, for example, Pollock, *First Book of Jurisprudence*, 23–7, on history bringing into question whether there was any necessary association between law and state-imposed sanction; at 27 he concluded that 'Law is enforced by the State because it is law; it is not law merely because the State enforces it'.

[51] See also below, 317–18, on neglect of past thought.

[52] *Constitutional History*, 100–101. Note further especially Pollock and Maitland, i. 181–2; also *Collected Papers*, i. 3–4.

[53] *Lectures*, 850; note the comments of Lobban, *Common Law*, 235, Rumble, *Doing Austin Justice*, 83–4.

jurisprudence'.[54] This was unacceptable to Maitland, because the specifics were essential for understanding legal development, and legal development was of significance not just for past law but also for the present. Writing of the twelfth-century view that the tenant for a term of years did not have a free tenement, and therefore could not bring the assize of novel disseisin, he comments that when an alternative action was developed for the termor in the thirteenth century, 'it was too late to say that the termor had a free tenement or was a freeholder. This episode had important consequences; it rules the terminology of our law even at the present day'.[55]

To Maitland, Austin's lack of interest in the process of legal development would also have been manifest in the limited treatment of topics that Maitland himself considered central to law and legal history, topics also in some cases difficult to reconcile with Austin's general jurisprudence.[56] Most significant were matters of procedure and their relationship to developments in substantive law.[57] At the start of *The Forms of Action*, Maitland says:

> Let us remember one of Maine's most striking phrases, 'So great is the ascendancy of the Law of Actions in the infancy of the Courts of Justice, that substantive law has at first the look of being gradually secreted in the interstices of procedure'. Assuredly this is true of our real property law, it has been secreted in the interstices of the forms of action. The system of Forms of Action or the Writ System is the most important characteristic of English medieval law, and it was not abolished until its piecemeal destruction in the nineteenth century.[58]

Austin's lack of discussion of such issues, his apparent lack of interest in them, made his explanations in Maitland's eyes at most insufficient, more probably worthless: 'J.A. = 0'.

[54] Note Rumble, *Doing Austin Justice*, 32, 80–81.

[55] Pollock and Maitland, i. 358; see also below, 313.

[56] See also below, 310, on trusts and corporations.

[57] See also, for example, *Collected Papers*, i. 484, ii. 474, 476. On the significance of '"mere matters of procedure"' compared to 'what may seem the weightier matters of jurisprudence', note further Pollock and Maitland, ii. 673–4.

[58] *Forms of Action*, 1; at 63 he refers to this as Maine's 'good saying'. See also, for example, *Forms of Action*, 22, 'The formula of the Novel Disseisin contains terms which in course of time will give birth to a great deal of law'; 38, concerning the new writ *quare ejecit infra terminum*, 'there is no legislation, no intention to give a new right, merely a new remedy; but as you see the character of the old right is being changed, it is ceasing to be a merely contractual *jus in personam*'.

Maitland's second major accusation in the *Encyclopaedia Britannica* was that Austin was 'too ignorant of the English, the Roman and every other system of law to make any considerable addition to the sum of knowledge'.[59] This makes clear the value that Maitland attached to the factual products of research, but knowledge was valuable not simply in itself. Although not named, Austin is surely at least one of the objects of Maitland's withering comment that 'Our neighbours' conception of the province of jurisprudence has its advantages as well as its disadvantages. . . . [T]he theorising is often done by men who have that close grasp of concrete modern fact which comes of a minute and practical study of legal systems'.[60]

Given the extensive references to Roman law in the *Lectures*, Maitland's view may come as a surprise, and it also differed markedly from Austin's self-assessment. Austin praised Roman law – 'Turning from the study of the English to the study of the Roman law, you escape from the empire of chaos and darkness, to a world which seems by comparison, the region of order and light'[61] – and was proud of his study of it:

> This is not a hasty surmise, but the result of a careful and ample induction, founded on a most diligent study of the Institutes of Gaius and of Justinian, and an attentive perusal of the Pandects or Digest of the latter. Nor is this opinion confined to myself; otherwise I should, of course, feel much less confidence in its correctness. But I share it with such men as Thibaut and Feuerbach, men of indefatigable perseverance and of a sagacity never surpassed.[62]

In Austin's view, failure to study Roman law helped to explain failings of even the greatest of thinkers:

> If Bentham had ever given to Roman law the attention it well deserves, he would have found that his own distinction [between general and special codes] precisely tallied with that [between the law of things and the law of persons] which he rejects with unmeasured and what, in spite of my veneration for Mr. Bentham, I must call *ignorant*, disdain.[63]

Given Maitland's greater willingness to criticise those whom he considered harsh critics, one must wonder whether this sentence explains Maitland's own use of the word 'ignorant' with reference to Austin in the *Encyclopaedia Britannica.*

[59] See above, 296. Cf. Pollock to writing to Holmes in 1899: 'I am a little bit disappointed that you only say Austin did not know *enough* law'; *Pollock–Holmes Letters*, i. 94.

[60] *Collected Papers*, iii. 315–16. [61] *Lectures*, 58. [62] *Lectures*, 383–4.

[63] *Lectures*, 692.

How are we to judge among these conflicting assessments of Austin's Roman learning? Details of Austin's studies of the subject are limited, but he certainly was working on Roman law at least at an elementary level in 1821–2, with John Stuart Mill as his pupil, and in Bonn in 1827–8.[64] He had an extensive library of relevant works. It included an 1823 copy of the *Institutes of Gaius*, edited by Goeschen, a copy he is said to have annotated extensively. This work is particularly prominent in the footnotes to Austin's *Lectures*, a prominence presumably influenced by the excitement that the recent publication of *Gaius* had generated. Andrew Lewis has concluded that 'Austin's grasp and interest in Roman law was considerable, going beyond what might have been found elsewhere in England at the time'.[65]

However, Maitland's comment, if perhaps overstated, remains explicable, especially if Austin's Roman learning is judged from the viewpoint of the 1890s rather than the 1820s or 1830s. Austin probably seemed over-reliant on modern writers on Roman law, curiously limited in his use of the *Digest*.[66] This in turn may have restricted his appreciation of the methods of Roman jurists and have led him to overemphasise the systematisation of Roman law.[67] What we cannot tell from Maitland's explicit statements is whether he was aware of, or himself had uncovered, errors in Austin's Roman learning.[68]

64 A. Lewis, '"Darkening the fair face of Roman law": Austin and Roman Law', in *Legacy of John Austin's Jurisprudence*, eds. Freeman and Mindus, 41–9, at 42–5; M. H. Hoeflich, *Roman and Civil Law and the Development of Anglo-American Jurisprudence in the Nineteenth Century* (Athens, GA, 1997), 11–13; Morison, *John Austin*, 19–20.

65 Lewis, 'Austin and Roman Law', 49.

66 Note Hoeflich, *Roman and Civil Law*, 13, 43; cf. Lewis, 'Austin and Roman Law', 41.

67 Note *Lectures*, 1081: 'I by no means mean to put the study of Roman Law on a level in point of importance with that of the Aristotelic Logic (for the Roman Law is not *necessary*): but in the respect now under consideration, it bears the same relation to law and morals, which the school logic bears to philosophy'. Hoeflich, *Roman and Civil Law*, 11–26, 45, 48, argues that the main influence of Roman and Civil Law on Austin was regarding method and arrangement rather than substance; Austin, he suggests, used such law as an 'ordering principle'. Any such ordering principle must clearly have a strong conceptual element, in this case founded on Roman law.

68 See Lewis, 'Austin and Roman Law', 49, for an example of a weakness in Austin's use of Roman law. Note *Lectures*, 499–500, for Austin correcting himself on a point of Roman law made in his previous lecture. The degree to which Maitland accepted all aspects of Austin's defintion of the distinction between *jus in rem* and *jus in personam* (e.g. *Lectures*, 369–71) is uncertain; he would certainly have been worried by the discussion of the subject at *Lectures*, 786–7, where Austin stated that 'the right of the master, against third parties, to his slave, servant, or apprentice, is a right *in rem* over or to a *person* [as opposed to over or to a thing]'. I would like to thank Magnus Ryan for his advice on this point. Cf. Austin's

What then of English law?[69] Austin's *Lectures* may on occasion lose some of the reader's confidence in the author's grasp of Common Law, with statements such as 'there are (I think) cases of this kind in our own law, though I cannot at this instant recall them'.[70] Maitland will certainly have picked up errors in Austin's treatment of English law of the past,[71] and may also have been worried by some of Austin's treatment of the law of his own time.[72]

Austin's lack of factual knowledge and his lack of historical awareness were related weaknesses in Maitland's eyes. Maitland was emphatic on the lack of determinacy in legal development; historical detail and historical process could be crucially connected.[73] Precise and extensive knowledge was therefore necessary for explanation. Sometimes this related to history outside law,[74] sometimes to internal legal development. Thus, in his essay on 'The Law of Real Property', he wrote, 'Our distinction between the two kinds of property [real and personal] is not to be explained by any jural necessity, it is the outcome of a long chapter of accidents'.[75] In his lectures on *The Forms of Action*, he looked at the relationship and development of the actions of mort d'ancestor and aiel, besaiel and cosinage, and commented that 'the story is instructive; it illustrates what I may call the irrational element in the history of the forms of action, the element of chance in legal history'.[76]

definitions with, for example, B. Nicholas, *An Introduction to Roman Law* (Oxford, 1962), 100. Maitland exaggerated the degree of his own ignorance of Roman law; see, for example, *Letters*, ii. no. 37.

[69] See below, 313–14, on Austin's overall attitude to Common Law.

[70] *Lectures*, 505. Note also *Lectures*, 500, for Austin correcting himself on a point of English law made in his previous lecture. Austin, of course, did not prepare the *Lectures* for publication; his hesitations and self-corrections may have worried a reader of the publish text more than they had a listener to the original lecture.

[71] *Lectures*, 530, on Bracton (also corrected in a footnote by the editor of the fifth edition of the *Lectures*).

[72] Note Austin, *Lectures*, 795, treating estates for life and leases for terms of years together; here his definition of property allows him to over-rule a distinction that Maitland would have considered important; cf. above, 304. For estates for life and leases for years, note, for example, J. Williams, *Principles of the Law of Real Property* (London, 1845), 5–10; R. Preston, *An Elementary Treatise on Estates* (2 vols., London, 1820–27). I would like to thank Professor Stuart Anderson for advice on this point.

[73] Note also *Letters*, ii. no. 3. [74] See, for example, Pollock and Maitland, i. 80.

[75] *Collected Papers*, i. 171.

[76] *Forms of Action*, 25. The unpredictability of legal development might produce apparent paradox, for example, with both jury and parliament starting, in Maitland's views, as royal tools not guardians of freedom; see, for example, Pollock and Maitland, i. 142, on the jury. Note also, for example, Pollock and Maitland, i. 253: 'just while it is becoming little

So far I have concentrated on Maitland's criticisms explicit in the *Encyclopaedia Britannica* article, but there are others that further explain the strength of his rejection of Austin. Maitland criticised central elements in Austin's definition of positive law as command emanating from a sovereign distinct from a body of people habitually obedient to it. Thus, particularly in his Introduction to his translation of Gierke and in his lectures on *Constitutional History*, Maitland commented adversely on Austin's view of sovereignty.[77] In part his objections were philosophical, as in the following passage where Maitland was clearly siding with Gierke:

> it will be gathered also that the set of thoughts about Law and Sovereignty into which Englishmen were lectured by John Austin appears to Dr Gierke as a past stage. For him Sovereignty is an attribute, not of some part of the State, but of the *Gesammtperson*, the whole organized community. For him it is as impossible to make the State logically prior to the Law (*Recht*) as to make Law logically prior to the State, since each exists in, for and by the other.[78]

Such objections challenged Austin's view of the relationship of sovereignty and law.

Other objections were more factual, questioning Austin's view of where sovereignty lies, which may, but need not necessarily, have implications for the relationship of law and sovereignty.[79] We have already seen Maitland take issue with application of Austin's notion of sovereignty to the past,[80] but he was also unconvinced by the arguments relating to the present. He found that sovereign powers did not and probably could not act as an Austinian sovereign should:

> Even the right or power to impose taxes [on colonies] has never been abandoned, though it is not exercised. Students of Austin's Jurisprudence may find some interest in noticing this case: the sovereign body habitually refrains from making laws of a certain class and must suspect that if it made such laws they would not be obeyed.[81]

better than a misnomer to speak of military tenure, the law about military tenure is being evolved, but as a part rather of our private than of our public law'.

77 *Encyclopaedia Britannica*, 603, mentions Austin on sovereignty, but without very significant comment; Austin is paired with Hobbes.

78 Introduction to Gierke, *Political Theories*, xliii; see below, n. 173, for the passage that follows this quotation, and below, 310, on trusts and corporations. Note also Morison, *John Austin*, 3.

79 Note *Constitutional History*, 530.

80 See above, 303. Note also, for example, Pollock and Maitland, ii. 3.

81 *Constitutional History*, 339.

The last sentence clearly plays on, and questions, Austin's notion of the habit of obedience in relation to sovereignty.

The issue of the habit of obedience may also have increased Maitland's worries regarding Austin's inclusion of the electors of the members of the House of Commons within the sovereign body. He may have thought it an inconsistency: could a group of people in one aspect be sovereign, in another have a habit of obedience to the sovereign? One strongly suspects that Maitland endorsed Sidgwick's comment that 'Austin's statements on this point appear to me hopelessly confused and inconsistent'.[82] Furthermore, the inclusion of the electors in the sovereign body did not seem to match reality. In his *Constitutional History*, Maitland tells his audience:

> Now Austin himself had, as I daresay you know, a curious doctrine about the sovereignty of this realm; instead of holding that the sovereign body consisted of the king, the lords and the representatives of the commons assembled in parliament, he held that it consisted of the king, the lords and the electors: he treats the members of the House of Commons as mere delegates of the electors. This seems to me a singularly profitless speculation. Suppose that the present parliament were to make a statute contrary to the strongest wishes and well-founded expectations of those who elected it; doubtless the statute would be law; the courts would treat it as law and would not for one instant permit a suggestion that parliament had exceeded its power by betraying (if you will) the trust that was imposed on it.[83]

At least for constitutional matters, Maitland preferred an approach that might be seen as containing 'legal realist' elements, and certainly one that regards law as a prediction of outcome. A telling passage in the *Constitutional History* begins: 'We have then to distinguish at every step what is matter of law, from what is not matter of law, from what is a

[82] Sidgwick, *Elements of Politics*, 29 n. 2; see further 27–9 for criticism of Austin's views of sovereignty as too simple and not matching reality. At 29, Sidgwick states that 'while I adopt substantially Austin's conception of the relation of Law to Government, as applied to the civil law of a modern political community in its latest stage, I prefer in stating it to avoid the difficulties of Austin's notion of sovereignty. The question "where supreme power ultimately resides" is one that it is most important to ask with regard to any political society: but it is a question to which, in my opinion, any simple general answer is liable to be misleading'.

[83] *Constitutional History*, 530; the criticism of Austin continues throughout this long paragraph. See Rumble, *Doing Austin Justice*, 235–7, for Bryce's criticism of Austin's treatment of sovereignty: Austin's view failed to fit the facts, and most sovereigns past or present were not unlimited.

matter of custom or convention'. Such an approach may seem thoroughly Austinian. However, Maitland continues:

> The two are intimately intertwined; as Mr Dicey has shown in his excellent lectures on the Constitution . . . the customs or conventions of our constitution derive their force, a force which is often felt to be quite as strong as the force of law, from the fact that they are so much mixed up with law that they could hardly be violated without a violation of law. We must therefore keep this distinction before us, and whenever we come to a rule ask ourselves whether it be law or no, ask ourselves what would happen if it were broken – would anybody be punished, and if so how, or would there merely be a general outcry that a departure had been made from sound constitutional precedent?[84]

Note that the closing question is not whether anyone in theory should or could be punished, but whether anyone in reality would be.[85]

Moreover, Maitland was unconvinced that the command view of law was universally applicable. Rather, where it existed, it was the product of history:

> From the Norman Conquest onwards, England seems marked out as the country in which men, so soon as they begin to philosophise, will endeavour to prove that all law is the command of a 'sovereign one', or a 'sovereign many'. They may be somewhat shocked when in the seventeenth century Hobbes states this theory in trenchant terms and combines it with many unpopular doctrines. But the way for Hobbes had been prepared of old. In the days of Edward I the text-writer whom we call Britton had put the common law into the king's mouth: all legal rules might be stated as royal commands.[86]

Nor could the sovereign command view explain how elements of law emerged from the practices of communities, notably elements such as trusts and corporations, central to Maitland's writings particularly in the last decade of his life.[87]

84 *Constitutional History*, 342; the passage that follows the one quoted is also of considerable relevance. See A. V. Dicey, *Introduction to the Study of the Law of the Constitution* (8th edition, London, 1915), 68–74, for criticism of Austin on sovereignty.

85 Note also *Pollock–Holmes Letters*, i. 3 (Pollock to Holmes in 1876): 'On the notice anent Austin, I thoroughly agree that the only definition of law for a lawyer's purposes is something which the Court will enforce'. Maitland too must have been aware of Holmes' views.

86 *Collected Papers*, ii. 481; however, compare this passage with that cited above, 303, and below, 325, on thirteenth-century views of law.

87 See, for example, F. W. Maitland, *State, Trust and Corporation*, eds. D. Runciman and M. Ryan (Cambridge, 2003); *Letters*, i. no. 366; Introduction to Gierke, *Political Theories*, xxx–xxxii, xxxviii; Pollock and Maitland, i. 669–71.

Related to this is Maitland's concern with Austin's views of custom and judge-made law, which Austin sometimes called 'judiciary law'. Again there is potential inconsistency in Austin's statements. Sometimes he was very clear in his preference for legislation: 'no judicious or candid man will doubt or dispute for a moment, that a well-made statute is incomparably superior to a rule of judiciary law'.[88] Elsewhere, however, he expressed the view that, in practice, judge-made law could be better than legislation, and perhaps by implication better than poor legislation:

> I cannot understand how any person who has considered the subject can suppose that society could possibly have gone on if judges had not legislated, or that there is any danger whatever in allowing that power which they have in fact exercised, to make up for the negligence or the incapacity of the avowed legislator. That part of the law of every country which was made by judges has been far better made than that part which consists of statutes enacted by the legislature.[89]

It was in part through judges that custom could, in Austin's terms, become law properly so called:

> a merely *moral*, or merely customary rule, may take the quality of a *legal* rule in two ways: – it may be adopted by a sovereign or subordinate legislature, and turned into a law in the direct mode; or it may be taken as a ground of a judicial decision, which afterwards obtains as a precedent; and in this case it is converted into a law after the judicial fashion. In whichever of these ways it becomes a legal rule, the law into which it is turned emanates from the sovereign or subordinate legislature or judge, which transmutes the moral or imperfect rule into a legal or perfect one.[90]

In this sense, 'customs constitute a distinct species of law, custom, or the persons with whom the custom originated, are authors or sources of law',

[88] *Lectures*, 661.

[89] *Province*, ed. Rumble, 163, forming part of the closing passage of a long note appended to *Lecture* V. See further Lobban, 'Austin and the Germans', 263–6, *Oxford History*, XI, 86–7, 90.

[90] *Lectures*, 536. See further, for example, *Province*, ed. Rumble, 36, 141; *Lectures*, 538: 'Law styled customary, then, is not to be considered a distinct kind of law. It is nothing but judiciary law founded on an anterior custom. As *merely* customary law (in the loose and improper sense of the term law), or rather as *merely* positive morality, it comes immediately from the subject members of the community by whom it was observed spontaneously or without compulsion by the State; but *as positive law*, it comes immediately from the Sovereign or subordinate judges who transmute the moral and imperfect into legal and perfect rules'. On Austin's view of the role of judges in the development of Common Law norms, note also Lobban, *Common Law*, 242–3, concluding that 'Austin was thus clearly aware of the nature of common law adjudication and its method of abstracting rules from circumstance'.

although the sovereign was the ultimate author of all law.[91] In this process lawyers too had an important part, and Austin wrote of 'law originating in custom, or floating traditionally amongst lawyers (as in England it is well known that there is much law constantly manufacturing at the bar, which in time is adopted by the judges, and by them again emitted to the bar)'.[92]

Two related arguments are essential for Austin to reconcile these positions with the sovereign command model of law. First, judges are delegates of the sovereign: 'the portion of the sovereign power which lies at [the judge's] disposition is merely delegated. The rules which he makes derive their legal force from authority given by the state: an authority which the state may confer expressly, but which it commonly imparts in the way of acquiescence'.[93] Second, the notion of delegation has to be broad. The following quotation primarily concerns subordinate legislatures, but must also apply to judges:

> The power of subordinate legislation granted to a subordinate legislature, is conferred by the sovereign legislature expressly or tacitly. If it be granted or admitted by written or oral declaration, it is conferred by the sovereign *expressly*. The sovereign confers it *tacitly*, by any conduct (not consisting in such declaration) which necessarily supposes that he acknowledges or admits it. For example, if he enforce a law made by a subordinate legislature, or permits his Courts of Justice to enforce that law, his positive or negative conduct necessarily supposes that he acknowledges a power of legalisation in the immediate author of the law.[94]

The idea of tacit conferment allows non-intervention to signify delegation. Maitland and others were unconvinced: the argument was both conceptually flawed and descriptively misleading.[95]

[91] *Lectures*, 510–11.

[92] *Lectures*, 513. Note also, for example, *Lectures*, 544, 546–7, 634–5. See further Lobban, 'Austin and the Germans', 265.

[93] *Province*, ed. Rumble, 35. [94] *Lectures*, 521–2.

[95] Sir Frederick Pollock, 'Law and Command', *Law Magazine* 1 (1872), 189–205, at 198: 'If we once admit that the sovereign has nothing to do with making the custom into law beyond a general silent assent, then it is surely the better way to refer the validity of the custom at once to the assent of those who made it, for after all the existence and power of the sovereign depend directly or indirectly . . . on the assent of the nation, and when the nation, or some part of it, makes a rule to itself by a gradual and indefinite consent, it seems hardly needful to suppose that such consent becomes operative by a feigned transmission through the sovereign'. For other late nineteenth-century criticisms of Austin's position see *Oxford History*, XI, 126–7. Note further Morison, *John Austin*, 3. For Maitland on sources of jurisdiction in medieval England see below, 325–6.

We have now looked at Maitland's main stated grounds for his criticism of Austin, but others can be explored. I leave until the conclusion of the paper the issue of what might be described as Maitland's intellectual temperament. There may also have been some general differences of belief, for example, on the positions that Austin gave to the principle of utility and to God.[96] However, I here limit myself to human law.

Maitland felt that Austin's 'general jurisprudence' neglected law's organic nature. To his students, Maitland said the following:

> Writers on general jurisprudence are largely concerned with the classification of legal rules. This is a very important task, and to their efforts we owe a great deal . . . But do not get into the way of thinking of law as consisting of a number of independent compartments, one of which is labelled constitutional, another administrative, another criminal, another property, so that you can learn the contents of one compartment and know nothing as to what is in the others. No, law is a body, a living body, every member of which is connected with and depends upon every other member. There is no science which deals with the foot, or the hand, or the heart. Science deals with the body as a whole, and with every part of it as related to the whole.[97]

He made the same point as to the relationship of past and present law:

> When we speak of a body of law, we use a metaphor so apt that it is hardly a metaphor. We picture to ourselves a being that lives and grows, that preserves its identity while every atom of which it is composed is subject to a ceaseless process of change, decay, and renewal. At any given moment of time – for example, in the present year – it may, indeed, seem to us that our legislators have, and freely exercise, an almost boundless power of doing what they will with the laws under which we live; and yet we know that, do what they may, their work will become an organic part of an already existing system.[98]

A related point is that Maitland may have taken statements in Austin's writings as showing him out of sympathy with Common Law as it was in reality. Thus Austin wrote:

96 See *Province*, for example, 13, 14, 80 and *Lectures* II and IV. On Austin and religion see L. Hamburger and J. Hamburger, *Troubled Lives: John and Sarah Austin* (Toronto, 1985), 41–2, 170–71; on God in his legal thought, note, for example, W. E. Rumble, 'Nineteenth-Century Perceptions of John Austin: Utilitarianism and the Reviews of The Province of Jurisprudence Determined', *Utilitas* 3 (1991), 199–216, at 210–15. For Maitland and Christianity see, for example, *Letters*, i. no. 437.

97 *Constitutional History*, 539.

98 *Collected Papers*, ii. 417. Note also Pollock and Maitland, ii. 561, on the forms of action.

> I will venture to affirm, that no other body of Law, obtaining in a civilized community, has so little of consistency and symmetry as our own. Hence its enormous bulk; and (what is infinitely worse than its mere bulk) the utter impossibility of conceiving it with distinctness and precision. If you would know the English Law, you must know all the details which make up the mess. For it has none of those large *coherent* principles which are a sure *index* to details. And since details are infinite, it is manifest that no man (let his industry be what it may) can compass the whole system. Consequently, the knowledge of an English Lawyer, is nothing but a beggarly account of scraps and fragments. His memory may be stored with numerous particulars, but of the Law as a whole, and of the mutual relations of its parts, he has not a conception.[99]

Critical as Maitland could be of aspects of Common Law, this passage may have suggested to him that Austin was unwilling to understand how Common Law worked. Its tone differs from, for example, Maitland's view of English real property law as 'archaism tempered by metaphysics'.[100] In addition, Austin's criticisms of Common Law may have struck Maitland as incompatible with Austin's profession that his subject was law as it is, rather than law as it should be.[101] Just as Austin's general jurisprudence could omit elements of past law as particularities of history, sometimes the nature of Common Law could likewise allow its exclusion.[102]

A further problem, then, is the aptness, the very possibility, of 'general jurisprudence'. Once more there are some possible inconsistencies in Austin's writings. His normal position is clear:

> I mean . . . by General Jurisprudence, the science concerned with the exposition of the principles, notions, and distinctions which are common to systems of law: understanding by systems of law, the ampler and maturer systems which, by reason of their amplitude and maturity, are pre-eminently pregnant with instruction.[103]

[99] *Lectures*, 467–8; note the comments on this passage in Rumble, *Doing Austin Justice*, 95–6. The extent of Austin's sympathy for Common Law has been debated, and his attitude to current English law and to the ideal workings of Common Law seems ambivalent; the assessment of Austin's attitude to Common Law, for example, in Lobban, *Oxford History*, XI, 72–3, is more sympathetic than was Maitland's.

[100] 'Two Lectures Delivered by F.W. Maitland', *Cambridge Law Journal* 24 (1966), 54–74, at 67.

[101] Note also Rumble, *Doing Austin Justice*, 96; Morison, *John Austin*, 2. For Austin's criticising English law see also, for example, *Lectures*, 601, on bringing suit: 'In England, the mess of complication and absurdity is somewhat thicker than it was in ancient Rome'.

[102] Note *Lectures*, 488.

[103] *Lectures*, 1073. He recognised that such a limitation of 'Universal Jurisprudence' involved a 'verbal impropriety' (see Rumble, *Doing Austin Justice*, 31); one may feel that this is not the type of 'verbal impropriety' that Austin would have passed over in arguments

However, as the last clause indicates, the concentration on 'ampler and maturer systems' was at least partly because they provided clearer materials, not because all the principles and distinctions of general jurisprudence were peculiar to those systems. Elsewhere Austin stated that some are 'common to all systems; – to the scanty and crude systems of rude societies, and the ampler and maturer systems of refined communities'.[104] Maitland considered that a jurisprudence only applying to certain sorts of legal system could not be regarded as general.[105] He also differed from Austin on the degree of similarity between legal systems. Thus, Austin confidently wrote:

> so numerous . . . are the principles common to systems of law, that a lawyer who has mastered the law which obtains in his country, has mastered implicitly most of the substance of law which obtains in any other community. So that the difficulty with which a lawyer, versed in the law of his own country, apprehends the law of another, is rather the result of differences between the terms of the systems, rather than of substantial or real differences between their maxims and rules.[106]

Maitland considered such views misguided.[107] In the *Encyclopaedia Britannica* he wrote that 'the revived study of Germanic law in Germany, which was just beginning in Austin's day, seems to be showing that the scheme of Roman jurisprudence is not the scheme into which English law will run without distortion'. Apparent similarities between systems, for example, similarities of vocabulary, might be deceptive: 'On the whole the lesson of this part of our legal history should be that it is very dangerous to play with foreign terms unless we know very well what we are about'.[108]

Finally, therefore, let us contrast Austin and Maitland's attitudes to language. Austin was very willing to dispense with common usage, or even normal legal usage, in favour of precise terminology based on his own definitions; phrases such as 'so called' and 'properly speaking' abound.[109]

proposed by others. He might well have seen it as indicating an argument flawed not only in its expression.

104 *Lectures*, 1072. Note the comments of Rumble, *Doing Austin Justice*, 84, and more generally at 157–60.

105 See above, 297, 303–4, below, 319.

106 *Lectures*, 1085; also see, for example, 1081.

107 See, for example, Pollock and Maitland, ii. 40–41, 44. Note also the editor's comment on a specific point in *Lectures*, 838–9.

108 *Forms of Action*, 63; cf. Maine, below, 322. See also below, 318.

109 See above, 298; see also, for example, *Province*, ed. Rumble, 11; *Lectures*, 523, 524, 746. For Austin's view that difficulties arise from vagueness of definition see, for example, *Province*, ed. Rumble, 176.

However, he was not entirely consistent in this respect, muddying some arguments by allowing looser classification or taking into consideration frequent usage.[110] More worrying to Maitland would have been Austin's happiness with overruling ordinary usage even when that usage might be significant, and with choosing a single definition even when it did not reflect legal usage;[111] Austin thereby ignored usage that might reveal thinking. This reflected another element of Austin's ahistoricism, his privileging of his own analytic framework over that of the laws he was seeking to explain.[112]

Furthermore, Austin himself found that terminological precision had limits.[113] Admitting that common usage might employ the word 'law' for a specific rather than a general order, he ended the particular discussion with the sentence 'and hence the difficulty of drawing a distinct boundary between laws and occasional commands'.[114] He also had to admit that words might be used with a broad or, by implication, a narrow signification: 'Every *law* or *rule* (taken with the largest signification which can be given to the term *properly*) is a *command*. Or, rather, laws or rules, properly so called, are a *species* of commands'.[115] Unsurprisingly, but unfortunately, he does not discuss the broad and the narrow signification of the term 'properly', thereby abandoning his quest for precision. Similarly, definition might produce distinctions that later had to be overridden in the process of arranging arguments. Thus, having carefully distinguished laws properly so called from improper laws, he found at the start of the fifth lecture of the *Province* that he had to 'distribute laws or rules under two classes: First, laws properly so called, with such improper laws as are closely analogous to the proper; second, those improper laws which are remotely analogous to the proper'; note again the use of

110 *Province*, ed. Rumble, 31: 'Acts on the part of legislatures to *explain* positive law, can scarcely be called laws, in the proper signification of the term.... But, this notwithstanding, they are frequently styled laws; *declaratory* laws, or declaratory statutes. They must, therefore, be noted as forming an exception to the proposition "that laws are a species of commands"'. Here Austin has created a problem for himself by pulling back from the idea that such explanatory matter cannot be properly called laws, taking common usage into account, and therefore having to declare them an exception to his definition of laws properly-so-called. Note also, for example, *Province*, ed. Rumble, 19.

111 See, for example, *Lectures*, 440. Note the discussion in Rumble, *Doing Austin Justice*, 87–9, 156–7.

112 Cf. Maitland's approach, below, 317–18.

113 See, for example, *Province*, ed. Rumble, 173; Lobban, *Common Law*, 234–5; Morison, *John Austin*, 77, 90.

114 *Province*, ed. Rumble, 26.

115 *Province*, ed. Rumble, 21.

qualifiers – this time 'closely' and 'remotely' – that indicate the range of a term or classification.[116]

Maitland had a very different attitude to language. He was unwilling to set aside the language of the laws and the people he was studying; sympathetic engagement with such language was essential if one was to make 'the thoughts of our forefathers . . . thinkable once more'.[117] Therefore:

> we ought to hesitate long before we condemn Bracton, and those founders of the common law whose spokesman he was, for calling the tenant in demesne an owner and proprietor of an immovable thing. Only three courses were open to them: (1) to deny that any land in England is owned: (2) to ascribe the ownership of the whole country to the king: (3) to hold that an owner is nonetheless an owner because he and his land owe services to the king or to some other lord. We can hardly doubt that they were right in choosing the third path; the second plunges into obvious falsehood; the first leads to a barren paradox.[118]

He sought not single definitions, single proper usages, but an awareness of variety and flexibility of signification: 'The one word *dominium* has to assume so many shades of meaning'.[119] This was true at any one time, and across time.

To explain the past as comprehensibly and as accurately as possible required an interplay between past vocabulary and modern terminology.[120] There was no simple solution. Modern terminology might fail in a particular instance: 'though it may be impossible for us to explain the distinction [between manor and vill] by any general terms of modern jurisprudence, it existed'.[121] Or use of modern classification might be apologetic in tone: 'though this distinction is one that we make, rather than one that we find made for us'.[122] Or it might be playful: 'we shall, for example, pass

116 *Province*, ed. Rumble, 15, and note also 157.

117 F. W. Maitland, *Domesday Book and Beyond* (Cambridge, 1897), 520.

118 Pollock and Maitland, ii. 4–5. Note also, for example, Pollock and Maitland, i. 438. Maitland's efforts to understand past views may be compared with the rather hectoring tone that Austin sometimes adopted; see, for example, *Lectures*, 540, on a passage of Julian in the *Digest* concerning custom being positive law: 'without pausing to analyse the passage, I shall briefly remark on a few of the errors with which it overflows'.

119 Pollock and Maitland, ii. 4. Note also, for example, Pollock and Maitland, ii. 31, 33–4, on seisin.

120 See further J. G. H. Hudson, 'Maitland and Anglo-Norman Law', in *The History of English Law: Centenary Essays on 'Pollock and Maitland'*, ed. J. G. H. Hudson (Oxford for the British Academy, 1996), 21–46, at 32–4. Note also, for example, Pollock and Maitland, ii. 1, 34–5, 255–6, 260, 453, 598.

121 Pollock and Maitland, i. 608.

122 Pollock and Maitland, ii. 1.

backwards and forwards between civil and criminal procedure, just because most modern writers have sedulously kept them apart'.[123] 'Whether [*Bracton*] would have ascribed "absolute ownership" we do not know. Might he not have asked whether in such a context "absolute" is anything better than an unmeaning expletive?'[124] Thoughts and practices must be teased from language and definition, with anachronism to be minimised but still inevitable.

Austin seems to have held that language, with sufficient care, could be forced to give precisely the meaning that he wanted. Maitland's attitude was very different: 'language is no mere instrument which we can control at will; it controls us'.[125] Maitland was writing before Wittgenstein and the other great linguistic theorists of the twentieth century. However, it does seem significant that he found a weakness in Austin's belief in the precision of language, a weakness which was going to form one point of entry for H. L. A. Hart's critique in *The Concept of Law*, a critique inspired by a later and rather different John or J. L. Austin.[126]

II. Maitland and Maine

Maitland's views of Austin can be illuminated by his response to Maine. It is a simplification but not a falsehood to say that many who reacted against Austin looked to Maine instead.[127] As Leslie Stephen wrote in his book on *The English Utilitarians*, 'Austin's star set as Maine's rose'.[128] Some sought to reconcile the arguments of Austin and Maine by taking the former as applicable to the end-point of the legal development about which the latter wrote, but others questioned even this possibility. For Stephen, it was clear that the two methods ought to be 'correlative rather than antagonistic. . . . A sound theory of origins and growth should be perfectly compatible with a sound theory of the actual order. But whether the two systems actually present that harmony is another

[123] Pollock and Maitland, ii. 573 n. 7. [124] Pollock and Maitland, ii. 6.

[125] Pollock and Maitland, i. 87. Maitland is here talking about the effect of the coming of French with the Norman conquerors, but probably the passage concerned and certainly Maitland's other statements allow the broad interpretation that I here give to the quotation.

[126] See H. L. A. Hart, *The Concept of Law* (Oxford, 1961), esp. 13–17, 121–32, 234.

[127] For possibilities other than the choice between Austin and Maine see, for example, Lobban, 'Legal Theory', 560–4, for natural law.

[128] Stephen, *English Utilitarians*, 320.

question'.[129] Maine himself may have been willing to consider that Austin's ideas might apply to developed legal systems,[130] but criticised his lack of historical perspective and hence the lack of universality of his 'general jurisprudence'.[131]

Maitland sometimes praised Maine in public and in print. We have already heard him quote Maine's 'good saying' about substantive law being secreted in the 'interstices' of procedure.[132] In his inaugural lecture he spoke:

> Of the great man [Maine] who when that science [of comparative jurisprudence] exists will be honoured as its prophet, and its herald, of the great man whom we have lost, may I say this? – His wonderful modesty, his dislike of all that looked like parade or pedantry, the fascination of his beautiful style are apt to conceal the width and depth of his reading. He was much more than learned, but then he was learned, very learned in law of all sorts and kinds. It is only through learning wide and deep, tough and technical, that we can safely approach those world-wide questions that he raised or criticize the answers that he found for them.[133]

Yet such praise contrasts with much else Maitland said of Maine: it may be that the public stage led him to emphasise the positive elements of his opinion; it may also be that his own further work led him to modify his view of Maine. His criticisms can be split into three elements: mistakes on matters of detail; weaknesses in Maine's picture of historical development; and failings of method.[134]

In 1901, Maitland wrote to Pollock:

> You spoke of Maine. Well, I always talk of him with reluctance, for on the few occasions on which I sought to verify his statements of fact I came to

129 Stephen, *English Utilitarians*, 333–4; see also Rumble, *Doing Austin Justice*, 169.

130 See *Oxford History*, XI, 107; W. Twining, 'Maine and Legal Education: A Comment', in *The Victorian Achievement of Sir Henry Maine*, ed. A. Diamond (Cambridge, 1991), 209–16, 210–11.

131 H. S. Maine, 'Roman Law and Legal Education', *Cambridge Essays* (London, 1856), 1–29, at 2: 'It is not because our own jurisprudence and that of Rome were *once* alike that they ought to be studied together – it is because they *will be* alike. It is because all laws, however dissimilar in their infancy, tend to resemble each other in their maturity; and because we in England are slowly, and perhaps unconsciously or unwillingly, but still steadily and certainly accustoming ourselves to the same modes of legal thought and to the same conceptions of legal principle to which the Roman jurisconsults had attained after centuries of accumulated experience and unwearied cultivation'.

132 See above, 304.

133 *Collected Papers*, i. 486–7.

134 *Letters*, i. no. 97 to Vinogradoff (1891): 'Perhaps you will become an idol like Maine – who can tell? I hardly wish you this fate, though you might like it for a fortnight'.

> the conclusion that he trusted much to a memory that played him tricks and rarely looked back at a book that he had once read: e.g. his story about the position of the half-blood in the Law of Normandy seems to me a mere dream that is contradicted by every version of the custumal.[135]

Pollock's own volume, *Introduction and Notes to Sir Henry Maine's "Ancient Law"*, published in 1906, has several mentions of Maitland correcting Maine: the proportion of *Bracton* taken from Justinian's *Corpus*, the prohibition of Roman law teaching in England, tensions between Common Law and Roman law and their respective lawyers, village communities.[136]

Pollock also cited Maitland against Maine's view of historical development: 'we are learning that the attempt to construct a normal programme for all portions of mankind is idle and unscientific'.[137] Maine emphasised the series of stages through which his 'progressive societies' passed.[138] Maitland was willing to talk in terms of patterns of development,[139] albeit aware that patterns in the past were at least in part created by the beholder in the present,[140] but he did not accept Maine's picture. Not all societies need pass through the same stages: 'To suppose that the family law of every nation needs traverse the same route, this is an unwarrantable hypothesis. To construct some fated scheme of successive stages which shall comprise every arrangement that may yet be discovered among backward peoples, this is a hopeless task'.[141] Routes might be different, and even on a single route, stages might be leapt, for example, through the appropriation of alien ideas.[142]

135 *Letters*, i. no. 279; note Pollock and Maitland, ii. 305. See also, for example, *Collected Papers*, iii. 460.

136 See Sir Frederick Pollock, *Introduction and Notes to Sir Henry Maine's "Ancient Law"* (2nd edition, London, 1908), 18–20, 51; note also 36, 39.

137 Pollock, *Introduction and Notes*, 32.

138 Note, however, expressions of caution in Maine; see, for example, *Ancient Law* (London, 1861), 269: 'It is not of course intended to insist that these different forms of the Village-Community represent distinct stages in a process of transmutation which has been everywhere accomplished in the same manner'. On Maine's evolutionism, note A. D. J. MacFarlane, 'Some Contributions of Maine to History and Anthropology', in *Victorian Achievement*, ed. Diamond, 111–42, at 137–41.

139 Note Pollock and Maitland, ii. 447: 'A premature simplicity imposed from above'.

140 See, for example, Pollock and Maitland, i. 75: 'along what must seem to us a destined path of progress'.

141 Pollock and Maitland, ii. 255.

142 Maitland, *Domesday Book and Beyond*, 345, quoted by Pollock, *Introduction and Notes*, 29.

In addition, Maitland doubted whether Maine had correctly identified the stages and their order even for the societies that he had studied. This was particularly so with Maine's emphatic argument that the family was the essential unit of early society and law, the importance of the individual only gradually increasing.[143] So Maitland comments that he had become 'sceptical about "the family" as a legal "unit"',[144] and, on a related issue, that 'if we look at the doings of our law courts, we may feel inclined to reverse a famous judgement and to say that while the individual is the unit of ancient, the corporation is the unit of modern law'.[145]

Maitland, moreover, was worried about the methods and materials that Maine used to create his picture of *Ancient Law*. He would have felt that Maine, like Austin, was too willing to take Roman law as the archetype of mature legal systems, to generalise from it with insufficient justification.[146] He was suspicious of the way in which Maine and his disciples sought to identify survivals of early law in later practices; it was not that such survivals did not exist,[147] but rather that some practices identified as such were in fact much more recent creations:

> Some quaint group of facts having been discovered in times that are yet recent, some group of facts which seems to be out of harmony with its modern surroundings, we are – so I venture to think – too often asked to infer without sufficient investigation that these phenomena are and must be enormously ancient, primitive, archaic, prehistoric, 'pre-Aryan'.[148]

An associated concern was the conflation of disparate evidence to create a misleading picture: 'I have a special dread of those theorists who are trying to fill up the dark ages of medieval history with laws collected from the barbarian tribes that have been observed in modern days'.[149] Any historical specificity, crucial in Maitland's eyes, was thereby neglected.

143 See especially Pollock and Maitland, ii. 240–5; S. D. White, 'Maitland on Family and Kinship', in *History of English Law*, ed. Hudson, 91–113; MacFarlane, 'Some Contributions of Maine', 116.

144 *Letters*, i. no. 123.

145 F. W. Maitland, *Township and Borough* (Cambridge, 1898), 15; see also Pollock and Maitland, i. 616–30, 687–8.

146 See above, n. 131, for Maine justifying his treating Roman law as typical of other mature legal systems. Note also Hoeflich, *Roman and Civil Law*, 78–85; P. G. Stein, 'Maine and Legal Education', in *Victorian Achievement*, ed. Diamond, 195–208; R. C. J. Cocks, *Sir Henry Maine: a Study in Victorian Jurisprudence* (Cambridge, 1988), 23.

147 See, for example, Pollock and Maitland, ii. 14, 291.

148 *Collected Papers*, ii. 314.

149 *Collected Papers*, iii. 300.

Finally, Maitland was worried by the neglect of the thinking of those studied. This hid the difficulty of understanding other societies, their functioning and development. Such was a fundamental problem of interpretation, although one also easily mocked in simpler terms of anachronism:

> Sir Henry Maine has said that 'the family, in fact, was a Corporation'. But then he has also told us that 'the Patriarch, for we must not yet call him the Pater-familias', was a 'trustee of his children and kindred', and 'in the eye of the law' represented the collective body. This patriarchal trustee, who represents a corporation, looks to me, I must confess it, suspiciously modern. He may be a savage, but he is in full evening dress. At any rate he is an individual man; and, if he is treated as trustee and representative, there is law enough for individuals and to spare. If we speak, we must speak with words; if we think, we must think with thoughts. We are moderns and our words and thoughts can not but be modern. Perhaps, as Mr Gilbert once suggested, it is too late for us to be early English. Every thought will be too sharp, every word will imply too many contrasts. We must, it is to be feared, use many words and qualify our every statement until we have almost contradicted it. The outcome will not be so graceful, so lucid, as Maine's Ancient Law.[150]

The struggle for the modern author was again one both of thought and of language.

Maitland's criticisms of Maine, therefore, have very marked similarities to his criticisms of Austin. There was the problem of accuracy and knowledge. In his inaugural, Maitland said that 'there is nothing that sets a man thinking and writing to such good effect about a system of law and its history as an acquaintance however slight with other systems and their history', but qualified this by remarking that 'there is not much "comparative jurisprudence" for those who do not know thoroughly well the things to be compared'.[151] Detail was important because of the variety and lack of determinacy of legal development. His view of legal history was very different from Maine's historical jurisprudence. Soon after the first publication of the *History of English Law*, Maitland wrote to Dicey:

[150] *Township and Borough*, 21–2.

[151] *Collected Papers*, i. 489; see also above, 297 n. 27. Cf. P. Stein, *Legal Evolution: The Story of an Idea* (Cambridge, 1980), 110: 'Maitland showed that Maine's schemes were too ambitious and were built on too narrow a base in fact. But he did not reject Maine's aims or the value of the comparative method, which Maitland himself used to considerable effect in regard to specific legal notions, such as the Corporation'.

> I have not for many years past believed in what calls itself historical jurisprudence. The only direct utility of legal history (I say nothing of its thrilling interest) lies in the lesson that each generation has an enormous power of shaping its own law.... I get more and more wrapped up in the middle ages but the only utilitarian justification that I ever urge *in foro conscientiae*, is that if history is to do its liberating work it must be as true to fact as it can possibly make itself and true to fact it will not be if it begins to think what lessons it can teach.[152]

III. Jurisprudence and legal history

Finally, let us briefly consider whether Maitland's rejection of some of Austin's arguments, his preference for a somewhat wider, more flexible view of the province of law, is reflected in his legal history. It is important not to exaggerate the breadth of Maitland's approach, particularly on certain subjects. Stephen White has shown how Maitland used a restricted view of legal history in his attack on Maine's arguments concerning the development of the family:

> Maitland achieved his polemical goal by abandoning the comparative method that Maine had used in melding evidence about many 'Indo-European societies' into a single evolutionary schema and by constructing, instead, a court-centred, judge-centred, state-centred national legal history in which kinship groups were almost invisible as active forces capable of shaping their own legal history and appeared, instead, as the passive subjects of external regulation by the state and its judges.... Because, in the *History of English Law*, Maitland evidently concurred with Pollock in sharply distinguishing 'rules of law' from 'common rules of morals and manners' and in equating 'law', for the purposes of historical inquiry with 'the sum of rules administered by courts of justice', and not with custom, he found no place in the legal history of the family, as later historians sometimes have, for the study of how people other than judges thought about kinship and used it in practice to legitimate claims on others.[153]

Such a critique of Maitland might seem to call into question arguments made earlier in this paper concerning Maitland's rejection of Austin's view of law. However, as White suggests, Maitland was here using a particular approach to legal history for particular polemical purposes. On some other topics he took a broader approach, paying more attention to

[152] *Letters*, ii. no. 116. Note also Cocks, *Sir Henry Maine*, at 144–5.
[153] White, 'Maitland on Family and Kinship', 94–5.

'the hundred forces which play upon our legal history'.[154] He was not rejecting the idea that important aspects of law at certain times were affected by the authority of the ruler and the decisions of the judges whom the ruler appointed; rather, he rejected Austin's view that sovereign command was by definition the essence of law.

Let us return then to Maitland and Austin, and look at passages where Maitland discusses notions of rights in ways that engage with and criticise Austin.[155] In a letter to Sidgwick he wrote: 'Since your youths won't ask you questions I dare to send you one – about the meaning of a "right", by which of course I mean a legal right. I don't know well how to answer it myself: the language of "our books" is not so precise as it might be'.[156] For Austin, the sovereign was an essential party to every legal right.[157] Maitland did not accept this view, certainly not its application to the past: 'We hesitate before we describe the serf as rightless even as against his lord, and, if we infer want of right from want of remedy, we feel that we may be doing violence to the thoughts of a generation which saw little

[154] Pollock and Maitland, i. 80; cf. White, 'Maitland on Family and Kinship', 95: 'Though keenly aware of "the hundred forces which play upon our legal history", he excluded many of them from his own writings about the family.... His discussion of family law centred on the analysis of the legal rights accorded to individual family members by English judges, who, he believed, had the power to shape the family because, by Angevin times if not earlier, they were sitting on "a bold high-handed court which wields the might of strong kingship"'. For subjects where Maitland pays greater attention to external history see, for example, Pollock and Maitland, i. 252–82 (tenure by knight service); 594–605 (the manor). See below, 325, on Maitland paying attention to courts other than the kings.

[155] Note also *Collected Papers*, i. 59–60.

[156] *Letters*, i. no. 38; see above, 296, for this letter beginning with the sentence 'Your dealings with Austin are very delightful to me, for the formal jurisprudent sits heavy upon us and you will deprive him of his terrors'.

[157] See, for example, *Province*, ed. Rumble, 235: 'To every legal right, there are three several parties: namely, a party bearing the right; a party burthened with the relative duty; and a sovereign government setting the law through which the right and the duty are respectively conferred and imposed'. Note also *Lectures*, 343–5, 396–7, 400. Cf. Pollock, *First Book of Jurisprudence*, 65: 'According to that view of the nature of law which regards it as the command of a supreme political authority and nothing else, it is difficult to ascribe rights, and barely possible to ascribe duties, to the State. But as we do not consider such a view to rest on any sound foundation, we are not concerned here with its consequences'. Maitland appears also not to have accepted Austin's argument, or at least its universal applicability, that 'a sovereign government... has no *legal* rights (in the proper acceptation of the term) *against its own subjects*'; *Province*, ed. Rumble, 230. Cf., for example, Pollock and Maitland, i. 68, 346, 384, 512–13; note also Morison, *John Austin*, 114.

difference between law and custom'.[158] As a result, he was unwilling to have the protection offered to villeins removed from the field of law, as he stated in the following passage, its Austinian terms within quotation marks:

> tenure in villeinage is protected, and if we choose to say that it is protected by 'positive morality' rather than by 'law properly so called,' we are bound to add that it is protected by a morality which keeps a court, which uses legal forms, which is conceived as law, or as something akin to law.[159]

Maitland emphasises the importance of courts other than the king's:

> The point that I should like emphasized – but perhaps you are coming to this – is that not having remedies in the King's own court is not equivalent to not having rights.[160]

> Think for one moment of the copyholder, or of his predecessor the tenant in villeinage; he was not protected in his holding by the king's court, still to regard him as without rights would be a perversion of history.[161]

Austin might have responded by arguing that the manorial court tacitly received its authority from the sovereign,[162] but we have already suggested that Maitland was unwilling to accept this argument about tacit delegation in general, and he certainly did not accept it with reference to the manorial court. Austin's argument was contradicted by thirteenth-century views, which held that 'seignorial jurisdiction has two roots – (1) the delegation of royal powers, (2) the relation between lord and tenants';[163] 'mere tenure gives to every lord, who has the means of exercising it, a jurisdiction over his tenant; his tenant is his justiciable'.[164] And:

158 Pollock and Maitland, i. 430; see also i. 224.

159 Pollock and Maitland, i. 361. See also Pollock and Maitland, i. 379: 'Had the tenant in villeinage heritable rights? Of rights recognized by the king's courts we have not to speak; but the manorial court frequently admitted that his rights were heritable, at least against all but the lord'. Note further, for example, Pollock and Maitland, i. 376–7, 385 ('protected by law, or by custom which has all the force of law . . . '), 387, 400–402.

160 *Letters*, i. no. 50 (to Vinogradoff, 1888).

161 *Forms of Action*, 8. See also, for example, Pollock and Maitland, i. 416–17.

162 See, for example, *Lectures*, 394: 'Every legal duty arises from a *Command*, signified, expressly or tacitly, by the *Sovereign* of a given Society'.

163 Pollock and Maitland, i. 571.

164 Pollock and Maitland, i. 585; the passage goes on to note royal control of this jurisdiction regarding freeholders, thereby implying the absence of royal control regarding villeins. See also Pollock and Maitland, i. 586.

> We have to form the notion of different spheres of jurisdiction, and this must colour our treatment of important private rights. It is not enough to say that a man has a right in land: we must add that it is, or is not, a right protected by the king's courts, for although it may be ignored there, still it may be protected by other courts, for example by the court of the manor. Nor is this the result of a mere division of labour such as at the present day may send petty cases to petty tribunals. The various courts have their roots in various principles, in various rights, the rights of the king, of the church, of feudal lords, of ancient communities.[165]

Such a broad use of the term 'right' is, of course, one point on which Maitland has subsequently been criticised by Thorne and, more particularly, by Milsom. It is through emphasis on sovereign enforcement and on rights good against the world that Milsom has attacked Maitland's description of the development of property law. Maitland had, he argues, lost sight of the personal, pre-dated the development of the proprietal:

> Seisin was originally the feudal investiture, the acceptance of the heritage from the lord. Before fees became hereditary, it was necessary to take a re-grant from the lord of the fee: for this re-grant seisin was afterwards substituted. Now this must necessarily have been a merely voluntary act.

However, that is not Milsom, but none other than John Austin, almost two centuries ago.[166] Maitland, the critic of Maine, would have been pleased to find that views of the law of the past did not evolve in any single, unidirectional, pattern.

IV. Conclusion

I have deliberately not made central to this paper the issue of whether Maitland's criticisms of Austin were justified. Some certainly have regarded Maitland as having missed Austin's significance. Notable amongst these is Buckland in his generally very sympathetic tribute to Maitland:

> where he saw defects in scholarship he was rather blind to real merits. He saw that Austin was not really a master of either English or Roman law, and he saw also that the main ideas expressed by Austin were all the work of his predecessors. Accordingly he arrived at the opinion which he expressed in the equation – J. A. = 0. I cannot but think that this is to ignore the real significance of Austin. Austin did, once for all, as Bentham had not wholly succeeded in doing, compel attention to the actual facts of the modern

[165] Pollock and Maitland, i. 528. [166] *Lectures*, 893.

> English conception of law, and drove from our books the half-thought-out matter which served for a philosophy of law in this country under the influence of Blackstone.[167]

Such a view may suggest that Maitland's reaction to Austin was in part a matter of intellectual temperament. Throughout his academic career Maitland displayed an interest in abstract thought, particularly in the area of political theory. In 1885, soon after his appointment to a Readership in Law at Cambridge, he wrote to Alfred Marshall, 'Sometimes I wish that I could give up lecturing about law and once more prepare myself for the Moral Science Tripos at your feet and Sidgwick's'.[168] However, this interest and this power of abstract thought were accompanied by a suspicion of grand explanatory and descriptive schemes, what in his early dissertation on liberty he referred to as theories clothed in universal terms.[169] This was a matter of intellectual principle[170]:

> The fault... of the would-be scientific procedure of our sociologists lies in the too frequent attempt to obtain a set of 'laws' by the study of only one class of phenomena.... Now I will not utterly deny the possibility of some such science of the very early stages in human progress. I know too little about the materials to do that. But even in this region I think it plain that our scientific people have been far too hasty in their laws. When this evidence about barbarians gets into the men who have been trained in a severe school of history and who have been taught by experience to look upon all the social phenomena as interdependent it begins to prove far less than it used to prove. Each case begins to look very unique...[171]

167 W. W. Buckland, 'F. W. Maitland', *Cambridge Law Journal*, 1 (1923), 279–301, at 293. Note further Buckland, 'Maitland', 293–4: 'In like manner, and, I suppose, for the same reason, Maitland undervalued Maine. Maine was not exact or profound either as a lawyer or as an historian. Much of what he says of Roman law is misleading. So is much of what he says of medieval law. Maitland saw this, and did not give, as it seems to me, enough weight to Maine's merits and achievements. He did not give him enough credit for directing men's minds at a time when historical research attracted few men in this country, and historical research in comparative law few men anywhere, to the problems to be solved and to the interest of comparative law. Even the beauty of his exposition, which had so much to do with his influence, was obscured to Maitland because of his inaccuracies. He did not, again, recognize that Maine was a great force, whose influence, unlike Austin's, spread beyond English-speaking countries'. For recent assessment of Austin more favourable than Maitland's see, for example, Lobban, *Common Law*, 257.

168 *Letters*, i. no. 13.

169 *Collected Papers*, i. 2. Note also Maitland's attack on Herbert Spencer; *Collected Papers*, i. 247–303.

170 Note also *Collected Papers*, iii. 303: 'I do regret the suggestion that at the present time the student of history should hope for and aim at ever wider and wider generalizations'.

171 *Collected Papers*, iii. 294–5.

At the same time, we see a political or moral principle at work: if Maitland found faults in certain universalising theories, he felt obliged to demonstrate their weaknesses in order to forestall the harm that they might do. This is manifest in his resistance to the universal applicability of the command view of law. Of men in the thirteenth century not having such a view he wrote:

> And well for us is it that this was so, for had they looked about for some such sovereign man or sovereign body as Austin's theory requires, there can be little doubt that our king would have become an absolute monarch, a true sovereign ruler in Austin's sense – the assembly of prelates and magnates was much too vague a body, and a body much too dependent for its constitution on the king's will to be recognized as the depositary of sovereign power.[172]

In Maitland's view, England had narrowly escaped a reception of Roman law and its potentially tyrannous effects; he was maintaining a similar defence in his critique of Austin.[173]

[172] *Constitutional History*, 101; see also Pollock and Maitland, i. 182.

[173] On the dangers of Roman or 'Byzantine' law see, for example, his article in *Encyclopaedia Britannica*, 605; F. W. Maitland, *English Law and the Renaissance* (Cambridge, 1901); Hudson, 'Maitland and Anglo-Norman Law', 25. Note also Introduction to Gierke, *Political Theories*, xliii: 'Some would warn us that in future the less we say about a supralegal, suprajural plenitude of power concentrated in a single point at Westminster – concentrated in one single organ of an increasingly complex commonwealth – the better for that commonwealth may be the days that are coming'.

INDEX

Abbott, CJ, 276–277
Abridgement (Fitzherbert), 73
absolute power, 36–37, 38, 43
Adam
  dominion over Eve, 197–198
  as world's first ruler, 200
Adam of Redlingfeld, 7
Adgore, Gregory, 30
adultery, 129–132, 133–134, 135, 136–137, 138
Against Aristogeiton (Demosthenes), 103
Alanus, 195
Alciato, Andreas, 112
Alighieri, Dante, 158
Amphiteatrum Legale (1690), 61
Ancient Law (Maine), 321
Anglo-Hanseatic relations (1474–1603), 170–191
  Bremen conference (1603), 170–178
  consultations by Louvain jurists (1553), 182–186
  Hanseatic memorandum, 186–190
    arguments on privileges in, 189
    closing pages, 188
    first part of, 187
    legal concepts and principles in, 188–189
    second part of, 187
    technical legal register of, 190
    traditional legal thinking in, 188
  King's subjection to civil law in, 178, 179–182
  legal arguments in support of Hanse, 178–179
  Utrecht Peace Treaty (1474), 170–178
Antiquity & Original of the Court of Chancery (Snagg), 50–51
Archbishop of Cologne, 212, 216, 223
Archeion, 42–45, 50
Archeion (Lambarde), 37–39
Argumentum ab Auctoritate, 62–69
Aristotle, 62, 63, 70
Ashley, Francis, 58–59
Asinio, 67
assize, of novel disseisin, 9–10
Atkin, Lord, 290
Atwood v. *Small*, 244
auctor, 72
auctoritates, 62
Augustine, Saint, 65
Austin, John, 293–328
  on Bentham, 300
  on common law, 313–314
  common views with Maitland, 299
  on feudalism, 303–304
  on general jurisprudence, 313, 314–315
  historical law and, 299–300
  on historical school of jurisprudence, 300
  inconsistencies in arguments, 295
  on judiciary law, 311–312
  on jurisprudence, 323–326
  Maitland's criticisms of, 295–318
    ahistoricism, 303
    Constitutional History of England lecture and, 297, 303, 309–310
    Encyclopaedia Britannica article and, 296–297, 299–301, 305–308, 315
    English law and, 307

Austin, John (*cont.*)
    History of English Law footnote, 297
    in Introduction to translation of Gierke, 298, 300, 308
  on manorial courts, 325–326
  on positive law, 294
  on Roman law, 305–306
  on sovereign command model of law, 312
  on sovereignty, 294–295, 308–309, 324–326
  use of language and terminology, 315–318
Austin's Case, 79
Austria, 231
authority, 60–84
  arguments from, 62–69
    in England, 69–74
    in Middle Ages, 62–69
  of Chancery, 33–59
    before late 1570s, 35–41
  conciliar, in Scotland, 140–169
    historical perspective, 141–150
    juridical perspective, 150–158
    theological perspective, 159–169
  of law, 71
  of medieval and modern lawyers, 64
  necessary vs. probable, 64
  precedent and, 74–83
  of Roman jurists, 64

Babell, Robert, 25
Bacon, Francis, 40
Bacon, Nicholas, 39, 41
Baker, J.H., 13, 275, 283
Baldus de Ubaldis, 94
Baldwin, Charles, 225, 226–227
Baldwyn, Anne, 25
Baldwyn, John, 25
Baldwyn v. *Marmyon*, 25
Balfour, James, 125–126
Banyster v. *Trussel* (1596), 79
Baron, Eguinare, 112–115
Baron de Bode
  death of, 212–213
  family's pursuit of claims, 212–213
  refuge in France, 212
Baron de Bode's Case, 212–249
  claim before the commissioners, 214–222
    Clement's claim, 216–222
    commissioners for claims on France, 214–216
    Convention 7 and, 214
    Convention 13 and, 214
  claim in common law courts, 236–247
    mandamus, 237–238
    petition of right in, 238–244
    return to parliament, 244–247
  political pressure in, 222–236
    Clement's debts/desperation and, 234–236
    on Hill's select committee, 227–234
    on Treasury, 223–227
Bartolus of Sassoferrato, 63, 94
Basilikon doron (James VI), 140, 162, 163, 165
Bassynwayt v. *Mannoke*, 27
bastardy, 136
Bate, William, 11
Beaton, David, 125
Beaumont v. *Cavell*, 25
Bell, Thomas, 69
Bellon, Jean, 64
Benett v. *Hert*, 27
Benn, Anthony, 55–56
Bentham, Jeremy, 300
Bergen, 173
Bigelow, Melville, 298
Bill of Rights (1689), 251
Board of Customs, 254
Board of Customs and Excise, 257
Board of Excise, 254
Board of Inland Revenue, 254
Board of Stamps, 254
Board of Stamps and Taxes, 255–256
Board of Taxes, 254
Bodin, Jean, 34
  and controversy of 1615/16, 54–59
  on equity, 52
  on estates of England, 49

influence on
Ashley, 58–59
Benn, 55–56
James I, 56–58
on oath of kings, 49
Republique, 45–48, 57
Boece, Hector, 142, 143
Bohier, Nicolas, 68
Bonard, Alfred de, 239
Book of Rates, 253
boule, 146
Boulston's Case, 80
Bourdieu, James, 228
Boyd, Ker & Co., 215
Brabazon, Roger, 7
Bracton, 69, 71, 303
Brende v. *Odemse*, 25
Breton, William, 26
Brewster v. *Grene*, 27
Brooke, Richard, 25
Brougham, Lord, 244
Brown v. *Howseden*, 31
Brudenell, Robert, 23
Brudenell v. *Worsop*, 23
Bruges conferences (1520–21), 171
Buchanan, George, 141–148
on lords of session, 154–155
Rerum Scoticarum historia, 141–148, 166
Buckley v. *Thomas* (1555), 75
Buckmaster, Lord, 289
Budé, 67
Bunting v. *Lepingwell*, 81
Burge, William, 278
Burn, Richard, 278
Burrow, John, 301
Byrne & Co. v. *Leon van Tienhoven & Co.* (1880), 281
Byrne v. *Leon van Tienhoven & Co.*, 287, 288

Caccialupi, Giovanni Battista, 63
Callistratus, 151, 152
Calvin's Case, 218
Cambridgeshire eyre (1286), 4, 8
canon law, 36–37, 120. *See also* law
on bastardy, 136, 137
contradictions with Roman law, 94–95
judicial discretion and, 157–158
Kirk's rejection of, 126
learned laws and, 94
on marriage, 135, 137
minor non tenetur and, 92–93
mos Italicus and, 95
pre-Tridentine, 121, 124–125, 138
privilegium fori in, 93–94
on reconciliation, 136–137
Scots consistorial law and, 121, 127, 128–129
use by Scots lawyers prior to 1560s, 90
Cantiuncula, Claudius, 65
Carion, Johann, 207
Carpzov, Benedict, 69
Caryll, John, 25
Case of Commendams, 58
Case of Impositions on Cloth, The (1559), 36–37
Case of the Marshalsea, The, 77, 78–79, 82
Castlereagh, Viscount, 214
Catholic Church, 86, 120, 122, 124
Cellarius, Christoph, 209
Chalke, William, 26
Chalmers, David, 87, 100, 143
on confusion of texts in medieval laws, 101–102
Dictionary of Scotch Law, 100
Epistles, 100, 105–107
on learning and history of Scots law, 107–110
Chancellor
absolute power and, 36–37
analogy between Roman praetor and, 46
authority of, 50–51
equitable powers of, 47
as instrument of King's prerogative, 40–41, 44
King's conscience and, 51
Lambarde's view on powers of, 44
petition of right and, 238–244
Snagg's view on, 50–51

Chancery
  absolute power and, 36–37
  authority of, 33–51, 59
    before late 1570s, 35–41
  in controversy of 1615/16, 54–59
  emergence of jurisdiction with prerogative, 36
  as keeper of king's conscience, 51
  per legem terrae requirements of Magna Carta, compliance with, 50
  prerogative from 1578, 41–52
    Lambarde's view, 42–48
    Morice's reading of, 48–50
    Snagg's reading of, 50–51
  prerogative in 1595–1615, 51, 52–53
Chancery bills, 14
Charnock v. *Worsley*, 76
Cheyney v. *Godfrey*, 52
Chronica (Carion), 207
Church of Scotland
  consistorial jurisdiction, 120, 123, 124
  law of God and, 131–132
  reconciliation and, 136
Cicero, 62, 149
civil law
  Anglo-Hanseatic relations and, 178–179, 180, 184
  canon law and, 127, 153
  commmon law and, 160–161
  conscience and, 141–148
  in France, 113, 153
  ius gentium and, 160–161
  James I on, 160–161
  King's subjection to, 178, 179–182
  in Scotland, 155, 156–157, 168
  Utrecht Peace Treaty and, 183–185
claims, pre-1154, 2
Cockburn, Alexander, 92–93
Cokayn, Francis, 23
Coke, Edward, 73, 76–77, 78, 79, 163
  on argument from authority, 80–82
  Commentary on Littleton, 81
  dismissal as Chief Justice, 33
  Eighth Reports, 58
  Fourth Reports, 81
  Third Reports, 80, 82
Cole v. *Rawe*, 21
Colebrooke, Henry, 283–291
Colgate v. *Blyth* (1586), 80
College of Justice, 89, 91, 94, 105, 107, 110, 141
commandments of God, 132
Commendator of St Andrews Priory v. *Bishop of Dunkeld* (1542), 93–94
commentaria bipertita, 113
Commentaries (Plowden), 73
Commissaries of Edinburgh, 121–122, 124, 127–128
  Divorce Act and, 134
  as inheritor of consistorial jurisdication of Catholic Church, 138
  jurisdiction, 128–129
  law of God and, 131–132
  Scottish Protestant divorce and, 129–131
Commissioners of Woods and Forests, 224, 225
Common Bench case, 2, 5, 8–9
common law
  Austin's views on, 307, 313–314
  authority of law and, 71
  Chancellor's authority and, 44
  civil law and, 160–161
  courts, 54, 56–57
  equity and, 161
  freehold land and, 15
  role of authorities in, 82
  vs. statute, 11
  statutory remedy to, 5
  unwritten, 46
common pleas, 1
common property, 194–195
  medicine as, 257
  natural law and, 195
  negative, 205
communia negativa, 205
communis opinio, 65
Compagnie des Salines de l'Est, 217
Compendium of the Laws of Scotland (Chalmers), 87
conscience, of king/monarch, 51
Constitutio Deo Auctore (Justinian), 102–103

Constitutional History of England, 297, 309–310
copyhold land, 25–26
Corpus Iuris Canonici, 135–136
Corpus Iuris Civilis, 94–95, 97, 106, 109, 153
Corpus Iuris (Justinian), 63–64
Cottenham, Lord, 239
Count de Wall's Case, 229
Court of Common Pleas, 75
Courte of Chauncerye, 38
Cox v. *Troy* (1822), 276–277, 288
Craig, Thomas, 127, 150–158
 on custom as source of law, 152–153
 Ius feudale, 127, 166
 on juridical discretion, 157–158
 on lords of session, 154–157
 on treatment of feudal land tenure, 153–154
Cranworth, Lord, 245
Crawfurd v. *Crawfurd* (1564), 136
Cromwell, Henry, 39

Dalton v. *Bishop of Ely*, 80
Danzig, 182–186
Darnall, Edith, 27
Darwin, Charles, 300
Davison, Christopher, 22, 27
Dawborne v. *Garbrand* (1595), 52–53
Dawson, John, 67
de Afflictis, Matthaeus, 66
de Donis, 6
De imperandi authoritate, et Christiana obedientia, libri quatuor (Sara), 197
De iure belli (Gentili), 188
de Leeuw, Elbert, 182
De Natura Legis Naturae (Fortescue), 36
De quattuor summis imperiis (Sleidanus), 207
De Richelieu, Duke, 214–216, 217
De statu hominum naturali (Pufendorf), 202–204
Decisiones (de Afflictis), 66
Decretals of Gregory IX, 135–136, 138
Decretum (Gratian), 194–195
Demosthenes, 103
Denman, George, 246, 247
Denman, Lord, 240, 241–242
Derry v. *Peek*, 289
Dialogus, 145, 147, 149
Dibb v. *Brooke & Sons* (1894), 274
Dicey, Albert Venn, 322–323
Dictionary of Scotch Law (Chalmers), 87, 100
Digest of Justinian, 92, 108, 137, 138, 146, 163
Digest of the Law of Contracts (Leake), 287
Direction or Preparative to the Study of the Law (Fulbeck), 73–74, 80
divorce, 120, 121, 124, 129–131, 133–134, 135, 136–137
Divorce Act of 1573, 133–134
Doctor and Student (St. German), 35, 73
Doctor Leyfield's Case, 79
Dodderidge, John, 82
Donoghue v. *Stevenson* (1932), 289–290
Dormand v. *Langham*, 21
dower case, in 1291, 8–9
Drew v. *Chalke*, 26
Drummond, James, 228–229
Drummond's Case, 230
Duchy of Lancaster, 53
Dudley, Edmund, 25
Duke of Burgundy, 175
Duke of Wellington, 214–216, 234
Dunlop v. *Brown* (1564/5), 135
Duxbury, Neil, 280, 281–282
Dyer's Reports, 77, 79

Earl of Northumberland's Case, The, 80
Ebden v. *Paris*, 21
Ecclesiastical Law (Burn), 278
Edgell v. *Day* (1865), 274
Edward I, 2, 174
Edward the Confessor, 69
Edward VI, 171, 179
Egerton, Thomas, 79
Egerton v. *Tychet*, 31
Eighth Reports (Coke), 58
ekklesia, 146
Eldon, Lord, 278

Elizabeth, 40
  Hanse's delegates and, 178
Ellenborough, Lord, 277
Ellesmere, Lord, 51, 78, 164
Empson, William, 227
Encyclopaedia Britannica, 296–297, 299–301, 305–308, 315
England, arguments from authority in, 69–74
Englefield's Case, 73
English law, authority of treatises in, 274–292
English Lawyer, The (Dodderidge), 82
English Utilitarians, The (Leslie), 318
Epistles (Chalmers), 100, 105–107
equitable jurisdiction, 140–169
equity
  Bodin's discussion of, 52
  Chancery and, 35–41
  civil law and, 156–157
  commmon law and, 161, 299–300
  French law and, 155–156
  jurisdiction and, 51, 52–53
  justice and, 94
  law and, 55–56
  legal truth and, 97
  lex terrae and, 58–59
  minor non tenetur rule and, 91
  natural, 163, 166
  prerogative explanation for, 41–52
  reason, 154
  reason and, 106–107, 109, 115
  Roman law and, 109, 163
  sovereignty and, 47, 54
Esher, Lord, 281
Essex, William, 23
Eston, John, 21
Everaerts, Nicolas, 64, 65
Exchequer Chamber, 243
Exposition of the Kinges Prerogative, 73
Eyre, Stephen, 26

Farmer v. *Glyn-Jones*, 259–260, 263, 267, 269
Feeld, Robert, 26
Feeld v. *Breton*, 26
feoffments, 15, 21–22, 29
Ferrers, Edward, 23
Fettiplace, Thomas, 25
Filmer, Robert
  on Adam as first ruler, 200
  Patriarcha, 198–199
Finlaison, John, 235
First Book of Discipline, 131
Fitzherbert, Anthony, 73
Fleming v. *Fleming* (1569), 137
Floren, 67
Follett, William, 228, 231, 232
Fonblanque, John, 230–231, 232
Fontana, Agostino, 61
Fortescue, J., 36
Foster v. *Wheeler* (1887), 280
Fountain, William, 25
France, 67
  commissioners for claims on, 214–216
  laws, 112–115, 155–156
Francogallia (Hotman), 149
Frederick, Charles Auguste Louis. See Baron de Bode
Frederick, Clement, 212–213, 216
  debts and desperation of, 234–236
  nationality of, 246
  pressure on Treasury, 223–227
Frederick, Clement (younger), 212–213, 243, 247
Frederick, William, 235
freehold land, 20–25
  active uses of, 18
French law, 112–115, 155–156
Frodshame v. *Lundysche*, 30
Frowyk, Thomas, 73
Fry, Edward, 283
Fulbeck, William, 73–74, 80
Fundamenta juris naturae (Thomasius), 205

Galen, 70
Gammarus, Peter, 64
general jurisprudence, 313, 314–315
Gentili, Alberico, 74, 80, 188
Germany, 67
Gierke, O., 298
Gifford, Lord, 221
Girardot, Marie, 221

Gisborne, Thomas, 233
Gisze, George, 175
Glorious Revolution, 228
Gloucester (1278), statute of, 5
  c.4, 4, 5
Glyn-Jones, William, 259–260
Gorla, Gino, 60
governmental power, 192–211
  biblical past and, 206–211
  natural law and, 194–195
  natural state and, 202–206
  sacred history and, 196–201
  universal history and, 206–211
Grant, William, 232
Gratian, 194–195
Greenlands v. *Wilmhurst* (1913), 279
Gregory, Saint, 65
Gregory IX, 135–136
Greynfeld, Thomas, 21
Guildhall, 174

habeas corpus, 53
Hales v. *Sheriffs of London*, 27
Hall, John, 22, 27
Hamilton, John, 124–125
Hamilton v. *Maxwell & Lindsay*, 137
Hannibal, 142
Hanse
  conflict with English commercial interests, 172
  English export trade and, 175
  Hanseatic memorandum, 186–190
    arguments on privileges in, 189
    closing pages, 188
    first part of, 187
    legal concepts and principles in, 188–189
    second part of, 187
    technical legal register of, 190
    traditional legal thinking in, 188
  legal arguments in support of, 178–179
  loss of privileges in England, 176
  Louvain jurists, 182–186
  mission for restoration of privileges, 176
  origins of, 173
  royal grants to German merchants, 173–174
  submission to civil law, 178–179
Harcourt, Vernon, 246
Hardy v. *Rutherford*, 130–131
Harvey, Gabriel, 54
Hatton, Christopher, 51
Hengham, CJ, 10
Henry I, 1
Henry II, 1
Henry III, 6
Henry VII, 25
Henry VIII, 171, 178–179
Henryson, Edward, 100, 126
  on confusion of texts in medieval laws, 101–102
  Preface, 100, 102–105
Hermogenian, 151
Hervy, George, 20
Hill, Matthew Davenport, 227–234, 237, 241
Hill v. *Reardon*, 221
Hippocrates, 63, 70
Hispanus, Laurentius, 195, 201
Historia sine parente (Ludewig), 208–209
Historia universalis (Cellarius), 209
Historiae Philippicae (Trogus), 142
History of English Law (Maitland), 297, 302, 323–324
Hobbes, Thomas, 193
Holbein the Younger, 175
Holy Roman Empire, 177, 188
Homer, 63–64
Homo ante et post lapsem (Locke), 201
Hooker, Richard, 199
Hotman, of François, 149
House of Commons, 40
House of Lords, 39–40, 243
Howard, J., 7
Howseden, William, 31
Hummel, Matthew, 239
Huntington, John, 22
Hyll, John, 21

Impey, Elijah, 215
In re Wellborne, 280
Incest Act of 1567, 132

individual property, divine creation of, 195–196
Inglis, Robert, 224
Inland Revenue Laboratory, 254
Insolvent Debtors Court, 235
Institutes of Gaius, 306
Institutiones Jurisprudentiae Divinae (Thomasius), 205–206
Institutions of the Law of Scotland (Stair), 166–167
inter vivos arrangement, 21–22, 28
Introduction and Notes to Sir Henry Maine's 'Ancient Law' (Pollock), 320
Introduction to the History of the Principal Kingdoms and States of Europe, An (Pufendorf), 207
Isidor of Seville, 193
ius commune, 63–64, 96–98, 106–107
Ius Feudale (Craig), 127, 150–158, 166
ius gentium, 106
ius scriptum, 108
Ives, E.W., 13

James I, 40–41, 51, 56–58
  Basilikon doron, 162, 163, 165
  on civil law, 160–161
  on lords of session, 159, 161–162
  Trew Law of Free Monarchies, 160
James II, 228
James V, 92
James VI, 140
Jane Tyrrel's Case (1557), 18
Jarman, Thomas, 278
Jenner, Herbert, 229, 230
Jessel, George, 282
John of Berwick, 8
John of Bredicot, 8–9
John XXII, Pope, 197
judicial interpretation, in the late thirteenth and early fourteenth centuries, 1–12
judiciary law, 310
jurisdiction, 18–19
  of Chancery, 36, 38, 39, 40, 51, 52–53, 56, 57
  of Church of Scotland, 120, 123, 124, 138
  of Commissaries of Edinburgh, 121, 128–129
  consistorial, 120, 123, 124, 138
  equitable, 140–169
  of lords of session, 89, 155, 156–157
  Papal Jurisdiction Act of 1560, 129, 132–133
  seignorial, 325–326
  Summary Jurisdiction Acts, 267
jurisprudence, historical school of, 300
Justinian, 106
  Constitutio Deo Auctore, 102–103
  Corpus Iuris, 63–64

Kekewich, Arthur, 280, 283
King of England
  absolute power and, 36–37
  Chancery as keeper of king's conscience, 51
  subjection to civil law, 178, 179–182
King's Bench, 1, 7
Kirk, 120, 123, 138
Knight v. *Boughton* (1844), 278
Kuttner, Stephan, 195
Kynnersley, Thomas, 212

Lambarde, William, 37–39
  analogy between Chancellor and Roman praetor, 46
  Archeion, 42–48, 50
  prerogative model of Chancery, 52
Langslow, Robert, 234
law
  authority of, 71
  canon. See canon law
  common law. See common law
  French, 112–115, 155–156
  medieval laws in 1566, 100–110
  natural. See natural law
  out-of-date, 101–102
  past and present law, 313
  positive, 294
  property. See property law
  Roman. See Roman law
  sovereign command model of, 312
law of God, 131–132, 138
Law of Oblivion, 122, 123, 129

Leake, Stephen, 287
Lee v. *Byrde*, 23
legal authorities, as instruments of conflict managememt, 170–191
legislation
  Divorce Act. See Divorce Act of 1573
  force of *lex* and, 66
  judicial interpretation of, 1–12
  judiciary law and, 294
  in late thirteenth and early fourteenth century England, 1–12
  Medicine Stamp Act (1812). See Medicine Stamp Act (1812)
  out-of-date, 101–102
  of Reformation Parliament, 128, 132–133, 148
  science of, 294
  in Scotland, 85–119
  of Scottish kings, 143
  subordinate, 311–312
  in Tudor times, 13
Leicestershire eyre (1284), 10
Lent parliament of 1299, 8
Leoninus, Elbertus, 182
Leslie, John (Bishop of Ross), 87, 100, 143
lettres de jussion, 114
lex Regia, 108
lex terrae, 58
libri Feudorum, 94
limitation dates, 1–2
  Westminster I statute (1275), 2
Lindley, 281
lit de justice, 114
Little, Clement, 126
Littleton, Thomas de, 73
Locke, John, 199–201
Lodge v. *Lysely* (1832), 277
Lord Chancellor. See chancellor
Lord Dacre's Case (1535), 15
Lord Daubeney v. *Osgood*, 23
lords of session, 89, 98–100
  attitudes to local laws prior to 1556, 98–100
  canon law and, 93–94
  ius commune and, 97
  James I on, 159, 161–162
  jurisdiction of, 89, 155, 156–157
  medieval laws and, 100
  minor non tenetur rule and, 91, 92
Lords of the Congregation (Scotland), 122
Louet, Georges, 68
Lovetot, John de, 3
Low Countries, 173, 176, 182
Ludewig, Johann Peter, 208–209
Lushington, 229
Lutheranism, 126
Lyndhurst, Lord, 244, 245, 278

Mackenzie, George, 147
MacMillan, Lord, 289–290
Magna Carta, 1
  dower case and, 8–9
  per legem terrae requirements of, 50
  plea roll enrolment and, 10–11
Maine, Henry, 318–323
  Ancient Law, 321
  on development of family, 323–324
  on family as corporation, 322
  on historical development, 320
  Maitland's criticisms of, 318–323
Maitland, Frederic William, 293–328
  on command view of law, 310
  common views with Austin, 299
  criticisms of Austin, 295–318
    ahistoricism, 303
    Constitutional History of England lecture and, 297, 303, 309–310
    Encyclopaedia Britannica article and, 296–297, 299–301, 305–308, 315
    English law, 307
    History of English Law footnote, 297
    in Introduction to translation of Gierke, 298, 300, 308
    Roman law, 305–306
  criticisms of Maine, 318–323
  Forms of Action lectures, 302, 304
  on general jurisprudence, 313, 314–315
  on importance of courts other than king's, 325

Maitland, Frederic William (*cont.*)
judgements on influence of past legal developments, 302
on judiciary law, 311–312
on jurisprudence, 323–326
'Law of Real Property', 307
letters
Bigelow, 298
to Dicey, 322–323
to Pollock, 296–297, 319–320
to Sidgwick, 296, 324
to Stephen, 296
on past and present law, 313
on property law, 326
on Roman law, 305–306
on sovereignty, 308–309, 324–326
use of language and terminology, 315–318
Maitland, Richard, 100
Maitland, Robert, 126
Maitland, Thomas, 144
Mannoke, John, 26
Margery, widow of Philip of Bredicot, 8–9
Marlborough (1267), statute of, c. 28 of, 3
marriage, 120, 121
bastardy and, 133
canon law on, 135
irregular, 135
payment of money in, 27
Marriage Act of 1567, 132–134
Martin, Andrew, 227
Martin v. *Marhsall* (1615), 53
martyrology, 71
Mary, Queen of Scots, 85, 87, 105, 121, 128
Mary of Guise, 86
Mary Tudor, Queen of France, 176
Mashh, William, 21
McClachelan v. *Laird of Lewmond* (1547), 99
Medicine Stamp Act (1812), 250–273
extra-statutory concessions, 257–262
bulk purchase of medicines, 257–258
dispensing concessions, 258
statutory exemptions, 259–262
interpretation of provisions in extra-statutory concession, 257–262
internal or external use, 255
proprietary right, 256–257
recommendation for relief of human ailments, 255–256
schedules, 255
medicine stamp duty, 250–273
administrative action, 254–262
bureaucratic law-making and, 266–270
legality of revenue practice in, 263–266
overview, 250–251
quack medicines and, 252–253
statutory framework, 251–253
Melanchton, Philip, 207
Melbourne, Lord, 236
Mennwenek, Thomas, 21
Mennwenek v. *Wylgarn*, 21
Merchants Adventurers, 176, 177, 186–187
Merlin, Philippe Antoine, 226
Mertlage, 71
Michaelmas, 2, 53, 58, 76
Middle Temple, 17
Middlesex eyre, action of cosinage in (1274), 3
Milan, 67
Mill, John Stuart, 306
Milsom, Stroud Francis, 326
minor non tenetur rule, 91, 92
Moile v. *Kirton*, 20
monarch, conscience of, 51
Montagu Chambers, 245
Monteagle, Lord, 245
Moore, Francis, 51, 73
More, John, 23
More, Thomas, 179
More chancellorship (1529–32), 14
More v. *Eyre*, 26
More v. *Kyrkeham*, 20
Morice, James, 41–42, 48–50
on oath of kings, 49
Morley, Thomas, 70
Morton v. *Morton*, 133
mos Gallicus, 112

mos Italicus, 94–97, 102–105, 107
Moses, 153
Motives concerning Romish Faith and Religion (Bell), 69
Mudaeus, Gabriel, 182

Naples, 66, 67
Natura Brevium, 77
Natural History of Society (Smith), 209
natural law, 117, 118, 194–195
  common property and, 195
  governmental power and, 194–195
  learned laws and, 155
  postlapsarian, 195
  property rights and, 195, 201
  Roman law and, 182
  sacred history and, 204, 205
natural law and, 195
negative common property, 205
Netherlands, 67
Nicholas of Stillingfleet v. *Parnel de Coygners*, 6–7
Norman, William, 21
Northamptonshire eyre, action of annual rent in (1285), 3–4
Novgorod, 173

Observations on the Acts of Parliament (Mackenzie), 147
O'Connell, Daniel, 233
Of the Lawes of Ecclesiastical Polity (Hooker), 199
Old Natura Brevium, 73
ordinary power, 36–37

Papal Jurisdiction Act of 1560, 129, 132–133
Pardessus, Jean, 276
Paris, Philip, 22
Parlement, 114
Parliament
  authority of, 13–32
  Baron de Bode's Case in, 240
  Law of Oblivion and, 122
  Medicine Stamp Act (1812), 252
  Reformation, 123, 128, 132–133
  revenue practice and, 263–266
  tax law and, 251
Parr v. *Wanton*, 20
paternal monarchies, 199
Patriarcha (Filmer), 198–199
personal property, uses of, 18–19
Philip II, 176
Philip of Bredicot, 8–9
Phillimore, Joseph, 227, 237
Piedmont, 66, 67
Pilkington's Case, 220
plea rolls, 10–11
Plowden, Edmund, 72, 73
Plummer, Thomas, 275–276
Pollock, Frederick, 280–281, 282, 286–287, 288–291, 296–297, 319–320
Pomponius, 151, 152
Portugal, 67
positive law, 294
postnati, 163, 164
Pothier, Robert Joseph, 229, 276–277, 286, 287–288
power, 36–37
Practicks (Sinclair), 90, 94–99
Praerogativa Regis, 41–42
praetorian prefecture, 113
precedent, 74–83
preeminence, 48
Preface (Henryson), 100, 102–105
Prerogativa Regis, 73
prerogative, 41–52
  from 1578, 41–52
    Lambarde's view, 42–48
    Morice's reading of, 48–50
    Snagg's reading of, 50–51
  in 1595–1615, 51, 52–53
  in controversy of 1615/16, 54–59
  emergence of Chancery's jurisdiction with, 36
  pre-eminence and, 48
  property law and, 34
  types of, 37
Principles of Contract (Pollock), 280–281, 287
privilege, 188

Privy Council, 122, 123, 124
claims on France and, 215
Clement's claims and, 220–222, 237, 244, 246
Commissaries of Edinburgh and, 130, 138
Drummond's claims and, 228–229
Hanseatic privileges and, 176
unsettled claims and, 225, 227
probouleuma, 146
Proclamation of Leith, 123
Profitable Book, 73
property law
forms of action and, 304
Maitland's view of, 314, 326
prerogatives and, 34
Prostestant Reformers, 86
prudentium auctoritas, 163
Pufendorf, Samuel, 196
De statu hominum naturali, 202–204
Introduction to the History of the Principal Kingdoms and States of Europe, An, 207
Purgatorio, 158

quack medicines, 252–253
Queen's Advocate v. *Morton* (1543), 91
Queen's Bench, 240, 241
Quia Emptores of 1290, 9

R v. *Ion*, 279
Ratcliff's Case, 76
ratio legis, 73–74
rebuc sic stantibus principle, 189
reconciliation, 136–137
Reformation crisis of 1559, 120, 123, 128
Reformation Parliament (Scotland), 123, 128, 132–133
Regiam Majestatem, 90, 91
Reichskammergericht, 67
Repertoire de Jurisprudence, 226
Republique (Bodin), 45–48, 57
Rerum Scoticarum historia (Buchanan), 141–148, 166
Responsa Prudentum, 162, 163
Rex Angliae, 179
rex in regno suo est imperator principle, 105–106, 109
Rhineland, 173
Richmond, Thomas, 219
Robert of Nailston, 11
Rodger, Alan (Baron Rodger of Earlsferry), 289–290
Roger of Mersea and his wife Isabel v. *Joan the wife of Robert Cope*, 10
Rolfe, Robert, 233
Roman law
consistorial law and, 121
contradictions with canon law, 94–95
Eguinare Baron on, 110–117
equity and, 109, 299–300
learned laws and, 94
Maitland's vs. Austin's views on, 305–306
minor non tenetur and, 92–93
mos Italicus and, 95
vs. Scot laws, 107–110
Romanus, Aegidus, 165
Rommilly, Samuel, 218
Romulus (founder of Rome), 108
Rondeau, Arthur, 228
Rosenthal, Alexander, 200
Rosentritt, G.C.H., 239
Rota, 66
Rowe, John, 21
Rowley, John, 26
Rowley v. *Taylour*, 26
Rule of Reason, The (Wilson), 70

sacred history, 196–201
Sacrum Consilium, 66, 68
Saham, J., 3–5
Sambach v. *Dalston* (1635), 17
Saravia, Adrian, 197
Savigny, Friedrich Carl von, 210
Scaccia, Sigismundo, 67
scire facias, writ of, 7
Scotland
conciliar authority in, 140–169
historical perspective, 141–150
juridical perspective, 150–158
theological perspective, 159–169
consistorial law, 120–139

equitable jurisdiction in, 140–169
legal context prior to 1560s, 89–100
'commoun law', 91–94
laws of Scottish realm, 91–94
Lords' attitudes, 98–100
Sinclair's *Practicks*, 94–98
legislation and authority in, 85–119
medieval laws in 1566, 100–110
Chalmers' *Epistles* and, 105–107
confusion of texts, 101
Henryson's *Preface* and, 102–105
history of, 107–110
problems of out-of-date laws, 101–102
Protestant Reformers in, 86
Reformation, authority in, 110–117
clergy and nobility in, 115–117
Scotorum historia (Boece), 142
Seaton v. *Cockburns*, 92–93
seisin, 2, 326
Septimius Severus, Emperor, 144
Session
canon law and, 93–94
as College of Justice, 89
ius commune and, 97
local laws and, 98–100, 118
medieval laws and, 100
minor non tenetur rule and, 91, 92
Scot laws and, 116
Shadwell, Launcelot, 222, 229
Shelley's Case, 73
Sherard, George, 27
Sherard, Thomas, 27
Sherard v. *Mayor of London*, 27
Sherrard, George, 22
Sherrard, Thomas, 22
Sherrard v. *Mayor of London*, 22
Sidgwick, Henry, 296, 324
Sinclair, John, 90, 94–99, 124
Sir William Pelham's Case, 73
Slade v. *Drake*, 78, 79
Slade's Case, 76–77
Sleidanus, Johannes, 207
Smith, Adam, 209
Snagg, Robert, 41, 50–51
Antiquity & Original of the Court of Chancery, 50–51
sovereignty, 189
of artists, 158
Austin's views on, 294–295, 308–309, 324–326
equity and, 47, 54
of king's judges, 152
law-making as indication of, 48
legislative, 117, 118, 119, 168
Maitland's views on, 308–309, 324–326
parliamentary, 243
positive law and, 294–295
power to amend laws and, 47, 48
privilege principle and, 189
Renaissance notions of sovereignty, 88
Speach (James I), 56–58
Spring Rice, Thomas, 227, 233, 235
St. German, Christopher, 35
St. Leonards, Lord, 277, 280
Stair, Viscount, 166–167, 168
Stamp Commissioners, 254
Stanley, E.G., 224
Star Chamber, 161
statute 3 Hen. VII, c. 4 (1487), 16
Statute of Enrolments (1536), 15–16
Statute of Fines (1299), c. 1 of, 8
Statute of Marlborough, c. 29 of, 314
Statute of Uses (1536), 13–32
active uses of freehold land and, 18
draftsman of, 16–17
evidence of pleadings, 20–32
chattels personal, 26–27
copyhold land, 25–26
freehold land, 20–25
terms of years, 25–26
express conveyances to uses and, 16
feoffments and, 15
passive use of leases and, 17–18
uses of personal property and, 18–19
Statute of Westminster I (1275)
c. 38 of, 2
c. 40 of, 5
c. 50 of, 42–48
Steelyard, 178, 186
Stephen, Leslie, 296, 318
Stevenson v. *McLean* (1880), 288
Stewart, Jane, 133
Stowel v. *Lord Zouch*, 72

Stukelegh v. *Eston*, 21
Stumm v. *Dixon & Co.* (1889), 281
stylus curiae, 68
Suffolk eyre (1287), 10
Sugden, Edward B., 279
Sugden's Vendors and Purchasers, 274, 280
Summary Jurisdiction Acts, 267
Symbolaeographia (West), 35

tailzies, 99
Taylor, M.A., 224
Tenterden, Lord, 276–277
Tenures (Littleton), 73
Tesauro, Antonio, 66, 67
Thesifer, Frederick, 240
Thomas of Siddington, 3–4
Thomasius, Christian, 205–206
Thorne, Samuel, 326
Thornton v. *Dick*, 277
Thornton v. *Sanderson*, 136
Toker, Walter, 21
Toolbooth of Edinburgh, 128
Topica (Everaerts), 64, 65
Topica Legalia (Cantiuncula), 65
Topics (Aristotle), 62
Tourneur, Timothy, 40–41, 56
Treasury, 223–227
Treatise on Obligations and Contracts, Part 1 (Colebrooke), 283
Treatise on Persons (Pothier), 229
treatises
  authority in English law in, 274–292
  judicial caution in use of, 281–283
  living authors as authority in, 275–281
  writers' perspectives on, 283
Treaty of Commerce, 214–216
Treaty of Lunéville (1801), 231
Treaty of Münster, 226, 231, 240
Treaty of Paris (1814), 214–216
Treaty of Westphalia, 231
Tresham's Case, 73
Trew Law of Free Monarchies, 160
Trinity term (1291), 8–9
Trogus, Pompeius, 142
Truro, Lord, 243, 244
Turner v. *Turner* (1819), 275–276
Two Treatises on Government (Locke), 200
Tyrrel's Case (1557), 15

Union Bank v. *Munster* (1887), 280
Universal History from the Earliest Account of Time (1730), 209
Utrecht Peace Treaty (1474), 170–178, 183–185, 187

van der Muyden, Gabriel, 182
Vaughell v. *Gibbs*, 21
Vigelius, Nicolas, 64
Virgil, 63–64, 158
Vogenauer, Stefan, 80
Vultejus, Hermann, 67

Waddington, H., 240
Walsh, Robert, 23
Warburton, Henry, 234
Wars of the Congregation, 122
Waterhouse v. *Woodstreet* (1597), 75
West, William, 35, 38
Westminster I (1275), statute of, c. 39 of, 2
Westminster II (1285), statute of, 6
  c. 1 of, 10
  c. 2 of, 7
  c. 45 of, 7
Westminster Review, 301
Weyland, Thomas, 5
Wheeler, John, 186–187
White, Stephen, 323–324
Whitsun, 1–2
Whyteley v. *Hall*, 31
Wilde, Thomas (Lord Truro), 243
Willcock, John, 136
William I, 69
William of Ockham, 196
William son of William de Ferrers v. *Henry le Porter and his wife Ismania*, 5
Williams, Bishop, 51
Williams, Ian, 75, 78
Williams, John, 275
Williams, Vaughnan, 274, 279
Willies, Edward, 235
Wilshire, John, 24

Wilson, Thomas, 70
Wimbish v. *Talboys*, 79
Windsor, Anderew, 25
Winram, John, 124–125
Withy v. *Mangles* (1843), 278
Wolsey, Cardinal, 180
Wosley chancellorship (1515–29), 14
Wray, Christopher, 17
Wren v. *Wetyngham*, 24
Wright, Lord, 290
writ of right, claimant counts in, 1
Wyse, Robert, 31

Year Books, 71, 73, 77, 79
Yorkshire Banking Co. v. *Beatson* (1879), 283

For EU product safety concerns, contact us at Calle de José Abascal, 56–1°, 28003 Madrid, Spain or eugpsr@cambridge.org.

www.ingramcontent.com/pod-product-compliance
Lightning Source LLC
LaVergne TN
LVHW011528200926
848484LV00001B/192

* 9 7 8 1 1 0 7 1 2 2 2 7 7 *